Just The facts101 Textbook Key Facts

Luxembourg Insolvency (Bankruptcy) Laws and Regulations Handbook: Strategic Information and Basic Laws

by Cram101
Texbook NOT Included

Table of Contents

Just The Facts101

Exam Prep for

Luxembourg Insolvency (Bankruptcy) Laws and Regulations Handbook: Strategic Information and Basic Laws

Just The Facts101 Exam Prep is your link from
the textbook and lecture to your exams.

Just The Facts101 Exam Preps are unauthorized and comprehensive reviews of your textbooks.

Just The Facts101 Exam Prep

eAIN 438848

Foundations of Business

A business, also known as an enterprise, agency or a firm, is an entity involved in the provision of goods and/or services to consumers. Businesses are prevalent in capitalist economies, where most of them are privately owned and provide goods and services to customers in exchange for other goods, services, or money.

:: Marketing techniques ::

__________ is the activity of dividing a broad consumer or business market, normally consisting of existing and potential customers, into sub-groups of consumers based on some type of shared characteristics. In dividing or segmenting markets, researchers typically look for common characteristics such as shared needs, common interests, similar lifestyles or even similar demographic profiles. The overall aim of segmentation is to identify high yield segments – that is, those segments that are likely to be the most profitable or that have growth potential – so that these can be selected for special attention .

Exam Probability: **Medium**

1. *Answer choices:*

(see index for correct answer)

- a. Prize
- b. Market segmentation
- c. Programmatic marketing
- d. AIDA

Guidance: level 1

:: Mereology ::

_________ , in the abstract, is what belongs to or with something, whether as an attribute or as a component of said thing. In the context of this article, it is one or more components , whether physical or incorporeal, of a person`s estate; or so belonging to, as in being owned by, a person or jointly a group of people or a legal entity like a corporation or even a society. Depending on the nature of the _________ , an owner of _________ has the right to consume, alter, share, redefine, rent, mortgage, pawn, sell, exchange, transfer, give away or destroy it, or to exclude others from doing these things, as well as to perhaps abandon it; whereas regardless of the nature of the _________ , the owner thereof has the right to properly use it , or at the very least exclusively keep it.

Exam Probability: **Low**

2. *Answer choices:*

(see index for correct answer)

- a. Property
- b. Gunk
- c. Mereological essentialism
- d. Meronomy

Guidance: level 1

:: Debt ::

_________ is when something, usually money, is owed by one party, the borrower or _________ or, to a second party, the lender or creditor. _________ is a deferred payment, or series of payments, that is owed in the future, which is what differentiates it from an immediate purchase. The _________ may be owed by sovereign state or country, local government, company, or an individual. Commercial _________ is generally subject to contractual terms regarding the amount and timing of repayments of principal and interest. Loans, bonds, notes, and mortgages are all types of _________ . The term can also be used metaphorically to cover moral obligations and other interactions not based on economic value. For example, in Western cultures, a person who has been helped by a second person is sometimes said to owe a " _________ of gratitude" to the second person.

Exam Probability: **High**

3. *Answer choices:*
(see index for correct answer)

- a. Charge-off
- b. Creditor
- c. Phantom debt
- d. Debt

Guidance: level 1

:: ::

_________ refers to a business or organization attempting to acquire goods or services to accomplish its goals. Although there are several organizations that attempt to set standards in the _________ process, processes can vary greatly between organizations. Typically the word " _________ " is not used interchangeably with the word "procurement", since procurement typically includes expediting, supplier quality, and transportation and logistics in addition to _________ .

Exam Probability: **Medium**

4. *Answer choices:*
(see index for correct answer)

- a. corporate values
- b. cultural
- c. open system
- d. functional perspective

Guidance: level 1

:: Commercial item transport and distribution ::

A _________ is a commitment or expectation to perform some action in general or if certain circumstances arise. A _________ may arise from a system of ethics or morality, especially in an honor culture. Many duties are created by law, sometimes including a codified punishment or liability for non-performance. Performing one`s _________ may require some sacrifice of self-interest.

Exam Probability: **High**

5. *Answer choices:*

(see index for correct answer)

- a. Wine shipping laws in the United States
- b. Shuttle tanker
- c. Containerized housing unit
- d. Duty

Guidance: level 1

:: E-commerce ::

__________ is the activity of buying or selling of products on online services or over the Internet. Electronic commerce draws on technologies such as mobile commerce, electronic funds transfer, supply chain management, Internet marketing, online transaction processing, electronic data interchange , inventory management systems, and automated data collection systems.

Exam Probability: **Low**

6. *Answer choices:*

(see index for correct answer)

- a. Address Verification System
- b. Mobilpenge
- c. Auction software
- d. E-commerce

Guidance: level 1

:: Non-profit technology ::

Instituto del Tercer Mundo is a Non-Governmental Organization that performs information, communication and education activities. __________ , which was established in 1989, shares the same secretariat and coordinating personnel as Social Watch and is based in Montevideo, Uruguay.

Exam Probability: **High**

7. *Answer choices:*

(see index for correct answer)

- a. OpenDocument Foundation
- b. ITeM
- c. Clinical Data Interchange Standards Consortium
- d. The Rosetta Foundation

Guidance: level 1

:: Marketing ::

A _________ is a group of customers within a business`s serviceable available market at which a business aims its marketing efforts and resources. A _________ is a subset of the total market for a product or service. The _________ typically consists of consumers who exhibit similar characteristics and are considered most likely to buy a business`s market offerings or are likely to be the most profitable segments for the business to service.

Exam Probability: **Low**

8. *Answer choices:*

(see index for correct answer)

- a. Target market
- b. Davie-Brown Index
- c. Landing page
- d. History of marketing

Guidance: level 1

:: International trade ::

_________ or globalisation is the process of interaction and integration among people, companies, and governments worldwide. As a complex and multifaceted phenomenon, _________ is considered by some as a form of capitalist expansion which entails the integration of local and national economies into a global, unregulated market economy. _________ has grown due to advances in transportation and communication technology. With the increased global interactions comes the growth of international trade, ideas, and culture. _________ is primarily an economic process of interaction and integration that`s associated with social and cultural aspects. However, conflicts and diplomacy are also large parts of the history of _________ , and modern _________ .

Exam Probability: **Low**

9. *Answer choices:*

(see index for correct answer)

- a. African Diamond Producers Association

- b. Globalization
- c. Balanced trade
- d. Cartaz

Guidance: level 1

:: Business ::

__________ is a trade policy that does not restrict imports or exports; it can also be understood as the free market idea applied to international trade. In government, __________ is predominantly advocated by political parties that hold liberal economic positions while economically left-wing and nationalist political parties generally support protectionism, the opposite of __________ .

Exam Probability: **High**

10. *Answer choices:*

(see index for correct answer)

- a. Free trade
- b. Certified Business Continuity Professional
- c. Organizational life cycle
- d. Business development

Guidance: level 1

:: Management ::

The term __________ refers to measures designed to increase the degree of autonomy and self-determination in people and in communities in order to enable them to represent their interests in a responsible and self-determined way, acting on their own authority. It is the process of becoming stronger and more confident, especially in controlling one`s life and claiming one`s rights. __________ as action refers both to the process of self- __________ and to professional support of people, which enables them to overcome their sense of powerlessness and lack of influence, and to recognize and use their resources. To do work with power.

Exam Probability: **High**

11. *Answer choices:*

(see index for correct answer)

- a. Formula for change

- b. Supplier performance management
- c. Continuous-flow manufacturing
- d. Duality

Guidance: level 1

:: Budgets ::

A _________ is a financial plan for a defined period, often one year. It may also include planned sales volumes and revenues, resource quantities, costs and expenses, assets, liabilities and cash flows. Companies, governments, families and other organizations use it to express strategic plans of activities or events in measurable terms.

Exam Probability: **High**

12. *Answer choices:*
(see index for correct answer)

- a. Budget set
- b. Budget
- c. Film budgeting
- d. Railway Budget

Guidance: level 1

:: Management ::

_________ is the practice of initiating, planning, executing, controlling, and closing the work of a team to achieve specific goals and meet specific success criteria at the specified time.

Exam Probability: **High**

13. *Answer choices:*
(see index for correct answer)

- a. Professional performances
- b. Project management
- c. Completed Staff Work
- d. Continuous monitoring

Guidance: level 1

:: Analysis ::

_________ is the process of breaking a complex topic or substance into smaller parts in order to gain a better understanding of it. The technique has been applied in the study of mathematics and logic since before Aristotle , though _________ as a formal concept is a relatively recent development.

Exam Probability: **High**

14. *Answer choices:*
(see index for correct answer)

- a. SWOQe
- b. Analytical quality control
- c. Proximity analysis
- d. Analysis

Guidance: level 1

:: Classification systems ::

_________ is the practice of comparing business processes and performance metrics to industry bests and best practices from other companies. Dimensions typically measured are quality, time and cost.

Exam Probability: **Medium**

15. *Answer choices:*
(see index for correct answer)

- a. Structural Classification of Proteins database
- b. China Time-honored Brand
- c. Benchmarking
- d. World Reference Base for Soil Resources

Guidance: level 1

:: Management ::

_________ is a process by which entities review the quality of all factors involved in production. ISO 9000 defines _________ as "A part of quality management focused on fulfilling quality requirements".

Exam Probability: **Low**

16. *Answer choices:*
(see index for correct answer)

- a. Success-oriented management
- b. Shamrock Organization
- c. Marketing plan
- d. Quality control

Guidance: level 1

:: Association of Southeast Asian Nations ::

The Association of Southeast Asian Nations is a regional intergovernmental organization comprising ten countries in Southeast Asia, which promotes intergovernmental cooperation and facilitates economic, political, security, military, educational, and sociocultural integration among its members and other countries in Asia. It also regularly engages other countries in the Asia-Pacific region and beyond. A major partner of Shanghai Cooperation Organisation, _________ maintains a global network of alliances and dialogue partners and is considered by many as a global powerhouse, the central union for cooperation in Asia-Pacific, and a prominent and influential organization. It is involved in numerous international affairs, and hosts diplomatic missions throughout the world.

Exam Probability: **Medium**

17. *Answer choices:*
(see index for correct answer)

- a. Emblem of the Association of Southeast Asian Nations
- b. The ASEAN Way
- c. ASEAN
- d. ASEAN Human Rights Declaration

Guidance: level 1

:: Management ::

_________ is the identification, evaluation, and prioritization of risks followed by coordinated and economical application of resources to minimize, monitor, and control the probability or impact of unfortunate events or to maximize the realization of opportunities.

Exam Probability: **Low**

18. *Answer choices:*

(see index for correct answer)

- a. Risk management
- b. Social risk management
- c. Force-field analysis
- d. Narcissistic leadership

Guidance: level 1

:: Production and manufacturing ::

__________ is a set of techniques and tools for process improvement. Though as a shortened form it may be found written as 6S, it should not be confused with the methodology known as 6S .

Exam Probability: **Medium**

19. *Answer choices:*

(see index for correct answer)

- a. Six Sigma
- b. Variable rate feeder
- c. Pre-shipment inspection
- d. Computer-aided process planning

Guidance: level 1

:: Marketing ::

A __________ is the quantity of payment or compensation given by one party to another in return for one unit of goods or services.. A __________ is influenced by both production costs and demand for the product. A __________ may be determined by a monopolist or may be imposed on the firm by market conditions.

Exam Probability: **Low**

20. *Answer choices:*

(see index for correct answer)

- a. Price
- b. Product sabotage
- c. Discoverability

- d. Marketing brochure

Guidance: level 1

:: Mathematical finance ::

In economics and finance, _________ , also known as present discounted value, is the value of an expected income stream determined as of the date of valuation. The _________ is always less than or equal to the future value because money has interest-earning potential, a characteristic referred to as the time value of money, except during times of negative interest rates, when the _________ will be more than the future value. Time value can be described with the simplified phrase, "A dollar today is worth more than a dollar tomorrow". Here, `worth more` means that its value is greater. A dollar today is worth more than a dollar tomorrow because the dollar can be invested and earn a day`s worth of interest, making the total accumulate to a value more than a dollar by tomorrow. Interest can be compared to rent. Just as rent is paid to a landlord by a tenant without the ownership of the asset being transferred, interest is paid to a lender by a borrower who gains access to the money for a time before paying it back. By letting the borrower have access to the money, the lender has sacrificed the exchange value of this money, and is compensated for it in the form of interest. The initial amount of the borrowed funds is less than the total amount of money paid to the lender.

Exam Probability: **Medium**

21. *Answer choices:*

(see index for correct answer)

- a. Consumer math
- b. Present value
- c. Implied volatility
- d. QuantLib

Guidance: level 1

:: Stock market ::

The _________ of a corporation is all of the shares into which ownership of the corporation is divided. In American English, the shares are commonly known as " _________ s". A single share of the _________ represents fractional ownership of the corporation in proportion to the total number of shares. This typically entitles the _________ holder to that fraction of the company's earnings, proceeds from liquidation of assets , or voting power, often dividing these up in proportion to the amount of money each _________ holder has invested. Not all _________ is necessarily equal, as certain classes of _________ may be issued for example without voting rights, with enhanced voting rights, or with a certain priority to receive profits or liquidation proceeds before or after other classes of shareholders.

Exam Probability: **Medium**

22. *Answer choices:*

(see index for correct answer)

- a. Microexchanges
- b. Stock exchange
- c. Stock
- d. Seeking Alpha

Guidance: level 1

:: Market research ::

_________ , an acronym for Information through Disguised Experimentation is an annual market research fair conducted by the students of IIM-Lucknow. Students create games and use various other simulated environments to capture consumers' subconscious thoughts. This innovative method of market research removes the sensitization effect that might bias peoples answers to questions. This ensures that the most truthful answers are captured to research questions. The games are designed in such a way that the observers can elicit all the required information just by observing and noting down the behaviour and the responses of the participants.

Exam Probability: **Medium**

23. *Answer choices:*

(see index for correct answer)

- a. IModerate
- b. Market research

- c. Market surveillance
- d. Multivariate landing page optimization

Guidance: level 1

:: ::

An _________ is the production of goods or related services within an economy. The major source of revenue of a group or company is the indicator of its relevant _________ . When a large group has multiple sources of revenue generation, it is considered to be working in different industries. Manufacturing _________ became a key sector of production and labour in European and North American countries during the Industrial Revolution, upsetting previous mercantile and feudal economies. This came through many successive rapid advances in technology, such as the production of steel and coal.

Exam Probability: **Medium**

24. *Answer choices:*

(see index for correct answer)

- a. open system
- b. surface-level diversity
- c. imperative
- d. hierarchical

Guidance: level 1

:: Loans ::

In finance, a _________ is the lending of money by one or more individuals, organizations, or other entities to other individuals, organizations etc. The recipient incurs a debt, and is usually liable to pay interest on that debt until it is repaid, and also to repay the principal amount borrowed.

Exam Probability: **Medium**

25. *Answer choices:*

(see index for correct answer)

- a. Student Loan Guarantor
- b. Loan
- c. Marketing assistance loans

- d. Home equity line of credit

Guidance: level 1

:: National accounts ::

__________ is a monetary measure of the market value of all the final goods and services produced in a period of time, often annually. GDP per capita does not, however, reflect differences in the cost of living and the inflation rates of the countries; therefore using a basis of GDP per capita at purchasing power parity is arguably more useful when comparing differences in living standards between nations.

Exam Probability: **High**

26. *Answer choices:*

(see index for correct answer)

- a. capital formation
- b. Fixed capital
- c. Gross domestic product

Guidance: level 1

:: Commerce ::

__________ relates to "the exchange of goods and services, especially on a large scale". It includes legal, economic, political, social, cultural and technological systems that operate in a country or in international trade.

Exam Probability: **Medium**

27. *Answer choices:*

(see index for correct answer)

- a. Deal transaction
- b. Country commercial guides
- c. Commerce
- d. Return merchandise authorization

Guidance: level 1

:: Marketing ::

_________ is based on a marketing concept which can be adopted by an organization as a strategy for business expansion. Where implemented, a franchisor licenses its know-how, procedures, intellectual property, use of its business model, brand, and rights to sell its branded products and services to a franchisee. In return the franchisee pays certain fees and agrees to comply with certain obligations, typically set out in a Franchise Agreement.

Exam Probability: **Medium**

28. *Answer choices:*

(see index for correct answer)

- a. Product proliferation
- b. Franchising
- c. Kronos Effect
- d. Fifth screen

Guidance: level 1

:: Statistical terminology ::

_________ is the magnitude or dimensions of a thing. _________ can be measured as length, width, height, diameter, perimeter, area, volume, or mass.

Exam Probability: **High**

29. *Answer choices:*

(see index for correct answer)

- a. Error bar
- b. Noncentrality parameter
- c. Random variate
- d. Univariate

Guidance: level 1

:: Quality management ::

_________ ensures that an organization, product or service is consistent. It has four main components: quality planning, quality assurance, quality control and quality improvement. _________ is focused not only on product and service quality, but also on the means to achieve it. _________ , therefore, uses quality assurance and control of processes as well as products to achieve more consistent quality.What a customer wants and is willing to pay for it determines quality. It is written or unwritten commitment to a known or unknown consumer in the market . Thus, quality can be defined as fitness for intended use or, in other words, how well the product performs its intended function

Exam Probability: **Low**

30. *Answer choices:*

(see index for correct answer)

- a. External quality assessment
- b. European Quality in Social Services
- c. Test bay
- d. Indian Register Quality Systems

Guidance: level 1

:: Interest rates ::

An _________ is the amount of interest due per period, as a proportion of the amount lent, deposited or borrowed . The total interest on an amount lent or borrowed depends on the principal sum, the _________ , the compounding frequency, and the length of time over which it is lent, deposited or borrowed.

Exam Probability: **Medium**

31. *Answer choices:*

(see index for correct answer)

- a. Bank rate
- b. Interest rate
- c. Annual effective discount rate
- d. Amortising swap

Guidance: level 1

:: Project management ::

_________ is the right to exercise power, which can be formalized by a state and exercised by way of judges, appointed executives of government, or the ecclesiastical or priestly appointed representatives of a God or other deities.

Exam Probability: **High**

32. *Answer choices:*

(see index for correct answer)

- a. PM Declaration of Interdependence
- b. Authority
- c. P3M3
- d. Project sponsorship

Guidance: level 1

:: ::

Competition arises whenever at least two parties strive for a goal which cannot be shared: where one`s gain is the other`s loss .

Exam Probability: **High**

33. *Answer choices:*

(see index for correct answer)

- a. imperative
- b. Competitor
- c. Character
- d. hierarchical

Guidance: level 1

:: Stock market ::

_________ is freedom from, or resilience against, potential harm caused by others. Beneficiaries of _________ may be of persons and social groups, objects and institutions, ecosystems or any other entity or phenomenon vulnerable to unwanted change by its environment.

Exam Probability: **Medium**

34. *Answer choices:*
(see index for correct answer)

- a. Security
- b. Witching hour
- c. Abnormal return
- d. Big boy letter

Guidance: level 1

:: Generally Accepted Accounting Principles ::

In accounting, _________ is the income that a business have from its normal business activities, usually from the sale of goods and services to customers. _________ is also referred to as sales or turnover.Some companies receive _________ from interest, royalties, or other fees. _________ may refer to business income in general, or it may refer to the amount, in a monetary unit, earned during a period of time, as in "Last year, Company X had _________ of $42 million". Profits or net income generally imply total _________ minus total expenses in a given period. In accounting, in the balance statement it is a subsection of the Equity section and _________ increases equity, it is often referred to as the "top line" due to its position on the income statement at the very top. This is to be contrasted with the "bottom line" which denotes net income .

Exam Probability: **Medium**

35. *Answer choices:*
(see index for correct answer)

- a. Paid in capital
- b. Pro forma
- c. Matching principle
- d. Indian Accounting Standards

Guidance: level 1

:: ::

An _________ is a contingent motivator. Traditional _________ s are extrinsic motivators which reward actions to yield a desired outcome. The effectiveness of traditional _________ s has changed as the needs of Western society have evolved. While the traditional _________ model is effective when there is a defined procedure and goal for a task, Western society started to require a higher volume of critical thinkers, so the traditional model became less effective. Institutions are now following a trend in implementing strategies that rely on intrinsic motivations rather than the extrinsic motivations that the traditional _________ s foster.

Exam Probability: **High**

36. *Answer choices:*

(see index for correct answer)

- a. hierarchical perspective
- b. surface-level diversity
- c. imperative
- d. open system

Guidance: level 1

:: Payments ::

A _________ is the trade of value from one party to another for goods, or services, or to fulfill a legal obligation.

Exam Probability: **Medium**

37. *Answer choices:*

(see index for correct answer)

- a. Tuition payments
- b. Subsidy
- c. Payment
- d. Market transition payments

Guidance: level 1

:: Stock market ::

A _________ , securities exchange or bourse, is a facility where stock brokers and traders can buy and sell securities, such as shares of stock and bonds and other financial instruments. _________ s may also provide for facilities the issue and redemption of such securities and instruments and capital events including the payment of income and dividends. Securities traded on a _________ include stock issued by listed companies, unit trusts, derivatives, pooled investment products and bonds. _________ s often function as "continuous auction" markets with buyers and sellers consummating transactions via open outcry at a central location such as the floor of the exchange or by using an electronic trading platform.

Exam Probability: **Low**

38. *Answer choices:*

(see index for correct answer)

- a. Stock Catalyst
- b. Stock exchange
- c. CNBC Ticker
- d. Yellow strip

Guidance: level 1

:: Employment ::

The _________ is an individual`s metaphorical "journey" through learning, work and other aspects of life. There are a number of ways to define _________ and the term is used in a variety of ways.

Exam Probability: **Medium**

39. *Answer choices:*

(see index for correct answer)

- a. Active ageing
- b. Clodomir Santos de Morais
- c. Employer Registration
- d. Career

Guidance: level 1

:: Meetings ::

An _________ is a group of people who participate in a show or encounter a work of art, literature , theatre, music , video games , or academics in any medium. _________ members participate in different ways in different kinds of art; some events invite overt _________ participation and others allowing only modest clapping and criticism and reception.

Exam Probability: **High**

40. *Answer choices:*
(see index for correct answer)

- a. Prayer meeting
- b. Awayday
- c. Agenda
- d. 2006 Russian March

Guidance: level 1

:: Business law ::

_________ is where a person`s financial liability is limited to a fixed sum, most commonly the value of a person`s investment in a company or partnership. If a company with _________ is sued, then the claimants are suing the company, not its owners or investors. A shareholder in a limited company is not personally liable for any of the debts of the company, other than for the amount already invested in the company and for any unpaid amount on the shares in the company, if any. The same is true for the members of a _________ partnership and the limited partners in a limited partnership. By contrast, sole proprietors and partners in general partnerships are each liable for all the debts of the business .

Exam Probability: **High**

41. *Answer choices:*
(see index for correct answer)

- a. Uniform Commercial Code
- b. Limited liability
- c. Duty of fair representation
- d. Board of directors

Guidance: level 1

:: Business terms ::

A _________ is a short statement of why an organization exists, what its overall goal is, identifying the goal of its operations: what kind of product or service it provides, its primary customers or market, and its geographical region of operation. It may include a short statement of such fundamental matters as the organization`s values or philosophies, a business`s main competitive advantages, or a desired future state—the "vision".

Exam Probability: **High**

42. *Answer choices:*

(see index for correct answer)

- a. Mission statement
- b. Personal selling
- c. Strategic partner
- d. back office

Guidance: level 1

:: Television commercials ::

_________ is a characteristic that distinguishes physical entities that have biological processes, such as signaling and self-sustaining processes, from those that do not, either because such functions have ceased , or because they never had such functions and are classified as inanimate. Various forms of _________ exist, such as plants, animals, fungi, protists, archaea, and bacteria. The criteria can at times be ambiguous and may or may not define viruses, viroids, or potential synthetic _________ as "living". Biology is the science concerned with the study of _________ .

Exam Probability: **Low**

43. *Answer choices:*

(see index for correct answer)

- a. Lamp
- b. Yeh Dil Maange More!
- c. Life
- d. The Pizza Head Show

Guidance: level 1

:: Insolvency ::

_________ is a legal process through which people or other entities who cannot repay debts to creditors may seek relief from some or all of their debts. In most jurisdictions, _________ is imposed by a court order, often initiated by the debtor.

Exam Probability: **Low**

44. *Answer choices:*

(see index for correct answer)

- a. Conservatorship
- b. Bankruptcy
- c. Liquidator
- d. Insolvency law of Russia

Guidance: level 1

:: Workplace ::

_________ is asystematic determination of a subject`s merit, worth and significance, using criteria governed by a set of standards. It can assist an organization, program, design, project or any other intervention or initiative to assess any aim, realisable concept/proposal, or any alternative, to help in decision-making; or to ascertain the degree of achievement or value in regard to the aim and objectives and results of any such action that has been completed. The primary purpose of _________ , in addition to gaining insight into prior or existing initiatives, is to enable reflection and assist in the identification of future change.

Exam Probability: **Medium**

45. *Answer choices:*

(see index for correct answer)

- a. Workplace strategy
- b. Toxic workplace
- c. Workplace violence
- d. Evaluation

Guidance: level 1

:: Stock market ::

_________ is a form of corporate equity ownership, a type of security. The terms voting share and ordinary share are also used frequently in other parts of the world; " _________ " being primarily used in the United States. They are known as Equity shares or Ordinary shares in the UK and other Commonwealth realms. This type of share gives the stockholder the right to share in the profits of the company, and to vote on matters of corporate policy and the composition of the members of the board of directors.

Exam Probability: **High**

46. *Answer choices:*

(see index for correct answer)

- a. Common stock
- b. European Depositary Receipt
- c. Ada TV
- d. Penny stock

Guidance: level 1

:: Alchemical processes ::

In chemistry, a _________ is a special type of homogeneous mixture composed of two or more substances. In such a mixture, a solute is a substance dissolved in another substance, known as a solvent. The mixing process of a _________ happens at a scale where the effects of chemical polarity are involved, resulting in interactions that are specific to solvation. The _________ assumes the phase of the solvent when the solvent is the larger fraction of the mixture, as is commonly the case. The concentration of a solute in a _________ is the mass of that solute expressed as a percentage of the mass of the whole _________ . The term aqueous _________ is when one of the solvents is water.

Exam Probability: **Medium**

47. *Answer choices:*

(see index for correct answer)

- a. Corporification
- b. Putrefaction
- c. Solution
- d. Putrefying bacteria

Guidance: level 1

:: Bribery ::

_________ is the act of giving or receiving something of value in exchange for some kind of influence or action in return, that the recipient would otherwise not offer. _________ is defined by Black`s Law Dictionary as the offering, giving, receiving, or soliciting of any item of value to influence the actions of an official or other person in charge of a public or legal duty. Essentially, _________ is offering to do something for someone for the expressed purpose of receiving something in exchange. Gifts of money or other items of value which are otherwise available to everyone on an equivalent basis, and not for dishonest purposes, is not _________ . Offering a discount or a refund to all purchasers is a legal rebate and is not _________ . For example, it is legal for an employee of a Public Utilities Commission involved in electric rate regulation to accept a rebate on electric service that reduces their cost for electricity, when the rebate is available to other residential electric customers. Giving the rebate to influence them to look favorably on the electric utility`s rate increase applications, however, would be considered _________ .

Exam Probability: **Low**

48. *Answer choices:*

(see index for correct answer)

- a. Caribbean Football Union corruption scandal
- b. Bribery
- c. GSIS-Meralco bribery case
- d. Cunningham scandal

Guidance: level 1

:: Project management ::

In political science, an _________ is a means by which a petition signed by a certain minimum number of registered voters can force a government to choose to either enact a law or hold a public vote in parliament in what is called indirect _________ , or under direct _________ , the proposition is immediately put to a plebiscite or referendum, in what is called a Popular initiated Referendum or citizen-initiated referendum).

Exam Probability: **Medium**

49. *Answer choices:*
(see index for correct answer)

- a. Libyan Project Management Association
- b. Resource leveling
- c. Initiative
- d. Project governance

Guidance: level 1

:: International trade ::

An _________ is a good brought into a jurisdiction, especially across a national border, from an external source. The party bringing in the good is called an _________ er. An _________ in the receiving country is an export from the sending country. _________ ation and exportation are the defining financial transactions of international trade.

Exam Probability: **Medium**

50. *Answer choices:*
(see index for correct answer)

- a. Linder hypothesis
- b. Special drawing rights
- c. Mutual recognition agreement
- d. Comparative advantage

Guidance: level 1

:: Management ::

In business, a _________ is the attribute that allows an organization to outperform its competitors. A _________ may include access to natural resources, such as high-grade ores or a low-cost power source, highly skilled labor, geographic location, high entry barriers, and access to new technology.

Exam Probability: **High**

51. *Answer choices:*
(see index for correct answer)

- a. Jarratt report
- b. Competitive advantage
- c. Management buyout
- d. Records manager

Guidance: level 1

:: Monopoly (economics) ::

A _________ is a form of intellectual property that gives its owner the legal right to exclude others from making, using, selling, and importing an invention for a limited period of years, in exchange for publishing an enabling public disclosure of the invention. In most countries _________ rights fall under civil law and the _________ holder needs to sue someone infringing the _________ in order to enforce his or her rights. In some industries _________ s are an essential form of competitive advantage; in others they are irrelevant.

Exam Probability: **Low**

52. *Answer choices:*

(see index for correct answer)

- a. Revenue-cap regulation
- b. Coercive monopoly
- c. Privatization
- d. Demonopolization

Guidance: level 1

:: Debt ::

_________ is the trust which allows one party to provide money or resources to another party wherein the second party does not reimburse the first party immediately , but promises either to repay or return those resources at a later date. In other words, _________ is a method of making reciprocity formal, legally enforceable, and extensible to a large group of unrelated people.

Exam Probability: **Low**

53. *Answer choices:*

(see index for correct answer)

- a. Medical debt
- b. Creditor
- c. Debt compliance
- d. Debit commission

Guidance: level 1

:: ::

Some scenarios associate "this kind of planning" with learning "life skills".Schedules are necessary, or at least useful, in situations where individuals need to know what time they must be at a specific location to receive a specific service, and where people need to accomplish a set of goals within a set time period.

Exam Probability: **Medium**

54. *Answer choices:*

(see index for correct answer)

- a. hierarchical perspective
- b. cultural
- c. imperative
- d. Scheduling

Guidance: level 1

:: Marketing analytics ::

__________ is a long-term, forward-looking approach to planning with the fundamental goal of achieving a sustainable competitive advantage. Strategic planning involves an analysis of the company`s strategic initial situation prior to the formulation, evaluation and selection of market-oriented competitive position that contributes to the company`s goals and marketing objectives.

Exam Probability: **Medium**

55. *Answer choices:*

(see index for correct answer)

- a. marketing dashboard
- b. Marketing strategy
- c. Advertising adstock
- d. Marketing performance measurement and management

Guidance: level 1

:: Stochastic processes ::

_________ is a system of rules that are created and enforced through social or governmental institutions to regulate behavior. It has been defined both as "the Science of Justice" and "the Art of Justice". _________ is a system that regulates and ensures that individuals or a community adhere to the will of the state. State-enforced _________ s can be made by a collective legislature or by a single legislator, resulting in statutes, by the executive through decrees and regulations, or established by judges through precedent, normally in common _________ jurisdictions. Private individuals can create legally binding contracts, including arbitration agreements that may elect to accept alternative arbitration to the normal court process. The formation of _________ s themselves may be influenced by a constitution, written or tacit, and the rights encoded therein. The _________ shapes politics, economics, history and society in various ways and serves as a mediator of relations between people.

Exam Probability: **Low**

56. *Answer choices:*

(see index for correct answer)

- a. Preferential attachment
- b. Mean value analysis
- c. Rough path
- d. Chinese restaurant process

Guidance: level 1

:: Rhetoric ::

_________ is the pattern of narrative development that aims to make vivid a place, object, character, or group. _________ is one of four rhetorical modes , along with exposition, argumentation, and narration. In practice it would be difficult to write literature that drew on just one of the four basic modes.

Exam Probability: **Medium**

57. *Answer choices:*

(see index for correct answer)

- a. Fiction-writing mode
- b. Master suppression techniques
- c. Description
- d. Politicards

Guidance: level 1

:: ::

__________ is the collection of techniques, skills, methods, and processes used in the production of goods or services or in the accomplishment of objectives, such as scientific investigation. __________ can be the knowledge of techniques, processes, and the like, or it can be embedded in machines to allow for operation without detailed knowledge of their workings. Systems applying __________ by taking an input, changing it according to the system`s use, and then producing an outcome are referred to as __________ systems or technological systems.

Exam Probability: **High**

58. *Answer choices:*

(see index for correct answer)

- a. similarity-attraction theory
- b. deep-level diversity
- c. levels of analysis
- d. Technology

Guidance: level 1

:: Economic globalization ::

__________ is an agreement in which one company hires another company to be responsible for a planned or existing activity that is or could be done internally,and sometimes involves transferring employees and assets from one firm to another.

Exam Probability: **Low**

59. *Answer choices:*

(see index for correct answer)

- a. Outsourcing
- b. global financial

Guidance: level 1

Management

Management is the administration of an organization, whether it is a business, a not-for-profit organization, or government body. Management includes the activities of setting the strategy of an organization and coordinating the efforts of its employees (or of volunteers) to accomplish its objectives through the application of available resources, such as financial, natural, technological, and human resources.

:: Project management ::

A _________ is a type of bar chart that illustrates a project schedule, named after its inventor, Henry Gantt , who designed such a chart around the years 1910–1915. Modern _________ s also show the dependency relationships between activities and current schedule status.

Exam Probability: **High**

1. *Answer choices:*

(see index for correct answer)

- a. Multidisciplinary approach
- b. Gantt chart
- c. Project blog
- d. Assumption-based planning

Guidance: level 1

:: Autonomy ::

In developmental psychology and moral, political, and bioethical philosophy, _________ is the capacity to make an informed, uncoerced decision. Autonomous organizations or institutions are independent or self-governing. _________ can also be defined from a human resources perspective, where it denotes a level of discretion granted to an employee in his or her work. In such cases, _________ is known to generally increase job satisfaction. _________ is a term that is also widely used in the field of medicine — personal _________ is greatly recognized and valued in health care.

Exam Probability: **High**

2. *Answer choices:*
(see index for correct answer)

- a. Rhex
- b. Autonomy
- c. Learner autonomy
- d. Consent

Guidance: level 1

:: Business law ::

A _________ is a group of people who jointly supervise the activities of an organization, which can be either a for-profit business, nonprofit organization, or a government agency. Such a board's powers, duties, and responsibilities are determined by government regulations and the organization's own constitution and bylaws. These authorities may specify the number of members of the board, how they are to be chosen, and how often they are to meet.

Exam Probability: **Medium**

3. *Answer choices:*
(see index for correct answer)

- a. Whitewash waiver
- b. Board of directors
- c. Commercial law
- d. Chattel mortgage

Guidance: level 1

:: Organizational behavior ::

In organizational behavior and industrial and organizational psychology, _________ is an individual`s psychological attachment to the organization. The basis behind many of these studies was to find ways to improve how workers feel about their jobs so that these workers would become more committed to their organizations. _________ predicts work variables such as turnover, organizational citizenship behavior, and job performance. Some of the factors such as role stress, empowerment, job insecurity and employability, and distribution of leadership have been shown to be connected to a worker`s sense of _________ .

Exam Probability: **High**

4. *Answer choices:*

(see index for correct answer)

- a. Organizational commitment
- b. Micro-initiative
- c. Self-policing
- d. Administrative Behavior

Guidance: level 1

:: Human resource management ::

_________ , also known as management by results , was first popularized by Peter Drucker in his 1954 book The Practice of Management. _________ is the process of defining specific objectives within an organization that management can convey to organization members, then deciding on how to achieve each objective in sequence. This process allows managers to take work that needs to be done one step at a time to allow for a calm, yet productive work environment. This process also helps organization members to see their accomplishments as they achieve each objective, which reinforces a positive work environment and a sense of achievement. An important part of MBO is the measurement and comparison of an employee`s actual performance with the standards set. Ideally, when employees themselves have been involved with the goal-setting and choosing the course of action to be followed by them, they are more likely to fulfill their responsibilities.According to George S. Odiorne, the system of _________ can be described as a process whereby the superior and subordinate jointly identify common goals, define each individual`s major areas of responsibility in terms of the results expected of him or her, and use these measures as guides for operating the unit and assessing the contribution of each of its members.

Exam Probability: **Medium**

5. *Answer choices:*

(see index for correct answer)

- a. Simultaneous recruiting of new graduates
- b. Adaptive performance
- c. Senior management
- d. Management by objectives

Guidance: level 1

:: Marketing ::

_________ is the percentage of a market accounted for by a specific entity. In a survey of nearly 200 senior marketing managers, 67% responded that they found the revenue- "dollar _________ " metric very useful, while 61% found "unit _________ " very useful.

Exam Probability: **Low**

6. *Answer choices:*

(see index for correct answer)

- a. Next-best-action marketing
- b. Place branding
- c. Local store marketing
- d. Multicultural marketing

Guidance: level 1

:: Systems thinking ::

Systems theory is the interdisciplinary study of systems. A system is a cohesive conglomeration of interrelated and interdependent parts that is either natural or man-made. Every system is delineated by its spatial and temporal boundaries, surrounded and influenced by its environment, described by its structure and purpose or nature and expressed in its functioning. In terms of its effects, a system can be more than the sum of its parts if it expresses synergy or emergent behavior. Changing one part of the system usually affects other parts and the whole system, with predictable patterns of behavior. For systems that are self-learning and self-adapting, the positive growth and adaptation depend upon how well the system is adjusted with its environment. Some systems function mainly to support other systems by aiding in the maintenance of the other system to prevent failure. The goal of systems theory is systematically discovering a system`s dynamics, constraints, conditions and elucidating principles that can be discerned and applied to systems at every level of nesting, and in every field for achieving optimized equifinality.

Exam Probability: **Low**

7. *Answer choices:*

(see index for correct answer)

- a. Thought leader
- b. World Futures Studies Federation
- c. Ted Coombs
- d. Interdependence

Guidance: level 1

:: Organizational theory ::

_________ refers to both a body of non-elective government officials and an administrative policy-making group. Historically, a _________ was a government administration managed by departments staffed with non-elected officials. Today, _________ is the administrative system governing any large institution, whether publicly owned or privately owned. The public administration in many countries is an example of a _________ , but so is the centralized hierarchical structure of a business firm.

Exam Probability: **Low**

8. *Answer choices:*

(see index for correct answer)

- a. Organizational learning
- b. Swift trust
- c. Solid line reporting
- d. Bureaucracy

Guidance: level 1

:: Management occupations ::

_________ is the process of designing, launching and running a new business, which is often initially a small business. The people who create these businesses are called entrepreneurs.

Exam Probability: **Low**

9. *Answer choices:*

(see index for correct answer)

- a. entrepreneurial
- b. Apparatchik
- c. Councillor
- d. Chief reputation officer

Guidance: level 1

:: ::

In business strategy, _________ is establishing a competitive advantage by having the lowest cost of operation in the industry. _________ is often driven by company efficiency, size, scale, scope and cumulative experience .A _________ strategy aims to exploit scale of production, well-defined scope and other economies , producing highly standardized products, using advanced technology.In recent years, more and more companies have chosen a strategic mix to achieve market leadership. These patterns consist of simultaneous _________ , superior customer service and product leadership. Walmart has succeeded across the world due to its _________ strategy. The company has cut down on exesses at every point of production and thus are able to provide the consumers with quality products at low prices.

Exam Probability: **Low**

10. *Answer choices:*

(see index for correct answer)

- a. open system
- b. process perspective
- c. corporate values
- d. information systems assessment

Guidance: level 1

:: ::

A _________ is a leader`s method of providing direction, implementing plans, and motivating people. Various authors have proposed identifying many different _________ s as exhibited by leaders in the political, business or other fields. Studies on _________ are conducted in the military field, expressing an approach that stresses a holistic view of leadership, including how a leader`s physical presence determines how others perceive that leader. The factors of physical presence in this context include military bearing, physical fitness, confidence, and resilience. The leader`s intellectual capacity helps to conceptualize solutions and to acquire knowledge to do the job. A leader`s conceptual abilities apply agility, judgment, innovation, interpersonal tact, and domain knowledge. Domain knowledge encompasses tactical and technical knowledge as well as cultural and geopolitical awareness. Daniel Goleman in his article "Leadership that Gets Results" talks about six styles of leadership.

Exam Probability: **Medium**

11. *Answer choices:*

(see index for correct answer)

- a. Sarbanes-Oxley act of 2002
- b. Leadership style
- c. interpersonal communication
- d. process perspective

Guidance: level 1

:: Commercial item transport and distribution ::

In commerce, supply-chain management , the management of the flow of goods and services, involves the movement and storage of raw materials, of work-in-process inventory, and of finished goods from point of origin to point of consumption. Interconnected or interlinked networks, channels and node businesses combine in the provision of products and services required by end customers in a supply chain. Supply-chain management has been defined as the "design, planning, execution, control, and monitoring of supply-chain activities with the objective of creating net value, building a competitive infrastructure, leveraging worldwide logistics, synchronizing supply with demand and measuring performance globally."SCM practice draws heavily from the areas of industrial engineering, systems engineering, operations management, logistics, procurement, information technology, and marketing and strives for an integrated approach. Marketing channels play an important role in supply-chain management. Current research in supply-chain management is concerned with topics related to sustainability and risk management, among others. Some suggest that the "people dimension" of SCM, ethical issues, internal integration, transparency/visibility, and human capital/talent management are topics that have, so far, been underrepresented on the research agenda.

Exam Probability: **Medium**

12. *Answer choices:*

(see index for correct answer)

- a. Mid-stream operation
- b. Green logistics
- c. Spoke-hub distribution paradigm
- d. Courier software

Guidance: level 1

:: Packaging ::

In work place, _________ or job _________ means good ranking with the hypothesized conception of requirements of a role. There are two types of job _________ s: contextual and task. Task _________ is related to cognitive ability while contextual _________ is dependent upon personality. Task _________ are behavioral roles that are recognized in job descriptions and by remuneration systems, they are directly related to organizational _________ , whereas, contextual _________ are value based and additional behavioral roles that are not recognized in job descriptions and covered by compensation; they are extra roles that are indirectly related to organizational _________ . Citizenship _________ like contextual _________ means a set of individual activity/contribution that supports the organizational culture.

Exam Probability: **Medium**

13. *Answer choices:*

(see index for correct answer)

- a. Pullapart
- b. Envelope
- c. Boxtop
- d. Load securing

Guidance: level 1

:: Supply chain management terms ::

In business and finance, _________ is a system of organizations, people, activities, information, and resources involved inmoving a product or service from supplier to customer. _________ activities involve the transformation of natural resources, raw materials, and components into a finished product that is delivered to the end customer. In sophisticated _________ systems, used products may re-enter the _________ at any point where residual value is recyclable. _________ s link value chains.

Exam Probability: **Low**

14. *Answer choices:*

(see index for correct answer)

- a. Direct shipment
- b. Work in process

- c. Supply chain
- d. Most valuable customers

Guidance: level 1

:: ::

A _________ is a type of job aid used to reduce failure by compensating for potential limits of human memory and attention. It helps to ensure consistency and completeness in carrying out a task. A basic example is the "to do list". A more advanced _________ would be a schedule, which lays out tasks to be done according to time of day or other factors. A primary task in _________ is documentation of the task and auditing against the documentation.

Exam Probability: **Low**

15. *Answer choices:*

(see index for correct answer)

- a. Character
- b. process perspective
- c. Checklist
- d. personal values

Guidance: level 1

:: Project management ::

A _________ is a professional in the field of project management. _________ s have the responsibility of the planning, procurement and execution of a project, in any undertaking that has a defined scope, defined start and a defined finish; regardless of industry. _________ s are first point of contact for any issues or discrepancies arising from within the heads of various departments in an organization before the problem escalates to higher authorities. Project management is the responsibility of a _________ . This individual seldom participates directly in the activities that produce the end result, but rather strives to maintain the progress, mutual interaction and tasks of various parties in such a way that reduces the risk of overall failure, maximizes benefits, and minimizes costs.

Exam Probability: **High**

16. *Answer choices:*

(see index for correct answer)

- a. Project manager
- b. ISO 31000
- c. The Practice Standard for Scheduling
- d. Schedule chicken

Guidance: level 1

:: Financial risk ::

__________ is a type of risk faced by investors, corporations, and governments that political decisions, events, or conditions will significantly affect the profitability of a business actor or the expected value of a given economic action. __________ can be understood and managed with reasoned foresight and investment.

Exam Probability: **High**

17. *Answer choices:*

(see index for correct answer)

- a. Political risk
- b. Capital Requirements Directive
- c. Interest rate risk
- d. Reputational risk

Guidance: level 1

:: Life skills ::

__________ , emotional leadership , emotional quotient and __________ quotient , is the capability of individuals to recognize their own emotions and those of others, discern between different feelings and label them appropriately, use emotional information to guide thinking and behavior, and manage and/or adjust emotions to adapt to environments or achieve one`s goal.

Exam Probability: **Low**

18. *Answer choices:*

(see index for correct answer)

- a. coping mechanism
- b. Social intelligence
- c. Emotional intelligence

- d. multiple intelligence

Guidance: level 1

:: Employment compensation ::

_________ refers to various incentive plans introduced by businesses that provide direct or indirect payments to employees that depend on company's profitability in addition to employees' regular salary and bonuses. In publicly traded companies these plans typically amount to allocation of shares to employees. One of the earliest pioneers of _________ was Englishman Theodore Cooke Taylor, who is known to have introduced the practice in his woollen mills during the late 1800s .

Exam Probability: **Medium**

19. *Answer choices:*
(see index for correct answer)

- a. Gender pay gap
- b. Pension administration in the United States
- c. Profit sharing
- d. New York Disability Benefits Law

Guidance: level 1

:: ::

The _________ is an intergovernmental organization that is concerned with the regulation of international trade between nations. The WTO officially commenced on 1 January 1995 under the Marrakesh Agreement, signed by 124 nations on 15 April 1994, replacing the General Agreement on Tariffs and Trade , which commenced in 1948. It is the largest international economic organization in the world.

Exam Probability: **High**

20. *Answer choices:*
(see index for correct answer)

- a. World Trade Organization
- b. empathy
- c. Character
- d. hierarchical

Guidance: level 1

:: Evaluation ::

A _________ is an evaluation of a publication, service, or company such as a movie , video game , musical composition , book ; a piece of hardware like a car, home appliance, or computer; or an event or performance, such as a live music concert, play, musical theater show, dance show, or art exhibition. In addition to a critical evaluation, the _________ 's author may assign the work a rating to indicate its relative merit. More loosely, an author may _________ current events, trends, or items in the news. A compilation of _________ s may itself be called a _________ . The New York _________ of Books, for instance, is a collection of essays on literature, culture, and current affairs. National _________ , founded by William F. Buckley, Jr., is an influential conservative magazine, and Monthly _________ is a long-running socialist periodical.

Exam Probability: **High**

21. *Answer choices:*

(see index for correct answer)

- a. Review
- b. Quality assurance
- c. Problem
- d. Technology assessment

Guidance: level 1

:: Decision theory ::

Within economics the concept of _________ is used to model worth or value, but its usage has evolved significantly over time. The term was introduced initially as a measure of pleasure or satisfaction within the theory of utilitarianism by moral philosophers such as Jeremy Bentham and John Stuart Mill. But the term has been adapted and reapplied within neoclassical economics, which dominates modern economic theory, as a _________ function that represents a consumer's preference ordering over a choice set. As such, it is devoid of its original interpretation as a measurement of the pleasure or satisfaction obtained by the consumer from that choice.

Exam Probability: **Medium**

22. *Answer choices:*

(see index for correct answer)

- a. Weighted sum model
- b. Mental accounting
- c. Two-moment decision model
- d. Pignistic probability

Guidance: level 1

:: ::

_________ is a kind of action that occur as two or more objects have an effect upon one another. The idea of a two-way effect is essential in the concept of _________ , as opposed to a one-way causal effect. A closely related term is interconnectivity, which deals with the _________ s of _________ s within systems: combinations of many simple _________ s can lead to surprising emergent phenomena. _________ has different tailored meanings in various sciences. Changes can also involve _________ .

Exam Probability: **Low**

23. *Answer choices:*

(see index for correct answer)

- a. Character
- b. corporate values
- c. hierarchical
- d. Interaction

Guidance: level 1

:: ::

_________ or accountancy is the measurement, processing, and communication of financial information about economic entities such as businesses and corporations. The modern field was established by the Italian mathematician Luca Pacioli in 1494. _________ , which has been called the "language of business", measures the results of an organization`s economic activities and conveys this information to a variety of users, including investors, creditors, management, and regulators. Practitioners of _________ are known as accountants. The terms " _________ " and "financial reporting" are often used as synonyms.

Exam Probability: **Low**

24. *Answer choices:*
(see index for correct answer)

- a. corporate values
- b. functional perspective
- c. Sarbanes-Oxley act of 2002
- d. co-culture

Guidance: level 1

:: ::

In mathematics, a _________ is a relationship between two numbers indicating how many times the first number contains the second. For example, if a bowl of fruit contains eight oranges and six lemons, then the _________ of oranges to lemons is eight to six . Similarly, the _________ of lemons to oranges is 6:8 and the _________ of oranges to the total amount of fruit is 8:14 .

Exam Probability: **Medium**

25. *Answer choices:*
(see index for correct answer)

- a. cultural
- b. Ratio
- c. surface-level diversity
- d. levels of analysis

Guidance: level 1

:: Human resource management ::

__________ expands the capacity of individuals to perform in leadership roles within organizations. Leadership roles are those that facilitate execution of a company's strategy through building alignment, winning mindshare and growing the capabilities of others. Leadership roles may be formal, with the corresponding authority to make decisions and take responsibility, or they may be informal roles with little official authority .

Exam Probability: **Medium**

26. *Answer choices:*
(see index for correct answer)

- a. Leadership development
- b. Talent supply chain management
- c. Sham peer review
- d. Fresh tracks

Guidance: level 1

:: ::

A __________ is monetary compensation paid by an employer to an employee in exchange for work done. Payment may be calculated as a fixed amount for each task completed , or at an hourly or daily rate , or based on an easily measured quantity of work done.

Exam Probability: **Low**

27. *Answer choices:*
(see index for correct answer)

- a. imperative
- b. deep-level diversity
- c. surface-level diversity
- d. hierarchical perspective

Guidance: level 1

:: Human resource management ::

__________ , executive management, upper management, or a management team is generally a team of individuals at the highest level of management of an organization who have the day-to-day tasks of managing that organization — sometimes a company or a corporation.

Exam Probability: **Low**

28. *Answer choices:*

(see index for correct answer)

- a. Occupational Information Network
- b. Management due diligence
- c. Aspiring Minds
- d. Senior management

Guidance: level 1

:: ::

__________ refers to the confirmation of certain characteristics of an object, person, or organization. This confirmation is often, but not always, provided by some form of external review, education, assessment, or audit. Accreditation is a specific organization's process of __________ . According to the National Council on Measurement in Education, a __________ test is a credentialing test used to determine whether individuals are knowledgeable enough in a given occupational area to be labeled "competent to practice" in that area.

Exam Probability: **Low**

29. *Answer choices:*

(see index for correct answer)

- a. process perspective
- b. Certification
- c. cultural
- d. Character

Guidance: level 1

:: ::

The __________ is a political and economic union of 28 member states that are located primarily in Europe. It has an area of 4,475,757 km2 and an estimated population of about 513 million. The EU has developed an internal single market through a standardised system of laws that apply in all member states in those matters, and only those matters, where members have agreed to act as one. EU policies aim to ensure the free movement of people, goods, services and capital within the internal market, enact legislation in justice and home affairs and maintain common policies on trade, agriculture, fisheries and regional development. For travel within the Schengen Area, passport controls have been abolished. A monetary union was established in 1999 and came into full force in 2002 and is composed of 19 EU member states which use the euro currency.

Exam Probability: **High**

30. *Answer choices:*
(see index for correct answer)

- a. European Union
- b. similarity-attraction theory
- c. imperative
- d. deep-level diversity

Guidance: level 1

:: Evaluation ::

__________ is the practice of being honest and showing a consistent and uncompromising adherence to strong moral and ethical principles and values.In ethics, __________ is regarded as the honesty and truthfulness or accuracy of one`s actions. __________ can stand in opposition to hypocrisy, in that judging with the standards of __________ involves regarding internal consistency as a virtue, and suggests that parties holding within themselves apparently conflicting values should account for the discrepancy or alter their beliefs. The word __________ evolved from the Latin adjective integer, meaning whole or complete. In this context, __________ is the inner sense of "wholeness" deriving from qualities such as honesty and consistency of character. As such, one may judge that others "have __________ " to the extent that they act according to the values, beliefs and principles they claim to hold.

Exam Probability: **High**

31. *Answer choices:*

(see index for correct answer)

- a. Teaching and Learning International Survey
- b. Goddard College
- c. Princeton Application Repository for Shared-Memory Computers
- d. Ecological indicator

Guidance: level 1

:: Marketing ::

_________ or stock is the goods and materials that a business holds for the ultimate goal of resale .

Exam Probability: **High**

32. *Answer choices:*

(see index for correct answer)

- a. Inventory
- b. Price premium
- c. Content Curation Marketing
- d. DeusM

Guidance: level 1

:: Human resource management ::

_________ encompasses values and behaviors that contribute to the unique social and psychological environment of a business. The _________ influences the way people interact, the context within which knowledge is created, the resistance they will have towards certain changes, and ultimately the way they share knowledge. _________ represents the collective values, beliefs and principles of organizational members and is a product of factors such as history, product, market, technology, strategy, type of employees, management style, and national culture; culture includes the organization`s vision, values, norms, systems, symbols, language, assumptions, environment, location, beliefs and habits.

Exam Probability: **Low**

33. *Answer choices:*

(see index for correct answer)

- a. Organizational culture
- b. ROWE
- c. SLT Human Capital Solutions
- d. Management due diligence

Guidance: level 1

:: Management ::

A __________ is someone who engages in facilitation—any activity that makes a social process easy or easier. A __________ often helps a group of people to understand their common objectives and assists them to plan how to achieve these objectives; in doing so, the __________ remains "neutral", meaning he/she does not take a particular position in the discussion. Some __________ tools will try to assist the group in achieving a consensus on any disagreements that preexist or emerge in the meeting so that it has a strong basis for future action.

Exam Probability: **Low**

34. *Answer choices:*

(see index for correct answer)

- a. Concept of operations
- b. Facilitator
- c. Downstream
- d. Power structure

Guidance: level 1

:: ::

A __________ or sample __________ is a single measure of some attribute of a sample . It is calculated by applying a function to the values of the items of the sample, which are known together as a set of data.

Exam Probability: **High**

35. *Answer choices:*

(see index for correct answer)

- a. Character
- b. corporate values

- c. similarity-attraction theory
- d. levels of analysis

Guidance: level 1

:: Customs duties ::

A _________ is a tax on imports or exports between sovereign states. It is a form of regulation of foreign trade and a policy that taxes foreign products to encourage or safeguard domestic industry. _________ s are the simplest and oldest instrument of trade policy. Traditionally, states have used them as a source of income. Now, they are among the most widely used instruments of protection, along with import and export quotas.

Exam Probability: **Medium**

36. *Answer choices:*
(see index for correct answer)

- a. Tariff-rate quota
- b. Russian Customs Tariff
- c. You Are on Indian Land
- d. Tariff

Guidance: level 1

:: Television commercials ::

_________ is a phenomenon whereby something new and somehow valuable is formed. The created item may be intangible or a physical object .

Exam Probability: **Low**

37. *Answer choices:*
(see index for correct answer)

- a. Surfer
- b. ZADZADZ
- c. Creativity
- d. The Force

Guidance: level 1

:: Mereology ::

__________ , in the abstract, is what belongs to or with something, whether as an attribute or as a component of said thing. In the context of this article, it is one or more components , whether physical or incorporeal, of a person`s estate; or so belonging to, as in being owned by, a person or jointly a group of people or a legal entity like a corporation or even a society. Depending on the nature of the __________ , an owner of __________ has the right to consume, alter, share, redefine, rent, mortgage, pawn, sell, exchange, transfer, give away or destroy it, or to exclude others from doing these things, as well as to perhaps abandon it; whereas regardless of the nature of the __________ , the owner thereof has the right to properly use it , or at the very least exclusively keep it.

Exam Probability: **Low**

38. *Answer choices:*

(see index for correct answer)

- a. Mereotopology
- b. Property
- c. Mereological essentialism
- d. Mereological nihilism

Guidance: level 1

:: Human resource management ::

__________ means increasing the scope of a job through extending the range of its job duties and responsibilities generally within the same level and periphery. __________ involves combining various activities at the same level in the organization and adding them to the existing job. It is also called the horizontal expansion of job activities. This contradicts the principles of specialisation and the division of labour whereby work is divided into small units, each of which is performed repetitively by an individual worker and the responsibilities are always clear. Some motivational theories suggest that the boredom and alienation caused by the division of labour can actually cause efficiency to fall. Thus, __________ seeks to motivate workers through reversing the process of specialisation. A typical approach might be to replace assembly lines with modular work; instead of an employee repeating the same step on each product, they perform several tasks on a single item. In order for employees to be provided with __________ they will need to be retrained in new fields to understand how each field works.

Exam Probability: **Low**

39. *Answer choices:*

(see index for correct answer)

- a. Adecco Group North America
- b. Job enrichment
- c. Job enlargement
- d. Organizational chart

Guidance: level 1

:: Project management ::

Contemporary business and science treat as a __________ any undertaking, carried out individually or collaboratively and possibly involving research or design, that is carefully planned to achieve a particular aim.

Exam Probability: **Low**

40. *Answer choices:*

(see index for correct answer)

- a. Terms of reference
- b. Duration
- c. Concept note
- d. Project

Guidance: level 1

:: Business law ::

A __________ is an arrangement where parties, known as partners, agree to cooperate to advance their mutual interests. The partners in a __________ may be individuals, businesses, interest-based organizations, schools, governments or combinations. Organizations may partner to increase the likelihood of each achieving their mission and to amplify their reach. A __________ may result in issuing and holding equity or may be only governed by a contract.

Exam Probability: **Low**

41. *Answer choices:*

(see index for correct answer)

- a. Jurisdictional strike
- b. Retained interest
- c. Partnership
- d. Holder

Guidance: level 1

:: Planning ::

__________ is a high level plan to achieve one or more goals under conditions of uncertainty. In the sense of the "art of the general," which included several subsets of skills including tactics, siegecraft, logistics etc., the term came into use in the 6th century C.E. in East Roman terminology, and was translated into Western vernacular languages only in the 18th century. From then until the 20th century, the word " __________ " came to denote "a comprehensive way to try to pursue political ends, including the threat or actual use of force, in a dialectic of wills" in a military conflict, in which both adversaries interact.

Exam Probability: **Medium**

42. *Answer choices:*

(see index for correct answer)

- a. Strategy
- b. Group information management
- c. Enterprise architecture planning

- d. Commercial area

Guidance: level 1

:: ::

Business is the activity of making one`s living or making money by producing or buying and selling products . Simply put, it is "any activity or enterprise entered into for profit. It does not mean it is a company, a corporation, partnership, or have any such formal organization, but it can range from a street peddler to General Motors."

Exam Probability: **High**

43. *Answer choices:*

(see index for correct answer)

- a. Firm
- b. similarity-attraction theory
- c. interpersonal communication
- d. information systems assessment

Guidance: level 1

:: Management ::

A _________ is an idea of the future or desired result that a person or a group of people envisions, plans and commits to achieve. People endeavor to reach _________ s within a finite time by setting deadlines.

Exam Probability: **Low**

44. *Answer choices:*

(see index for correct answer)

- a. Corporate recovery
- b. Participative decision-making
- c. Goal
- d. Vorstand

Guidance: level 1

:: Cognitive biases ::

The _________ is a type of immediate judgement discrepancy, or cognitive bias, where a person making an initial assessment of another person, place, or thing will assume ambiguous information based upon concrete information. A simplified example of the _________ is when an individual noticing that the person in the photograph is attractive, well groomed, and properly attired, assumes, using a mental heuristic, that the person in the photograph is a good person based upon the rules of that individual's social concept. This constant error in judgment is reflective of the individual's preferences, prejudices, ideology, aspirations, and social perception. The _________ is an evaluation by an individual and can affect the perception of a decision, action, idea, business, person, group, entity, or other whenever concrete data is generalized or influences ambiguous information.

Exam Probability: **High**

45. *Answer choices:*

(see index for correct answer)

- a. Social comparison bias
- b. Rosy retrospection
- c. Halo effect
- d. Perceptual psychology

Guidance: level 1

:: ::

_________ involves decision making. It can include judging the merits of multiple options and selecting one or more of them. One can make a _________ between imagined options or between real options followed by the corresponding action. For example, a traveler might choose a route for a journey based on the preference of arriving at a given destination as soon as possible. The preferred route can then follow from information such as the length of each of the possible routes, traffic conditions, etc. The arrival at a _________ can include more complex motivators such as cognition, instinct, and feeling.

Exam Probability: **Medium**

46. *Answer choices:*

(see index for correct answer)

- a. hierarchical perspective
- b. Choice

- c. levels of analysis
- d. information systems assessment

Guidance: level 1

:: Production and manufacturing ::

__________ is a theory of management that analyzes and synthesizes workflows. Its main objective is improving economic efficiency, especially labor productivity. It was one of the earliest attempts to apply science to the engineering of processes and to management. __________ is sometimes known as Taylorism after its founder, Frederick Winslow Taylor.

Exam Probability: **High**

47. *Answer choices:*

(see index for correct answer)

- a. LPA512
- b. SERCOS III
- c. Product layout
- d. Reverse engineering

Guidance: level 1

:: International trade ::

__________ involves the transfer of goods or services from one person or entity to another, often in exchange for money. A system or network that allows __________ is called a market.

Exam Probability: **Medium**

48. *Answer choices:*

(see index for correct answer)

- a. Modalities
- b. Franz Oppenheimer
- c. Trade
- d. Open general licence

Guidance: level 1

:: Production and manufacturing ::

An __________ is a manufacturing process in which parts are added as the semi-finished assembly moves from workstation to workstation where the parts are added in sequence until the final assembly is produced. By mechanically moving the parts to the assembly work and moving the semi-finished assembly from work station to work station, a finished product can be assembled faster and with less labor than by having workers carry parts to a stationary piece for assembly.

Exam Probability: **High**

49. *Answer choices:*

(see index for correct answer)

- a. Variable rate feeder
- b. Plant layout study
- c. Product lifecycle management
- d. Changeover

Guidance: level 1

:: ::

__________ is the collection of mechanisms, processes and relations by which corporations are controlled and operated. Governance structures and principles identify the distribution of rights and responsibilities among different participants in the corporation and include the rules and procedures for making decisions in corporate affairs. __________ is necessary because of the possibility of conflicts of interests between stakeholders, primarily between shareholders and upper management or among shareholders.

Exam Probability: **Low**

50. *Answer choices:*

(see index for correct answer)

- a. process perspective
- b. hierarchical perspective
- c. Corporate governance
- d. surface-level diversity

Guidance: level 1

:: Product management ::

__________ s, also known as Shewhart charts or process-behavior charts, are a statistical process control tool used to determine if a manufacturing or business process is in a state of control.

Exam Probability: **Medium**

51. *Answer choices:*

(see index for correct answer)

- a. Discontinuation
- b. Coolanol
- c. Trademark distinctiveness
- d. Promise Index

Guidance: level 1

:: Time management ::

__________ is the process of planning and exercising conscious control of time spent on specific activities, especially to increase effectiveness, efficiency, and productivity. It involves a juggling act of various demands upon a person relating to work, social life, family, hobbies, personal interests and commitments with the finiteness of time. Using time effectively gives the person "choice" on spending/managing activities at their own time and expediency.

Exam Probability: **Low**

52. *Answer choices:*

(see index for correct answer)

- a. Time Trek
- b. Getting Things Done
- c. HabitRPG
- d. Time management

Guidance: level 1

:: Decision theory ::

A _________ is a decision support tool that uses a tree-like model of decisions and their possible consequences, including chance event outcomes, resource costs, and utility. It is one way to display an algorithm that only contains conditional control statements.

Exam Probability: **Low**

53. *Answer choices:*

(see index for correct answer)

- a. Price of stability
- b. Nash equilibrium
- c. Decision tree
- d. Binary decision

Guidance: level 1

:: Management ::

_________ is a process by which entities review the quality of all factors involved in production. ISO 9000 defines _________ as "A part of quality management focused on fulfilling quality requirements".

Exam Probability: **Low**

54. *Answer choices:*

(see index for correct answer)

- a. Extended enterprise
- b. Quality control
- c. Product Development and Systems Engineering Consortium
- d. Line management

Guidance: level 1

:: ::

A _________ is a fund into which a sum of money is added during an employee`s employment years, and from which payments are drawn to support the person`s retirement from work in the form of periodic payments. A _________ may be a "defined benefit plan" where a fixed sum is paid regularly to a person, or a "defined contribution plan" under which a fixed sum is invested and then becomes available at retirement age. _________ s should not be confused with severance pay; the former is usually paid in regular installments for life after retirement, while the latter is typically paid as a fixed amount after involuntary termination of employment prior to retirement.

Exam Probability: **Low**

55. *Answer choices:*

(see index for correct answer)

- a. hierarchical perspective
- b. Pension
- c. information systems assessment
- d. Character

Guidance: level 1

:: ::

_________ consists of using generic or ad hoc methods in an orderly manner to find solutions to problems. Some of the problem-solving techniques developed and used in philosophy, artificial intelligence, computer science, engineering, mathematics, or medicine are related to mental problem-solving techniques studied in psychology.

Exam Probability: **High**

56. *Answer choices:*

(see index for correct answer)

- a. Problem solving
- b. Sarbanes-Oxley act of 2002
- c. hierarchical
- d. empathy

Guidance: level 1

:: Leadership ::

_________ Theory, or the _________ Model, is a model created by Paul Hersey and Ken Blanchard, developed while working on Management of Organizational Behavior. The theory was first introduced in 1969 as "life cycle theory of leadership". During the mid-1970s, life cycle theory of leadership was renamed " _________ Theory."

Exam Probability: **Medium**

57. *Answer choices:*

(see index for correct answer)

- a. Situational leadership
- b. Three levels of leadership model
- c. Integral leadership
- d. Jewish leadership

Guidance: level 1

:: Management ::

_________ is an area of management concerned with designing and controlling the process of production and redesigning business operations in the production of goods or services. It involves the responsibility of ensuring that business operations are efficient in terms of using as few resources as needed and effective in terms of meeting customer requirements. _________ is primarily concerned with planning, organizing and supervising in the contexts of production, manufacturing or the provision of services.

Exam Probability: **High**

58. *Answer choices:*

(see index for correct answer)

- a. Operations management
- b. Task-oriented and relationship-oriented leadership
- c. Board of governors
- d. Identity formation

Guidance: level 1

:: Grounds for termination of employment ::

_________ is a habitual pattern of absence from a duty or obligation without good reason. Generally, _________ is unplanned absences. _________ has been viewed as an indicator of poor individual performance, as well as a breach of an implicit contract between employee and employer. It is seen as a management problem, and framed in economic or quasi-economic terms. More recent scholarship seeks to understand _________ as an indicator of psychological, medical, or social adjustment to work.

Exam Probability: **High**

59. *Answer choices:*

(see index for correct answer)

- a. Sleeping while on duty
- b. No call, no show
- c. Absenteeism
- d. Presidential Policy Directive 19

Guidance: level 1

Business law

Corporate law (also known as business law) is the body of law governing the rights, relations, and conduct of persons, companies, organizations and businesses. It refers to the legal practice relating to, or the theory of corporations. Corporate law often describes the law relating to matters which derive directly from the life-cycle of a corporation. It thus encompasses the formation, funding, governance, and death of a corporation.

:: ::

In international relations, __________ is – from the perspective of governments – a voluntary transfer of resources from one country to another.

Exam Probability: **Low**

1. *Answer choices:*
(see index for correct answer)

- a. information systems assessment
- b. Aid
- c. similarity-attraction theory
- d. cultural

Guidance: level 1

:: Legal procedure ::

__________, adjective law, or rules of court comprises the rules by which a court hears and determines what happens in civil, lawsuit, criminal or administrative proceedings. The rules are designed to ensure a fair and consistent application of due process or fundamental justice to all cases that come before a court.

Exam Probability: **High**

2. *Answer choices:*
(see index for correct answer)

- a. Procedural law
- b. Opening statement
- c. Closing argument
- d. appellate

Guidance: level 1

:: ::

The _________ is the highest court within the hierarchy of courts in many legal jurisdictions. Other descriptions for such courts include court of last resort, apex court, and high court of appeal. Broadly speaking, the decisions of a _________ are not subject to further review by any other court. _________ s typically function primarily as appellate courts, hearing appeals from decisions of lower trial courts, or from intermediate-level appellate courts.

Exam Probability: **Low**

3. *Answer choices:*

(see index for correct answer)

- a. similarity-attraction theory
- b. Sarbanes-Oxley act of 2002
- c. process perspective
- d. empathy

Guidance: level 1

:: Contract Clause case law ::

The _________ appears in the United States Constitution, Article I, section 10, clause 1. The clause prohibits a State from passing any law that "impairs the obligation of contracts" or "makes any thing but gold and silver coin a tender in payment of debts". It states.

Exam Probability: **Medium**

4. *Answer choices:*

(see index for correct answer)

- a. Smyth v. Ames
- b. Charles River Bridge v. Warren Bridge
- c. Fletcher v. Peck

Guidance: level 1

:: Contract law ::

Offer and acceptance analysis is a traditional approach in contract law. The offer and acceptance formula, developed in the 19th century, identifies a moment of formation when the parties are of one mind. This classical approach to contract formation has been modified by developments in the law of estoppel, misleading conduct, misrepresentation and unjust enrichment.

Exam Probability: **High**

5. *Answer choices:*

(see index for correct answer)

- a. Drop dead date
- b. Firm commitment
- c. Per minas
- d. Offeror

Guidance: level 1

:: Product liability ::

__________ is the area of law in which manufacturers, distributors, suppliers, retailers, and others who make products available to the public are held responsible for the injuries those products cause. Although the word "product" has broad connotations, __________ as an area of law is traditionally limited to products in the form of tangible personal property.

Exam Probability: **High**

6. *Answer choices:*

(see index for correct answer)

- a. Market share liability
- b. Product Liability Directive
- c. Chinese drywall
- d. Domestic Fuels Protection Act

Guidance: level 1

:: Competition regulators ::

The _________ is an independent agency of the United States government, established in 1914 by the _________ Act. Its principal mission is the promotion of consumer protection and the elimination and prevention of anticompetitive business practices, such as coercive monopoly. It is headquartered in the _________ Building in Washington, D.C.

Exam Probability: **Low**

7. *Answer choices:*
(see index for correct answer)

- a. United States Department of Justice Antitrust Division
- b. Federal Antimonopoly Service
- c. Federal Trade Commission
- d. Directorate-General for Competition

Guidance: level 1

:: Contract law ::

_________ , in human interactions, is a sincere intention to be fair, open, and honest, regardless of the outcome of the interaction. While some Latin phrases lose their literal meaning over centuries, this is not the case with bona fides; it is still widely used and interchangeable with its generally accepted modern-day English translation of _________ . It is an important concept within law and business. The opposed concepts are bad faith, mala fides and perfidy . In contemporary English, the usage of bona fides is synonymous with credentials and identity. The phrase is sometimes used in job advertisements, and should not be confused with the bona fide occupational qualifications or the employer`s _________ effort, as described below.

Exam Probability: **Low**

8. *Answer choices:*
(see index for correct answer)

- a. Verbal contract
- b. Good faith
- c. Contractual term
- d. Impracticability

Guidance: level 1

:: International trade ::

__________ involves the transfer of goods or services from one person or entity to another, often in exchange for money. A system or network that allows __________ is called a market.

Exam Probability: **High**

9. *Answer choices:*
(see index for correct answer)

- a. Authorized economic operator
- b. Trade
- c. International monetary systems
- d. Cross-border cooperation

Guidance: level 1

:: Psychometrics ::

__________ is a dynamic, structured, interactive process where a neutral third party assists disputing parties in resolving conflict through the use of specialized communication and negotiation techniques. All participants in __________ are encouraged to actively participate in the process. __________ is a "party-centered" process in that it is focused primarily upon the needs, rights, and interests of the parties. The mediator uses a wide variety of techniques to guide the process in a constructive direction and to help the parties find their optimal solution. A mediator is facilitative in that she/he manages the interaction between parties and facilitates open communication. __________ is also evaluative in that the mediator analyzes issues and relevant norms , while refraining from providing prescriptive advice to the parties .

Exam Probability: **Low**

10. *Answer choices:*
(see index for correct answer)

- a. Reaction time
- b. Mediation
- c. Structural equation modeling
- d. Quantitative marketing research

Guidance: level 1

:: Contract law ::

_________ of Contract is a legal term. In contract law, it is the implied ability of an individual to make a legally binding contract on behalf of an organization, by way of uniform or interaction with the public on behalf of that organization. When a person is wearing a uniform or nametag bearing the logo or trademark of a business or organization; or if that person is functioning in an obviously authorized capacity on behalf of a business or organization, that person carries an _________ of Contract. _________ is authority that is not express or written into the contract, but which the agent is assumed to have in order to transact the business of insurance for the principal. _________ is incidental to express authority since not every single detail of an agent`s authority can be spelled out in the written contract.

Exam Probability: **Medium**

11. *Answer choices:*

(see index for correct answer)

- a. Unconscionability
- b. Culpa in contrahendo
- c. Liquidated damages
- d. Implied authority

Guidance: level 1

:: Trade secrets ::

The _________ of 1996 was a 6 title Act of Congress dealing with a wide range of issues, including not only industrial espionage , but the insanity defense, matters regarding the Boys & Girls Clubs of America, requirements for presentence investigation reports, and the United States Sentencing Commission reports regarding encryption or scrambling technology, and other technical and minor amendments.

Exam Probability: **Low**

12. *Answer choices:*

(see index for correct answer)

- a. Rivendell Forest Prods. v. Georgia-Pacific Corp.
- b. Aromat
- c. DVD Copy Control Association, Inc. v. Bunner
- d. Economic Espionage Act

Guidance: level 1

:: ::

In common law legal systems, _________ is a principle or rule established in a previous legal case that is either binding on or persuasive for a court or other tribunal when deciding subsequent cases with similar issues or facts. Common-law legal systems place great value on deciding cases according to consistent principled rules, so that similar facts will yield similar and predictable outcomes, and observance of _________ is the mechanism by which that goal is attained. The principle by which judges are bound to _________ s is known as stare decisis. Common-law _________ is a third kind of law, on equal footing with statutory law and delegated legislation or regulatory law

.

Exam Probability: **Low**

13. *Answer choices:*

(see index for correct answer)

- a. Precedent
- b. similarity-attraction theory
- c. personal values
- d. Sarbanes-Oxley act of 2002

Guidance: level 1

:: Services management and marketing ::

A _________ or servicemark is a trademark used in the United States and several other countries to identify a service rather than a product.

Exam Probability: **High**

14. *Answer choices:*

(see index for correct answer)

- a. Integrated customer management
- b. Functional branding
- c. Industrialization of services business model
- d. Service mark

Guidance: level 1

:: United States federal public corruption crime ::

Mail fraud and _________ are federal crimes in the United States that involve mailing or electronically transmitting something associated with fraud. Jurisdiction is claimed by the federal government if the illegal activity crosses interstate or international borders.

Exam Probability: **High**

15. *Answer choices:*

(see index for correct answer)

- a. Racketeer Influenced and Corrupt Organizations Act
- b. RICO Act

Guidance: level 1

:: ::

An _________ is a written sworn statement of fact voluntarily made by an affiant or deponent under an oath or affirmation administered by a person authorized to do so by law. Such statement is witnessed as to the authenticity of the affiant's signature by a taker of oaths, such as a notary public or commissioner of oaths. An _________ is a type of verified statement or showing, or in other words, it contains a verification, meaning it is under oath or penalty of perjury, and this serves as evidence to its veracity and is required for court proceedings.

Exam Probability: **Low**

16. *Answer choices:*

(see index for correct answer)

- a. interpersonal communication
- b. levels of analysis
- c. open system
- d. corporate values

Guidance: level 1

:: Commercial item transport and distribution ::

_________ s may be negotiable or non-negotiable. Negotiable _________ s allow transfer of ownership of that commodity without having to deliver the physical commodity. See Delivery order.

Exam Probability: **High**

17. *Answer choices:*

(see index for correct answer)

- a. Worldscale
- b. Pallet jack
- c. Whiddy Island Disaster
- d. Warehouse receipt

Guidance: level 1

:: ::

_________ is widespread, interconnected digital technology. The term entered the popular culture from science fiction and the arts but is now used by technology strategists, security professionals, government, military and industry leaders and entrepreneurs to describe the domain of the global technology environment. Others consider _________ to be just a notional environment in which communication over computer networks occurs. The word became popular in the 1990s when the uses of the Internet, networking, and digital communication were all growing dramatically and the term " _________ " was able to represent the many new ideas and phenomena that were emerging. It has been called the largest unregulated and uncontrolled domain in the history of mankind, and is also unique because it is a domain created by people vice the traditional physical domains.

Exam Probability: **Medium**

18. *Answer choices:*

(see index for correct answer)

- a. corporate values
- b. cultural
- c. Cyberspace
- d. surface-level diversity

Guidance: level 1

:: Legal doctrines and principles ::

The __________ rule is a rule in the Anglo-American common law that governs what kinds of evidence parties to a contract dispute can introduce when trying to determine the specific terms of a contract. The rule also prevents parties who have reduced their agreement to a final written document from later introducing other evidence, such as the content of oral discussions from earlier in the negotiation process, as evidence of a different intent as to the terms of the contract. The rule provides that "extrinsic evidence is inadmissible to vary a written contract". The term "parol" derives from the Anglo-Norman French parol or parole, meaning "word of mouth" or "verbal", and in medieval times referred to oral pleadings in a court case.

Exam Probability: **Medium**

19. *Answer choices:*

(see index for correct answer)

- a. Parol evidence
- b. Attractive nuisance doctrine
- c. negligence
- d. Eminent domain

Guidance: level 1

:: Criminal law ::

__________ is the body of law that relates to crime. It proscribes conduct perceived as threatening, harmful, or otherwise endangering to the property, health, safety, and moral welfare of people inclusive of one's self. Most __________ is established by statute, which is to say that the laws are enacted by a legislature. __________ includes the punishment and rehabilitation of people who violate such laws. __________ varies according to jurisdiction, and differs from civil law, where emphasis is more on dispute resolution and victim compensation, rather than on punishment or rehabilitation. Criminal procedure is a formalized official activity that authenticates the fact of commission of a crime and authorizes punitive or rehabilitative treatment of the offender.

Exam Probability: **Low**

20. *Answer choices:*

(see index for correct answer)

- a. Self-incrimination

- b. Mala prohibita
- c. mitigating factor
- d. Criminal law

Guidance: level 1

:: ::

__________ s and acquisitions are transactions in which the ownership of companies, other business organizations, or their operating units are transferred or consolidated with other entities. As an aspect of strategic management, M&A can allow enterprises to grow or downsize, and change the nature of their business or competitive position.

Exam Probability: **Medium**

21. *Answer choices:*

(see index for correct answer)

- a. personal values
- b. co-culture
- c. Character
- d. Merger

Guidance: level 1

:: ::

An __________ is the production of goods or related services within an economy. The major source of revenue of a group or company is the indicator of its relevant __________ . When a large group has multiple sources of revenue generation, it is considered to be working in different industries. Manufacturing __________ became a key sector of production and labour in European and North American countries during the Industrial Revolution, upsetting previous mercantile and feudal economies. This came through many successive rapid advances in technology, such as the production of steel and coal.

Exam Probability: **Low**

22. *Answer choices:*

(see index for correct answer)

- a. imperative

- b. deep-level diversity
- c. co-culture
- d. Industry

Guidance: level 1

:: Contract law ::

In the United States, the _________ rule refers to the legal right for a buyer of goods to insist upon " _________ " by the seller. In a contract for the sale of goods, if the goods fail to conform exactly to the description in the contract the buyer may nonetheless accept the goods, or reject the goods, or reject the nonconforming part of the tender and accept the conforming part. The buyer does not have an unfettered ability to reject tender.

Exam Probability: **High**

23. *Answer choices:*
(see index for correct answer)

- a. Anticipatory breach
- b. Offeree
- c. Cost-plus-incentive fee
- d. End-user license agreement

Guidance: level 1

:: Business models ::

A _________ , _________ company or daughter company is a company that is owned or controlled by another company, which is called the parent company, parent, or holding company. The _________ can be a company, corporation, or limited liability company. In some cases it is a government or state-owned enterprise. In some cases, particularly in the music and book publishing industries, subsidiaries are referred to as imprints.

Exam Probability: **Low**

24. *Answer choices:*
(see index for correct answer)

- a. Product-service system
- b. Subsidiary
- c. Home business
- d. European Cooperative Society

Guidance: level 1

:: Contract law ::

In common law jurisdictions, an _________ is a contract law term for certain assurances that are presumed to be made in the sale of products or real property, due to the circumstances of the sale. These assurances are characterized as warranties irrespective of whether the seller has expressly promised them orally or in writing. They include an _________ of fitness for a particular purpose, an _________ of merchantability for products, _________ of workmanlike quality for services, and an _________ of habitability for a home.

Exam Probability: **High**

25. *Answer choices:*

(see index for correct answer)

- a. Talent holding deal
- b. Severability
- c. Contract B
- d. Parametric contract

Guidance: level 1

:: ::

_________ is a process under which executive or legislative actions are subject to review by the judiciary. A court with authority for _________ may invalidate laws, acts and governmental actions that are incompatible with a higher authority: an executive decision may be invalidated for being unlawful or a statute may be invalidated for violating the terms of a constitution. _________ is one of the checks and balances in the separation of powers: the power of the judiciary to supervise the legislative and executive branches when the latter exceed their authority. The doctrine varies between jurisdictions, so the procedure and scope of _________ may differ between and within countries.

Exam Probability: **High**

26. *Answer choices:*

(see index for correct answer)

- a. information systems assessment
- b. Judicial review
- c. corporate values
- d. functional perspective

Guidance: level 1

:: Film production ::

__________ is a legal term more comprehensive and of higher import than either warranty or "security". It most commonly designates a private transaction by means of which one person, to obtain some trust, confidence or credit for another, engages to be answerable for him. It may also designate a treaty through which claims, rights or possessions are secured. It is to be differentiated from the colloquial "personal __________ " in that a __________ is a legal concept which produces an economic effect. A personal __________ by contrast is often used to refer to a promise made by an individual which is supported by, or assured through, the word of the individual. In the same way, a __________ produces a legal effect wherein one party affirms the promise of another by promising to themselves pay if default occurs.

Exam Probability: **Medium**

27. *Answer choices:*
(see index for correct answer)

- a. First look deal
- b. Front projection effect
- c. Film editing
- d. Shoot and protect

Guidance: level 1

:: ::

A __________ is a formal presentation of a matter such as a complaint, indictment or bill of exchange. In early-medieval England, juries of __________ would hear inquests in order to establish whether someone should be presented for a crime.

Exam Probability: **Medium**

28. *Answer choices:*

(see index for correct answer)

- a. empathy
- b. Presentment
- c. process perspective
- d. information systems assessment

Guidance: level 1

:: Project management ::

A _________ is a source or supply from which a benefit is produced and it has some utility. _________ s can broadly be classified upon their availability—they are classified into renewable and non-renewable _________ s.Examples of non renewable _________ s are coal ,crude oil natural gas nuclear energy etc. Examples of renewable _________ s are air,water,wind,solar energy etc. They can also be classified as actual and potential on the basis of level of development and use, on the basis of origin they can be classified as biotic and abiotic, and on the basis of their distribution, as ubiquitous and localized . An item becomes a _________ with time and developing technology. Typically, _________ s are materials, energy, services, staff, knowledge, or other assets that are transformed to produce benefit and in the process may be consumed or made unavailable. Benefits of _________ utilization may include increased wealth, proper functioning of a system, or enhanced well-being. From a human perspective a natural _________ is anything obtained from the environment to satisfy human needs and wants. From a broader biological or ecological perspective a _________ satisfies the needs of a living organism .

Exam Probability: **High**

29. *Answer choices:*

(see index for correct answer)

- a. TargetProcess
- b. Effort management
- c. Theory Z of Ouchi
- d. Organizational project management

Guidance: level 1

:: ::

The _________ is the central philosophical concept in the deontological moral philosophy of Immanuel Kant. Introduced in Kant`s 1785 Groundwork of the Metaphysics of Morals, it may be defined as a way of evaluating motivations for action.

Exam Probability: **Low**

30. *Answer choices:*

(see index for correct answer)

- a. information systems assessment
- b. functional perspective
- c. Categorical imperative
- d. cultural

Guidance: level 1

:: ::

The _________ is an intergovernmental organization that is concerned with the regulation of international trade between nations. The WTO officially commenced on 1 January 1995 under the Marrakesh Agreement, signed by 124 nations on 15 April 1994, replacing the General Agreement on Tariffs and Trade , which commenced in 1948. It is the largest international economic organization in the world.

Exam Probability: **High**

31. *Answer choices:*

(see index for correct answer)

- a. World Trade Organization
- b. information systems assessment
- c. cultural
- d. open system

Guidance: level 1

:: Equity (law) ::

An assignment is a legal term used in the context of the law of contract and of property. In both instances, assignment is the process whereby a person, the assignor, transfers rights or benefits to another, the _________ . An assignment may not transfer a duty, burden or detriment without the express agreement of the _________ . The right or benefit being assigned may be a gift or it may be paid for with a contractual consideration such as money.

Exam Probability: **Medium**

32. *Answer choices:*

(see index for correct answer)

- a. Assignee
- b. assignor

Guidance: level 1

:: Information technology audit ::

_________ is the act of using a computer to take or alter electronic data, or to gain unlawful use of a computer or system. In the United States, _________ is specifically proscribed by the _________ and Abuse Act, which criminalizes computer-related acts under federal jurisdiction. Types of _________ include.

Exam Probability: **High**

33. *Answer choices:*

(see index for correct answer)

- a. David Coderre
- b. Information security audit
- c. Computer fraud
- d. Code audit

Guidance: level 1

:: Corporate finance ::

__________ is a contract law concept about the purchase of the release from a debt obligation. It is one of the methods by which parties to a contract may terminate their agreement. The release is completed by the transfer of valuable consideration that must not be the actual performance of the obligation itself. The accord is the agreement to discharge the obligation and the satisfaction is the legal "consideration" which binds the parties to the agreement. A valid accord does not discharge the prior contract; instead it suspends the right to enforce it in accordance with the terms of the accord contract, in which satisfaction, or performance of the contract will discharge both contracts . If the creditor breaches the accord, then the debtor will be able to bring up the existence of the accord in order to enjoin any action against him.

Exam Probability: **Low**

34. *Answer choices:*

(see index for correct answer)

- a. Capital structure
- b. Two-tier tender offer
- c. Corporate finance
- d. Accord and satisfaction

Guidance: level 1

:: Criminal procedure ::

__________ is the adjudication process of the criminal law. While __________ differs dramatically by jurisdiction, the process generally begins with a formal criminal charge with the person on trial either being free on bail or incarcerated, and results in the conviction or acquittal of the defendant. __________ can be either in form of inquisitorial or adversarial __________ .

Exam Probability: **Low**

35. *Answer choices:*

(see index for correct answer)

- a. Criminal procedure
- b. Exoneration

Guidance: level 1

:: Commerce ::

_________ relates to "the exchange of goods and services, especially on a large scale". It includes legal, economic, political, social, cultural and technological systems that operate in a country or in international trade.

Exam Probability: **Low**

36. *Answer choices:*

(see index for correct answer)

- a. Commerce
- b. Coincidence of wants
- c. Receipt
- d. Return merchandise authorization

Guidance: level 1

:: Insurance terms ::

_________ is the assumption by a third party of another party`s legal right to collect a debt or damages. It is a legal doctrine whereby one person is entitled to enforce the subsisting or revived rights of another for one`s own benefit. A right of _________ typically arises by operation of law, but can also arise by statute or by agreement. _________ is an equitable remedy, having first developed in the English Court of Chancery. It is a familiar feature of common law systems. Analogous doctrines exist in civil law jurisdictions.

Exam Probability: **High**

37. *Answer choices:*

(see index for correct answer)

- a. Subrogation
- b. Copayment
- c. Loss reserving
- d. Insurance bad faith

Guidance: level 1

:: ::

The _________ of 1977 is a United States federal law known primarily for two of its main provisions: one that addresses accounting transparency requirements under the Securities Exchange Act of 1934 and another concerning bribery of foreign officials. The Act was amended in 1988 and in 1998, and has been subject to continued congressional concerns, namely whether its enforcement discourages U.S. companies from investing abroad.

Exam Probability: **Medium**

38. *Answer choices:*

(see index for correct answer)

- a. Sarbanes-Oxley act of 2002
- b. functional perspective
- c. personal values
- d. interpersonal communication

Guidance: level 1

:: Real estate ::

_________, real estate, realty, or immovable property In English common law refers to landed properties belonging to some person. It include all structures, crops, buildings, machinery, wells, dams, ponds, mines, canals, and roads, among other things. The term is historic, arising from the now-discontinued form of action, which distinguish between _________ disputes and personal property disputes. Personal property was, and continues to refer to all properties that are not real properties.

Exam Probability: **Medium**

39. *Answer choices:*

(see index for correct answer)

- a. Private transfer fee
- b. Property condition assessment
- c. Rent control in the United States
- d. Immovable property

Guidance: level 1

:: Writs ::

In common law, a _________ is a formal _________ ten order issued by a body with administrative or judicial jurisdiction; in modern usage, this body is generally a court. Warrants, prerogative _________ s, and subpoenas are common types of _________ , but many forms exist and have existed.

Exam Probability: **High**

40. *Answer choices:*
(see index for correct answer)

- a. Qui tam
- b. Writ of execution
- c. Writ of assistance

Guidance: level 1

:: Business law ::

In the United States, the United Kingdom, Australia, Canada and South Africa, _________ relates to the doctrines of the law of agency. It is relevant particularly in corporate law and constitutional law. _________ refers to a situation where a reasonable third party would understand that an agent had authority to act. This means a principal is bound by the agent`s actions, even if the agent had no actual authority, whether express or implied. It raises an estoppel because the third party is given an assurance, which he relies on and would be inequitable for the principal to deny the authority given. _________ can legally be found, even if actual authority has not been given.

Exam Probability: **Medium**

41. *Answer choices:*
(see index for correct answer)

- a. Copyright transfer agreement
- b. Tax patent
- c. Apparent authority
- d. Firm offer

Guidance: level 1

:: Contract law ::

_________ is a legal process for collecting a monetary judgment on behalf of a plaintiff from a defendant. _________ allows the plaintiff to take the money or property of the debtor from the person or institution that holds that property . A similar legal mechanism called execution allows the seizure of money or property held directly by the debtor.

Exam Probability: **Low**

42. *Answer choices:*

(see index for correct answer)

- a. Reciprocal obligation
- b. Firm commitment
- c. Garnishment
- d. Samenlevingscontract

Guidance: level 1

:: Competition law ::

In competition law, a _________ is a market in which a particular product or service is sold. It is the intersection of a relevant product market and a relevant geographic market. The European Commission defines a _________ and its product and geographic components as follows.

Exam Probability: **Medium**

43. *Answer choices:*

(see index for correct answer)

- a. Commerce Act 1986
- b. European Union merger law
- c. Relevant market
- d. Antitrust law

Guidance: level 1

:: ::

A _________ is an individual or institution that legally owns one or more shares of stock in a public or private corporation. _________ s may be referred to as members of a corporation. Legally, a person is not a _________ in a corporation until their name and other details are entered in the corporation`s register of _________ s or members.

Exam Probability: **Medium**

44. *Answer choices:*
(see index for correct answer)

- a. similarity-attraction theory
- b. Character
- c. Shareholder
- d. levels of analysis

Guidance: level 1

:: Employment discrimination ::

_________ is a form of discrimination based on race, gender, religion, national origin, physical or mental disability, age, sexual orientation, and gender identity by employers. Earnings differentials or occupational differentiation—where differences in pay come from differences in qualifications or responsibilities—should not be confused with _________ . Discrimination can be intended and involve disparate treatment of a group or be unintended, yet create disparate impact for a group.

Exam Probability: **Low**

45. *Answer choices:*
(see index for correct answer)

- a. LGBT employment discrimination in the United States
- b. Employment discrimination
- c. New South Wales selection bias
- d. Employment discrimination law in the European Union

Guidance: level 1

:: Stock market ::

_________ is freedom from, or resilience against, potential harm caused by others. Beneficiaries of _________ may be of persons and social groups, objects and institutions, ecosystems or any other entity or phenomenon vulnerable to unwanted change by its environment.

Exam Probability: **High**

46. *Answer choices:*

(see index for correct answer)

- a. Penny stock
- b. Direct public offering
- c. Big boy letter
- d. Security

Guidance: level 1

:: United States corporate law ::

In tort law, a _________ is a legal obligation which is imposed on an individual requiring adherence to a standard of reasonable care while performing any acts that could foreseeably harm others. It is the first element that must be established to proceed with an action in negligence. The claimant must be able to show a _________ imposed by law which the defendant has breached. In turn, breaching a duty may subject an individual to liability. The _________ may be imposed by operation of law between individuals who have no current direct relationship but eventually become related in some manner, as defined by common law .

Exam Probability: **Low**

47. *Answer choices:*

(see index for correct answer)

- a. Corporate law in the United States
- b. Model Nonprofit Corporation Act
- c. NYSE Listed Company Manual
- d. New York Business Corporation Law

Guidance: level 1

:: Business ethics ::

__________ is a type of harassment technique that relates to a sexual nature and the unwelcome or inappropriate promise of rewards in exchange for sexual favors. __________ includes a range of actions from mild transgressions to sexual abuse or assault. Harassment can occur in many different social settings such as the workplace, the home, school, churches, etc. Harassers or victims may be of any gender.

Exam Probability: **High**

48. *Answer choices:*

(see index for correct answer)

- a. Wheelmen
- b. Sexual harassment
- c. Jewish business ethics
- d. Smart casual

Guidance: level 1

:: Contract law ::

Generally, a __________ is a loan or a credit transaction in which the lender acquires a security interest in collateral owned by the borrower and is entitled to foreclose on or repossess the collateral in the event of the borrower`s default. The terms of the relationship are governed by a contract, or security agreement. A common example would be a consumer who purchases a car on credit. If the consumer fails to make the payments on time, the lender will take the car and resell it, applying the proceeds of the sale toward the loan. Mortgages and deeds of trust are another example. In the United States, __________ s in personal property are governed by Article 9 of the Uniform Commercial Code .

Exam Probability: **Medium**

49. *Answer choices:*

(see index for correct answer)

- a. Community Benefits Agreement
- b. Executory contract
- c. Waiver
- d. Secured transaction

Guidance: level 1

:: ::

__________ , also referred to as orthostasis, is a human position in which the body is held in an upright position and supported only by the feet.

Exam Probability: **Medium**

50. *Answer choices:*

(see index for correct answer)

- a. Character
- b. co-culture
- c. Standing
- d. open system

Guidance: level 1

:: Intention ::

__________ is the mental element of a person`s intention to commit a crime; or knowledge that one`s action or lack of action would cause a crime to be committed. It is a necessary element of many crimes.

Exam Probability: **High**

51. *Answer choices:*

(see index for correct answer)

- a. bona fide
- b. Mens rea

Guidance: level 1

:: Monopoly (economics) ::

__________ is a category of property that includes intangible creations of the human intellect. __________ encompasses two types of rights: industrial property rights and copyright. It was not until the 19th century that the term " __________ " began to be used, and not until the late 20th century that it became commonplace in the majority of the world.

Exam Probability: **High**

52. *Answer choices:*

(see index for correct answer)

- a. Intellectual property
- b. Municipalization
- c. Market concentration
- d. Concentration ratio

Guidance: level 1

:: ::

In the law of evidence, a _________ of a particular fact can be made without the aid of proof in some situations. The invocation of a _________ shifts the burden of proof from one party to the opposing party in a court trial.

Exam Probability: **High**

53. *Answer choices:*

(see index for correct answer)

- a. corporate values
- b. similarity-attraction theory
- c. Presumption
- d. hierarchical

Guidance: level 1

:: Manufacturing ::

A _________ is a building for storing goods. _________ s are used by manufacturers, importers, exporters, wholesalers, transport businesses, customs, etc. They are usually large plain buildings in industrial parks on the outskirts of cities, towns or villages.

Exam Probability: **High**

54. *Answer choices:*

(see index for correct answer)

- a. AGO system
- b. Lights out
- c. Warehouse
- d. By-product

Guidance: level 1

:: Mereology ::

_________ , in the abstract, is what belongs to or with something, whether as an attribute or as a component of said thing. In the context of this article, it is one or more components , whether physical or incorporeal, of a person's estate; or so belonging to, as in being owned by, a person or jointly a group of people or a legal entity like a corporation or even a society. Depending on the nature of the _________ , an owner of _________ has the right to consume, alter, share, redefine, rent, mortgage, pawn, sell, exchange, transfer, give away or destroy it, or to exclude others from doing these things, as well as to perhaps abandon it; whereas regardless of the nature of the _________ , the owner thereof has the right to properly use it , or at the very least exclusively keep it.

Exam Probability: **High**

55. *Answer choices:*

(see index for correct answer)

- a. Mereological essentialism
- b. Mereological nihilism
- c. Property
- d. Non-wellfounded mereology

Guidance: level 1

:: Arbitration law ::

The United States Arbitration Act , more commonly referred to as the _________ or FAA, is an act of Congress that provides for judicial facilitation of private dispute resolution through arbitration. It applies in both state courts and federal courts, as was held constitutional in Southland Corp. v. Keating. It applies where the transaction contemplated by the parties "involves" interstate commerce and is predicated on an exercise of the Commerce Clause powers granted to Congress in the U.S. Constitution.

Exam Probability: **High**

56. *Answer choices:*

(see index for correct answer)

- a. Title 9 of the United States Code
- b. James A. Graham
- c. UNCITRAL Model Law on International Commercial Arbitration
- d. Federal Arbitration Act

Guidance: level 1

:: Utilitarianism ::

_________ is a family of consequentialist ethical theories that promotes actions that maximize happiness and well-being for the majority of a population. Although different varieties of _________ admit different characterizations, the basic idea behind all of them is to in some sense maximize utility, which is often defined in terms of well-being or related concepts. For instance, Jeremy Bentham, the founder of _________ , described utility as

Exam Probability: **Low**

57. *Answer choices:*

(see index for correct answer)

- a. The Collected Works of Jeremy Bentham
- b. Telishment
- c. Preference utilitarianism
- d. Utilitarianism

Guidance: level 1

:: Marketing ::

_________ comes from the Latin neg and otsia referring to businessmen who, unlike the patricians, had no leisure time in their industriousness; it held the meaning of business until the 17th century when it took on the diplomatic connotation as a dialogue between two or more people or parties intended to reach a beneficial outcome over one or more issues where a conflict exists with respect to at least one of these issues. Thus, _________ is a process of combining divergent positions into a joint agreement under a decision rule of unanimity.

Exam Probability: **Medium**

58. *Answer choices:*

(see index for correct answer)

- a. Negotiation
- b. City marketing
- c. Primary research
- d. Cult brand

Guidance: level 1

:: ::

_________ refers to a business or organization attempting to acquire goods or services to accomplish its goals. Although there are several organizations that attempt to set standards in the _________ process, processes can vary greatly between organizations. Typically the word " _________ " is not used interchangeably with the word "procurement", since procurement typically includes expediting, supplier quality, and transportation and logistics in addition to _________ .

Exam Probability: **Low**

59. *Answer choices:*

(see index for correct answer)

- a. similarity-attraction theory
- b. levels of analysis
- c. Purchasing
- d. Character

Guidance: level 1

Finance

Finance is a field that is concerned with the allocation (investment) of assets and liabilities over space and time, often under conditions of risk or uncertainty. Finance can also be defined as the science of money management. Participants in the market aim to price assets based on their risk level, fundamental value, and their expected rate of return. Finance can be split into three sub-categories: public finance, corporate finance and personal finance.

:: Banking ::

A __________ is a financial institution that accepts deposits from the public and creates credit. Lending activities can be performed either directly or indirectly through capital markets. Due to their importance in the financial stability of a country, __________ s are highly regulated in most countries. Most nations have institutionalized a system known as fractional reserve __________ ing under which __________ s hold liquid assets equal to only a portion of their current liabilities. In addition to other regulations intended to ensure liquidity, __________ s are generally subject to minimum capital requirements based on an international set of capital standards, known as the Basel Accords.

Exam Probability: **Low**

1. *Answer choices:*

(see index for correct answer)

- a. International Academy of Retail Banking
- b. Transactional account
- c. Bank
- d. Village banking

Guidance: level 1

:: Financial crises ::

A _________ is any of a broad variety of situations in which some financial assets suddenly lose a large part of their nominal value. In the 19th and early 20th centuries, many financial crises were associated with banking panics, and many recessions coincided with these panics. Other situations that are often called financial crises include stock market crashes and the bursting of other financial bubbles, currency crises, and sovereign defaults. Financial crises directly result in a loss of paper wealth but do not necessarily result in significant changes in the real economy .

Exam Probability: **High**

2. *Answer choices:*

(see index for correct answer)

- a. Currency crisis
- b. Financial crisis
- c. United Copper
- d. Bad bank

Guidance: level 1

:: Business economics ::

_________ is one of the constituents of a leasing calculus or operation. It describes the future value of a good in terms of absolute value in monetary terms and it is sometimes abbreviated into a percentage of the initial price when the item was new.

Exam Probability: **Low**

3. *Answer choices:*

(see index for correct answer)

- a. Business ecosystem
- b. Consumer economy
- c. Residual value
- d. Inclusive business finance

Guidance: level 1

:: Income taxes ::

An _________ is a tax imposed on individuals or entities that varies with respective income or profits . _________ generally is computed as the product of a tax rate times taxable income. Taxation rates may vary by type or characteristics of the taxpayer.

Exam Probability: **Medium**

4. *Answer choices:*

(see index for correct answer)

- a. Income Tax Act 2007
- b. Income splitting
- c. Personal allowance
- d. Income tax

Guidance: level 1

:: Business law ::

A _________ is a group of people who jointly supervise the activities of an organization, which can be either a for-profit business, nonprofit organization, or a government agency. Such a board`s powers, duties, and responsibilities are determined by government regulations and the organization`s own constitution and bylaws. These authorities may specify the number of members of the board, how they are to be chosen, and how often they are to meet.

Exam Probability: **High**

5. *Answer choices:*

(see index for correct answer)

- a. License
- b. Double ticketing
- c. Board of directors
- d. Enhanced use lease

Guidance: level 1

:: Debt ::

_________ is when something, usually money, is owed by one party, the borrower or _________ or, to a second party, the lender or creditor. _________ is a deferred payment, or series of payments, that is owed in the future, which is what differentiates it from an immediate purchase. The _________ may be owed by sovereign state or country, local government, company, or an individual. Commercial _________ is generally subject to contractual terms regarding the amount and timing of repayments of principal and interest. Loans, bonds, notes, and mortgages are all types of _________ . The term can also be used metaphorically to cover moral obligations and other interactions not based on economic value. For example, in Western cultures, a person who has been helped by a second person is sometimes said to owe a " _________ of gratitude" to the second person.

Exam Probability: **Low**

6. *Answer choices:*
(see index for correct answer)

- a. Sum certain
- b. Debt adjustment
- c. Default trap
- d. Debt

Guidance: level 1

:: ::

In marketing, a _________ is a ticket or document that can be redeemed for a financial discount or rebate when purchasing a product.

Exam Probability: **High**

7. *Answer choices:*
(see index for correct answer)

- a. similarity-attraction theory
- b. Coupon
- c. corporate values
- d. functional perspective

Guidance: level 1

:: Financial ratios ::

In finance, the __________ , also known as the acid-test ratio is a type of liquidity ratio which measures the ability of a company to use its near cash or quick assets to extinguish or retire its current liabilities immediately. Quick assets include those current assets that presumably can be quickly converted to cash at close to their book values. It is the ratio between quickly available or liquid assets and current liabilities.

Exam Probability: **Low**

8. *Answer choices:*

(see index for correct answer)

- a. CROCI
- b. Quick ratio
- c. Like for like
- d. Days payable outstanding

Guidance: level 1

:: Debt ::

A __________ is a monetary amount owed to a creditor that is unlikely to be paid and, or which the creditor is not willing to take action to collect for various reasons, often due to the debtor not having the money to pay, for example due to a company going into liquidation or insolvency. There are various technical definitions of what constitutes a __________ , depending on accounting conventions, regulatory treatment and the institution provisioning. In the USA, bank loans with more than ninety days` arrears become "problem loans". Accounting sources advise that the full amount of a __________ be written off to the profit and loss account or a provision for __________ s as soon as it is foreseen.

Exam Probability: **Medium**

9. *Answer choices:*

(see index for correct answer)

- a. Debtors Anonymous
- b. Bad debt
- c. Arrears
- d. Money disorders

Guidance: level 1

:: Finance ::

The _________ of a corporation is the accumulated net income of the corporation that is retained by the corporation at a particular point of time, such as at the end of the reporting period. At the end of that period, the net income at that point is transferred from the Profit and Loss Account to the _________ account. If the balance of the _________ account is negative it may be called accumulated losses, retained losses or accumulated deficit, or similar terminology.

Exam Probability: **Low**

10. *Answer choices:*

(see index for correct answer)

- a. Asset-backed commercial paper program
- b. Currency converter
- c. Rational herding
- d. Retained earnings

Guidance: level 1

:: ::

The _________ is a private, non-profit organization standard-setting body whose primary purpose is to establish and improve Generally Accepted Accounting Principles within the United States in the public`s interest. The Securities and Exchange Commission designated the FASB as the organization responsible for setting accounting standards for public companies in the US. The FASB replaced the American Institute of Certified Public Accountants` Accounting Principles Board on July 1, 1973.

Exam Probability: **High**

11. *Answer choices:*

(see index for correct answer)

- a. hierarchical
- b. Financial Accounting Standards Board
- c. deep-level diversity
- d. information systems assessment

Guidance: level 1

:: International taxation ::

__________ is the levying of tax by two or more jurisdictions on the same declared income , asset , or financial transaction . Double liability is mitigated in a number of ways, for example.

Exam Probability: **Medium**

12. *Answer choices:*

(see index for correct answer)

- a. Foreign personal holding company
- b. Double taxation
- c. Differential tax analysis
- d. Tax equalization

Guidance: level 1

:: Pharmaceutical industry ::

A __________ is a document in which data collected for a clinical trial is first recorded. This data is usually later entered in the case report form. The International Conference on Harmonisation of Technical Requirements for Registration of Pharmaceuticals for Human Use guidelines define __________ s as "original documents, data, and records." __________ s contain source data, which is defined as "all information in original records and certified copies of original records of clinical findings, observations, or other activities in a clinical trial necessary for the reconstruction and evaluation of the trial."

Exam Probability: **Low**

13. *Answer choices:*

(see index for correct answer)

- a. Source document
- b. Clinical Practice Research Datalink
- c. RAJ Pharma
- d. Big Pharma conspiracy theory

Guidance: level 1

:: ::

_________ or accountancy is the measurement, processing, and communication of financial information about economic entities such as businesses and corporations. The modern field was established by the Italian mathematician Luca Pacioli in 1494. _________ , which has been called the "language of business", measures the results of an organization`s economic activities and conveys this information to a variety of users, including investors, creditors, management, and regulators. Practitioners of _________ are known as accountants. The terms " _________ " and "financial reporting" are often used as synonyms.

Exam Probability: **Low**

14. *Answer choices:*

(see index for correct answer)

- a. hierarchical
- b. levels of analysis
- c. Accounting
- d. process perspective

Guidance: level 1

:: Funds ::

_________ value is the value of an entity`s assets minus the value of its liabilities, often in relation to open-end or mutual funds, since shares of such funds registered with the U.S. Securities and Exchange Commission are redeemed at their _________ value. It is also a key figure with regard to hedge funds and venture capital funds when calculating the value of the underlying investments in these funds by investors. This may also be the same as the book value or the equity value of a business. _________ value may represent the value of the total equity, or it may be divided by the number of shares outstanding held by investors, thereby representing the _________ value per share.

Exam Probability: **Medium**

15. *Answer choices:*

(see index for correct answer)

- a. Inter Pipeline
- b. Iraq Relief and Reconstruction Fund
- c. Net asset

- d. S. W. Mitchell Capital

Guidance: level 1

:: ::

An __________ is a comprehensive report on a company`s activities throughout the preceding year. __________ s are intended to give shareholders and other interested people information about the company`s activities and financial performance. They may be considered as grey literature. Most jurisdictions require companies to prepare and disclose __________ s, and many require the __________ to be filed at the company`s registry. Companies listed on a stock exchange are also required to report at more frequent intervals .

Exam Probability: **High**

16. *Answer choices:*

(see index for correct answer)

- a. interpersonal communication
- b. empathy
- c. co-culture
- d. Annual report

Guidance: level 1

:: Finance ::

__________ is a field that is concerned with the allocation of assets and liabilities over space and time, often under conditions of risk or uncertainty. __________ can also be defined as the art of money management. Participants in the market aim to price assets based on their risk level, fundamental value, and their expected rate of return. __________ can be split into three sub-categories: public __________ , corporate __________ and personal __________ .

Exam Probability: **Low**

17. *Answer choices:*

(see index for correct answer)

- a. Finance
- b. Stock buyback
- c. Stock market prediction

- d. Yield

Guidance: level 1

:: Stock market ::

A _________ or stock divide increases the number of shares in a company. The price is adjusted such that the before and after market capitalization of the company remains the same and dilution does not occur. Options and warrants are included.

Exam Probability: **Low**

18. *Answer choices:*

(see index for correct answer)

- a. Immediate or cancel
- b. Nifty Fifty
- c. Intermarket sweep order
- d. Xetra

Guidance: level 1

:: Mereology ::

_________ , in the abstract, is what belongs to or with something, whether as an attribute or as a component of said thing. In the context of this article, it is one or more components , whether physical or incorporeal, of a person`s estate; or so belonging to, as in being owned by, a person or jointly a group of people or a legal entity like a corporation or even a society. Depending on the nature of the _________ , an owner of _________ has the right to consume, alter, share, redefine, rent, mortgage, pawn, sell, exchange, transfer, give away or destroy it, or to exclude others from doing these things, as well as to perhaps abandon it; whereas regardless of the nature of the _________ , the owner thereof has the right to properly use it , or at the very least exclusively keep it.

Exam Probability: **High**

19. *Answer choices:*

(see index for correct answer)

- a. Gunk

- b. Meronomy
- c. Non-wellfounded mereology
- d. Mereotopology

Guidance: level 1

:: ::

In finance, return is a profit on an investment. It comprises any change in value of the investment, and/or cash flows which the investor receives from the investment, such as interest payments or dividends. It may be measured either in absolute terms or as a percentage of the amount invested. The latter is also called the holding period return.

Exam Probability: **High**

20. *Answer choices:*

(see index for correct answer)

- a. similarity-attraction theory
- b. surface-level diversity
- c. deep-level diversity
- d. cultural

Guidance: level 1

:: ::

__________ is the collection of mechanisms, processes and relations by which corporations are controlled and operated. Governance structures and principles identify the distribution of rights and responsibilities among different participants in the corporation and include the rules and procedures for making decisions in corporate affairs. __________ is necessary because of the possibility of conflicts of interests between stakeholders, primarily between shareholders and upper management or among shareholders.

Exam Probability: **Low**

21. *Answer choices:*

(see index for correct answer)

- a. Corporate governance
- b. process perspective
- c. hierarchical
- d. co-culture

Guidance: level 1

:: ::

__________ , often abbreviated as B/E in finance, is the point of balance making neither a profit nor a loss. The term originates in finance but the concept has been applied in other fields.

Exam Probability: **Medium**

22. *Answer choices:*

(see index for correct answer)

- a. surface-level diversity
- b. Break-even
- c. similarity-attraction theory
- d. interpersonal communication

Guidance: level 1

:: Finance ::

A __________ , publicly-traded company, publicly-held company, publicly-listed company, or public limited company is a corporation whose ownership is dispersed among the general public in many shares of stock which are freely traded on a stock exchange or in over-the-counter markets. In some jurisdictions, public companies over a certain size must be listed on an exchange. A __________ can be listed or unlisted .

Exam Probability: **Medium**

23. *Answer choices:*

(see index for correct answer)

- a. Offshore financial centre
- b. Debt restructuring
- c. Senior stretch loan
- d. Underwriting spread

Guidance: level 1

:: ::

In business, economics or investment, market _________ is a market`s feature whereby an individual or firm can quickly purchase or sell an asset without causing a drastic change in the asset`s price. _________ is about how big the trade-off is between the speed of the sale and the price it can be sold for. In a liquid market, the trade-off is mild: selling quickly will not reduce the price much. In a relatively illiquid market, selling it quickly will require cutting its price by some amount.

Exam Probability: **Low**

24. *Answer choices:*
(see index for correct answer)

- a. imperative
- b. functional perspective
- c. Liquidity
- d. open system

Guidance: level 1

:: Management accounting ::

_________ are costs that are not directly accountable to a cost object . _________ may be either fixed or variable. _________ include administration, personnel and security costs. These are those costs which are not directly related to production. Some _________ may be overhead. But some overhead costs can be directly attributed to a project and are direct costs.

Exam Probability: **Low**

25. *Answer choices:*
(see index for correct answer)

- a. Indirect costs
- b. Institute of Certified Management Accountants
- c. Management accounting in supply chains
- d. Double counting

Guidance: level 1

:: Stock market ::

The _________ of a corporation is all of the shares into which ownership of the corporation is divided. In American English, the shares are commonly known as " _________ s". A single share of the _________ represents fractional ownership of the corporation in proportion to the total number of shares. This typically entitles the _________ holder to that fraction of the company's earnings, proceeds from liquidation of assets , or voting power, often dividing these up in proportion to the amount of money each _________ holder has invested. Not all _________ is necessarily equal, as certain classes of _________ may be issued for example without voting rights, with enhanced voting rights, or with a certain priority to receive profits or liquidation proceeds before or after other classes of shareholders.

Exam Probability: **Low**

26. *Answer choices:*

(see index for correct answer)

- a. Underwriting contract
- b. Stock
- c. Red herring prospectus
- d. Prime Standard

Guidance: level 1

:: Fundamental analysis ::

_________ is the monetary value of earnings per outstanding share of common stock for a company.

Exam Probability: **Low**

27. *Answer choices:*

(see index for correct answer)

- a. Equity value
- b. Public float
- c. economic Value Added
- d. Continuing value

Guidance: level 1

:: ::

_________ is a political and social philosophy promoting traditional social institutions in the context of culture and civilization. The central tenets of _________ include tradition, human imperfection, organic society, hierarchy, authority, and property rights. Conservatives seek to preserve a range of institutions such as religion, parliamentary government, and property rights, with the aim of emphasizing social stability and continuity. The more traditional elements—reactionaries—oppose modernism and seek a return to "the way things were".

Exam Probability: **Low**

28. *Answer choices:*

(see index for correct answer)

- a. Conservatism
- b. similarity-attraction theory
- c. Sarbanes-Oxley act of 2002
- d. cultural

Guidance: level 1

:: Asset ::

In accounting, a _________ is any asset which can reasonably be expected to be sold, consumed, or exhausted through the normal operations of a business within the current fiscal year or operating cycle . Typical _________ s include cash, cash equivalents, short-term investments , accounts receivable, stock inventory, supplies, and the portion of prepaid liabilities which will be paid within a year.In simple words, assets which are held for a short period are known as _________ s. Such assets are expected to be realised in cash or consumed during the normal operating cycle of the business.

Exam Probability: **Medium**

29. *Answer choices:*

(see index for correct answer)

- a. Current asset
- b. Fixed asset

Guidance: level 1

:: Generally Accepted Accounting Principles ::

Financial statements prepared and presented by a company typically follow an external standard that specifically guides their preparation. These standards vary across the globe and are typically overseen by some combination of the private accounting profession in that specific nation and the various government regulators. Variations across countries may be considerable, making cross-country evaluation of financial data challenging.

Exam Probability: **High**

30. *Answer choices:*

(see index for correct answer)

- a. Generally accepted accounting principles
- b. Cash method of accounting
- c. Pro forma
- d. Paid in capital

Guidance: level 1

:: Costs ::

In microeconomic theory, the __________ , or alternative cost, of making a particular choice is the value of the most valuable choice out of those that were not taken. In other words, opportunity that will require sacrifices.

Exam Probability: **Low**

31. *Answer choices:*

(see index for correct answer)

- a. Opportunity cost
- b. Repugnancy costs
- c. Cost of products sold
- d. Road Logistics Costing in South Africa

Guidance: level 1

:: Elementary geometry ::

The _________ is the front of an animal`s head that features three of the head`s sense organs, the eyes, nose, and mouth, and through which animals express many of their emotions. The _________ is crucial for human identity, and damage such as scarring or developmental deformities affects the psyche adversely.

Exam Probability: **High**

32. *Answer choices:*

(see index for correct answer)

- a. Reflection symmetry
- b. Euclidean geometry
- c. Hypotenuse
- d. Equidistant

Guidance: level 1

:: Actuarial science ::

_________ is the addition of interest to the principal sum of a loan or deposit, or in other words, interest on interest. It is the result of reinvesting interest, rather than paying it out, so that interest in the next period is then earned on the principal sum plus previously accumulated interest. _________ is standard in finance and economics.

Exam Probability: **High**

33. *Answer choices:*

(see index for correct answer)

- a. John Graunt
- b. Age stratification
- c. Maximum life span
- d. Compound interest

Guidance: level 1

:: ::

_________ is the process whereby a business sets the price at which it will sell its products and services, and may be part of the business`s marketing plan. In setting prices, the business will take into account the price at which it could acquire the goods, the manufacturing cost, the market place, competition, market condition, brand, and quality of product.

Exam Probability: **Low**

34. *Answer choices:*

(see index for correct answer)

- a. levels of analysis
- b. Pricing
- c. co-culture
- d. hierarchical

Guidance: level 1

:: Monopoly (economics) ::

A _________ is a form of intellectual property that gives its owner the legal right to exclude others from making, using, selling, and importing an invention for a limited period of years, in exchange for publishing an enabling public disclosure of the invention. In most countries _________ rights fall under civil law and the _________ holder needs to sue someone infringing the _________ in order to enforce his or her rights. In some industries _________ s are an essential form of competitive advantage; in others they are irrelevant.

Exam Probability: **Medium**

35. *Answer choices:*

(see index for correct answer)

- a. Natural monopoly
- b. Monopoly
- c. Contestable market
- d. Network effect

Guidance: level 1

:: Accounting terminology ::

_________ are liabilities that reflect expenses that have not yet been paid or logged under accounts payable during an accounting period; in other words, a company's obligation to pay for goods and services that have been provided for which invoices have not yet been received. Examples would include accrued wages payable, accrued sales tax payable, and accrued rent payable.

Exam Probability: **Medium**

36. *Answer choices:*

(see index for correct answer)

- a. Enterprise liquidity
- b. Accrued liabilities
- c. Accounting equation
- d. Checkoff

Guidance: level 1

:: ::

_________ Corporation was an American energy, commodities, and services company based in Houston, Texas. It was founded in 1985 as a merger between Houston Natural Gas and InterNorth, both relatively small regional companies. Before its bankruptcy on December 3, 2001, _________ employed approximately 29,000 staff and was a major electricity, natural gas, communications and pulp and paper company, with claimed revenues of nearly $101 billion during 2000. Fortune named _________ "America's Most Innovative Company" for six consecutive years.

Exam Probability: **Low**

37. *Answer choices:*

(see index for correct answer)

- a. Enron
- b. functional perspective
- c. personal values
- d. deep-level diversity

Guidance: level 1

:: Marketing ::

A _________ is something that is necessary for an organism to live a healthy life. _________ s are distinguished from wants in that, in the case of a _________ , a deficiency causes a clear adverse outcome: a dysfunction or death. In other words, a _________ is something required for a safe, stable and healthy life while a want is a desire, wish or aspiration. When _________ s or wants are backed by purchasing power, they have the potential to become economic demands.

Exam Probability: **Medium**

38. *Answer choices:*

(see index for correct answer)

- a. Inventory
- b. MARC USA
- c. Need
- d. Buyer decision process

Guidance: level 1

:: ::

An _________ is an asset that lacks physical substance. It is defined in opposition to physical assets such as machinery and buildings. An _________ is usually very hard to evaluate. Patents, copyrights, franchises, goodwill, trademarks, and trade names. The general interpretation also includes software and other intangible computer based assets are all examples of _________ s. _________ s generally—though not necessarily—suffer from typical market failures of non-rivalry and non-excludability.

Exam Probability: **High**

39. *Answer choices:*

(see index for correct answer)

- a. Intangible asset
- b. surface-level diversity
- c. deep-level diversity
- d. co-culture

Guidance: level 1

:: Actuarial science ::

The _________ is the greater benefit of receiving money now rather than an identical sum later. It is founded on time preference.

Exam Probability: **Medium**

40. *Answer choices:*

(see index for correct answer)

- a. Esscher principle
- b. Decrement table
- c. Experience modifier
- d. Time value of money

Guidance: level 1

:: Planning ::

_________ is a high level plan to achieve one or more goals under conditions of uncertainty. In the sense of the "art of the general," which included several subsets of skills including tactics, siegecraft, logistics etc., the term came into use in the 6th century C.E. in East Roman terminology, and was translated into Western vernacular languages only in the 18th century. From then until the 20th century, the word " _________ " came to denote "a comprehensive way to try to pursue political ends, including the threat or actual use of force, in a dialectic of wills" in a military conflict, in which both adversaries interact.

Exam Probability: **Medium**

41. *Answer choices:*

(see index for correct answer)

- a. Territorialist School
- b. Group information management
- c. Concept driven strategy
- d. Strategy

Guidance: level 1

:: Banking ::

A _________ is a financial account maintained by a bank for a customer. A _________ can be a deposit account, a credit card account, a current account, or any other type of account offered by a financial institution, and represents the funds that a customer has entrusted to the financial institution and from which the customer can make withdrawals. Alternatively, accounts may be loan accounts in which case the customer owes money to the financial institution.

Exam Probability: **Medium**

42. *Answer choices:*

(see index for correct answer)

- a. Bank account
- b. Representative APR
- c. Clap note
- d. U-turn

Guidance: level 1

:: Expense ::

_________ relates to the cost of borrowing money. It is the price that a lender charges a borrower for the use of the lender`s money. On the income statement, _________ can represent the cost of borrowing money from banks, bond investors, and other sources. _________ is different from operating expense and CAPEX, for it relates to the capital structure of a company, and it is usually tax-deductible.

Exam Probability: **Medium**

43. *Answer choices:*

(see index for correct answer)

- a. Business overhead expense disability insurance
- b. Stock option expensing
- c. Freight expense
- d. Interest expense

Guidance: level 1

:: Retirement ::

An _________ is a series of payments made at equal intervals. Examples of annuities are regular deposits to a savings account, monthly home mortgage payments, monthly insurance payments and pension payments. Annuities can be classified by the frequency of payment dates. The payments may be made weekly, monthly, quarterly, yearly, or at any other regular interval of time.

Exam Probability: **Medium**

44. *Answer choices:*

(see index for correct answer)

- a. Cash balance plan
- b. Stakeholder pension scheme
- c. Aging in place
- d. Annuity

Guidance: level 1

:: Generally Accepted Accounting Principles ::

_________ is the accounting classification of an account. It is part of double-entry book-keeping technique.

Exam Probability: **Medium**

45. *Answer choices:*

(see index for correct answer)

- a. Normal balance
- b. Net profit
- c. Income statement
- d. Depreciation

Guidance: level 1

:: Project management ::

Some scenarios associate "this kind of planning" with learning "life skills". _________ s are necessary, or at least useful, in situations where individuals need to know what time they must be at a specific location to receive a specific service, and where people need to accomplish a set of goals within a set time period.

Exam Probability: **Medium**

46. *Answer choices:*

(see index for correct answer)

- a. Financial plan
- b. Schedule
- c. Aggregate project plan
- d. Logical framework approach

Guidance: level 1

:: Institutional investors ::

A _________ is an investment fund that pools capital from accredited investors or institutional investors and invests in a variety of assets, often with complex portfolio-construction and risk management techniques. It is administered by a professional investment management firm, and often structured as a limited partnership, limited liability company, or similar vehicle. _________ s are generally distinct from mutual funds and regarded as alternative investments, as their use of leverage is not capped by regulators, and distinct from private equity funds, as the majority of _________ s invest in relatively liquid assets. However, funds which operate similarly to _________ s but are regulated similarly to mutual funds are available and known as liquid alternative investments.

Exam Probability: **Medium**

47. *Answer choices:*

(see index for correct answer)

- a. SSBT OD05 Omnibus
- b. Admiral Administration
- c. Hedge fund
- d. Sampension

Guidance: level 1

:: Loans ::

In finance, a __________ is the lending of money by one or more individuals, organizations, or other entities to other individuals, organizations etc. The recipient incurs a debt, and is usually liable to pay interest on that debt until it is repaid, and also to repay the principal amount borrowed.

Exam Probability: **High**

48. *Answer choices:*

(see index for correct answer)

- a. Full documentation loan
- b. Mortgage loan
- c. Package loan
- d. Commodity loan rate

Guidance: level 1

:: Interest ::

In finance, __________ is the interest on a bond or loan that has accumulated since the principal investment, or since the previous coupon payment if there has been one already.

Exam Probability: **High**

49. *Answer choices:*

(see index for correct answer)

- a. Penal interest
- b. Interest at maturity
- c. Riba
- d. Accrued interest

Guidance: level 1

:: Investment ::

__________ , and investment appraisal, is the planning process used to determine whether an organization`s long term investments such as new machinery, replacement of machinery, new plants, new products, and research development projects are worth the funding of cash through the firm`s capitalization structure . It is the process of allocating resources for major capital, or investment, expenditures. One of the primary goals of __________ investments is to increase the value of the firm to the shareholders.

Exam Probability: **High**

50. *Answer choices:*

(see index for correct answer)

- a. APMEX
- b. Separately managed account
- c. Unified managed account
- d. Uncompensated risk

Guidance: level 1

:: Business law ::

__________ is where a person`s financial liability is limited to a fixed sum, most commonly the value of a person`s investment in a company or partnership. If a company with __________ is sued, then the claimants are suing the company, not its owners or investors. A shareholder in a limited company is not personally liable for any of the debts of the company, other than for the amount already invested in the company and for any unpaid amount on the shares in the company, if any. The same is true for the members of a __________ partnership and the limited partners in a limited partnership. By contrast, sole proprietors and partners in general partnerships are each liable for all the debts of the business .

Exam Probability: **High**

51. *Answer choices:*

(see index for correct answer)

- a. Process agent
- b. Commercial law
- c. Unfair business practices
- d. Forged endorsement

Guidance: level 1

:: E-commerce ::

A _________ is a plastic payment card that can be used instead of cash when making purchases. It is similar to a credit card, but unlike a credit card, the money is immediately transferred directly from the cardholder`s bank account when performing a transaction.

Exam Probability: **High**

52. *Answer choices:*

(see index for correct answer)

- a. Debit card
- b. BuildDirect
- c. Great Online Shopping Festival
- d. Mobile commerce service provider

Guidance: level 1

:: ::

Pharmaceutical _________ is the creation of a particular pharmaceutical product to fit the unique need of a patient. To do this, _________ pharmacists combine or process appropriate ingredients using various tools.

Exam Probability: **High**

53. *Answer choices:*

(see index for correct answer)

- a. functional perspective
- b. corporate values
- c. interpersonal communication
- d. Compounding

Guidance: level 1

:: Markets (customer bases) ::

In economics, _________ is the economic price for which a good or service is offered in the marketplace. It is of interest mainly in the study of microeconomics. Market value and _________ are equal only under conditions of market efficiency, equilibrium, and rational expectations.

Exam Probability: **Medium**

54. *Answer choices:*

(see index for correct answer)

- a. Perfect market
- b. Captive market
- c. Market price
- d. Economic equilibrium

Guidance: level 1

:: Debt ::

A _________ is a party that has a claim on the services of a second party. It is a person or institution to whom money is owed. The first party, in general, has provided some property or service to the second party under the assumption that the second party will return an equivalent property and service. The second party is frequently called a debtor or borrower. The first party is called the _________, which is the lender of property, service, or money.

Exam Probability: **Medium**

55. *Answer choices:*

(see index for correct answer)

- a. Creditor
- b. Debt
- c. Asset protection
- d. Internal debt

Guidance: level 1

:: Public finance ::

__________ is the process by which the monetary authority of a country, typically the central bank or currency board, controls either the cost of very short-term borrowing or the money supply, often targeting inflation rate or interest rate to ensure price stability and general trust in the currency.

Exam Probability: **Low**

56. *Answer choices:*

(see index for correct answer)

- a. Marginal cost of public funds
- b. Association of Public Treasurers of the United States and Canada
- c. Monetary policy
- d. Budget Code of Russia

Guidance: level 1

:: Financial regulatory authorities of the United States ::

The __________ is the revenue service of the United States federal government. The government agency is a bureau of the Department of the Treasury, and is under the immediate direction of the Commissioner of Internal Revenue, who is appointed to a five-year term by the President of the United States. The IRS is responsible for collecting taxes and administering the Internal Revenue Code, the main body of federal statutory tax law of the United States. The duties of the IRS include providing tax assistance to taxpayers and pursuing and resolving instances of erroneous or fraudulent tax filings. The IRS has also overseen various benefits programs, and enforces portions of the Affordable Care Act.

Exam Probability: **Medium**

57. *Answer choices:*

(see index for correct answer)

- a. Federal Deposit Insurance Corporation
- b. Internal Revenue Service
- c. Municipal Securities Rulemaking Board
- d. National Credit Union Administration

Guidance: level 1

:: Business law ::

A __________ is an arrangement where parties, known as partners, agree to cooperate to advance their mutual interests. The partners in a __________ may be individuals, businesses, interest-based organizations, schools, governments or combinations. Organizations may partner to increase the likelihood of each achieving their mission and to amplify their reach. A __________ may result in issuing and holding equity or may be only governed by a contract.

Exam Probability: **Low**

58. *Answer choices:*

(see index for correct answer)

- a. Partnership
- b. Advertising regulation
- c. Board of directors
- d. Starting a Business Index

Guidance: level 1

:: ::

A __________ is any person who contracts to acquire an asset in return for some form of consideration.

Exam Probability: **Medium**

59. *Answer choices:*

(see index for correct answer)

- a. Buyer
- b. interpersonal communication
- c. empathy
- d. levels of analysis

Guidance: level 1

Human resource management

Human resource (HR) management is the strategic approach to the effective management of organization workers so that they help the business gain a competitive advantage. It is designed to maximize employee performance in service of an employer's strategic objectives. HR is primarily concerned with the management of people within organizations, focusing on policies and on systems. HR departments are responsible for overseeing employee-benefits design, employee recruitment, training and development, performance appraisal, and rewarding (e.g., managing pay and benefit systems). HR also concerns itself with organizational change and industrial relations, that is, the balancing of organizational practices with requirements arising from collective bargaining and from governmental laws.

:: Production and manufacturing ::

_________ is a set of techniques and tools for process improvement. Though as a shortened form it may be found written as 6S, it should not be confused with the methodology known as 6S .

Exam Probability: **Medium**

1. *Answer choices:*

(see index for correct answer)

- a. Transfer cars
- b. STEP-NC
- c. Engineering validation test
- d. Woodworking machine

Guidance: level 1

:: Income ::

In business and accounting, net income is an entity`s income minus cost of goods sold, expenses and taxes for an accounting period. It is computed as the residual of all revenues and gains over all expenses and losses for the period, and has also been defined as the net increase in shareholders` equity that results from a company`s operations. In the context of the presentation of financial statements, the IFRS Foundation defines net income as synonymous with profit and loss. The difference between revenue and the cost of making a product or providing a service, before deducting overheads, payroll, taxation, and interest payments. This is different from operating income .

Exam Probability: **Medium**

2. *Answer choices:*

(see index for correct answer)

- a. Stipend
- b. IRD asset
- c. Family income
- d. Per capita income

Guidance: level 1

:: ::

An _________ is a person temporarily or permanently residing in a country other than their native country. In common usage, the term often refers to professionals, skilled workers, or artists taking positions outside their home country, either independently or sent abroad by their employers, who can be companies, universities, governments, or non-governmental organisations. Effectively migrant workers, they usually earn more than they would at home, and less than local employees. However, the term ` _________ ` is also used for retirees and others who have chosen to live outside their native country. Historically, it has also referred to exiles.

Exam Probability: **High**

3. *Answer choices:*

(see index for correct answer)

- a. Expatriate
- b. similarity-attraction theory
- c. interpersonal communication
- d. hierarchical perspective

Guidance: level 1

:: Industrial agreements ::

A _________ , in labor relations, is a group of employees with a clear and identifiable community of interests who are represented by a single labor union in collective bargaining and other dealings with management. Examples would be non-management professors, law enforcement professionals, blue-collar workers, clerical and administrative employees, etc. Geographic location as well as the number of facilities included in _________ s can be at issue during representation cases.

Exam Probability: **Low**

4. *Answer choices:*
(see index for correct answer)

- a. Bargaining unit
- b. McCrone Agreement
- c. WorkChoices
- d. Collective bargaining

Guidance: level 1

:: Parental leave ::

_________ , or family leave, is an employee benefit available in almost all countries. The term " _________ " may include maternity, paternity, and adoption leave; or may be used distinctively from "maternity leave" and "paternity leave" to describe separate family leave available to either parent to care for small children. In some countries and jurisdictions, "family leave" also includes leave provided to care for ill family members. Often, the minimum benefits and eligibility requirements are stipulated by law.

Exam Probability: **Medium**

5. *Answer choices:*
(see index for correct answer)

- a. Parental leave
- b. Pregnant Workers Directive
- c. Parental leave economics
- d. Maternity and Parental Leave, etc Regulations 1999

Guidance: level 1

:: Management ::

A _________ is a method or technique that has been generally accepted as superior to any alternatives because it produces results that are superior to those achieved by other means or because it has become a standard way of doing things, e.g., a standard way of complying with legal or ethical requirements.

Exam Probability: **High**

6. *Answer choices:*

(see index for correct answer)

- a. Earned schedule
- b. Best practice
- c. Dynamic enterprise modeling
- d. Community management

Guidance: level 1

:: Management ::

_________ is a technique used by some employers to rotate their employees` assigned jobs throughout their employment. Employers practice this technique for a number of reasons. It was designed to promote flexibility of employees and to keep employees interested into staying with the company/organization which employs them. There is also research that shows how _________ s help relieve the stress of employees who work in a job that requires manual labor.

Exam Probability: **High**

7. *Answer choices:*

(see index for correct answer)

- a. Cynefin
- b. Relational view
- c. Job rotation
- d. Goals Breakdown Structure

Guidance: level 1

:: Employment compensation ::

A __________ , also known as a flexible spending arrangement, is one of a number of tax-advantaged financial accounts, resulting in payroll tax savings. Before the Patient Protection and Affordable Care Act, one significant disadvantage to using an FSA was that funds not used by the end of the plan year were forfeited to the employer, known as the "use it or lose it" rule. Under the terms of the Affordable Care Act, a plan may permit an employee to carry over up to $500 into the following year without losing the funds.

Exam Probability: **High**

8. *Answer choices:*

(see index for correct answer)

- a. Flexible spending account
- b. Prevailing wage
- c. Salary cap
- d. Federal Salary Council

Guidance: level 1

:: Sexual harassment in the United States ::

In law, a __________ , reasonable man, or the man on the Clapham omnibus is a hypothetical person of legal fiction crafted by the courts and communicated through case law and jury instructions.

Exam Probability: **Low**

9. *Answer choices:*

(see index for correct answer)

- a. Charol Shakeshaft
- b. Blakey v. Continental Airlines
- c. Sandy Gallin
- d. Reasonable person

Guidance: level 1

:: ::

A _________ is a fund into which a sum of money is added during an employee`s employment years, and from which payments are drawn to support the person`s retirement from work in the form of periodic payments. A _________ may be a "defined benefit plan" where a fixed sum is paid regularly to a person, or a "defined contribution plan" under which a fixed sum is invested and then becomes available at retirement age. _________ s should not be confused with severance pay; the former is usually paid in regular installments for life after retirement, while the latter is typically paid as a fixed amount after involuntary termination of employment prior to retirement.

Exam Probability: **High**

10. *Answer choices:*

(see index for correct answer)

- a. process perspective
- b. interpersonal communication
- c. levels of analysis
- d. Pension

Guidance: level 1

:: Meetings ::

A _________ is a formal meeting of the representatives of different countries, constituent states, organizations, trade unions, political parties or other groups. The term, originally denoting a parley during battle in the Late Middle Ages, is derived from the Latin _________ us.

Exam Probability: **Low**

11. *Answer choices:*

(see index for correct answer)

- a. Carlton Club meeting
- b. Congress
- c. Convocation
- d. Audience

Guidance: level 1

:: Human resource management ::

This term is often used in an employment or human resources context where rather than terminating employees for first or minor infractions, there is a system of escalating responses intended to correct the negative behavior rather than to punish the employee.

Exam Probability: **High**

12. *Answer choices:*

(see index for correct answer)

- a. Progressive discipline
- b. Human resource policies
- c. Technical performance measure
- d. Management by objectives

Guidance: level 1

:: Human resource management ::

_________ is a continual process used to align the needs and priorities of the organization with those of its workforce to ensure it can meet its legislative, regulatory, service and production requirements and organizational objectives. _________ enables evidence based workforce development strategies.

Exam Probability: **Medium**

13. *Answer choices:*

(see index for correct answer)

- a. Employee retention
- b. Onboarding
- c. Workforce planning
- d. Person specification

Guidance: level 1

:: Labour law ::

An _________ is special or specified circumstances that partially or fully exempt a person or organization from performance of a legal obligation so as to avoid an unreasonable or disproportionate burden or obstacle.

Exam Probability: **High**

14. *Answer choices:*

(see index for correct answer)

- a. Individual capacity
- b. Vesting
- c. Undue hardship
- d. International Association of Labour Law Journals

Guidance: level 1

:: ::

__________ is a form of government characterized by strong central power and limited political freedoms. Individual freedoms are subordinate to the state and there is no constitutional accountability and rule of law under an authoritarian regime. Authoritarian regimes can be autocratic with power concentrated in one person or it can be more spread out between multiple officials and government institutions. Juan Linz`s influential 1964 description of __________ characterized authoritarian political systems by four qualities.

Exam Probability: **Low**

15. *Answer choices:*

(see index for correct answer)

- a. Sarbanes-Oxley act of 2002
- b. Authoritarianism
- c. personal values
- d. functional perspective

Guidance: level 1

:: Employment compensation ::

An _________ is an employee benefit program that assists employees with personal problems and/or work-related problems that may impact their job performance, health, mental and emotional well-being. EAPs generally offer free and confidential assessments, short-term counseling, referrals, and follow-up services for employees and their household members. EAP counselors also work in a consultative role with managers and supervisors to address employee and organizational challenges and needs. Many corporations, academic institution and/or government agencies are active in helping organizations prevent and cope with workplace violence, trauma, and other emergency response situations. There is a variety of support programs offered for employees. Even though EAPs are mainly aimed at work-related problems, there are a variety of programs that can assist with problems outside of the workplace. EAPs have grown over the years, and are more desirable economically and socially.

Exam Probability: **Medium**

16. *Answer choices:*

(see index for correct answer)

- a. Agency Workers Regulations 2010
- b. Explanation of benefits
- c. Compensation of employees
- d. Personal income

Guidance: level 1

:: ::

A _________ is monetary compensation paid by an employer to an employee in exchange for work done. Payment may be calculated as a fixed amount for each task completed , or at an hourly or daily rate , or based on an easily measured quantity of work done.

Exam Probability: **High**

17. *Answer choices:*

(see index for correct answer)

- a. Wage
- b. Sarbanes-Oxley act of 2002
- c. personal values
- d. open system

Guidance: level 1

:: Trade unions ::

A _________ is an association of workers forming a legal unit or legal personhood, usually called a "bargaining unit", which acts as bargaining agent and legal representative for a unit of employees in all matters of law or right arising from or in the administration of a collective agreement. Labour unions typically fund the formal organisation, head office, and legal team functions of the labour union through regular fees or union dues. The delegate staff of the labour union representation in the workforce are made up of workplace volunteers who are appointed by members in democratic elections.

Exam Probability: **High**

18. *Answer choices:*

(see index for correct answer)

- a. LabourStart
- b. Union busting
- c. Paper local
- d. Trade union

Guidance: level 1

:: Occupational safety and health law ::

The _________ of 1970 is a US labor law governing the federal law of occupational health and safety in the private sector and federal government in the United States. It was enacted by Congress in 1970 and was signed by President Richard Nixon on December 29, 1970. Its main goal is to ensure that employers provide employees with an environment free from recognized hazards, such as exposure to toxic chemicals, excessive noise levels, mechanical dangers, heat or cold stress, or unsanitary conditions. The Act created the Occupational Safety and Health Administration and the National Institute for Occupational Safety and Health .

Exam Probability: **High**

19. *Answer choices:*

(see index for correct answer)

- a. Mines and Collieries Act 1842
- b. Employment Standards Act
- c. Employment Standards Act of British Columbia

- d. Occupational Safety and Health Act 1994

Guidance: level 1

:: Employee relations ::

__________ is a fundamental concept in the effort to understand and describe, both qualitatively and quantitatively, the nature of the relationship between an organization and its employees. An "engaged employee" is defined as one who is fully absorbed by and enthusiastic about their work and so takes positive action to further the organization`s reputation and interests. An engaged employee has a positive attitude towards the organization and its values. In contrast, a disengaged employee may range from someone doing the bare minimum at work , up to an employee who is actively damaging the company`s work output and reputation.

Exam Probability: **High**

20. *Answer choices:*

(see index for correct answer)

- a. employee stock ownership
- b. Employee engagement
- c. Employee motivation
- d. Employee surveys

Guidance: level 1

:: Human resource management ::

__________ refers to the ability of an organization to retain its employees. __________ can be represented by a simple statistic . However, many consider __________ as relating to the efforts by which employers attempt to retain the employees in their workforce. In this sense, retention becomes the strategies rather than the outcome.

Exam Probability: **Medium**

21. *Answer choices:*

(see index for correct answer)

- a. Administrative services organization
- b. Skills management
- c. Managerial assessment of proficiency

- d. Senior management

Guidance: level 1

:: Business ethics ::

In United States labor law, a __________ exists when one`s behavior within a workplace creates an environment that is difficult or uncomfortable for another person to work in, due to discrimination. Common complaints in sexual harassment lawsuits include fondling, suggestive remarks, sexually-suggestive photos displayed in the workplace, use of sexual language, or off-color jokes. Small matters, annoyances, and isolated incidents are usually not considered to be statutory violations of the discrimination laws. For a violation to impose liability, the conduct must create a work environment that would be intimidating, hostile, or offensive to a reasonable person. An employer can be held liable for failing to prevent these workplace conditions, unless it can prove that it attempted to prevent the harassment and that the employee failed to take advantage of existing harassment counter-measures or tools provided by the employer.

Exam Probability: **High**

22. *Answer choices:*
(see index for correct answer)

- a. Third-party technique
- b. Terror-free investing
- c. Hostile work environment
- d. Proceedings of the International Association for Business and Society

Guidance: level 1

:: ::

On December 31, 2016, Xerox separated its business process service operations into a new publicly traded company, Conduent. Xerox focuses on its document technology and document outsourcing business, and continues to trade on the NYSE. On January 31, 2018, Xerox announced that it would sell a controlling stake to Fujifilm, which has maintained a joint venture in the Asia-Pacific region known as Fuji Xerox.

Exam Probability: **High**

23. *Answer choices:*

(see index for correct answer)

- a. similarity-attraction theory
- b. corporate values
- c. surface-level diversity
- d. hierarchical

Guidance: level 1

:: Occupational safety and health organizations ::

The _________ is the United States federal agency responsible for conducting research and making recommendations for the prevention of work-related injury and illness. NIOSH is part of the Centers for Disease Control and Prevention within the U.S. Department of Health and Human Services.

Exam Probability: **Low**

24. *Answer choices:*

(see index for correct answer)

- a. NEBOSH
- b. NIOSH Education and Research Centers
- c. Migration and Health Research Center
- d. Scientific Committee on Occupational Exposure Limit Values

Guidance: level 1

:: ::

_________ refers to the overall process of attracting, shortlisting, selecting and appointing suitable candidates for jobs within an organization. _________ can also refer to processes involved in choosing individuals for unpaid roles. Managers, human resource generalists and _________ specialists may be tasked with carrying out _________, but in some cases public-sector employment agencies, commercial _________ agencies, or specialist search consultancies are used to undertake parts of the process. Internet-based technologies which support all aspects of _________ have become widespread.

Exam Probability: **High**

25. *Answer choices:*

(see index for correct answer)

- a. empathy
- b. cultural
- c. hierarchical
- d. information systems assessment

Guidance: level 1

:: Labour relations ::

An _________ is a place of employment at which one is not required to join or financially support a union as a condition of hiring or continued employment. _________ is also known as a merit shop.

Exam Probability: **Low**

26. *Answer choices:*

(see index for correct answer)

- a. Passfield Memorandum
- b. European Trade Union Confederation
- c. Open shop
- d. Worker center

Guidance: level 1

:: Human resource management ::

_________ is a flexible hours schedule that allows workers to alter workday start and finish times. In contrast to traditional work arrangements that require employees to work a standard 9 a.m. to 5 p.m. day, _________ typically involves a "core" period of the day during which employees are required to be at work , and a "bandwidth" period within which all required hours must be worked . The working day outside of the "core" period is "flexible time", in which employees can choose when they work, subject to achieving total daily, weekly or monthly hours within the "bandwidth" period set by employers, and subject to the necessary work being done. The total working time required of employees on _________ schedules is the same as that required under traditional work schedules. A _________ policy allows staff to determine when they will work, while a flexplace policy allows staff to determine where they will work. Advantages include allowing employees to coordinate their work hours with public transport schedules, with the schedules of their children, and with daily traffic patterns to avoid high congestion times such as rush hour. Some claim that flexible working will change the nature of the way we work. The idea of _________ was invented by Christel Kammerer.

Exam Probability: **Low**

27. *Answer choices:*

(see index for correct answer)

- a. Incentive program
- b. Flextime
- c. Organizational culture
- d. Vendor on premises

Guidance: level 1

:: Unemployment ::

The _________ is the negative relationship between the levels of unemployment and wages that arises when these variables are expressed in local terms. According to David Blanchflower and Andrew Oswald , the _________ summarizes the fact that "A worker who is employed in an area of high unemployment earns less than an identical individual who works in a region with low joblessness."

Exam Probability: **Medium**

28. *Answer choices:*

(see index for correct answer)

- a. Mount Street Club
- b. Phillips curve
- c. Employment protection legislation
- d. Growth recession

Guidance: level 1

:: Industrial relations ::

_________ or employee satisfaction is a measure of workers` contentedness with their job, whether or not they like the job or individual aspects or facets of jobs, such as nature of work or supervision. _________ can be measured in cognitive , affective , and behavioral components. Researchers have also noted that _________ measures vary in the extent to which they measure feelings about the job . or cognitions about the job .

Exam Probability: **Medium**

29. *Answer choices:*

(see index for correct answer)

- a. Job satisfaction
- b. Workforce Investment Board
- c. Injury prevention
- d. Industrial violence

Guidance: level 1

:: Job interview ::

A _________ is a job interview in which the applicant is presented with a challenging business scenario that he/she must investigate and propose a solution to. _________ s are designed to test the candidate`s analytical skills and "soft" skills within a realistic business context. The case is often a business situation or a business case that the interviewer has worked on in real life.

Exam Probability: **Low**

30. *Answer choices:*

(see index for correct answer)

- a. Mock interview
- b. Exit interview
- c. Informational interview
- d. SOARA

Guidance: level 1

:: Human resource management ::

__________ refers to the ratio of the number of job positions to the number of job applicants and is used in the context of selection and recruitment.

Exam Probability: **Low**

31. *Answer choices:*

(see index for correct answer)

- a. Workforce sciences
- b. Disciplinary probation
- c. Professional employer organization
- d. Selection ratio

Guidance: level 1

:: ::

__________ is the process of collecting, analyzing and/or reporting information regarding the performance of an individual, group, organization, system or component. __________ is not a new concept, some of the earliest records of human activity relate to the counting or recording of activities.

Exam Probability: **Low**

32. *Answer choices:*

(see index for correct answer)

- a. personal values
- b. surface-level diversity
- c. Sarbanes-Oxley act of 2002
- d. process perspective

Guidance: level 1

:: United States employment discrimination case law ::

__________ , 524 U.S. 775 , is a US labor law case of the United States Supreme Court in which the Court identified the circumstances under which an employer may be held liable under Title VII of the Civil Rights Act of 1964 for the acts of a supervisory employee whose sexual harassment of subordinates has created a hostile work environment amounting to employment discrimination. The court held that "an employer is vicariously liable for actionable discrimination caused by a supervisor, but subject to an affirmative defense looking to the reasonableness of the employer`s conduct as well as that of a plaintiff victim."

Exam Probability: **Low**

33. *Answer choices:*

(see index for correct answer)

- a. Ricci v. DeStefano
- b. Executive Order 11375
- c. Gross v. FBL Financial Services, Inc.
- d. Dothard v. Rawlinson

Guidance: level 1

:: ::

__________ is the amount of time someone works beyond normal working hours. The term is also used for the pay received for this time. Normal hours may be determined in several ways.

Exam Probability: **Low**

34. *Answer choices:*

(see index for correct answer)

- a. hierarchical perspective
- b. similarity-attraction theory
- c. empathy
- d. Overtime

Guidance: level 1

:: Training ::

_________ is action or inaction that is regulated to be in accordance with a particular system of governance. _________ is commonly applied to regulating human and animal behavior, and furthermore, it is applied to each activity-branch in all branches of organized activity, knowledge, and other fields of study and observation. _________ can be a set of expectations that are required by any governing entity including the self, groups, classes, fields, industries, or societies.

Exam Probability: **Medium**

35. *Answer choices:*
(see index for correct answer)

- a. Hypoventilation training
- b. Training
- c. Instructor-led training
- d. Discipline

Guidance: level 1

:: Unemployment ::

_________ is the support service provided by responsible organizations, keen to support individuals who are exiting the business – to help former employees transition to new jobs and help them re-orient themselves in the job market. A consultancy firm usually provides the _________ services which are paid for by the former employer and are achieved usually through practical advice, training materials and workshops. Some companies may offer psychological support.

Exam Probability: **High**

36. *Answer choices:*
(see index for correct answer)

- a. Hysteresis
- b. Outplacement
- c. Employment-to-population ratio
- d. Functional finance

Guidance: level 1

:: Majority–minority relations ::

_________ , also known as reservation in India and Nepal, positive discrimination / action in the United Kingdom, and employment equity in Canada and South Africa, is the policy of promoting the education and employment of members of groups that are known to have previously suffered from discrimination. Historically and internationally, support for _________ has sought to achieve goals such as bridging inequalities in employment and pay, increasing access to education, promoting diversity, and redressing apparent past wrongs, harms, or hindrances.

Exam Probability: **High**

37. *Answer choices:*
(see index for correct answer)

- a. cultural dissonance
- b. Affirmative action
- c. cultural Relativism

Guidance: level 1

:: Employment ::

_________ is the probability that an individual will keep his/her job; a job with a high level of _________ is such that a person with the job would have a small chance of losing it.

Exam Probability: **High**

38. *Answer choices:*
(see index for correct answer)

- a. Working parent
- b. Job security
- c. Working holiday visa
- d. Split shift

Guidance: level 1

:: Self ::

_________ is a conscious or subconscious process in which people attempt to influence the perceptions of other people about a person, object or event. They do so by regulating and controlling information in social interaction. It was first conceptualized by Erving Goffman in 1959 in The Presentation of Self in Everyday Life, and then was expanded upon in 1967. An example of _________ theory in play is in sports such as soccer. At an important game, a player would want to showcase themselves in the best light possible, because there are college recruiters watching. This person would have the flashiest pair of cleats and try and perform their best to show off their skills. Their main goal may be to impress the college recruiters in a way that maximizes their chances of being chosen for a college team rather than winning the game.

Exam Probability: **Low**

39. *Answer choices:*

(see index for correct answer)

- a. Egocentrism
- b. Impression management
- c. Self-presentation
- d. a person

Guidance: level 1

:: Trade unions in the United States ::

The _________ is a labor union in the United States and Canada. Formed in 1903 by the merger of The Team Drivers International Union and The Teamsters National Union, the union now represents a diverse membership of blue-collar and professional workers in both the public and private sectors. The union had approximately 1.3 million members in 2013. Formerly known as the _________ , Chauffeurs, Warehousemen and Helpers of America, the IBT is a member of the Change to Win Federation and Canadian Labour Congress.

Exam Probability: **High**

40. *Answer choices:*

(see index for correct answer)

- a. Working America
- b. International Brotherhood of Teamsters
- c. Teaching Assistants Association
- d. Tennessee Nurses Association

Guidance: level 1

:: Teams ::

A _________ usually refers to a group of individuals who work together from different geographic locations and rely on communication technology such as email, FAX, and video or voice conferencing services in order to collaborate. The term can also refer to groups or teams that work together asynchronously or across organizational levels. Powell, Piccoli and Ives define _________ s as "groups of geographically, organizationally and/or time dispersed workers brought together by information and telecommunication technologies to accomplish one or more organizational tasks." According to Ale Ebrahim et. al. , _________ s can also be defined as "small temporary groups of geographically, organizationally and/or time dispersed knowledge workers who coordinate their work predominantly with electronic information and communication technologies in order to accomplish one or more organization tasks."

Exam Probability: **High**

41. *Answer choices:*

(see index for correct answer)

- a. Team-building
- b. team composition

Guidance: level 1

:: Human resource management ::

_________ involves improving the effectiveness of organizations and the individuals and teams within them. Training may be viewed as related to immediate changes in organizational effectiveness via organized instruction, while development is related to the progress of longer-term organizational and employee goals. While _________ technically have differing definitions, the two are oftentimes used interchangeably and/or together. _________ has historically been a topic within applied psychology but has within the last two decades become closely associated with human resources management, talent management, human resources development, instructional design, human factors, and knowledge management.

Exam Probability: **High**

42. *Answer choices:*

(see index for correct answer)

- a. Attendance management
- b. Randstad Holding
- c. Training and development
- d. Selection ratio

Guidance: level 1

:: Employment of foreign-born ::

__________ refers to the international labor pool of workers, including those employed by multinational companies and connected through a global system of networking and production, immigrant workers, transient migrant workers, telecommuting workers, those in export-oriented employment, contingent work or other precarious employment. As of 2012, the global labor pool consisted of approximately 3 billion workers, around 200 million unemployed.

Exam Probability: **Medium**

43. *Answer choices:*

(see index for correct answer)

- a. Global workforce
- b. Reverse brain drain
- c. L-1 visa
- d. Human capital flight

Guidance: level 1

:: ::

In production, research, retail, and accounting, a _________ is the value of money that has been used up to produce something or deliver a service, and hence is not available for use anymore. In business, the _________ may be one of acquisition, in which case the amount of money expended to acquire it is counted as _________ . In this case, money is the input that is gone in order to acquire the thing. This acquisition _________ may be the sum of the _________ of production as incurred by the original producer, and further _________ s of transaction as incurred by the acquirer over and above the price paid to the producer. Usually, the price also includes a mark-up for profit over the _________ of production.

Exam Probability: **High**

44. *Answer choices:*

(see index for correct answer)

- a. Cost
- b. functional perspective
- c. process perspective
- d. open system

Guidance: level 1

:: Options (finance) ::

_________ is a contractual agreement between a corporation and recipients of phantom shares that bestow upon the grantee the right to a cash payment at a designated time or in association with a designated event in the future, which payment is to be in an amount tied to the market value of an equivalent number of shares of the corporation`s stock. Thus, the amount of the payout will increase as the stock price rises, and decrease if the stock falls, but without the recipient actually receiving any stock. Like other forms of stock-based compensation plans, _________ broadly serves to align the interests of recipients and shareholders, incent contribution to share value, and encourage the retention or continued participation of contributors. Recipients are typically employees, but may also be directors, third-party vendors, or others.

Exam Probability: **High**

45. *Answer choices:*

(see index for correct answer)

- a. Naked put
- b. Chicago Options Associates
- c. Phantom stock
- d. Put option

Guidance: level 1

:: Validity (statistics) ::

__________ is the extent to which a test accurately measures what it is supposed to measure. In the fields of psychological testing and educational testing, "validity refers to the degree to which evidence and theory support the interpretations of test scores entailed by proposed uses of tests". Although classical models divided the concept into various "validities" , the currently dominant view is that validity is a single unitary construct.

Exam Probability: **Low**

46. *Answer choices:*

(see index for correct answer)

- a. Nomological network
- b. Discriminant validity
- c. Face validity
- d. Test validity

Guidance: level 1

:: Stress ::

__________ means beneficial stress—either psychological, physical , or biochemical/radiological .

Exam Probability: **High**

47. *Answer choices:*

(see index for correct answer)

- a. Compassion fatigue
- b. Psychotic break
- c. Coping
- d. Surgical stress

Guidance: level 1

:: Termination of employment ::

The _________ of 1988 is a US labor law which protects employees, their families, and communities by requiring most employers with 100 or more employees to provide 60 calendar-day advance notification of plant closings and mass layoffs of employees, as defined in the Act. In 2001, there were about 2,000 mass layoffs and plant closures which were subject to WARN advance notice requirements and which affected about 660,000 employees.

Exam Probability: **Medium**

48. *Answer choices:*
(see index for correct answer)

- a. Worker Adjustment and Retraining Notification Act
- b. Termination of Employment Convention, 1982
- c. The Disposable American
- d. Pink slip

Guidance: level 1

:: Project management ::

Some scenarios associate "this kind of planning" with learning "life skills". _________ s are necessary, or at least useful, in situations where individuals need to know what time they must be at a specific location to receive a specific service, and where people need to accomplish a set of goals within a set time period.

Exam Probability: **High**

49. *Answer choices:*
(see index for correct answer)

- a. Project governance
- b. Feature-driven development
- c. Rapid Results
- d. Project manufacturing

Guidance: level 1

:: Labor ::

The workforce or labour force is the labour pool in employment. It is generally used to describe those working for a single company or industry, but can also apply to a geographic region like a city, state, or country. Within a company, its value can be labelled as its "Workforce in Place". The workforce of a country includes both the employed and the unemployed. The labour force participation rate, LFPR , is the ratio between the labour force and the overall size of their cohort . The term generally excludes the employers or management, and can imply those involved in manual labour. It may also mean all those who are available for work.

Exam Probability: **High**

50. *Answer choices:*

(see index for correct answer)

- a. Entry-level job
- b. Factors of production
- c. Hot desking
- d. Roughneck

Guidance: level 1

:: Workplace ::

A _________ , also referred to as a performance review, performance evaluation, development discussion, or employee appraisal is a method by which the job performance of an employee is documented and evaluated. _________ s are a part of career development and consist of regular reviews of employee performance within organizations.

Exam Probability: **Medium**

51. *Answer choices:*

(see index for correct answer)

- a. labour turnover
- b. Workplace deviance
- c. Performance appraisal
- d. Feminisation of the workplace

Guidance: level 1

:: Employment compensation ::

_________ is time off from work that workers can use to stay home to address their health and safety needs without losing pay. Paid _________ is a statutory requirement in many nations. Most European, many Latin American, a few African and a few Asian countries have legal requirements for paid _________ .

Exam Probability: **Medium**

52. *Answer choices:*

(see index for correct answer)

- a. Pay Bands
- b. Paid time off
- c. Non-wage labour costs
- d. Commission

Guidance: level 1

:: Labor ::

_________ s are workers whose main capital is knowledge. Examples include programmers, physicians, pharmacists, architects, engineers, scientists, design thinkers, public accountants, lawyers, and academics, and any other white-collar workers, whose line of work requires the one to "think for a living".

Exam Probability: **Low**

53. *Answer choices:*

(see index for correct answer)

- a. Hot desking
- b. Anti-capitalism
- c. Knowledge worker
- d. Labor notes

Guidance: level 1

:: Employment compensation ::

__________ is a notional derivative of a Health Reimbursement Arrangement , a type of US employer-funded health benefit plan that reimburses employees for out-of-pocket medical expenses and, in limited cases, to pay for health insurance plan premiums.

Exam Probability: **Medium**

54. *Answer choices:*
(see index for correct answer)

- a. Family wage
- b. Health Reimbursement Account
- c. Golden handcuffs
- d. Scanlon plan

Guidance: level 1

:: ::

A __________ , medical practitioner, medical doctor, or simply doctor, is a professional who practises medicine, which is concerned with promoting, maintaining, or restoring health through the study, diagnosis, prognosis and treatment of disease, injury, and other physical and mental impairments. __________ s may focus their practice on certain disease categories, types of patients, and methods of treatment—known as specialities—or they may assume responsibility for the provision of continuing and comprehensive medical care to individuals, families, and communities—known as general practice. Medical practice properly requires both a detailed knowledge of the academic disciplines, such as anatomy and physiology, underlying diseases and their treatment—the science of medicine—and also a decent competence in its applied practice—the art or craft of medicine.

Exam Probability: **Medium**

55. *Answer choices:*
(see index for correct answer)

- a. Character
- b. corporate values
- c. co-culture
- d. interpersonal communication

Guidance: level 1

:: Educational assessment and evaluation ::

An _________ is a component of a competence to do a certain kind of work at a certain level. Outstanding _________ can be considered "talent". An _________ may be physical or mental. _________ is inborn potential to do certain kinds of work whether developed or undeveloped. Ability is developed knowledge, understanding, learned or acquired abilities or attitude. The innate nature of _________ is in contrast to skills and achievement, which represent knowledge or ability that is gained through learning.

Exam Probability: **High**

56. *Answer choices:*

(see index for correct answer)

- a. Bologna Process
- b. Aptitude
- c. Test preparation
- d. National Academic Recognition Information Centre

Guidance: level 1

:: ::

_________ is the means to see, hear, or become aware of something or someone through our fundamental senses. The term _________ derives from the Latin word perceptio, and is the organization, identification, and interpretation of sensory information in order to represent and understand the presented information, or the environment.

Exam Probability: **Medium**

57. *Answer choices:*

(see index for correct answer)

- a. levels of analysis
- b. hierarchical
- c. personal values
- d. co-culture

Guidance: level 1

:: Organizational behavior ::

_________ is the state or fact of exclusive rights and control over property, which may be an object, land/real estate or intellectual property. _________ involves multiple rights, collectively referred to as title, which may be separated and held by different parties.

Exam Probability: **Low**

58. *Answer choices:*

(see index for correct answer)

- a. Administrative Behavior
- b. Counterproductive norms
- c. Positive organizational behavior
- d. Organizational citizenship behavior

Guidance: level 1

:: Occupational safety and health ::

A safety data sheet , _________ , or product safety data sheet is a document that lists information relating to occupational safety and health for the use of various substances and products. SDSs are a widely used system for cataloging information on chemicals, chemical compounds, and chemical mixtures. SDS information may include instructions for the safe use and potential hazards associated with a particular material or product, along with spill-handling procedures. SDS formats can vary from source to source within a country depending on national requirements.

Exam Probability: **Low**

59. *Answer choices:*

(see index for correct answer)

- a. Hot work
- b. Nutec
- c. Herbert William Heinrich
- d. Global Alliance for Clean Cookstoves

Guidance: level 1

Information systems

Information systems (IS) are formal, sociotechnical, organizational systems designed to collect, process, store, and distribute information. In a sociotechnical perspective Information Systems are composed by four components: technology, process, people and organizational structure.

:: Data quality ::

_________ or data cleaning is the process of detecting and correcting corrupt or inaccurate records from a record set, table, or database and refers to identifying incomplete, incorrect, inaccurate or irrelevant parts of the data and then replacing, modifying, or deleting the dirty or coarse data. _________ may be performed interactively with data wrangling tools, or as batch processing through scripting.

Exam Probability: **High**

1. *Answer choices:*

(see index for correct answer)

- a. One-for-one checking
- b. Information quality
- c. Data cleansing
- d. Input mask

Guidance: level 1

:: Domain name system ::

_________ , Inc. is an American company based in Reston, Virginia, United States that operates a diverse array of network infrastructure, including two of the Internet's thirteen root nameservers, the authoritative registry for the .com, .net, and .name generic top-level domains and the .cc and .tv country-code top-level domains, and the back-end systems for the .jobs, .gov, and .edu top-level domains. _________ also offers a range of security services, including managed DNS, distributed denial-of-service attack mitigation and cyber-threat reporting.

Exam Probability: **High**

2. *Answer choices:*

(see index for correct answer)

- a. ARPA Host Name Server Protocol
- b. Dynamic DNS
- c. Zone file
- d. Public Suffix List

Guidance: level 1

:: Classification systems ::

_________ is the practice of comparing business processes and performance metrics to industry bests and best practices from other companies. Dimensions typically measured are quality, time and cost.

Exam Probability: **High**

3. *Answer choices:*

(see index for correct answer)

- a. Benchmarking
- b. Taxon in disguise
- c. Bordeaux Wine Official Classification of 1855
- d. Climate classification

Guidance: level 1

:: Sound recording ::

__________ is a medium for magnetic recording, made of a thin, magnetizable coating on a long, narrow strip of plastic film. It was developed in Germany in 1928, based on magnetic wire recording. Devices that record and play back audio and video using __________ are tape recorders and video tape recorders respectively. A device that stores computer data on __________ is known as a tape drive.

Exam Probability: **Medium**

4. *Answer choices:*

(see index for correct answer)

- a. Headroom
- b. Magnetic tape
- c. Alignment level
- d. CX

Guidance: level 1

:: Information technology audit ::

__________ is the act of using a computer to take or alter electronic data, or to gain unlawful use of a computer or system. In the United States, __________ is specifically proscribed by the __________ and Abuse Act, which criminalizes computer-related acts under federal jurisdiction. Types of __________ include.

Exam Probability: **High**

5. *Answer choices:*

(see index for correct answer)

- a. Computer fraud
- b. Computer forensics
- c. National Information Infrastructure Protection Act
- d. Information security audit

Guidance: level 1

:: Costs ::

In economics, __________ is the total economic cost of production and is made up of variable cost, which varies according to the quantity of a good produced and includes inputs such as labour and raw materials, plus fixed cost, which is independent of the quantity of a good produced and includes inputs that cannot be varied in the short term: fixed costs such as buildings and machinery, including sunk costs if any. Since cost is measured per unit of time, it is a flow variable.

Exam Probability: **Medium**

6. *Answer choices:*

(see index for correct answer)

- a. Search cost
- b. Total cost
- c. Cost of products sold
- d. Further processing cost

Guidance: level 1

:: Information technology ::

__________ is the use of computers to store, retrieve, transmit, and manipulate data, or information, often in the context of a business or other enterprise. IT is considered to be a subset of information and communications technology . An __________ system is generally an information system, a communications system or, more specifically speaking, a computer system – including all hardware, software and peripheral equipment – operated by a limited group of users.

Exam Probability: **Low**

7. *Answer choices:*

(see index for correct answer)

- a. Information technology
- b. ActivEcho
- c. Iomart Group plc
- d. Software-based Storage

Guidance: level 1

:: Digital rights management ::

__________ tools or technological protection measures are a set of access control technologies for restricting the use of proprietary hardware and copyrighted works. DRM technologies try to control the use, modification, and distribution of copyrighted works , as well as systems within devices that enforce these policies.

Exam Probability: **Low**

8. *Answer choices:*
(see index for correct answer)

- a. Rightscorp, Inc.
- b. The Right to Read
- c. ByteShield
- d. Digital rights management

Guidance: level 1

:: Automatic identification and data capture ::

__________ is the trademark for a type of matrix barcode first designed in 1994 for the automotive industry in Japan. A barcode is a machine-readable optical label that contains information about the item to which it is attached. In practice, __________ s often contain data for a locator, identifier, or tracker that points to a website or application. A __________ uses four standardized encoding modes to store data efficiently; extensions may also be used.

Exam Probability: **Medium**

9. *Answer choices:*
(see index for correct answer)

- a. HipVoice
- b. Omni-ID
- c. SILVIA
- d. Noisy channel model

Guidance: level 1

:: Payment systems ::

_________ is a mobile phone-based money transfer, financing and microfinancing service, launched in 2007 by Vodafone for Safaricom and Vodacom, the largest mobile network operators in Kenya and Tanzania. It has since expanded to Afghanistan, South Africa, India and in 2014 to Romania and in 2015 to Albania. _________ allows users to deposit, withdraw, transfer money and pay for goods and services easily with a mobile device.

Exam Probability: **Medium**

10. *Answer choices:*

(see index for correct answer)

- a. M-Pesa
- b. Cardsave
- c. Bankgiro
- d. WorldPay

Guidance: level 1

:: Virtual reality ::

An _________ , a concept in Hinduism that means "descent", refers to the material appearance or incarnation of a deity on earth. The relative verb to "alight, to make one`s appearance" is sometimes used to refer to any guru or revered human being.

Exam Probability: **Low**

11. *Answer choices:*

(see index for correct answer)

- a. The Sword of Damocles
- b. Gouraud shading
- c. Blaxxun
- d. Avatar

Guidance: level 1

:: Infographics ::

A _________ is a symbolic representation of information according to visualization technique. _________ s have been used since ancient times, but became more prevalent during the Enlightenment. Sometimes, the technique uses a three-dimensional visualization which is then projected onto a two-dimensional surface. The word graph is sometimes used as a synonym for _________ .

Exam Probability: **Low**

12. *Answer choices:*

(see index for correct answer)

- a. Texture advection
- b. Coat of arms
- c. Diagram
- d. Creately

Guidance: level 1

:: E-commerce ::

_________ is the activity of buying or selling of products on online services or over the Internet. Electronic commerce draws on technologies such as mobile commerce, electronic funds transfer, supply chain management, Internet marketing, online transaction processing, electronic data interchange , inventory management systems, and automated data collection systems.

Exam Probability: **Low**

13. *Answer choices:*

(see index for correct answer)

- a. Point of sale
- b. Maritime E-Commerce Association
- c. Mobile payment
- d. ICOCA

Guidance: level 1

:: Network management ::

__________ is the process of administering and managing computer networks. Services provided by this discipline include fault analysis, performance management, provisioning of networks and maintaining the quality of service. Software that enables network administrators to perform their functions is called __________ software.

Exam Probability: **Low**

14. *Answer choices:*

(see index for correct answer)

- a. Network administrator
- b. Java Management Extensions
- c. Fault management
- d. Network management

Guidance: level 1

:: Network theory ::

A __________ is a social structure made up of a set of social actors , sets of dyadic ties, and other social interactions between actors. The __________ perspective provides a set of methods for analyzing the structure of whole social entities as well as a variety of theories explaining the patterns observed in these structures. The study of these structures uses __________ analysis to identify local and global patterns, locate influential entities, and examine network dynamics.

Exam Probability: **Low**

15. *Answer choices:*

(see index for correct answer)

- a. Weighted network
- b. Assortativity
- c. Complex network
- d. Social network

Guidance: level 1

:: World Wide Web ::

A __________ is a document that is suitable to act as a web resource on the World Wide Web. In order to graphically display a __________ , a web browser is needed. This is a type of software that can retrieve __________ s from the Internet. When accessed by a web browser it may be displayed as a __________ on a monitor or mobile device. Typical __________ s are hypertext documents which contain hyperlinks, often referred to as links, for browsing to other __________ s.

Exam Probability: **Low**

16. *Answer choices:*
(see index for correct answer)

- a. Stanford Web Credibility Project
- b. Socialcasting
- c. Online video analytics
- d. Google Dashboard

Guidance: level 1

:: E-commerce ::

__________ , and its now-deprecated predecessor, Secure Sockets Layer , are cryptographic protocols designed to provide communications security over a computer network. Several versions of the protocols find widespread use in applications such as web browsing, email, instant messaging, and voice over IP . Websites can use TLS to secure all communications between their servers and web browsers.

Exam Probability: **High**

17. *Answer choices:*
(see index for correct answer)

- a. Associate-O-Matic
- b. Government-to-citizen
- c. Storenvy
- d. Transport Layer Security

Guidance: level 1

:: ::

The __________ , commonly known as the Web, is an information system where documents and other web resources are identified by Uniform Resource Locators , which may be interlinked by hypertext, and are accessible over the Internet. The resources of the WWW may be accessed by users by a software application called a web browser.

Exam Probability: **High**

18. *Answer choices:*
(see index for correct answer)

- a. Character
- b. similarity-attraction theory
- c. World Wide Web
- d. empathy

Guidance: level 1

:: Fault tolerance ::

__________ is the property that enables a system to continue operating properly in the event of the failure of some of its components. If its operating quality decreases at all, the decrease is proportional to the severity of the failure, as compared to a naively designed system, in which even a small failure can cause total breakdown. __________ is particularly sought after in high-availability or life-critical systems. The ability of maintaining functionality when portions of a system break down is referred to as graceful degradation.

Exam Probability: **Medium**

19. *Answer choices:*
(see index for correct answer)

- a. Fault tolerance
- b. Redundancy
- c. Fail-safe
- d. Double switching

Guidance: level 1

:: Supply chain management ::

ERP is usually referred to as a category of business management software — typically a suite of integrated applications—that an organization can use to collect, store, manage, and interpret data from these many business activities.

Exam Probability: **Medium**

20. *Answer choices:*
(see index for correct answer)

- a. ISO/PAS 28000
- b. Enterprise resource planning
- c. Supply network operations
- d. Delivery Reliability

Guidance: level 1

:: Satellite navigation systems ::

_________ Galilei was an Italian astronomer, physicist and engineer, sometimes described as a polymath. _________ has been called the "father of observational astronomy", the "father of modern physics", the "father of the scientific method", and the "father of modern science".

Exam Probability: **Low**

21. *Answer choices:*
(see index for correct answer)

- a. Advanced driver assistance systems
- b. Assisted GPS
- c. United States v. Pineda-Moreno
- d. Galileo

Guidance: level 1

:: ::

_________ is a free email service developed by Google. Users can access _________ on the web and using third-party programs that synchronize email content through POP or IMAP protocols. _________ started as a limited beta release on April 1, 2004 and ended its testing phase on July 7, 2009.

Exam Probability: **Medium**

22. *Answer choices:*

(see index for correct answer)

- a. imperative
- b. open system
- c. similarity-attraction theory
- d. Gmail

Guidance: level 1

:: Metadata ::

_________ s usage can be discovered by inspection of software applications or application data files through a process of manual or automated Application Discovery and Understanding. Once _________ s are discovered they can be registered in a metadata registry.

Exam Probability: **High**

23. *Answer choices:*

(see index for correct answer)

- a. Exchangeable image file format
- b. Mail Isolation Control and Tracking
- c. Property equivalence
- d. Data element

Guidance: level 1

:: Network analyzers ::

A _________ , meaning "meat eater" , is an organism that derives its energy and nutrient requirements from a diet consisting mainly or exclusively of animal tissue, whether through predation or scavenging. Animals that depend solely on animal flesh for their nutrient requirements are called obligate _________ s while those that also consume non-animal food are called facultative _________ s. Omnivores also consume both animal and non-animal food, and, apart from the more general definition, there is no clearly defined ratio of plant to animal material that would distinguish a facultative _________ from an omnivore. A _________ at the top of the food chain, not preyed upon by other animals, is termed an apex predator.

Exam Probability: **Low**

24. *Answer choices:*

(see index for correct answer)

- a. Microsoft Network Monitor
- b. Kismet
- c. MTR
- d. Carnivore

Guidance: level 1

:: Stochastic processes ::

_________ in its modern meaning is a "new idea, creative thoughts, new imaginations in form of device or method". _________ is often also viewed as the application of better solutions that meet new requirements, unarticulated needs, or existing market needs. Such _________ takes place through the provision of more-effective products, processes, services, technologies, or business models that are made available to markets, governments and society. An _________ is something original and more effective and, as a consequence, new, that "breaks into" the market or society. _________ is related to, but not the same as, invention, as _________ is more apt to involve the practical implementation of an invention to make a meaningful impact in the market or society, and not all _________ s require an invention. _________ often manifests itself via the engineering process, when the problem being solved is of a technical or scientific nature. The opposite of _________ is exnovation.

Exam Probability: **High**

25. *Answer choices:*

(see index for correct answer)

- a. D/M/1 queue
- b. Innovation
- c. Gaussian process
- d. Random structure function

Guidance: level 1

:: Virtual economies ::

__________ is an online virtual world, developed and owned by the San Francisco-based firm Linden Lab and launched on June 23, 2003. By 2013, __________ had approximately one million regular users; at the end of 2017 active user count totals "between 800,000 and 900,000". In many ways, __________ is similar to massively multiplayer online role-playing games; however, Linden Lab is emphatic that their creation is not a game: "There is no manufactured conflict, no set objective".

Exam Probability: **High**

26. *Answer choices:*

(see index for correct answer)

- a. Habbo
- b. Virtual economy
- c. Second Life
- d. ArcheAge

Guidance: level 1

:: Information systems ::

__________ are formal, sociotechnical, organizational systems designed to collect, process, store, and distribute information. In a sociotechnical perspective, __________ are composed by four components: task, people, structure , and technology.

Exam Probability: **Low**

27. *Answer choices:*

(see index for correct answer)

- a. E-GMS
- b. Information systems
- c. Intelligent decision support system
- d. CountrySTAT

Guidance: level 1

:: Commercial item transport and distribution ::

In commerce, supply-chain management , the management of the flow of goods and services, involves the movement and storage of raw materials, of work-in-process inventory, and of finished goods from point of origin to point of consumption. Interconnected or interlinked networks, channels and node businesses combine in the provision of products and services required by end customers in a supply chain. Supply-chain management has been defined as the "design, planning, execution, control, and monitoring of supply-chain activities with the objective of creating net value, building a competitive infrastructure, leveraging worldwide logistics, synchronizing supply with demand and measuring performance globally."SCM practice draws heavily from the areas of industrial engineering, systems engineering, operations management, logistics, procurement, information technology, and marketing and strives for an integrated approach. Marketing channels play an important role in supply-chain management. Current research in supply-chain management is concerned with topics related to sustainability and risk management, among others. Some suggest that the "people dimension" of SCM, ethical issues, internal integration, transparency/visibility, and human capital/talent management are topics that have, so far, been underrepresented on the research agenda.

Exam Probability: **Low**

28. *Answer choices:*

(see index for correct answer)

- a. Dock
- b. Delivery order
- c. Weigh station
- d. Supply chain management

Guidance: level 1

:: Google services ::

A blog is a discussion or informational website published on the World Wide Web consisting of discrete, often informal diary-style text entries . Posts are typically displayed in reverse chronological order, so that the most recent post appears first, at the top of the web page. Until 2009, blogs were usually the work of a single individual, occasionally of a small group, and often covered a single subject or topic. In the 2010s, "multi-author blogs" emerged, featuring the writing of multiple authors and sometimes professionally edited. MABs from newspapers, other media outlets, universities, think tanks, advocacy groups, and similar institutions account for an increasing quantity of blog traffic. The rise of Twitter and other "microblogging" systems helps integrate MABs and single-author blogs into the news media. Blog can also be used as a verb, meaning to maintain or add content to a blog.

Exam Probability: **Medium**

29. *Answer choices:*

(see index for correct answer)

- a. Google Reader
- b. Blogger
- c. Google News Archive
- d. Vevo

Guidance: level 1

:: ::

Sustainability is the process of people maintaining change in a balanced environment, in which the exploitation of resources, the direction of investments, the orientation of technological development and institutional change are all in harmony and enhance both current and future potential to meet human needs and aspirations. For many in the field, sustainability is defined through the following interconnected domains or pillars: environment, economic and social, which according to Fritjof Capra is based on the principles of Systems Thinking. Sub-domains of _________ development have been considered also: cultural, technological and political. While _________ development may be the organizing principle for sustainability for some, for others, the two terms are paradoxical . _________ development is the development that meets the needs of the present without compromising the ability of future generations to meet their own needs. Brundtland Report for the World Commission on Environment and Development introduced the term of _________ development.

Exam Probability: **High**

30. *Answer choices:*

(see index for correct answer)

- a. empathy
- b. hierarchical perspective
- c. process perspective
- d. Sustainable

Guidance: level 1

:: ::

A _________ is the event in which two or more bodies exert forces on each other in about a relatively short time. Although the most common use of the word _________ refers to incidents in which two or more objects collide with great force, the scientific use of the term implies nothing about the magnitude of the force.

Exam Probability: **High**

31. *Answer choices:*

(see index for correct answer)

- a. hierarchical perspective
- b. information systems assessment
- c. Collision

- d. process perspective

Guidance: level 1

:: Computer networking ::

_________ is a method of grouping data that is transmitted over a digital network into packets. Packets are made of a header and a payload. Data in the header are used by networking hardware to direct the packet to its destination where the payload is extracted and used by application software. _________ is the primary basis for data communications in computer networks worldwide.

Exam Probability: **High**

32. *Answer choices:*

(see index for correct answer)

- a. Out-of-band data
- b. RendezVous Routing Daemon
- c. Physical layer
- d. Federal Networking Council

Guidance: level 1

:: Information systems ::

A _________ is an information system that supports business or organizational decision-making activities. DSSs serve the management, operations and planning levels of an organization and help people make decisions about problems that may be rapidly changing and not easily specified in advance—i.e. unstructured and semi-structured decision problems. _________ s can be either fully computerized or human-powered, or a combination of both.

Exam Probability: **High**

33. *Answer choices:*

(see index for correct answer)

- a. Document engineering
- b. Physical Internet
- c. Association for Information Systems
- d. Decision support system

Guidance: level 1

:: Mereology ::

_________ , in the abstract, is what belongs to or with something, whether as an attribute or as a component of said thing. In the context of this article, it is one or more components , whether physical or incorporeal, of a person`s estate; or so belonging to, as in being owned by, a person or jointly a group of people or a legal entity like a corporation or even a society. Depending on the nature of the _________ , an owner of _________ has the right to consume, alter, share, redefine, rent, mortgage, pawn, sell, exchange, transfer, give away or destroy it, or to exclude others from doing these things, as well as to perhaps abandon it; whereas regardless of the nature of the _________ , the owner thereof has the right to properly use it , or at the very least exclusively keep it.

Exam Probability: **High**

34. *Answer choices:*
(see index for correct answer)

- a. Simple
- b. Mereological nihilism
- c. Property
- d. Mereology

Guidance: level 1

:: Telecommunication theory ::

In reliability theory and reliability engineering, the term _________ has the following meanings.

Exam Probability: **Low**

35. *Answer choices:*
(see index for correct answer)

- a. Medium-power talker
- b. Received noise power
- c. Availability
- d. Asynchronous operation

Guidance: level 1

:: Industrial design ::

Across the many fields concerned with _________ , including information science, computer science, human-computer interaction, communication, and industrial design, there is little agreement over the meaning of the term " _________ ", although all are related to interaction with computers and other machines with a user interface.

Exam Probability: **Low**

36. *Answer choices:*

(see index for correct answer)

- a. Interactivity
- b. Bauhaus
- c. Productionisation
- d. Solid Ground Curing

Guidance: level 1

:: Reputation management ::

A _________ is an astronomical object consisting of a luminous spheroid of plasma held together by its own gravity. The nearest _________ to Earth is the Sun. Many other _________ s are visible to the naked eye from Earth during the night, appearing as a multitude of fixed luminous points in the sky due to their immense distance from Earth. Historically, the most prominent _________ s were grouped into constellations and asterisms, the brightest of which gained proper names. Astronomers have assembled _________ catalogues that identify the known _________ s and provide standardized stellar designations. However, most of the estimated 300 sextillion _________ s in the Universe are invisible to the naked eye from Earth, including all _________ s outside our galaxy, the Milky Way.

Exam Probability: **High**

37. *Answer choices:*

(see index for correct answer)

- a. Get Satisfaction
- b. Infamy
- c. personal brand
- d. Star

Guidance: level 1

:: Outsourcing ::

A service-level agreement is a commitment between a service provider and a client. Particular aspects of the service – quality, availability, responsibilities – are agreed between the service provider and the service user. The most common component of SLA is that the services should be provided to the customer as agreed upon in the contract. As an example, Internet service providers and telcos will commonly include _________ s within the terms of their contracts with customers to define the level of service being sold in plain language terms. In this case the SLA will typically have a technical definition in mean time between failures , mean time to repair or mean time to recovery ; identifying which party is responsible for reporting faults or paying fees; responsibility for various data rates; throughput; jitter; or similar measurable details.

Exam Probability: **High**

38. *Answer choices:*
(see index for correct answer)

- a. Service level agreement
- b. Counsel On Call
- c. Media Process Outsourcing
- d. IQor

Guidance: level 1

:: Information technology management ::

_________ concerns a cycle of organizational activity: the acquisition of information from one or more sources, the custodianship and the distribution of that information to those who need it, and its ultimate disposition through archiving or deletion.

Exam Probability: **Medium**

39. *Answer choices:*
(see index for correct answer)

- a. Service Integration Maturity Model
- b. Enterprise information management
- c. OPIDIS
- d. Information management

Guidance: level 1

:: Google services ::

__________ is a time-management and scheduling calendar service developed by Google. It became available in beta release April 13, 2006, and in general release in July 2009, on the web and as mobile apps for the Android and iOS platforms.

Exam Probability: **High**

40. *Answer choices:*

(see index for correct answer)

- a. Zygote Body
- b. AdSense
- c. Google Alerts
- d. Google Calendar

Guidance: level 1

:: SQL ::

SQL is a domain-specific language used in programming and designed for managing data held in a relational database management system , or for stream processing in a relational data stream management system . It is particularly useful in handling structured data where there are relations between different entities/variables of the data. SQL offers two main advantages over older read/write APIs like ISAM or VSAM. First, it introduced the concept of accessing many records with one single command; and second, it eliminates the need to specify how to reach a record, e.g. with or without an index.

Exam Probability: **Medium**

41. *Answer choices:*

(see index for correct answer)

- a. SQL:1999
- b. Structured type
- c. SQL/Schemata
- d. Data definition

Guidance: level 1

:: Game artificial intelligence ::

In computer science, _________ , sometimes called machine intelligence, is intelligence demonstrated by machines, in contrast to the natural intelligence displayed by humans and animals. Colloquially, the term " _________ " is used to describe machines that mimic "cognitive" functions that humans associate with other human minds, such as "learning" and "problem solving".

Exam Probability: **Low**

42. *Answer choices:*

(see index for correct answer)

- a. Artificial intelligence
- b. Negascout
- c. Jump point search
- d. Chinook

Guidance: level 1

:: Virtual economies ::

_________ Inc. is an American social game developer running social video game services founded in April 2007 and headquartered in San Francisco, California, United States. The company primarily focuses on mobile and social networking platforms. _________ states its mission as "connecting the world through games."

Exam Probability: **High**

43. *Answer choices:*

(see index for correct answer)

- a. Pioneer
- b. Spiral Knights
- c. Final Fantasy XI
- d. Geewa

Guidance: level 1

:: ::

A _________ is a knowledge base website on which users collaboratively modify content and structure directly from the web browser. In a typical _________ , text is written using a simplified markup language and often edited with the help of a rich-text editor.

Exam Probability: **High**

44. *Answer choices:*

(see index for correct answer)

- a. Wiki
- b. information systems assessment
- c. cultural
- d. surface-level diversity

Guidance: level 1

:: Management ::

In business, a _________ is the attribute that allows an organization to outperform its competitors. A _________ may include access to natural resources, such as high-grade ores or a low-cost power source, highly skilled labor, geographic location, high entry barriers, and access to new technology.

Exam Probability: **High**

45. *Answer choices:*

(see index for correct answer)

- a. Competitive advantage
- b. Behavioral risk management
- c. Radical transparency
- d. Operations management

Guidance: level 1

:: Data management ::

A _________ is a place where you can store data. Commonly used to refer to a column in a database or a field in a data entry form or web form.

Exam Probability: **Medium**

46. *Answer choices:*
(see index for correct answer)

- a. Database transaction
- b. Linear medium
- c. UI data binding
- d. Data field

Guidance: level 1

:: Business models ::

__________ , a portmanteau of the words "free" and "premium", is a pricing strategy by which a product or service is provided free of charge, but money is charged for additional features, services, or virtual or physical goods. The business model has been in use by the software industry since the 1980s as a licensing scheme. A subset of this model used by the video game industry is called free-to-play.

Exam Probability: **Medium**

47. *Answer choices:*
(see index for correct answer)

- a. Artel
- b. One stop shop
- c. Subscription business model
- d. Entreship

Guidance: level 1

:: Security compliance ::

A __________ is a communicated intent to inflict harm or loss on another person. A __________ is considered an act of coercion. __________ s are widely observed in animal behavior, particularly in a ritualized form, chiefly in order to avoid the unnecessary physical violence that can lead to physical damage or the death of both conflicting parties.

Exam Probability: **Medium**

48. *Answer choices:*
(see index for correct answer)

- a. 201 CMR 17.00

- b. Threat
- c. Attack
- d. Vulnerability

Guidance: level 1

:: Automatic identification and data capture ::

__________ uses electromagnetic fields to automatically identify and track tags attached to objects. The tags contain electronically stored information. Passive tags collect energy from a nearby RFID reader`s interrogating radio waves. Active tags have a local power source and may operate hundreds of meters from the RFID reader. Unlike a barcode, the tag need not be within the line of sight of the reader, so it may be embedded in the tracked object. RFID is one method of automatic identification and data capture .

Exam Probability: **Medium**

49. *Answer choices:*

(see index for correct answer)

- a. Radio fingerprinting
- b. Clipped tag
- c. IBeacon
- d. Radio-frequency identification

Guidance: level 1

:: Data quality ::

_________ is the maintenance of, and the assurance of the accuracy and consistency of, data over its entire life-cycle, and is a critical aspect to the design, implementation and usage of any system which stores, processes, or retrieves data. The term is broad in scope and may have widely different meanings depending on the specific context even under the same general umbrella of computing. It is at times used as a proxy term for data quality, while data validation is a pre-requisite for _________ . _________ is the opposite of data corruption. The overall intent of any _________ technique is the same: ensure data is recorded exactly as intended and upon later retrieval, ensure the data is the same as it was when it was originally recorded. In short, _________ aims to prevent unintentional changes to information. _________ is not to be confused with data security, the discipline of protecting data from unauthorized parties.

Exam Probability: **High**

50. *Answer choices:*

(see index for correct answer)

- a. Data truncation
- b. Data Quality Campaign
- c. Database preservation
- d. Data integrity

Guidance: level 1

:: Service-oriented (business computing) ::

_________ is a style of software design where services are provided to the other components by application components, through a communication protocol over a network. The basic principles of _________ are independent of vendors, products and technologies.A service is a discrete unit of functionality that can be accessed remotely and acted upon and updated independently, such as retrieving a credit card statement online.

Exam Probability: **High**

51. *Answer choices:*

(see index for correct answer)

- a. Service-oriented architecture
- b. Service-oriented transformation
- c. Web Service Choreography

- d. Microsoft BizTalk Server

Guidance: level 1

:: Finance ::

_________ is a financial estimate intended to help buyers and owners determine the direct and indirect costs of a product or system. It is a management accounting concept that can be used in full cost accounting or even ecological economics where it includes social costs.

Exam Probability: **Medium**

52. *Answer choices:*

(see index for correct answer)

- a. Treasury management
- b. Portfolio optimization
- c. Fine
- d. Total cost of ownership

Guidance: level 1

:: Ubiquitous computing ::

A _________ , chip card, or integrated circuit card is a physical electronic authorization device, used to control access to a resource. It is typically a plastic credit card sized card with an embedded integrated circuit. Many _________ s include a pattern of metal contacts to electrically connect to the internal chip. Others are contactless, and some are both. _________ s can provide personal identification, authentication, data storage, and application processing. Applications include identification, financial, mobile phones , public transit, computer security, schools, and healthcare. _________ s may provide strong security authentication for single sign-on within organizations. Several nations have deployed _________ s throughout their populations.

Exam Probability: **High**

53. *Answer choices:*

(see index for correct answer)

- a. Syledis

- b. Personal and Ubiquitous Computing
- c. Contactless smart card
- d. Smart card

Guidance: level 1

:: Survey methodology ::

An _________ is a conversation where questions are asked and answers are given. In common parlance, the word " _________ " refers to a one-on-one conversation between an _________ er and an _________ ee. The _________ er asks questions to which the _________ ee responds, usually so information may be transferred from _________ ee to _________ er . Sometimes, information can be transferred in both directions. It is a communication, unlike a speech, which produces a one-way flow of information.

Exam Probability: **Medium**

54. *Answer choices:*
(see index for correct answer)

- a. Interview
- b. National Health Interview Survey
- c. American Association for Public Opinion Research
- d. Coverage error

Guidance: level 1

:: Data transmission ::

In telecommunications and computing, _________ is the number of bits that are conveyed or processed per unit of time.

Exam Probability: **Low**

55. *Answer choices:*
(see index for correct answer)

- a. Transmission time
- b. Digital Audio Control Protocol
- c. IF-MAP
- d. Dynamic Packet Transport

Guidance: level 1

:: Information technology management ::

__________ is a good-practice framework created by international professional association ISACA for information technology management and IT governance. __________ provides an implementable "set of controls over information technology and organizes them around a logical framework of IT-related processes and enablers."

Exam Probability: **Medium**

56. *Answer choices:*

(see index for correct answer)

- a. Data warehouse appliance
- b. COBIT
- c. Configuration management database
- d. ERP for IT

Guidance: level 1

:: Computer access control protocols ::

An __________ is a type of computer communications protocol or cryptographic protocol specifically designed for transfer of authentication data between two entities. It allows the receiving entity to authenticate the connecting entity as well as authenticate itself to the connecting entity by declaring the type of information needed for authentication as well as syntax. It is the most important layer of protection needed for secure communication within computer networks.

Exam Probability: **Medium**

57. *Answer choices:*

(see index for correct answer)

- a. RADIUS
- b. Authentication protocol
- c. SPNEGO
- d. Simple Authentication and Security Layer

Guidance: level 1

:: ::

A web _________ or Internet _________ is a software system that is designed to carry out web search , which means to search the World Wide Web in a systematic way for particular information specified in a web search query. The search results are generally presented in a line of results, often referred to as _________ results pages . The information may be a mix of web pages, images, videos, infographics, articles, research papers and other types of files. Some _________ s also mine data available in databases or open directories. Unlike web directories, which are maintained only by human editors, _________ s also maintain real-time information by running an algorithm on a web crawler.Internet content that is not capable of being searched by a web _________ is generally described as the deep web.

Exam Probability: **Medium**

58. *Answer choices:*

(see index for correct answer)

- a. functional perspective
- b. personal values
- c. cultural
- d. corporate values

Guidance: level 1

:: ::

_________ rate is the ratio of users who click on a specific link to the number of total users who view a page, email, or advertisement. It is commonly used to measure the success of an online advertising campaign for a particular website as well as the effectiveness of email campaigns.

Exam Probability: **Low**

59. *Answer choices:*

(see index for correct answer)

- a. co-culture
- b. imperative
- c. Click-through
- d. Sarbanes-Oxley act of 2002

Guidance: level 1

Marketing

Marketing is the study and management of exchange relationships. Marketing is the business process of creating relationships with and satisfying customers. With its focus on the customer, marketing is one of the premier components of business management.
Marketing is defined by the American Marketing Association as "the activity, set of institutions, and processes for creating, communicating, delivering, and exchanging offerings that have value for customers, clients, partners, and society at large."

:: ::

__________ , or auditory perception, is the ability to perceive sounds by detecting vibrations, changes in the pressure of the surrounding medium through time, through an organ such as the ear. The academic field concerned with __________ is auditory science.

Exam Probability: **Medium**

1. *Answer choices:*

(see index for correct answer)

- a. Character
- b. Hearing
- c. cultural
- d. empathy

Guidance: level 1

:: Direct marketing ::

__________ is a form of direct marketing using databases of customers or potential customers to generate personalized communications in order to promote a product or service for marketing purposes. The method of communication can be any addressable medium, as in direct marketing.

Exam Probability: **Low**

2. *Answer choices:*

(see index for correct answer)

- a. Peter Lemongello
- b. Telemarketing
- c. Database marketing
- d. Warm market

Guidance: level 1

:: Consumer behaviour ::

__________ refers to the ability of a company or product to retain its customers over some specified period. High __________ means customers of the product or business tend to return to, continue to buy or in some other way not defect to another product or business, or to non-use entirely. Selling organizations generally attempt to reduce customer defections. __________ starts with the first contact an organization has with a customer and continues throughout the entire lifetime of a relationship and successful retention efforts take this entire lifecycle into account. A company`s ability to attract and retain new customers is related not only to its product or services, but also to the way it services its existing customers, the value the customers actually generate as a result of utilizing the solutions, and the reputation it creates within and across the marketplace.

Exam Probability: **Low**

3. *Answer choices:*

(see index for correct answer)

- a. Shopping while black
- b. Geodemography
- c. Cocooning
- d. Homo consumericus

Guidance: level 1

:: Monopoly (economics) ::

The _________ of 1890 was a United States antitrust law that regulates competition among enterprises, which was passed by Congress under the presidency of Benjamin Harrison.

Exam Probability: **Low**

4. *Answer choices:*

(see index for correct answer)

- a. Average cost pricing
- b. Monopoly
- c. Herfindahl index
- d. Tesco Town

Guidance: level 1

:: ::

Business is the activity of making one`s living or making money by producing or buying and selling products . Simply put, it is "any activity or enterprise entered into for profit. It does not mean it is a company, a corporation, partnership, or have any such formal organization, but it can range from a street peddler to General Motors."

Exam Probability: **High**

5. *Answer choices:*

(see index for correct answer)

- a. Character
- b. Firm
- c. similarity-attraction theory
- d. information systems assessment

Guidance: level 1

:: Brand management ::

__________ refers to the extent to which customers are able to recall or recognise a brand. __________ is a key consideration in consumer behavior, advertising management, brand management and strategy development. The consumer`s ability to recognise or recall a brand is central to purchasing decision-making. Purchasing cannot proceed unless a consumer is first aware of a product category and a brand within that category. Awareness does not necessarily mean that the consumer must be able to recall a specific brand name, but he or she must be able to recall sufficient distinguishing features for purchasing to proceed. For instance, if a consumer asks her friend to buy her some gum in a "blue pack", the friend would be expected to know which gum to buy, even though neither friend can recall the precise brand name at the time.

Exam Probability: **Medium**

6. *Answer choices:*

(see index for correct answer)

- a. Brand report card
- b. BrandActive
- c. Brand awareness
- d. Branded content

Guidance: level 1

:: Competition regulators ::

The __________ is an independent agency of the United States government, established in 1914 by the __________ Act. Its principal mission is the promotion of consumer protection and the elimination and prevention of anticompetitive business practices, such as coercive monopoly. It is headquartered in the __________ Building in Washington, D.C.

Exam Probability: **Low**

7. *Answer choices:*

(see index for correct answer)

- a. Jersey Competition Regulatory Authority
- b. Federal Trade Commission
- c. Competition Appeal Tribunal
- d. Fair Trade Commission

Guidance: level 1

:: Marketing ::

A __________ is something that is necessary for an organism to live a healthy life. __________ s are distinguished from wants in that, in the case of a __________ , a deficiency causes a clear adverse outcome: a dysfunction or death. In other words, a __________ is something required for a safe, stable and healthy life while a want is a desire, wish or aspiration. When __________ s or wants are backed by purchasing power, they have the potential to become economic demands.

Exam Probability: **Medium**

8. *Answer choices:*

(see index for correct answer)

- a. Franchising
- b. Packshot
- c. Online lead generation
- d. Need

Guidance: level 1

:: Debt ::

__________ is the trust which allows one party to provide money or resources to another party wherein the second party does not reimburse the first party immediately , but promises either to repay or return those resources at a later date. In other words, __________ is a method of making reciprocity formal, legally enforceable, and extensible to a large group of unrelated people.

Exam Probability: **Medium**

9. *Answer choices:*

(see index for correct answer)

- a. Debt crisis
- b. Default trap
- c. Borrowing base
- d. Tax benefits of debt

Guidance: level 1

:: Strategic alliances ::

A _________ is an agreement between two or more parties to pursue a set of agreed upon objectives needed while remaining independent organizations. A _________ will usually fall short of a legal partnership entity, agency, or corporate affiliate relationship. Typically, two companies form a _________ when each possesses one or more business assets or have expertise that will help the other by enhancing their businesses. _________ s can develop in outsourcing relationships where the parties desire to achieve long-term win-win benefits and innovation based on mutually desired outcomes.

Exam Probability: **High**

10. *Answer choices:*

(see index for correct answer)

- a. Defensive termination
- b. Bridge Alliance
- c. International joint venture
- d. Cross-licensing

Guidance: level 1

:: Information technology ::

_________ is the use of computers to store, retrieve, transmit, and manipulate data, or information, often in the context of a business or other enterprise. IT is considered to be a subset of information and communications technology . An _________ system is generally an information system, a communications system or, more specifically speaking, a computer system – including all hardware, software and peripheral equipment – operated by a limited group of users.

Exam Probability: **High**

11. *Answer choices:*

(see index for correct answer)

- a. Levi, Ray %26 Shoup
- b. ISO/IEC JTC 1/SC 25
- c. Infocommunications
- d. Information technology

Guidance: level 1

:: Public relations ::

__________ is the public visibility or awareness for any product, service or company. It may also refer to the movement of information from its source to the general public, often but not always via the media. The subjects of __________ include people , goods and services, organizations, and works of art or entertainment.

Exam Probability: **High**

12. *Answer choices:*

(see index for correct answer)

- a. Information subsidy
- b. Sparkpr
- c. Upstate California
- d. Publicity

Guidance: level 1

:: Product development ::

In business and engineering, __________ covers the complete process of bringing a new product to market. A central aspect of NPD is product design, along with various business considerations. __________ is described broadly as the transformation of a market opportunity into a product available for sale. The product can be tangible or intangible , though sometimes services and other processes are distinguished from "products." NPD requires an understanding of customer needs and wants, the competitive environment, and the nature of the market.Cost, time and quality are the main variables that drive customer needs. Aiming at these three variables, innovative companies develop continuous practices and strategies to better satisfy customer requirements and to increase their own market share by a regular development of new products. There are many uncertainties and challenges which companies must face throughout the process. The use of best practices and the elimination of barriers to communication are the main concerns for the management of the NPD .

Exam Probability: **Low**

13. *Answer choices:*

(see index for correct answer)

- a. New product development
- b. Material selection
- c. Engineering design management
- d. Modular function deployment

Guidance: level 1

:: Economic globalization ::

__________ is an agreement in which one company hires another company to be responsible for a planned or existing activity that is or could be done internally,and sometimes involves transferring employees and assets from one firm to another.

Exam Probability: **Medium**

14. *Answer choices:*
(see index for correct answer)

- a. Outsourcing
- b. global financial

Guidance: level 1

:: Project management ::

A __________ is a source or supply from which a benefit is produced and it has some utility. __________ s can broadly be classified upon their availability—they are classified into renewable and non-renewable __________ s.Examples of non renewable __________ s are coal ,crude oil natural gas nuclear energy etc. Examples of renewable __________ s are air,water,wind,solar energy etc. They can also be classified as actual and potential on the basis of level of development and use, on the basis of origin they can be classified as biotic and abiotic, and on the basis of their distribution, as ubiquitous and localized . An item becomes a __________ with time and developing technology. Typically, __________ s are materials, energy, services, staff, knowledge, or other assets that are transformed to produce benefit and in the process may be consumed or made unavailable. Benefits of __________ utilization may include increased wealth, proper functioning of a system, or enhanced well-being. From a human perspective a natural __________ is anything obtained from the environment to satisfy human needs and wants. From a broader biological or ecological perspective a __________ satisfies the needs of a living organism .

Exam Probability: **Medium**

15. *Answer choices:*

(see index for correct answer)

- a. Waterfall model
- b. Initiative
- c. Resource
- d. American Society of Professional Estimators

Guidance: level 1

:: Marketing ::

__________ uses different marketing channels and tools in combination: Marketing communication channels focus on any way a business communicates a message to its desired market, or the market in general. A marketing communication tool can be anything from: advertising, personal selling, direct marketing, sponsorship, communication, and promotion to public relations.

Exam Probability: **High**

16. *Answer choices:*

(see index for correct answer)

- a. Adobe Experience Manager
- b. Marketing communications
- c. Customer equity
- d. Adobe Media Optimizer

Guidance: level 1

:: Business ::

In commerce, __________ is the product of an interaction between an organization and a customer over the duration of their relationship.This interaction is made up of three parts: the customer journey, the brand touchpoints the customer interacts with, and the environments the __________ s during their experience. A good __________ means that the individual`s experience during all points of contact matches the individual`s expectations. Gartner asserts the importance of managing the customer`s experience.

Exam Probability: **Medium**

17. *Answer choices:*
(see index for correct answer)

- a. Crowdsourcing
- b. Procurement PunchOut
- c. Intangible asset finance
- d. Attribution

Guidance: level 1

:: ::

Employment is a relationship between two parties, usually based on a contract where work is paid for, where one party, which may be a corporation, for profit, not-for-profit organization, co-operative or other entity is the employer and the other is the employee. Employees work in return for payment, which may be in the form of an hourly wage, by piecework or an annual salary, depending on the type of work an employee does or which sector she or he is working in. Employees in some fields or sectors may receive gratuities, bonus payment or stock options. In some types of employment, employees may receive benefits in addition to payment. Benefits can include health insurance, housing, disability insurance or use of a gym. Employment is typically governed by employment laws, regulations or legal contracts.

Exam Probability: **Medium**

18. *Answer choices:*
(see index for correct answer)

- a. Personnel
- b. Sarbanes-Oxley act of 2002
- c. co-culture
- d. personal values

Guidance: level 1

:: Product management ::

A __________ , trade mark, or trade-mark is a recognizable sign, design, or expression which identifies products or services of a particular source from those of others, although __________ s used to identify services are usually called service marks. The __________ owner can be an individual, business organization, or any legal entity. A __________ may be located on a package, a label, a voucher, or on the product itself. For the sake of corporate identity, __________ s are often displayed on company buildings. It is legally recognized as a type of intellectual property.

Exam Probability: **Low**

19. *Answer choices:*

(see index for correct answer)

- a. Service product management
- b. Trademark
- c. business name
- d. Mid-life update

Guidance: level 1

:: Costs ::

In economics, __________ is the total economic cost of production and is made up of variable cost, which varies according to the quantity of a good produced and includes inputs such as labour and raw materials, plus fixed cost, which is independent of the quantity of a good produced and includes inputs that cannot be varied in the short term: fixed costs such as buildings and machinery, including sunk costs if any. Since cost is measured per unit of time, it is a flow variable.

Exam Probability: **Medium**

20. *Answer choices:*

(see index for correct answer)

- a. Total cost of acquisition
- b. Customer Cost
- c. Manufacturing cost
- d. Flyaway cost

Guidance: level 1

:: ::

A __________ is a graphic mark, emblem, or symbol used to aid and promote public identification and recognition. It may be of an abstract or figurative design or include the text of the name it represents as in a wordmark.

Exam Probability: **High**

21. *Answer choices:*

(see index for correct answer)

- a. deep-level diversity
- b. functional perspective
- c. corporate values
- d. imperative

Guidance: level 1

:: ::

In communications and information processing, __________ is a system of rules to convert information—such as a letter, word, sound, image, or gesture—into another form or representation, sometimes shortened or secret, for communication through a communication channel or storage in a storage medium. An early example is the invention of language, which enabled a person, through speech, to communicate what they saw, heard, felt, or thought to others. But speech limits the range of communication to the distance a voice can carry, and limits the audience to those present when the speech is uttered. The invention of writing, which converted spoken language into visual symbols, extended the range of communication across space and time.

Exam Probability: **High**

22. *Answer choices:*

(see index for correct answer)

- a. functional perspective
- b. hierarchical perspective
- c. similarity-attraction theory
- d. Code

Guidance: level 1

:: ::

In business and engineering, new _________ covers the complete process of bringing a new product to market. A central aspect of NPD is product design, along with various business considerations. New _________ is described broadly as the transformation of a market opportunity into a product available for sale. The product can be tangible or intangible , though sometimes services and other processes are distinguished from "products." NPD requires an understanding of customer needs and wants, the competitive environment, and the nature of the market.Cost, time and quality are the main variables that drive customer needs. Aiming at these three variables, innovative companies develop continuous practices and strategies to better satisfy customer requirements and to increase their own market share by a regular development of new products. There are many uncertainties and challenges which companies must face throughout the process. The use of best practices and the elimination of barriers to communication are the main concerns for the management of the NPD .

Exam Probability: **High**

23. *Answer choices:*

(see index for correct answer)

- a. process perspective
- b. Product development
- c. deep-level diversity
- d. functional perspective

Guidance: level 1

:: ::

In a supply chain, a _________ , or a seller, is an enterprise that contributes goods or services. Generally, a supply chain _________ manufactures inventory/stock items and sells them to the next link in the chain. Today, these terms refer to a supplier of any good or service.

Exam Probability: **Medium**

24. *Answer choices:*

(see index for correct answer)

- a. Character
- b. deep-level diversity
- c. levels of analysis
- d. Vendor

Guidance: level 1

:: ::

The _________ is a U.S. business-focused, English-language international daily newspaper based in New York City. The Journal, along with its Asian and European editions, is published six days a week by Dow Jones & Company, a division of News Corp. The newspaper is published in the broadsheet format and online. The Journal has been printed continuously since its inception on July 8, 1889, by Charles Dow, Edward Jones, and Charles Bergstresser.

Exam Probability: **High**

25. *Answer choices:*
(see index for correct answer)

- a. hierarchical perspective
- b. levels of analysis
- c. Wall Street Journal
- d. information systems assessment

Guidance: level 1

:: Business models ::

A _________ is "an autonomous association of persons united voluntarily to meet their common economic, social, and cultural needs and aspirations through a jointly-owned and democratically-controlled enterprise". _________ s may include.

Exam Probability: **High**

26. *Answer choices:*
(see index for correct answer)

- a. Defensive patent aggregation
- b. The Community Company
- c. Inclusive business model
- d. Micro-enterprise

Guidance: level 1

:: Sales ::

_________ is a business discipline which is focused on the practical application of sales techniques and the management of a firm`s sales operations. It is an important business function as net sales through the sale of products and services and resulting profit drive most commercial business. These are also typically the goals and performance indicators of _________ .

Exam Probability: **Medium**

27. *Answer choices:*

(see index for correct answer)

- a. Sales management
- b. Sales process
- c. Voice-based marketing automation
- d. Closed-end leasing

Guidance: level 1

:: Business economics ::

In economics, _________ is demand for a factor of production or intermediate good that occurs as a result of the demand for another intermediate or final good. In essence, the demand for, say, a factor of production by a firm is dependent on the demand by consumers for the product produced by the firm. The term was first introduced by Alfred Marshall in his Principles of Economics in 1890.

Exam Probability: **Low**

28. *Answer choices:*

(see index for correct answer)

- a. Productivity model
- b. Monopoly wage
- c. Derived demand
- d. Cost object

Guidance: level 1

:: ::

In the broadest sense, _________ is any practice which contributes to the sale of products to a retail consumer. At a retail in-store level, _________ refers to the variety of products available for sale and the display of those products in such a way that it stimulates interest and entices customers to make a purchase.

Exam Probability: **Low**

29. *Answer choices:*

(see index for correct answer)

- a. process perspective
- b. information systems assessment
- c. surface-level diversity
- d. Merchandising

Guidance: level 1

:: ::

Market segmentation is the activity of dividing a broad consumer or business market, normally consisting of existing and potential customers, into sub-groups of consumers based on some type of shared characteristics. In dividing or segmenting markets, researchers typically look for common characteristics such as shared needs, common interests, similar lifestyles or even similar demographic profiles. The overall aim of segmentation is to identify high yield segments – that is, those segments that are likely to be the most profitable or that have growth potential – so that these can be selected for special attention .

Exam Probability: **Medium**

30. *Answer choices:*

(see index for correct answer)

- a. functional perspective
- b. information systems assessment
- c. interpersonal communication
- d. Market segments

Guidance: level 1

:: Legal terms ::

A _________ is a person who is called upon to issue a response to a communication made by another. The term is used in legal contexts, in survey methodology, and in psychological conditioning.

Exam Probability: **Medium**

31. *Answer choices:*

(see index for correct answer)

- a. Impleader
- b. Commanding precedent
- c. Mischief
- d. Incorporation of international law

Guidance: level 1

:: Generally Accepted Accounting Principles ::

In accounting, _________ is the income that a business have from its normal business activities, usually from the sale of goods and services to customers. _________ is also referred to as sales or turnover.Some companies receive _________ from interest, royalties, or other fees. _________ may refer to business income in general, or it may refer to the amount, in a monetary unit, earned during a period of time, as in "Last year, Company X had _________ of $42 million". Profits or net income generally imply total _________ minus total expenses in a given period. In accounting, in the balance statement it is a subsection of the Equity section and _________ increases equity, it is often referred to as the "top line" due to its position on the income statement at the very top. This is to be contrasted with the "bottom line" which denotes net income .

Exam Probability: **Medium**

32. *Answer choices:*

(see index for correct answer)

- a. Indian Accounting Standards
- b. Long-term liabilities
- c. Provision
- d. Revenue

Guidance: level 1

:: Business terms ::

A _________ is a short statement of why an organization exists, what its overall goal is, identifying the goal of its operations: what kind of product or service it provides, its primary customers or market, and its geographical region of operation. It may include a short statement of such fundamental matters as the organization's values or philosophies, a business's main competitive advantages, or a desired future state—the "vision".

Exam Probability: **High**

33. *Answer choices:*

(see index for correct answer)

- a. strategic plan
- b. Personal selling
- c. Mission statement
- d. year-to-date

Guidance: level 1

:: Retailing ::

A _________ is a self-service shop offering a wide variety of food, beverages and household products, organized into sections and shelves. It is larger and has a wider selection than earlier grocery stores, but is smaller and more limited in the range of merchandise than a hypermarket or big-box market.

Exam Probability: **High**

34. *Answer choices:*

(see index for correct answer)

- a. Pop-up retail
- b. Shopping list
- c. Street date
- d. Convenience store

Guidance: level 1

:: Brand management ::

In marketing, _________ is the analysis and planning on how a brand is perceived in the market. Developing a good relationship with the target market is essential for _________ . Tangible elements of _________ include the product itself; its look, price, and packaging, etc. The intangible elements are the experiences that the consumers share with the brand, and also the relationships they have with the brand. A brand manager would oversee all aspects of the consumer`s brand association as well as relationships with members of the supply chain.

Exam Probability: **Low**

35. *Answer choices:*

(see index for correct answer)

- a. Status brand
- b. Merck Consumer Health
- c. Superbrands
- d. Brand management

Guidance: level 1

:: Consumer theory ::

_________ is the quantity of a good that consumers are willing and able to purchase at various prices during a given period of time.

Exam Probability: **High**

36. *Answer choices:*

(see index for correct answer)

- a. Quality bias
- b. Induced consumption
- c. Rational addiction
- d. Marshallian demand function

Guidance: level 1

:: ::

__________ is a marketing communication that employs an openly sponsored, non-personal message to promote or sell a product, service or idea. Sponsors of __________ are typically businesses wishing to promote their products or services. __________ is differentiated from public relations in that an advertiser pays for and has control over the message. It differs from personal selling in that the message is non-personal, i.e., not directed to a particular individual. __________ is communicated through various mass media, including traditional media such as newspapers, magazines, television, radio, outdoor __________ or direct mail; and new media such as search results, blogs, social media, websites or text messages. The actual presentation of the message in a medium is referred to as an advertisement, or "ad" or advert for short.

Exam Probability: **Low**

37. *Answer choices:*

(see index for correct answer)

- a. Advertising
- b. Sarbanes-Oxley act of 2002
- c. levels of analysis
- d. cultural

Guidance: level 1

:: Marketing by medium ::

__________ or viral advertising is a business strategy that uses existing social networks to promote a product. Its name refers to how consumers spread information about a product with other people in their social networks, much in the same way that a virus spreads from one person to another. It can be delivered by word of mouth or enhanced by the network effects of the Internet and mobile networks.

Exam Probability: **Low**

38. *Answer choices:*

(see index for correct answer)

- a. Digital marketing
- b. Growth hacking
- c. Viral marketing
- d. Direct Text Marketing

Guidance: level 1

:: Promotion and marketing communications ::

A _________ is the intended audience or readership of a publication, advertisement, or other message. In marketing and advertising, it is a particular group of consumers within the predetermined target market, identified as the targets or recipients for a particular advertisement or message. Businesses that have a wide target market will focus on a specific _________ for certain messages to send, such as The Body Shops Mother`s Day advertisements, which were aimed at the children and spouses of women, rather than the whole market which would have included the women themselves.

Exam Probability: **Medium**

39. *Answer choices:*

(see index for correct answer)

- a. Television advertisement
- b. Puffery
- c. Hugin Group
- d. Direct mail

Guidance: level 1

:: Business law ::

A _________ is an arrangement where parties, known as partners, agree to cooperate to advance their mutual interests. The partners in a _________ may be individuals, businesses, interest-based organizations, schools, governments or combinations. Organizations may partner to increase the likelihood of each achieving their mission and to amplify their reach. A _________ may result in issuing and holding equity or may be only governed by a contract.

Exam Probability: **Low**

40. *Answer choices:*

(see index for correct answer)

- a. Equity of redemption
- b. Lex mercatoria
- c. Partnership
- d. Relational contract

Guidance: level 1

:: Project management ::

__________ is the right to exercise power, which can be formalized by a state and exercised by way of judges, appointed executives of government, or the ecclesiastical or priestly appointed representatives of a God or other deities.

Exam Probability: **High**

41. *Answer choices:*
(see index for correct answer)

- a. Authority
- b. Concept note
- c. Dependency
- d. Critical path drag

Guidance: level 1

:: Market research ::

__________ is an organized effort to gather information about target markets or customers. It is a very important component of business strategy. The term is commonly interchanged with marketing research; however, expert practitioners may wish to draw a distinction, in that marketing research is concerned specifically about marketing processes, while __________ is concerned specifically with markets.

Exam Probability: **Low**

42. *Answer choices:*
(see index for correct answer)

- a. Qualtrics
- b. Sociomapping
- c. Market research
- d. A/B testing

Guidance: level 1

:: Data ::

Data has two ways of being created or generated. The first is what is called `captured data`, and is found through purposeful investigation or analysis. The second is called `exhaust data`, and is gathered usually by machines or terminals as a secondary function. For example, cash registers, smartphones, and speedometers serve a main function but may collect data as a secondary task. Exhaustive data is usually too large or of little use to process and becomes `transient` or thrown away.

Exam Probability: **Medium**

43. *Answer choices:*

(see index for correct answer)

- a. Sonar
- b. One Source Networks
- c. S-LINK
- d. Infonomics

Guidance: level 1

:: ::

In production, research, retail, and accounting, a _________ is the value of money that has been used up to produce something or deliver a service, and hence is not available for use anymore. In business, the _________ may be one of acquisition, in which case the amount of money expended to acquire it is counted as _________ . In this case, money is the input that is gone in order to acquire the thing. This acquisition _________ may be the sum of the _________ of production as incurred by the original producer, and further _________ s of transaction as incurred by the acquirer over and above the price paid to the producer. Usually, the price also includes a mark-up for profit over the _________ of production.

Exam Probability: **Medium**

44. *Answer choices:*

(see index for correct answer)

- a. Sarbanes-Oxley act of 2002
- b. functional perspective
- c. co-culture
- d. Cost

Guidance: level 1

:: ::

A _________ is the process of presenting a topic to an audience. It is typically a demonstration, introduction, lecture, or speech meant to inform, persuade, inspire, motivate, or to build good will or to present a new idea or product. The term can also be used for a formal or ritualized introduction or offering, as with the _________ of a debutante. _________ s in certain formats are also known as keynote address.

Exam Probability: **High**

45. *Answer choices:*

(see index for correct answer)

- a. similarity-attraction theory
- b. imperative
- c. deep-level diversity
- d. Presentation

Guidance: level 1

:: Trade associations ::

A _________ , also known as an industry trade group, business association, sector association or industry body, is an organization founded and funded by businesses that operate in a specific industry. An industry _________ participates in public relations activities such as advertising, education, political donations, lobbying and publishing, but its focus is collaboration between companies. Associations may offer other services, such as producing conferences, networking or charitable events or offering classes or educational materials. Many associations are non-profit organizations governed by bylaws and directed by officers who are also members.

Exam Probability: **Low**

46. *Answer choices:*

(see index for correct answer)

- a. Marketing Research Association
- b. Promotion Marketing Association
- c. SCSI Trade Association
- d. Trade association

Guidance: level 1

:: Management ::

A __________ is an idea of the future or desired result that a person or a group of people envisions, plans and commits to achieve. People endeavor to reach __________ s within a finite time by setting deadlines.

Exam Probability: **Medium**

47. *Answer choices:*

(see index for correct answer)

- a. Event chain methodology
- b. Goal
- c. Power to the edge
- d. Competitive heterogeneity

Guidance: level 1

:: Industrial design ::

In physics and mathematics, the __________ of a mathematical space is informally defined as the minimum number of coordinates needed to specify any point within it. Thus a line has a __________ of one because only one coordinate is needed to specify a point on it for example, the point at 5 on a number line. A surface such as a plane or the surface of a cylinder or sphere has a __________ of two because two coordinates are needed to specify a point on it for example, both a latitude and longitude are required to locate a point on the surface of a sphere. The inside of a cube, a cylinder or a sphere is three- __________ al because three coordinates are needed to locate a point within these spaces.

Exam Probability: **Low**

48. *Answer choices:*

(see index for correct answer)

- a. Furniture
- b. Community design
- c. Chintz
- d. Dimension

Guidance: level 1

:: Brand management ::

Marketing communications uses different marketing channels and tools in combination: Marketing communication channels focus on any way a business communicates a message to its desired market, or the market in general. A marketing communication tool can be anything from: advertising, personal selling, direct marketing, sponsorship, communication, and promotion to public relations.

Exam Probability: **Low**

49. *Answer choices:*

(see index for correct answer)

- a. VCU Brandcenter
- b. Mascot
- c. Reputation marketing
- d. Brand specialist

Guidance: level 1

:: Management ::

The term _________ refers to measures designed to increase the degree of autonomy and self-determination in people and in communities in order to enable them to represent their interests in a responsible and self-determined way, acting on their own authority. It is the process of becoming stronger and more confident, especially in controlling one`s life and claiming one`s rights. _________ as action refers both to the process of self- _________ and to professional support of people, which enables them to overcome their sense of powerlessness and lack of influence, and to recognize and use their resources. To do work with power.

Exam Probability: **High**

50. *Answer choices:*

(see index for correct answer)

- a. Tata Management Training Centre
- b. Gemba
- c. Empowerment
- d. Behavioral risk management

Guidance: level 1

:: Marketing ::

__________ or stock is the goods and materials that a business holds for the ultimate goal of resale .

Exam Probability: **Medium**

51. *Answer choices:*

(see index for correct answer)

- a. Inventory
- b. Email production
- c. Adobe Experience Manager
- d. Market share

Guidance: level 1

:: Marketing techniques ::

__________ , also known as embedded marketing, is a marketing technique where references to specific brands or products are incorporated into another work, such as a film or television program, with specific promotional intent.

Exam Probability: **Low**

52. *Answer choices:*

(see index for correct answer)

- a. Product demonstration
- b. Unique perceived benefit
- c. Continuity marketing
- d. Product placement

Guidance: level 1

:: Marketing ::

__________ is the marketing of products that are presumed to be environmentally safe. It incorporates a broad range of activities, including product modification, changes to the production process, sustainable packaging, as well as modifying advertising. Yet defining __________ is not a simple task where several meanings intersect and contradict each other; an example of this will be the existence of varying social, environmental and retail definitions attached to this term. Other similar terms used are environmental marketing and ecological marketing.

Exam Probability: **Medium**

53. *Answer choices:*
(see index for correct answer)

- a. Price
- b. Green marketing
- c. Aftermarket
- d. Mass affluent

Guidance: level 1

:: Business planning ::

__________ is an organization's process of defining its strategy, or direction, and making decisions on allocating its resources to pursue this strategy. It may also extend to control mechanisms for guiding the implementation of the strategy. __________ became prominent in corporations during the 1960s and remains an important aspect of strategic management. It is executed by strategic planners or strategists, who involve many parties and research sources in their analysis of the organization and its relationship to the environment in which it competes.

Exam Probability: **Medium**

54. *Answer choices:*
(see index for correct answer)

- a. Strategic planning
- b. Exit planning
- c. Stakeholder management
- d. Open Options Corporation

Guidance: level 1

:: Marketing ::

A _________ is a group of customers within a business`s serviceable available market at which a business aims its marketing efforts and resources. A _________ is a subset of the total market for a product or service. The _________ typically consists of consumers who exhibit similar characteristics and are considered most likely to buy a business`s market offerings or are likely to be the most profitable segments for the business to service.

Exam Probability: **Medium**

55. *Answer choices:*

(see index for correct answer)

- a. Marketing activation
- b. Contribution margin-based pricing
- c. Target market
- d. Mass affluent

Guidance: level 1

:: ::

A _________ consists of one people who live in the same dwelling and share meals. It may also consist of a single family or another group of people. A dwelling is considered to contain multiple _________ s if meals or living spaces are not shared. The _________ is the basic unit of analysis in many social, microeconomic and government models, and is important to economics and inheritance.

Exam Probability: **Medium**

56. *Answer choices:*

(see index for correct answer)

- a. similarity-attraction theory
- b. interpersonal communication
- c. levels of analysis
- d. personal values

Guidance: level 1

:: ::

The _________ is an agreement signed by Canada, Mexico, and the United States, creating a trilateral trade bloc in North America. The agreement came into force on January 1, 1994, and superseded the 1988 Canada–United States Free Trade Agreement between the United States and Canada. The NAFTA trade bloc is one of the largest trade blocs in the world by gross domestic product.

Exam Probability: **High**

57. *Answer choices:*
(see index for correct answer)

- a. similarity-attraction theory
- b. functional perspective
- c. process perspective
- d. Sarbanes-Oxley act of 2002

Guidance: level 1

:: Services management and marketing ::

_________ is a specialised branch of marketing. _________ emerged as a separate field of study in the early 1980s, following the recognition that the unique characteristics of services required different strategies compared with the marketing of physical goods.

Exam Probability: **Low**

58. *Answer choices:*
(see index for correct answer)

- a. Service provider
- b. Reverse bounty
- c. Advanced 365
- d. Functional branding

Guidance: level 1

:: Financial economics ::

In management, business value is an informal term that includes all forms of value that determine the health and well-being of the firm in the long run. Business value expands concept of value of the firm beyond economic value to include other forms of value such as employee value, _________ , supplier value, channel partner value, alliance partner value, managerial value, and societal value. Many of these forms of value are not directly measured in monetary terms.

Exam Probability: **Low**

59. *Answer choices:*

(see index for correct answer)

- a. International finance
- b. Triangular arbitrage
- c. Mid price
- d. Customer value

Guidance: level 1

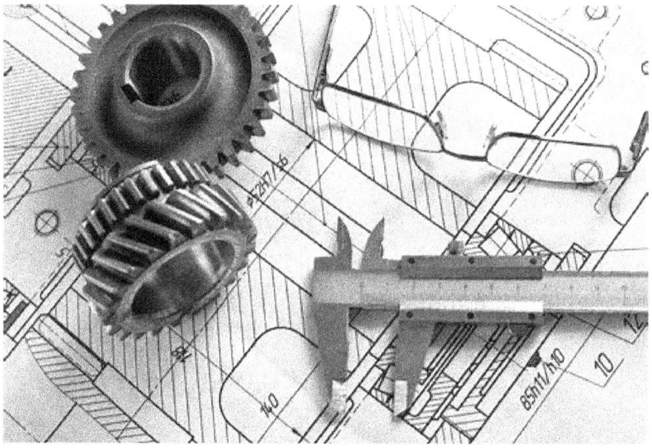

Manufacturing

Manufacturing is the production of merchandise for use or sale using labor and machines, tools, chemical and biological processing, or formulation. The term may refer to a range of human activity, from handicraft to high tech, but is most commonly applied to industrial design , in which raw materials are transformed into finished goods on a large scale. Such finished goods may be sold to other manufacturers for the production of other, more complex products, such as aircraft, household appliances, furniture, sports equipment or automobiles, or sold to wholesalers, who in turn sell them to retailers, who then sell them to end users and consumers.

:: Quality ::

_________ is a concept first outlined by quality expert Joseph M. Juran in publications, most notably Juran on _________ . Designing for quality and innovation is one of the three universal processes of the Juran Trilogy, in which Juran describes what is required to achieve breakthroughs in new products, services, and processes. Juran believed that quality could be planned, and that most quality crises and problems relate to the way in which quality was planned.

Exam Probability: **Medium**

1. *Answer choices:*

(see index for correct answer)

- a. Root cause analysis
- b. Secure Stations Scheme
- c. Quality by Design
- d. Primary/secondary quality distinction

Guidance: level 1

:: Management ::

An _________ is a loosely coupled, self-organizing network of firms that combine their economic output to provide products and services offerings to the market. Firms in the _________ may operate independently, for example, through market mechanisms, or cooperatively through agreements and contracts. They provide value added service or product to the OEM .

Exam Probability: **High**

2. *Answer choices:*

(see index for correct answer)

- a. Planning
- b. Defensive expenditures
- c. Extended enterprise
- d. Oriental management

Guidance: level 1

:: Gas technologies ::

A _________ is a rotary mechanical device that extracts energy from a fluid flow and converts it into useful work. The work produced by a _________ can be used for generating electrical power when combined with a generator. A _________ is a turbomachine with at least one moving part called a rotor assembly, which is a shaft or drum with blades attached. Moving fluid acts on the blades so that they move and impart rotational energy to the rotor. Early _________ examples are windmills and waterwheels.

Exam Probability: **High**

3. *Answer choices:*

(see index for correct answer)

- a. HEPA
- b. Air compressor
- c. Bicycle pump
- d. Turbine

Guidance: level 1

:: Manufacturing ::

A __________ is an object used to extend the ability of an individual to modify features of the surrounding environment. Although many animals use simple __________ s, only human beings, whose use of stone __________ s dates back hundreds of millennia, use __________ s to make other __________ s. The set of __________ s needed to perform different tasks that are part of the same activity is called gear or equipment.

Exam Probability: **Medium**

4. *Answer choices:*

(see index for correct answer)

- a. Reconfigurable Manufacturing System
- b. Tool
- c. Standard Motor Products
- d. Demand flow technology

Guidance: level 1

:: Management ::

A supply-chain network is an evolution of the basic supply chain. Due to rapid technological advancement, organisations with a basic supply chain can develop this chain into a more complex structure involving a higher level of interdependence and connectivity between more organisations, this constitutes a supply-chain network.

Exam Probability: **Medium**

5. *Answer choices:*

(see index for correct answer)

- a. Product breakdown structure
- b. Dominant design
- c. Supply management
- d. Project cost management

Guidance: level 1

:: Semiconductor companies ::

_________ Corporation is a Japanese multinational conglomerate corporation headquartered in Konan, Minato, Tokyo. Its diversified business includes consumer and professional electronics, gaming, entertainment and financial services. The company owns the largest music entertainment business in the world, the largest video game console business and one of the largest video game publishing businesses, and is one of the leading manufacturers of electronic products for the consumer and professional markets, and a leading player in the film and television entertainment industry. _________ was ranked 97th on the 2018 Fortune Global 500 list.

Exam Probability: **Medium**

6. *Answer choices:*

(see index for correct answer)

- a. CEITEC
- b. Sony
- c. Freescale Semiconductor
- d. Kodenshi AUK Group

Guidance: level 1

:: Production and manufacturing ::

_________ is a set of techniques and tools for process improvement. Though as a shortened form it may be found written as 6S, it should not be confused with the methodology known as 6S .

Exam Probability: **High**

7. *Answer choices:*

(see index for correct answer)

- a. Memo motion
- b. Six Sigma
- c. Joint product
- d. CTQ tree

Guidance: level 1

:: Lean manufacturing ::

_________ is the Sino-Japanese word for "improvement". In business, _________ refers to activities that continuously improve all functions and involve all employees from the CEO to the assembly line workers. It also applies to processes, such as purchasing and logistics, that cross organizational boundaries into the supply chain. It has been applied in healthcare, psychotherapy, life-coaching, government, and banking.

Exam Probability: **Low**

8. *Answer choices:*
(see index for correct answer)

- a. Just in sequence
- b. Kanban board
- c. JobShopLean
- d. Poka-yoke

Guidance: level 1

:: Management ::

_________ is an iterative four-step management method used in business for the control and continuous improvement of processes and products. It is also known as the Deming circle/cycle/wheel, the Shewhart cycle, the control circle/cycle, or plan–do–study–act . Another version of this _________ cycle is O _________ . The added "O" stands for observation or as some versions say: "Observe the current condition." This emphasis on observation and current condition has currency with the literature on lean manufacturing and the Toyota Production System. The _________ cycle, with Ishikawa's changes, can be traced back to S. Mizuno of the Tokyo Institute of Technology in 1959.

Exam Probability: **High**

9. *Answer choices:*
(see index for correct answer)

- a. Facilitator
- b. Allegiance
- c. Empowerment
- d. PDCA

Guidance: level 1

:: Inventory ::

The __________ is the level of inventory which triggers an action to replenish that particular inventory stock. It is a minimum amount of an item which a firm holds in stock, such that, when stock falls to this amount, the item must be reordered. It is normally calculated as the forecast usage during the replenishment lead time plus safety stock. In the EOQ model, it was assumed that there is no time lag between ordering and procuring of materials. Therefore the __________ for replenishing the stocks occurs at that level when the inventory level drops to zero and because instant delivery by suppliers, the stock level bounce back.

Exam Probability: **Low**

10. *Answer choices:*

(see index for correct answer)

- a. Order picking
- b. LIFO
- c. Stock mix
- d. Stock control

Guidance: level 1

:: Chemical processes ::

__________ is the understanding and application of the fundamental principles and laws of nature that allow us to transform raw material and energy into products that are useful to society, at an industrial level. By taking advantage of the driving forces of nature such as pressure, temperature and concentration gradients, as well as the law of conservation of mass, process engineers can develop methods to synthesize and purify large quantities of desired chemical products. __________ focuses on the design, operation, control, optimization and intensification of chemical, physical, and biological processes. __________ encompasses a vast range of industries, such as agriculture, automotive, biotechnical, chemical, food, material development, mining, nuclear, petrochemical, pharmaceutical, and software development. The application of systematic computer-based methods to __________ is "process systems engineering".

Exam Probability: **Low**

11. *Answer choices:*
(see index for correct answer)

- a. Emulsion polymerization
- b. SNOX process
- c. Calcium looping
- d. Selexol

Guidance: level 1

:: Quality management ::

__________ ensures that an organization, product or service is consistent. It has four main components: quality planning, quality assurance, quality control and quality improvement. __________ is focused not only on product and service quality, but also on the means to achieve it. __________ , therefore, uses quality assurance and control of processes as well as products to achieve more consistent quality.What a customer wants and is willing to pay for it determines quality. It is written or unwritten commitment to a known or unknown consumer in the market . Thus, quality can be defined as fitness for intended use or, in other words, how well the product performs its intended function

Exam Probability: **High**

12. *Answer choices:*
(see index for correct answer)

- a. Quality management
- b. Management by wandering around
- c. Quality policy
- d. Quality circle

Guidance: level 1

:: Data interchange standards ::

__________ is the concept of businesses electronically communicating information that was traditionally communicated on paper, such as purchase orders and invoices. Technical standards for EDI exist to facilitate parties transacting such instruments without having to make special arrangements.

Exam Probability: **High**

13. *Answer choices:*

(see index for correct answer)

- a. Domain Application Protocol
- b. ASC X12
- c. Interaction protocol
- d. Electronic data interchange

Guidance: level 1

:: Costs ::

In process improvement efforts, _________ or cost of quality is a means to quantify the total cost of quality-related efforts and deficiencies. It was first described by Armand V. Feigenbaum in a 1956 Harvard Business Review article.

Exam Probability: **Medium**

14. *Answer choices:*

(see index for correct answer)

- a. Further processing cost
- b. Economic cost
- c. Quality costs
- d. Direct materials cost

Guidance: level 1

:: Production economics ::

_________ is the creation of a whole that is greater than the simple sum of its parts. The term _________ comes from the Attic Greek word sea synergia from synergos, , meaning "working together".

Exam Probability: **Low**

15. *Answer choices:*

(see index for correct answer)

- a. Sectoral output
- b. Synergy
- c. Productive capacity
- d. Fragmentation

Guidance: level 1

:: Project management ::

_________ is the right to exercise power, which can be formalized by a state and exercised by way of judges, appointed executives of government, or the ecclesiastical or priestly appointed representatives of a God or other deities.

Exam Probability: **High**

16. *Answer choices:*

(see index for correct answer)

- a. Project Management Institute
- b. Authority
- c. The International Association of Project and Program Management
- d. Cone of Uncertainty

Guidance: level 1

:: ::

Catalysis is the process of increasing the rate of a chemical reaction by adding a substance known as a _________ , which is not consumed in the catalyzed reaction and can continue to act repeatedly. Because of this, only very small amounts of _________ are required to alter the reaction rate in principle.

Exam Probability: **High**

17. *Answer choices:*

(see index for correct answer)

- a. hierarchical perspective
- b. functional perspective
- c. open system
- d. Catalyst

Guidance: level 1

:: Unit operations ::

_________ is the process of separating the components or substances from a liquid mixture by using selective boiling and condensation. _________ may result in essentially complete separation , or it may be a partial separation that increases the concentration of selected components in the mixture. In either case, the process exploits differences in the volatility of the mixture`s components. In industrial chemistry, _________ is a unit operation of practically universal importance, but it is a physical separation process, not a chemical reaction.

Exam Probability: **Low**

18. *Answer choices:*

(see index for correct answer)

- a. Settling
- b. Theoretical plate
- c. Solvent impregnated resin
- d. Distillation

Guidance: level 1

:: Quality ::

The _________ , formerly the _________ Control , is a knowledge-based global community of quality professionals, with nearly 80,000 members dedicated to promoting and advancing quality tools, principles, and practices in their workplaces and communities.

Exam Probability: **Low**

19. *Answer choices:*

(see index for correct answer)

- a. Customer Service Excellence
- b. Software Engineering Process Group
- c. European Organization for Quality
- d. American Society for Quality

Guidance: level 1

:: Supply chain management ::

A _________ is a type of auction in which the traditional roles of buyer and seller are reversed. Thus, there is one buyer and many potential sellers. In an ordinary auction , buyers compete to obtain goods or services by offering increasingly higher prices. In contrast, in a _________ , the sellers compete to obtain business from the buyer and prices will typically decrease as the sellers underbid each other.

Exam Probability: **High**

20. *Answer choices:*

(see index for correct answer)

- a. Suppliers and Parts database
- b. competitive bidding
- c. Disintermediation
- d. Delivery Reliability

Guidance: level 1

:: Quality ::

A _________ is an initiating cause of either a condition or a causal chain that leads to an outcome or effect of interest. The term denotes the earliest, most basic, `deepest`, cause for a given behavior; most often a fault. The idea is that you can only see an error by its manifest signs. Those signs can be widespread, multitudinous, and convoluted, whereas the _________ leading to them often is a lot simpler.

Exam Probability: **Low**

21. *Answer choices:*

(see index for correct answer)

- a. Root cause analysis
- b. Software Engineering Process Group
- c. Society for Software Quality
- d. Dualistic Petri nets

Guidance: level 1

:: Promotion and marketing communications ::

The _________ of American Manufacturers, now ThomasNet, is an online platform for supplier discovery and product sourcing in the US and Canada. It was once known as the "big green books" and "Thomas Registry", and was a multi-volume directory of industrial product information covering 650,000 distributors, manufacturers and service companies within 67,000-plus industrial categories that is now published on ThomasNet.

Exam Probability: **Medium**

22. *Answer choices:*

(see index for correct answer)

- a. direct-mail
- b. Thomas Register
- c. Social network advertising
- d. Air Miles

Guidance: level 1

:: Fault-tolerant computer systems ::

_________ decision-making is a group decision-making process in which group members develop, and agree to support a decision in the best interest of the whole group or common goal. _________ may be defined professionally as an acceptable resolution, one that can be supported, even if not the "favourite" of each individual. It has its origin in the Latin word consensus , which is from consentio meaning literally feel together. It is used to describe both the decision and the process of reaching a decision. _________ decision-making is thus concerned with the process of deliberating and finalizing a decision, and the social, economic, legal, environmental and political effects of applying this process.

Exam Probability: **Low**

23. *Answer choices:*

(see index for correct answer)

- a. Lockstep
- b. Failure detector
- c. Processor array
- d. Paxos

Guidance: level 1

:: ::

In sales, commerce and economics, a _________ is the recipient of a good, service, product or an idea - obtained from a seller, vendor, or supplier via a financial transaction or exchange for money or some other valuable consideration.

Exam Probability: **Medium**

24. *Answer choices:*

(see index for correct answer)

- a. functional perspective
- b. levels of analysis
- c. cultural
- d. hierarchical perspective

Guidance: level 1

:: E-commerce ::

_________ is the activity of buying or selling of products on online services or over the Internet. Electronic commerce draws on technologies such as mobile commerce, electronic funds transfer, supply chain management, Internet marketing, online transaction processing, electronic data interchange , inventory management systems, and automated data collection systems.

Exam Probability: **High**

25. *Answer choices:*

(see index for correct answer)

- a. Carmudi
- b. DVD-by-mail
- c. E-commerce
- d. Ashley Ebner

Guidance: level 1

:: Data management ::

__________ refers to a data-driven improvement cycle used for improving, optimizing and stabilizing business processes and designs. The __________ improvement cycle is the core tool used to drive Six Sigma projects. However, __________ is not exclusive to Six Sigma and can be used as the framework for other improvement applications.

Exam Probability: **High**

26. *Answer choices:*

(see index for correct answer)

- a. VMDS
- b. Data virtualization
- c. DMAIC
- d. HyperLogLog

Guidance: level 1

:: Product development ::

In business and engineering, __________ covers the complete process of bringing a new product to market. A central aspect of NPD is product design, along with various business considerations. __________ is described broadly as the transformation of a market opportunity into a product available for sale. The product can be tangible or intangible , though sometimes services and other processes are distinguished from "products." NPD requires an understanding of customer needs and wants, the competitive environment, and the nature of the market.Cost, time and quality are the main variables that drive customer needs. Aiming at these three variables, innovative companies develop continuous practices and strategies to better satisfy customer requirements and to increase their own market share by a regular development of new products. There are many uncertainties and challenges which companies must face throughout the process. The use of best practices and the elimination of barriers to communication are the main concerns for the management of the NPD .

Exam Probability: **High**

27. *Answer choices:*

(see index for correct answer)

- a. Product line extension
- b. New product development
- c. Minimum viable product

- d. Brief

Guidance: level 1

:: Industrial equipment ::

_________ s are heat exchangers typically used to provide heat to the bottom of industrial distillation columns. They boil the liquid from the bottom of a distillation column to generate vapors which are returned to the column to drive the distillation separation. The heat supplied to the column by the _________ at the bottom of the column is removed by the condenser at the top of the column.

Exam Probability: **Low**

28. *Answer choices:*
(see index for correct answer)

- a. Thermal wheel
- b. Buell dryer
- c. Coiled tubing umbilical
- d. Reboiler

Guidance: level 1

:: Chemical reactions ::

A _________ is a process that leads to the chemical transformation of one set of chemical substances to another. Classically, _________ s encompass changes that only involve the positions of electrons in the forming and breaking of chemical bonds between atoms, with no change to the nuclei , and can often be described by a chemical equation. Nuclear chemistry is a sub-discipline of chemistry that involves the _________ s of unstable and radioactive elements where both electronic and nuclear changes can occur.

Exam Probability: **High**

29. *Answer choices:*
(see index for correct answer)

- a. Colorimetric analysis
- b. Hydrolysis
- c. Molecularity
- d. Substrate

Guidance: level 1

:: Industrial processes ::

A __________ is a device used for high-temperature heating. The name derives from Latin word fornax, which means oven. The heat energy to fuel a __________ may be supplied directly by fuel combustion, by electricity such as the electric arc __________ , or through induction heating in induction __________ s.

Exam Probability: **Low**

30. *Answer choices:*

(see index for correct answer)

- a. Glass-ceramic-to-metal seals
- b. Shrink-fitting
- c. Lead chamber process
- d. Spark plasma sintering

Guidance: level 1

:: Manufacturing ::

__________ or lean production, often simply "lean", is a systematic method for the minimization of waste within a manufacturing system without sacrificing productivity, which can cause problems. Lean also takes into account waste created through overburden and waste created through unevenness in work loads . Working from the perspective of the client who consumes a product or service, "value" is any action or process that a customer would be willing to pay for.

Exam Probability: **Low**

31. *Answer choices:*

(see index for correct answer)

- a. Engineering bill of materials
- b. PackML
- c. Manufacturing engineering
- d. Concrete plant

Guidance: level 1

:: Project management ::

In economics and business decision-making, a sunk cost is a cost that has already been incurred and cannot be recovered.

Exam Probability: **Medium**

32. *Answer choices:*

(see index for correct answer)

- a. Mandated lead arranger
- b. Sunk costs
- c. Project Management South Africa
- d. Project Management Professional

Guidance: level 1

:: Consortia ::

A _________ is an association of two or more individuals, companies, organizations or governments with the objective of participating in a common activity or pooling their resources for achieving a common goal.

Exam Probability: **Medium**

33. *Answer choices:*

(see index for correct answer)

- a. Southern New Jersey Rail Group
- b. Broadband Forum
- c. SCOPE Alliance
- d. CANARIE

Guidance: level 1

:: Asset ::

In financial accounting, an _________ is any resource owned by the business. Anything tangible or intangible that can be owned or controlled to produce value and that is held by a company to produce positive economic value is an _________ . Simply stated, _________ s represent value of ownership that can be converted into cash . The balance sheet of a firm records the monetary value of the _________ s owned by that firm. It covers money and other valuables belonging to an individual or to a business.

Exam Probability: **High**

34. *Answer choices:*

(see index for correct answer)

- a. Fixed asset
- b. Asset

Guidance: level 1

:: Production and manufacturing ::

_________ is a concept in purchasing and project management for securing the quality and timely delivery of goods and components.

Exam Probability: **Medium**

35. *Answer choices:*

(see index for correct answer)

- a. SafetyBUS p
- b. Expediting
- c. Accelerated aging
- d. Reverse engineering

Guidance: level 1

:: Management ::

A _________ is an idea of the future or desired result that a person or a group of people envisions, plans and commits to achieve. People endeavor to reach _________ s within a finite time by setting deadlines.

Exam Probability: **High**

36. *Answer choices:*
(see index for correct answer)

- a. Goal
- b. Economic production quantity
- c. Duality
- d. Outrage constraint

Guidance: level 1

:: Business planning ::

__________ is a critical component to the successful delivery of any project, programme or activity. A stakeholder is any individual, group or organization that can affect, be affected by, or perceive itself to be affected by a programme.

Exam Probability: **High**

37. *Answer choices:*
(see index for correct answer)

- a. Joint decision trap
- b. Community Futures
- c. Stakeholder management
- d. operational planning

Guidance: level 1

:: Building materials ::

__________ is an alloy of iron and carbon, and sometimes other elements. Because of its high tensile strength and low cost, it is a major component used in buildings, infrastructure, tools, ships, automobiles, machines, appliances, and weapons.

Exam Probability: **Medium**

38. *Answer choices:*
(see index for correct answer)

- a. Asphalt roll roofing
- b. Steel
- c. Fiber roll
- d. Opus albarium

Guidance: level 1

:: Quality assurance ::

The _________ is a United States-based nonprofit tax-exempt 501 organization that accredits more than 21,000 US health care organizations and programs. The international branch accredits medical services from around the world. A majority of US state governments recognize _________ accreditation as a condition of licensure for the receipt of Medicaid and Medicare reimbursements.

Exam Probability: **Low**

39. *Answer choices:*

(see index for correct answer)

- a. Certificate of Conformity to Technical Regulation
- b. Swiss quality label for further education institutions
- c. Certified Quality Engineer
- d. Technical Control Department

Guidance: level 1

:: Business process ::

_________ is the value to an enterprise which is derived from the techniques, procedures, and programs that implement and enhance the delivery of goods and services. _________ is one of the three components of structural capital, itself a component of intellectual capital. _________ can be seen as the value of processes to any entity, whether for profit or not-for profit, but is most commonly used in reference to for-profit entities.

Exam Probability: **High**

40. *Answer choices:*

(see index for correct answer)

- a. Real-time enterprise
- b. IDS Scheer
- c. Process capital
- d. Tenant screening

Guidance: level 1

:: ::

_________ refers to the confirmation of certain characteristics of an object, person, or organization. This confirmation is often, but not always, provided by some form of external review, education, assessment, or audit. Accreditation is a specific organization's process of _________ . According to the National Council on Measurement in Education, a _________ test is a credentialing test used to determine whether individuals are knowledgeable enough in a given occupational area to be labeled "competent to practice" in that area.

Exam Probability: **High**

41. *Answer choices:*

(see index for correct answer)

- a. empathy
- b. co-culture
- c. Character
- d. imperative

Guidance: level 1

:: Project management ::

_________ is a marketing activity that does an aggregate plan for the production process, in advance of 6 to 18 months, to give an idea to management as to what quantity of materials and other resources are to be procured and when, so that the total cost of operations of the organization is kept to the minimum over that period.

Exam Probability: **High**

42. *Answer choices:*

(see index for correct answer)

- a. Project Management Institute
- b. Task
- c. Aggregate planning
- d. Flexible product development

Guidance: level 1

:: ::

In a supply chain, a _________ , or a seller, is an enterprise that contributes goods or services. Generally, a supply chain _________ manufactures inventory/stock items and sells them to the next link in the chain. Today, these terms refer to a supplier of any good or service.

Exam Probability: **Medium**

43. *Answer choices:*

(see index for correct answer)

- a. information systems assessment
- b. Vendor
- c. personal values
- d. hierarchical perspective

Guidance: level 1

:: Production and manufacturing ::

_________ is the process of determining the production capacity needed by an organization to meet changing demands for its products. In the context of _________ , design capacity is the maximum amount of work that an organization is capable of completing in a given period. Effective capacity is the maximum amount of work that an organization is capable of completing in a given period due to constraints such as quality problems, delays, material handling, etc.

Exam Probability: **Medium**

44. *Answer choices:*

(see index for correct answer)

- a. Positive recall
- b. Foundation Fieldbus H1
- c. Highly accelerated stress audit
- d. Screw conveyor

Guidance: level 1

:: Finance ::

__________ is a financial estimate intended to help buyers and owners determine the direct and indirect costs of a product or system. It is a management accounting concept that can be used in full cost accounting or even ecological economics where it includes social costs.

Exam Probability: **High**

45. *Answer choices:*
(see index for correct answer)

- a. Isoelastic utility
- b. Total cost of ownership
- c. Double digital option
- d. Putty-putty

Guidance: level 1

:: Mereology ::

__________ , in the abstract, is what belongs to or with something, whether as an attribute or as a component of said thing. In the context of this article, it is one or more components , whether physical or incorporeal, of a person's estate; or so belonging to, as in being owned by, a person or jointly a group of people or a legal entity like a corporation or even a society. Depending on the nature of the __________ , an owner of __________ has the right to consume, alter, share, redefine, rent, mortgage, pawn, sell, exchange, transfer, give away or destroy it, or to exclude others from doing these things, as well as to perhaps abandon it; whereas regardless of the nature of the __________ , the owner thereof has the right to properly use it , or at the very least exclusively keep it.

Exam Probability: **Medium**

46. *Answer choices:*
(see index for correct answer)

- a. Gunk
- b. Non-wellfounded mereology
- c. Mereotopology
- d. Property

Guidance: level 1

:: Project management ::

A _________ is a team whose members usually belong to different groups, functions and are assigned to activities for the same project. A team can be divided into sub-teams according to need. Usually _________ s are only used for a defined period of time. They are disbanded after the project is deemed complete. Due to the nature of the specific formation and disbandment, _________ s are usually in organizations.

Exam Probability: **Low**

47. *Answer choices:*

(see index for correct answer)

- a. Point of total assumption
- b. Critical path drag
- c. Project team
- d. Project engineering

Guidance: level 1

:: Infographics ::

The _________ is a form used to collect data in real time at the location where the data is generated. The data it captures can be quantitative or qualitative. When the information is quantitative, the _________ is sometimes called a tally sheet.

Exam Probability: **Medium**

48. *Answer choices:*

(see index for correct answer)

- a. Diagram
- b. Cave5D
- c. Hazard symbol
- d. Graphicacy

Guidance: level 1

:: Industrial engineering ::

__________ , in its contemporary conceptualisation, is a comparison of perceived expectations of a service with perceived performance , giving rise to the equation SQ=P-E. This conceptualistion of _________ has its origins in the expectancy-disconfirmation paradigm.

Exam Probability: **High**

49. *Answer choices:*

(see index for correct answer)

- a. Service quality
- b. Response surface methodology
- c. Work Measurement
- d. Package testing

Guidance: level 1

:: Quality assurance ::

Organizations that issue credentials or certify third parties against official standards are themselves formally accredited by _________ bodies ; hence they are sometimes known as "accredited certification bodies". The _________ process ensures that their certification practices are acceptable, typically meaning that they are competent to test and certify third parties, behave ethically and employ suitable quality assurance.

Exam Probability: **Medium**

50. *Answer choices:*

(see index for correct answer)

- a. Load testing
- b. SUBSAFE
- c. Joint Commission
- d. Consolidated Standards of Reporting Trials

Guidance: level 1

:: Management ::

In inventory management, __________ is the order quantity that minimizes the total holding costs and ordering costs. It is one of the oldest classical production scheduling models. The model was developed by Ford W. Harris in 1913, but R. H. Wilson, a consultant who applied it extensively, and K. Andler are given credit for their in-depth analysis.

Exam Probability: **Medium**

51. *Answer choices:*
(see index for correct answer)

- a. Process management
- b. Economic order quantity
- c. Line of business
- d. Twelve leverage points

Guidance: level 1

:: Industrial engineering ::

The __________ is the design of any task that aims to describe or explain the variation of information under conditions that are hypothesized to reflect the variation. The term is generally associated with experiments in which the design introduces conditions that directly affect the variation, but may also refer to the design of quasi-experiments, in which natural conditions that influence the variation are selected for observation.

Exam Probability: **Low**

52. *Answer choices:*
(see index for correct answer)

- a. Institute of Industrial Engineers
- b. Operation chart
- c. Material flow
- d. Optimal design

Guidance: level 1

:: Management ::

__________ is a category of business activity made possible by software tools that aim to provide customers with both independence from vendors and better means for engaging with vendors. These same tools can also apply to individuals` relations with other institutions and organizations.

Exam Probability: **Low**

53. *Answer choices:*
(see index for correct answer)

- a. Iterative and incremental development
- b. Scenario planning
- c. Demand chain management
- d. Vendor relationship management

Guidance: level 1

:: Supply chain management ::

__________ is a core supply chain function and includes supply chain planning and supply chain execution capabilities. Specifically, __________ is the capability firms use to plan total material requirements. The material requirements are communicated to procurement and other functions for sourcing. __________ is also responsible for determining the amount of material to be deployed at each stocking location across the supply chain, establishing material replenishment plans, determining inventory levels to hold for each type of inventory , and communicating information regarding material needs throughout the extended supply chain.

Exam Probability: **Medium**

54. *Answer choices:*
(see index for correct answer)

- a. Transactional IT
- b. Dynamic discounting
- c. Service parts pricing
- d. Materials management

Guidance: level 1

:: Management accounting ::

__________ are costs that are not directly accountable to a cost object . __________ may be either fixed or variable. __________ include administration, personnel and security costs. These are those costs which are not directly related to production. Some __________ may be overhead. But some overhead costs can be directly attributed to a project and are direct costs.

Exam Probability: **Low**

55. *Answer choices:*

(see index for correct answer)

- a. Spend management
- b. Overhead
- c. Operating profit margin
- d. Indirect costs

Guidance: level 1

:: Non-parametric statistics ::

A __________ is an accurate representation of the distribution of numerical data. It is an estimate of the probability distribution of a continuous variable and was first introduced by Karl Pearson. It differs from a bar graph, in the sense that a bar graph relates two variables, but a __________ relates only one. To construct a __________ , the first step is to "bin" the range of values—that is, divide the entire range of values into a series of intervals—and then count how many values fall into each interval. The bins are usually specified as consecutive, non-overlapping intervals of a variable. The bins must be adjacent, and are often of equal size.

Exam Probability: **Medium**

56. *Answer choices:*

(see index for correct answer)

- a. Van der Waerden test
- b. L-estimator
- c. Semiparametric regression
- d. Mantel test

Guidance: level 1

:: Packaging ::

In work place, _________ or job _________ means good ranking with the hypothesized conception of requirements of a role. There are two types of job _________ s: contextual and task. Task _________ is related to cognitive ability while contextual _________ is dependent upon personality. Task _________ are behavioral roles that are recognized in job descriptions and by remuneration systems, they are directly related to organizational _________, whereas, contextual _________ are value based and additional behavioral roles that are not recognized in job descriptions and covered by compensation; they are extra roles that are indirectly related to organizational _________. Citizenship _________ like contextual _________ means a set of individual activity/contribution that supports the organizational culture.

Exam Probability: **Medium**

57. *Answer choices:*

(see index for correct answer)

- a. Cyperus tegetiformis
- b. Plastic bag
- c. Child-resistant packaging
- d. Performance

Guidance: level 1

:: Process management ::

_________ is a statistics package developed at the Pennsylvania State University by researchers Barbara F. Ryan, Thomas A. Ryan, Jr., and Brian L. Joiner in 1972. It began as a light version of OMNITAB 80, a statistical analysis program by NIST. Statistical analysis software such as _________ automates calculations and the creation of graphs, allowing the user to focus more on the analysis of data and the interpretation of results. It is compatible with other _________, Inc. software.

Exam Probability: **Medium**

58. *Answer choices:*

(see index for correct answer)

- a. Acceptable quality limit
- b. Defects per million opportunities
- c. Minitab
- d. Value grid

Guidance: level 1

:: Project management ::

__________ is a work methodology emphasizing the parallelisation of tasks , which is sometimes called simultaneous engineering or integrated product development using an integrated product team approach. It refers to an approach used in product development in which functions of design engineering, manufacturing engineering, and other functions are integrated to reduce the time required to bring a new product to market.

Exam Probability: **High**

59. *Answer choices:*

(see index for correct answer)

- a. Gantt chart
- b. Participatory impact pathways analysis
- c. Concurrent engineering
- d. Project cycle management

Guidance: level 1

Commerce

Commerce relates to "the exchange of goods and services, especially on a large scale." It includes legal, economic, political, social, cultural and technological systems that operate in any country or internationally.

:: Economic globalization ::

_________ is an agreement in which one company hires another company to be responsible for a planned or existing activity that is or could be done internally,and sometimes involves transferring employees and assets from one firm to another.

Exam Probability: **Medium**

1. *Answer choices:*

(see index for correct answer)

- a. global financial
- b. reshoring

Guidance: level 1

:: International trade ::

_________ involves the transfer of goods or services from one person or entity to another, often in exchange for money. A system or network that allows _________ is called a market.

Exam Probability: **High**

2. *Answer choices:*

(see index for correct answer)

- a. East forum Berlin
- b. Trade
- c. Import
- d. Export-led growth

Guidance: level 1

:: Service industries ::

_________ is travel for pleasure or business; also the theory and practice of touring, the business of attracting, accommodating, and entertaining tourists, and the business of operating tours. _________ may be international, or within the traveller's country. The World _________ Organization defines _________ more generally, in terms which go "beyond the common perception of _________ as being limited to holiday activity only", as people "traveling to and staying in places outside their usual environment for not more than one consecutive year for leisure and not less than 24 hours, business and other purposes".

Exam Probability: **Medium**

3. *Answer choices:*

(see index for correct answer)

- a. Pension Administration
- b. Excel Insurance Solutions
- c. Tourism
- d. Maid service

Guidance: level 1

:: Project management ::

In political science, an _________ is a means by which a petition signed by a certain minimum number of registered voters can force a government to choose to either enact a law or hold a public vote in parliament in what is called indirect _________ , or under direct _________ , the proposition is immediately put to a plebiscite or referendum, in what is called a Popular initiated Referendum or citizen-initiated referendum).

Exam Probability: **Low**

4. *Answer choices:*

(see index for correct answer)

- a. Effective Development Group
- b. Soft Costs
- c. Initiative
- d. Indian Institute of Project Management

Guidance: level 1

:: Minimum wage ::

A _________ is the lowest remuneration that employers can legally pay their workers—the price floor below which workers may not sell their labor. Most countries had introduced _________ legislation by the end of the 20th century.

Exam Probability: **Low**

5. *Answer choices:*

(see index for correct answer)

- a. Minimum wage in Taiwan
- b. Minimum Wage Fairness Act
- c. Guaranteed minimum income
- d. Minimum wage

Guidance: level 1

:: Game theory ::

To _________ is to make a deal between different parties where each party gives up part of their demand. In arguments, _________ is a concept of finding agreement through communication, through a mutual acceptance of terms—often involving variations from an original goal or desires.

Exam Probability: **Low**

6. *Answer choices:*

(see index for correct answer)

- a. Compromise
- b. Rationalizability
- c. Repeated game
- d. Job scheduling game

Guidance: level 1

:: ::

A __________ , or also known as foreman, overseer, facilitator, monitor, area coordinator, or sometimes gaffer, is the job title of a low level management position that is primarily based on authority over a worker or charge of a workplace. A __________ can also be one of the most senior in the staff at the place of work, such as a Professor who oversees a PhD dissertation. Supervision, on the other hand, can be performed by people without this formal title, for example by parents. The term __________ itself can be used to refer to any personnel who have this task as part of their job description.

Exam Probability: **Medium**

7. *Answer choices:*

(see index for correct answer)

- a. co-culture
- b. deep-level diversity
- c. functional perspective
- d. Supervisor

Guidance: level 1

:: Basic financial concepts ::

__________ is a sustained increase in the general price level of goods and services in an economy over a period of time.When the general price level rises, each unit of currency buys fewer goods and services; consequently, __________ reflects a reduction in the purchasing power per unit of money a loss of real value in the medium of exchange and unit of account within the economy. The measure of __________ is the __________ rate, the annualized percentage change in a general price index, usually the consumer price index, over time. The opposite of __________ is deflation.

Exam Probability: **Medium**

8. *Answer choices:*

(see index for correct answer)

- a. Base effect
- b. Inflation
- c. Leverage cycle
- d. Short interest

Guidance: level 1

:: Quality management ::

__________ ensures that an organization, product or service is consistent. It has four main components: quality planning, quality assurance, quality control and quality improvement. __________ is focused not only on product and service quality, but also on the means to achieve it. __________ , therefore, uses quality assurance and control of processes as well as products to achieve more consistent quality. What a customer wants and is willing to pay for it determines quality. It is written or unwritten commitment to a known or unknown consumer in the market . Thus, quality can be defined as fitness for intended use or, in other words, how well the product performs its intended function

Exam Probability: **Medium**

9. *Answer choices:*

(see index for correct answer)

- a. TL 9000
- b. ISO 9000
- c. Quality management
- d. External quality assessment

Guidance: level 1

:: ::

A __________ is a sworn body of people convened to render an impartial verdict officially submitted to them by a court, or to set a penalty or judgment. Modern juries tend to be found in courts to ascertain the guilt or lack thereof in a crime. In Anglophone jurisdictions, the verdict may be guilty or not guilty . The old institution of grand juries still exists in some places, particularly the United States, to investigate whether enough evidence of a crime exists to bring someone to trial.

Exam Probability: **High**

10. *Answer choices:*

(see index for correct answer)

- a. personal values
- b. open system

- c. Jury
- d. process perspective

Guidance: level 1

:: Business law ::

A __________ is a group of people who jointly supervise the activities of an organization, which can be either a for-profit business, nonprofit organization, or a government agency. Such a board`s powers, duties, and responsibilities are determined by government regulations and the organization`s own constitution and bylaws. These authorities may specify the number of members of the board, how they are to be chosen, and how often they are to meet.

Exam Probability: **Medium**

11. *Answer choices:*

(see index for correct answer)

- a. Secret rebate
- b. Board of directors
- c. Country of origin
- d. Apparent authority

Guidance: level 1

:: Payments ::

A __________ or government incentive is a form of financial aid or support extended to an economic sector generally with the aim of promoting economic and social policy. Although commonly extended from government, the term __________ can relate to any type of support – for example from NGOs or as implicit subsidies. Subsidies come in various forms including: direct and indirect .

Exam Probability: **Low**

12. *Answer choices:*

(see index for correct answer)

- a. KlickEx
- b. Market transition payments
- c. Subsidy

- d. Incentive payments

Guidance: level 1

:: Project management ::

__________ is the right to exercise power, which can be formalized by a state and exercised by way of judges, appointed executives of government, or the ecclesiastical or priestly appointed representatives of a God or other deities.

Exam Probability: **High**

13. *Answer choices:*

(see index for correct answer)

- a. Assumption-based planning
- b. Authority
- c. Project accounting
- d. Team performance management

Guidance: level 1

:: Management occupations ::

__________ ship is the process of designing, launching and running a new business, which is often initially a small business. The people who create these businesses are called __________ s.

Exam Probability: **Low**

14. *Answer choices:*

(see index for correct answer)

- a. Chief gaming officer
- b. County administrator
- c. Hayward
- d. General counsel

Guidance: level 1

:: Auctioneering ::

__________ are electronic auctions, which can be used by sellers to sell their items to many potential buyers. Sellers and buyers can be individuals, organizations etc.

Exam Probability: **Medium**

15. *Answer choices:*

(see index for correct answer)

- a. Dutch auction
- b. Virginity auction
- c. Auctionata
- d. Walton School of Auctioneering

Guidance: level 1

:: ::

A federation is a political entity characterized by a union of partially self-governing provinces, states, or other regions under a central __________ . In a federation, the self-governing status of the component states, as well as the division of power between them and the central government, is typically constitutionally entrenched and may not be altered by a unilateral decision of either party, the states or the federal political body. Alternatively, federation is a form of government in which sovereign power is formally divided between a central authority and a number of constituent regions so that each region retains some degree of control over its internal affairs. It is often argued that federal states where the central government has the constitutional authority to suspend a constituent state`s government by invoking gross mismanagement or civil unrest, or to adopt national legislation that overrides or infringe on the constituent states` powers by invoking the central government`s constitutional authority to ensure "peace and good government" or to implement obligations contracted under an international treaty, are not truly federal states.

Exam Probability: **Medium**

16. *Answer choices:*

(see index for correct answer)

- a. imperative
- b. process perspective
- c. Federal government

- d. Sarbanes-Oxley act of 2002

Guidance: level 1

:: Dot-com bubble ::

_________ , Inc., is a web search engine and web portal established in 1994, spun out of Carnegie Mellon University. _________ also encompasses a network of email, webhosting, social networking, and entertainment websites. The company is based in Waltham, Massachusetts, and is currently a subsidiary of Kakao.

Exam Probability: **Medium**

17. *Answer choices:*
(see index for correct answer)

- a. Lycos
- b. Dot-com company
- c. E-Dreams
- d. Think Tools

Guidance: level 1

:: ::

Competition law is a law that promotes or seeks to maintain market competition by regulating anti-competitive conduct by companies. Competition law is implemented through public and private enforcement. Competition law is known as " _________ law" in the United States for historical reasons, and as "anti-monopoly law" in China and Russia. In previous years it has been known as trade practices law in the United Kingdom and Australia. In the European Union, it is referred to as both _________ and competition law.

Exam Probability: **Medium**

18. *Answer choices:*
(see index for correct answer)

- a. empathy
- b. Antitrust
- c. Character
- d. imperative

Guidance: level 1

:: Information technology ::

_________ is the use of computers to store, retrieve, transmit, and manipulate data, or information, often in the context of a business or other enterprise. IT is considered to be a subset of information and communications technology . An _________ system is generally an information system, a communications system or, more specifically speaking, a computer system – including all hardware, software and peripheral equipment – operated by a limited group of users.

Exam Probability: **Medium**

19. *Answer choices:*

(see index for correct answer)

- a. Information technology
- b. Open collaboration
- c. Consumerization
- d. Geeks Without Bounds

Guidance: level 1

:: Strategic alliances ::

A _________ is an agreement between two or more parties to pursue a set of agreed upon objectives needed while remaining independent organizations. A _________ will usually fall short of a legal partnership entity, agency, or corporate affiliate relationship. Typically, two companies form a _________ when each possesses one or more business assets or have expertise that will help the other by enhancing their businesses. _________ s can develop in outsourcing relationships where the parties desire to achieve long-term win-win benefits and innovation based on mutually desired outcomes.

Exam Probability: **Low**

20. *Answer choices:*

(see index for correct answer)

- a. International joint venture
- b. Strategic alliance
- c. Management contract
- d. Bridge Alliance

Guidance: level 1

:: ::

__________ is the extraction of valuable minerals or other geological materials from the earth, usually from an ore body, lode, vein, seam, reef or placer deposit. These deposits form a mineralized package that is of economic interest to the miner.

Exam Probability: **High**

21. *Answer choices:*

(see index for correct answer)

- a. Mining
- b. hierarchical perspective
- c. Sarbanes-Oxley act of 2002
- d. levels of analysis

Guidance: level 1

:: Data interchange standards ::

__________ is the concept of businesses electronically communicating information that was traditionally communicated on paper, such as purchase orders and invoices. Technical standards for EDI exist to facilitate parties transacting such instruments without having to make special arrangements.

Exam Probability: **Medium**

22. *Answer choices:*

(see index for correct answer)

- a. Electronic data interchange
- b. Uniform Communication Standard
- c. Data Interchange Standards Association
- d. Domain Application Protocol

Guidance: level 1

:: Debt ::

_________ is the trust which allows one party to provide money or resources to another party wherein the second party does not reimburse the first party immediately , but promises either to repay or return those resources at a later date. In other words, _________ is a method of making reciprocity formal, legally enforceable, and extensible to a large group of unrelated people.

Exam Probability: **Low**

23. *Answer choices:*

(see index for correct answer)

- a. Debt-lag
- b. Credit
- c. Peak debt
- d. Arrears

Guidance: level 1

:: Management accounting ::

In economics, _________ s, indirect costs or overheads are business expenses that are not dependent on the level of goods or services produced by the business. They tend to be time-related, such as interest or rents being paid per month, and are often referred to as overhead costs. This is in contrast to variable costs, which are volume-related and unknown at the beginning of the accounting year. For a simple example, such as a bakery, the monthly rent for the baking facilities, and the monthly payments for the security system and basic phone line are _________ s, as they do not change according to how much bread the bakery produces and sells. On the other hand, the wage costs of the bakery are variable, as the bakery will have to hire more workers if the production of bread increases. Economists reckon _________ as a entry barrier for new entrepreneurs.

Exam Probability: **Low**

24. *Answer choices:*

(see index for correct answer)

- a. Hedge accounting
- b. Notional profit
- c. Direct material total variance
- d. Activity-based management

Guidance: level 1

:: ::

_________ is the process of removing or reducing state regulations, typically in the economic sphere. It is the repeal of governmental regulation of the economy. It became common in advanced industrial economies in the 1970s and 1980s, as a result of new trends in economic thinking about the inefficiencies of government regulation, and the risk that regulatory agencies would be controlled by the regulated industry to its benefit, and thereby hurt consumers and the wider economy.

Exam Probability: **Medium**

25. *Answer choices:*

(see index for correct answer)

- a. Deregulation
- b. empathy
- c. surface-level diversity
- d. deep-level diversity

Guidance: level 1

:: Accounting source documents ::

An _________ , bill or tab is a commercial document issued by a seller to a buyer, relating to a sale transaction and indicating the products, quantities, and agreed prices for products or services the seller had provided the buyer.

Exam Probability: **Medium**

26. *Answer choices:*

(see index for correct answer)

- a. Bank statement
- b. Credit memorandum
- c. Parcel audit
- d. Invoice

Guidance: level 1

:: Production economics ::

In economics long run is a theoretical concept where all markets are in equilibrium, and all prices and quantities have fully adjusted and are in equilibrium. The long run contrasts with the _________ where there are some constraints and markets are not fully in equilibrium.

Exam Probability: **Medium**

27. *Answer choices:*

(see index for correct answer)

- a. Robinson Crusoe economy
- b. Producer's risk
- c. Learning-by-doing
- d. Total factor productivity

Guidance: level 1

:: Management ::

A _________ is an idea of the future or desired result that a person or a group of people envisions, plans and commits to achieve. People endeavor to reach _________ s within a finite time by setting deadlines.

Exam Probability: **High**

28. *Answer choices:*

(see index for correct answer)

- a. Managing stage boundaries
- b. One in, one out policy
- c. Goal
- d. Maryland StateStat

Guidance: level 1

:: Industrial automation ::

_________ is the technology by which a process or procedure is performed with minimal human assistance. _________ or automatic control is the use of various control systems for operating equipment such as machinery, processes in factories, boilers and heat treating ovens, switching on telephone networks, steering and stabilization of ships, aircraft and other applications and vehicles with minimal or reduced human intervention.

Exam Probability: **Medium**

29. *Answer choices:*

(see index for correct answer)

- a. I/Gear
- b. Automated mining
- c. IODD
- d. Automation

Guidance: level 1

:: Behavior modification ::

In psychotherapy and mental health, _________ has a positive sense of empowering individuals, or a negative sense of encouraging dysfunctional behavior.

Exam Probability: **Low**

30. *Answer choices:*

(see index for correct answer)

- a. behavioural change
- b. Thought stopping

Guidance: level 1

:: Hospitality industry ::

__________ refers to the relationship between a guest and a host, wherein the host receives the guest with goodwill, including the reception and entertainment of guests, visitors, or strangers. Louis, chevalier de Jaucourt describes __________ in the Encyclopédie as the virtue of a great soul that cares for the whole universe through the ties of humanity.

Exam Probability: **Medium**

31. *Answer choices:*

(see index for correct answer)

- a. Hospitality
- b. Restaurant ware
- c. Travel insurance
- d. Restaurant rating

Guidance: level 1

:: Auctioneering ::

A __________ is a type of sealed-bid auction. Bidders submit written bids without knowing the bid of the other people in the auction. The highest bidder wins but the price paid is the second-highest bid. This type of auction is strategically similar to an English auction and gives bidders an incentive to bid their true value. The auction was first described academically by Columbia University professor William Vickrey in 1961 though it had been used by stamp collectors since 1893. In 1797 Johann Wolfgang von Goethe sold a manuscript using a sealed-bid, second-price auction.

Exam Probability: **Low**

32. *Answer choices:*

(see index for correct answer)

- a. How Much Wood Would a Woodchuck Chuck
- b. Bidding fee auction
- c. Wine auction
- d. Vickrey auction

Guidance: level 1

:: Business ethics ::

_________ is a type of harassment technique that relates to a sexual nature and the unwelcome or inappropriate promise of rewards in exchange for sexual favors. _________ includes a range of actions from mild transgressions to sexual abuse or assault. Harassment can occur in many different social settings such as the workplace, the home, school, churches, etc. Harassers or victims may be of any gender.

Exam Probability: **Low**

33. *Answer choices:*

(see index for correct answer)

- a. Journal of Business Ethics
- b. Earnings quality
- c. International Association for Business and Society
- d. Sexual harassment

Guidance: level 1

:: Packaging ::

In work place, _________ or job _________ means good ranking with the hypothesized conception of requirements of a role. There are two types of job _________ s: contextual and task. Task _________ is related to cognitive ability while contextual _________ is dependent upon personality. Task _________ are behavioral roles that are recognized in job descriptions and by remuneration systems, they are directly related to organizational _________ , whereas, contextual _________ are value based and additional behavioral roles that are not recognized in job descriptions and covered by compensation; they are extra roles that are indirectly related to organizational _________ . Citizenship _________ like contextual _________ means a set of individual activity/contribution that supports the organizational culture.

Exam Probability: **Low**

34. *Answer choices:*

(see index for correct answer)

- a. Fibrenap
- b. Box-sealing tape
- c. Record sleeve
- d. Envelope

Guidance: level 1

:: Information retrieval ::

__________ is a technique used by recommender systems. __________ has two senses, a narrow one and a more general one.

Exam Probability: **Low**

35. *Answer choices:*
(see index for correct answer)

- a. European Summer School in Information Retrieval
- b. Ness Computing
- c. DtSearch
- d. Collaborative filtering

Guidance: level 1

:: Dot-com bubble ::

__________ was an online grocery business that filed bankruptcy in 2001 after 3 years of operation and was later folded into Amazon.com. It was headquartered in Foster City, California, United States. It delivered products to customers` homes within a 30-minute window of their choosing. At its peak, it offered service in ten US markets: the San Francisco Bay Area; Dallas; Sacramento; San Diego; Los Angeles; Orange County, California; Chicago; Seattle; Portland, Oregon; and Atlanta, Georgia. The company had hoped to expand to 26 cities by 2001.

Exam Probability: **Medium**

36. *Answer choices:*
(see index for correct answer)

- a. DrinkExchange
- b. Epidemic Marketing
- c. Fucked Company
- d. Webvan

Guidance: level 1

:: Business models ::

A _________ , _________ company or daughter company is a company that is owned or controlled by another company, which is called the parent company, parent, or holding company. The _________ can be a company, corporation, or limited liability company. In some cases it is a government or state-owned enterprise. In some cases, particularly in the music and book publishing industries, subsidiaries are referred to as imprints.

Exam Probability: **Medium**

37. *Answer choices:*
(see index for correct answer)

- a. Brainsworking
- b. Subsidiary
- c. Premium business model
- d. 70/20/10 Model

Guidance: level 1

:: Monopoly (economics) ::

A _________ exists when a specific person or enterprise is the only supplier of a particular commodity. This contrasts with a monopsony which relates to a single entity's control of a market to purchase a good or service, and with oligopoly which consists of a few sellers dominating a market. Monopolies are thus characterized by a lack of economic competition to produce the good or service, a lack of viable substitute goods, and the possibility of a high _________ price well above the seller's marginal cost that leads to a high _________ profit. The verb monopolise or monopolize refers to the process by which a company gains the ability to raise prices or exclude competitors. In economics, a _________ is a single seller. In law, a _________ is a business entity that has significant market power, that is, the power to charge overly high prices. Although monopolies may be big businesses, size is not a characteristic of a _________ . A small business may still have the power to raise prices in a small industry .

Exam Probability: **Medium**

38. *Answer choices:*
(see index for correct answer)

- a. Bilateral monopoly
- b. Monopoly

- c. Quasi-rent
- d. Practice of law

Guidance: level 1

:: Production economics ::

In microeconomics, _________ are the cost advantages that enterprises obtain due to their scale of operation , with cost per unit of output decreasing with increasing scale.

Exam Probability: **Medium**

39. *Answer choices:*

(see index for correct answer)

- a. Socially optimal firm size
- b. Factor price
- c. Constant elasticity of transformation
- d. Multifactor productivity

Guidance: level 1

:: ::

In business, overhead or overhead expense refers to an ongoing expense of operating a business. Overheads are the expenditure which cannot be conveniently traced to or identified with any particular cost unit, unlike operating expenses such as raw material and labor. Therefore, overheads cannot be immediately associated with the products or services being offered, thus do not directly generate profits. However, overheads are still vital to business operations as they provide critical support for the business to carry out profit making activities. For example, _________ s such as the rent for a factory allows workers to manufacture products which can then be sold for a profit. Such expenses are incurred for output generally and not for particular work order; e.g., wages paid to watch and ward staff, heating and lighting expenses of factory, etc. Overheads are also very important cost element along with direct materials and direct labor.

Exam Probability: **High**

40. *Answer choices:*

(see index for correct answer)

- a. Character
- b. Overhead cost
- c. open system
- d. Sarbanes-Oxley act of 2002

Guidance: level 1

:: Real property law ::

A __________ is the grant of authority or rights, stating that the granter formally recognizes the prerogative of the recipient to exercise the rights specified. It is implicit that the granter retains superiority , and that the recipient admits a limited status within the relationship, and it is within that sense that __________ s were historically granted, and that sense is retained in modern usage of the term.

Exam Probability: **Medium**

41. *Answer choices:*

(see index for correct answer)

- a. Tenancy deposit schemes
- b. Charter
- c. Avenage
- d. Preemption

Guidance: level 1

:: ::

Business is the activity of making one`s living or making money by producing or buying and selling products . Simply put, it is "any activity or enterprise entered into for profit. It does not mean it is a company, a corporation, partnership, or have any such formal organization, but it can range from a street peddler to General Motors."

Exam Probability: **High**

42. *Answer choices:*

(see index for correct answer)

- a. process perspective
- b. personal values
- c. hierarchical
- d. Firm

Guidance: level 1

:: Scientific method ::

In the social sciences and life sciences, a _________ is a research method involving an up-close, in-depth, and detailed examination of a subject of study , as well as its related contextual conditions.

Exam Probability: **Medium**

43. *Answer choices:*

(see index for correct answer)

- a. Case study
- b. Causal research
- c. Preference test
- d. pilot project

Guidance: level 1

:: ::

_________ , in general use, is a devotion and faithfulness to a nation, cause, philosophy, country, group, or person. Philosophers disagree on what can be an object of _________ , as some argue that _________ is strictly interpersonal and only another human being can be the object of _________ . The definition of _________ in law and political science is the fidelity of an individual to a nation, either one`s nation of birth, or one`s declared home nation by oath .

Exam Probability: **High**

44. *Answer choices:*

(see index for correct answer)

- a. levels of analysis
- b. Sarbanes-Oxley act of 2002
- c. functional perspective
- d. cultural

Guidance: level 1

:: ::

__________ is both a research area and a practical skill encompassing the ability of an individual or organization to "lead" or guide other individuals, teams, or entire organizations. Specialist literature debates various viewpoints, contrasting Eastern and Western approaches to __________ , and also United States versus European approaches. U.S. academic environments define __________ as "a process of social influence in which a person can enlist the aid and support of others in the accomplishment of a common task".

Exam Probability: **Low**

45. *Answer choices:*
(see index for correct answer)

- a. interpersonal communication
- b. process perspective
- c. hierarchical perspective
- d. empathy

Guidance: level 1

:: Land value taxation ::

__________ , sometimes referred to as dry __________ , is the solid surface of Earth that is not permanently covered by water. The vast majority of human activity throughout history has occurred in __________ areas that support agriculture, habitat, and various natural resources. Some life forms have developed from predecessor species that lived in bodies of water.

Exam Probability: **High**

46. *Answer choices:*
(see index for correct answer)

- a. Georgism
- b. Land value tax
- c. Land
- d. Henry George

Guidance: level 1

:: ::

A trade union is an association of workers forming a legal unit or legal personhood, usually called a "bargaining unit", which acts as bargaining agent and legal representative for a unit of employees in all matters of law or right arising from or in the administration of a collective agreement. Labour unions typically fund the formal organisation, head office, and legal team functions of the labour union through regular fees or union dues. The delegate staff of the labour union representation in the workforce are made up of workplace volunteers who are appointed by members in democratic elections.

Exam Probability: **Medium**

47. *Answer choices:*

(see index for correct answer)

- a. hierarchical perspective
- b. deep-level diversity
- c. Labor union
- d. Character

Guidance: level 1

:: Supply chain management ::

A _________ is a type of auction in which the traditional roles of buyer and seller are reversed. Thus, there is one buyer and many potential sellers. In an ordinary auction , buyers compete to obtain goods or services by offering increasingly higher prices. In contrast, in a _________ , the sellers compete to obtain business from the buyer and prices will typically decrease as the sellers underbid each other.

Exam Probability: **Medium**

48. *Answer choices:*

(see index for correct answer)

- a. Global supply-chain finance
- b. National Centre for Cold-chain Development
- c. Gideon Hillman Consulting
- d. Enterprise carbon accounting

Guidance: level 1

:: ::

Business Model Canvas is a strategic management and lean startup template for developing new or documenting existing business models. It is a visual chart with elements describing a firm`s or product`s value proposition, infrastructure, customers, and finances. It assists firms in aligning their activities by illustrating potential trade-offs.

Exam Probability: **Medium**

49. *Answer choices:*
(see index for correct answer)

- a. hierarchical perspective
- b. similarity-attraction theory
- c. Sarbanes-Oxley act of 2002
- d. Cost structure

Guidance: level 1

:: Marketing ::

__________ or stock is the goods and materials that a business holds for the ultimate goal of resale .

Exam Probability: **High**

50. *Answer choices:*
(see index for correct answer)

- a. Business stature
- b. In-game advertising
- c. Geographical pricing
- d. Inventory

Guidance: level 1

:: Project management ::

Contemporary business and science treat as a __________ any undertaking, carried out individually or collaboratively and possibly involving research or design, that is carefully planned to achieve a particular aim.

Exam Probability: **Low**

51. *Answer choices:*
(see index for correct answer)

- a. Lean project management
- b. Project
- c. Gantt chart
- d. Project cycle management

Guidance: level 1

:: E-commerce ::

An __________ , or automated clearinghouse, is an electronic network for financial transactions, generally domestic low value payments. An ACH is a computer-based clearing house and settlement facility established to process the exchange of electronic transactions between participating financial institutions. It is a form of clearing house that is specifically for payments and may support both credit transfers and direct debits.

Exam Probability: **High**

52. *Answer choices:*
(see index for correct answer)

- a. Online wallet
- b. EPages
- c. Automated Clearing House
- d. Advance ship notice

Guidance: level 1

:: Auctioneering ::

Unlike sealed-bid auctions , an __________ is "open" or fully transparent, as the identity of all bidders is disclosed to each other during the auction. More generally, an auction mechanism is considered "English" if it involves an iterative process of adjusting the price in a direction that is unfavorable to the bidders . In contrast, a Dutch auction would adjust the price in a direction that favored the bidders .

Exam Probability: **Low**

53. *Answer choices:*
(see index for correct answer)

- a. Camden auction
- b. Vickrey auction
- c. Auctionata
- d. English auction

Guidance: level 1

:: ::

_________ is an American restaurant chain and international franchise which was founded in 1958 by Dan and Frank Carney. The company is known for its Italian-American cuisine menu, including pizza and pasta, as well as side dishes and desserts. _________ has 18,431 restaurants worldwide as of December 31, 2018, making it the world`s largest pizza chain in terms of locations. It is a subsidiary of Yum! Brands, Inc., one of the world`s largest restaurant companies.

Exam Probability: **Medium**

54. *Answer choices:*

(see index for correct answer)

- a. co-culture
- b. empathy
- c. cultural
- d. Pizza Hut

Guidance: level 1

:: Payment systems ::

_________ s are part of a payment system issued by financial institutions, such as a bank, to a customer that enables its owner to access the funds in the customer`s designated bank accounts, or through a credit account and make payments by electronic funds transfer and access automated teller machines . Such cards are known by a variety of names including bank cards, ATM cards, MAC , client cards, key cards or cash cards.

Exam Probability: **High**

55. *Answer choices:*

(see index for correct answer)

- a. Zimswitch

- b. Payment card
- c. BIPS
- d. Legal Electronic Data Exchange Standard

Guidance: level 1

:: Retailing ::

A __________ or trolley , also known by a variety of other names, is a cart supplied by a shop, especially supermarkets, for use by customers inside the shop for transport of merchandise to the checkout counter during shopping. In many cases customers can then also use the cart to transport their purchased goods to their vehicles, but some carts are designed to prevent them from leaving the shop.

Exam Probability: **High**

56. *Answer choices:*

(see index for correct answer)

- a. Stock rotation
- b. Buy Here Pay Here
- c. Shopping cart
- d. Gold Souq

Guidance: level 1

:: ::

__________ is a type of government support for the citizens of that society. __________ may be provided to people of any income level, as with social security , but it is usually intended to ensure that the poor can meet their basic human needs such as food and shelter. __________ attempts to provide poor people with a minimal level of well-being, usually either a free- or a subsidized-supply of certain goods and social services, such as healthcare, education, and vocational training.

Exam Probability: **High**

57. *Answer choices:*

(see index for correct answer)

- a. Welfare
- b. open system

- c. personal values
- d. functional perspective

Guidance: level 1

:: Public relations ::

__________ is the public visibility or awareness for any product, service or company. It may also refer to the movement of information from its source to the general public, often but not always via the media. The subjects of __________ include people , goods and services, organizations, and works of art or entertainment.

Exam Probability: **Medium**

58. *Answer choices:*

(see index for correct answer)

- a. Publicity
- b. Spin
- c. Public Relations Inquiry
- d. Lawfare

Guidance: level 1

:: ::

Advertising is a marketing communication that employs an openly sponsored, non-personal message to promote or sell a product, service or idea. Sponsors of advertising are typically businesses wishing to promote their products or services. Advertising is differentiated from public relations in that an advertiser pays for and has control over the message. It differs from personal selling in that the message is non-personal, i.e., not directed to a particular individual.Advertising is communicated through various mass media, including traditional media such as newspapers, magazines, television, radio, outdoor advertising or direct mail; and new media such as search results, blogs, social media, websites or text messages. The actual presentation of the message in a medium is referred to as an __________ , or "ad" or advert for short.

Exam Probability: **Medium**

59. *Answer choices:*

(see index for correct answer)

- a. hierarchical perspective
- b. Advertisement
- c. open system
- d. co-culture

Guidance: level 1

Business ethics

Business ethics (also known as corporate ethics) is a form of applied ethics or professional ethics, that examines ethical principles and moral or ethical problems that can arise in a business environment. It applies to all aspects of business conduct and is relevant to the conduct of individuals and entire organizations. These ethics originate from individuals, organizational statements or from the legal system. These norms, values, ethical, and unethical practices are what is used to guide business. They help those businesses maintain a better connection with their stakeholders.

:: ::

_________ is the means to see, hear, or become aware of something or someone through our fundamental senses. The term _________ derives from the Latin word perceptio, and is the organization, identification, and interpretation of sensory information in order to represent and understand the presented information, or the environment.

Exam Probability: **Medium**

1. *Answer choices:*

(see index for correct answer)

- a. surface-level diversity
- b. Perception
- c. process perspective
- d. imperative

Guidance: level 1

:: Corporate crime ::

_________ LLP, based in Chicago, was an American holding company. Formerly one of the "Big Five" accounting firms , the firm had provided auditing, tax, and consulting services to large corporations. By 2001, it had become one of the world`s largest multinational companies.

Exam Probability: **Medium**

2. *Answer choices:*
(see index for correct answer)

- a. Arthur Andersen
- b. Langbar International
- c. Corporate Manslaughter and Corporate Homicide Act 2007
- d. FirstEnergy

Guidance: level 1

:: Business ethics ::

The _________ are the names of two corporate codes of conduct, developed by the African-American preacher Rev. Leon Sullivan, promoting corporate social responsibility.

Exam Probability: **Medium**

3. *Answer choices:*
(see index for correct answer)

- a. Impact investing
- b. Sullivan principles
- c. Destructionism
- d. Foreign official

Guidance: level 1

:: Management ::

The term _________ refers to measures designed to increase the degree of autonomy and self-determination in people and in communities in order to enable them to represent their interests in a responsible and self-determined way, acting on their own authority. It is the process of becoming stronger and more confident, especially in controlling one`s life and claiming one`s rights. _________ as action refers both to the process of self- _________ and to professional support of people, which enables them to overcome their sense of powerlessness and lack of influence, and to recognize and use their resources. To do work with power.

Exam Probability: **Medium**

4. *Answer choices:*

(see index for correct answer)

- a. Empowerment
- b. Target culture
- c. Management Week
- d. Infrastructure asset management

Guidance: level 1

:: ::

Oriental Nicety, formerly _________ , Exxon Mediterranean, SeaRiver Mediterranean, S/R Mediterranean, Mediterranean, and Dong Fang Ocean, was an oil tanker that gained notoriety after running aground in Prince William Sound spilling hundreds of thousands of barrels of crude oil in Alaska. On March 24, 1989, while owned by the former Exxon Shipping Company, and captained by Joseph Hazelwood and First Mate James Kunkel bound for Long Beach, California, the vessel ran aground on the Bligh Reef resulting in the second largest oil spill in United States history. The size of the spill is estimated to have been 40,900 to 120,000 m3 , or 257,000 to 750,000 barrels. In 1989, the _________ oil spill was listed as the 54th largest spill in history.

Exam Probability: **High**

5. *Answer choices:*

(see index for correct answer)

- a. cultural
- b. Character
- c. Exxon Valdez

- d. deep-level diversity

Guidance: level 1

:: Labour law ::

An _________ is special or specified circumstances that partially or fully exempt a person or organization from performance of a legal obligation so as to avoid an unreasonable or disproportionate burden or obstacle.

Exam Probability: **High**

6. *Answer choices:*

(see index for correct answer)

- a. Undue hardship
- b. Bharat Forge Co Ltd v Uttam Manohar Nakate
- c. Occupational disease
- d. Love contract

Guidance: level 1

:: ::

The _________ Group is a global financial investment management and insurance company headquartered in Des Moines, Iowa.

Exam Probability: **High**

7. *Answer choices:*

(see index for correct answer)

- a. Principal Financial
- b. corporate values
- c. empathy
- d. open system

Guidance: level 1

:: Trade unions ::

A __________ was a group formed of private citizens to administer law and order where they considered governmental structures to be inadequate. The term is commonly associated with the frontier areas of the American West in the mid-19th century, where groups attacked cattle rustlers and gangs, and people at gold mining claims. As non-state organizations no functioning checks existed to protect against excessive force or safeguard due process from the committees. In the years prior to the Civil War, some committees worked to free slaves and transport them to freedom.

Exam Probability: **Medium**

8. *Answer choices:*
(see index for correct answer)

- a. International Labour Sports Federation
- b. Public-sector trade union
- c. Vigilance committee
- d. Local union

Guidance: level 1

:: Ethically disputed business practices ::

__________ is the trading of a public company's stock or other securities by individuals with access to nonpublic information about the company. In various countries, some kinds of trading based on insider information is illegal. This is because it is seen as unfair to other investors who do not have access to the information, as the investor with insider information could potentially make larger profits than a typical investor could make. The rules governing __________ are complex and vary significantly from country to country. The extent of enforcement also varies from one country to another. The definition of insider in one jurisdiction can be broad, and may cover not only insiders themselves but also any persons related to them, such as brokers, associates and even family members. A person who becomes aware of non-public information and trades on that basis may be guilty of a crime.

Exam Probability: **High**

9. *Answer choices:*
(see index for correct answer)

- a. Coffin ship
- b. Insider trading

- c. Spamming
- d. Sugging

Guidance: level 1

:: Majority–minority relations ::

It was established as axiomatic in anthropological research by Franz Boas in the first few decades of the 20th century and later popularized by his students. Boas first articulated the idea in 1887: "civilization is not something absolute, but ... is relative, and ... our ideas and conceptions are true only so far as our civilization goes". However, Boas did not coin the term.

Exam Probability: **High**

10. *Answer choices:*
(see index for correct answer)

- a. cultural dissonance
- b. positive discrimination
- c. Cultural relativism

Guidance: level 1

:: Corporations law ::

A normal _________ consists of various departments that contribute to the company`s overall mission and goals. Common departments include Marketing, [Finance, [[Operations managementOperations, Human Resource, and IT. These five divisions represent the major departments within a publicly traded company, though there are often smaller departments within autonomous firms. There is typically a CEO, and Board of Directors composed of the directors of each department. There are also company presidents, vice presidents, and CFOs.There is a great diversity in corporate forms as enterprises may range from single company to multi-corporate conglomerate. The four main _________ s are Functional, Divisional, Geographic, and the Matrix.Realistically, most corporations tend to have a “hybrid” structure, which is a combination of different models with one dominant strategy.

Exam Probability: **High**

11. *Answer choices:*
(see index for correct answer)

- a. Corporate structure
- b. Corporate lawyer
- c. Internal affairs doctrine
- d. Company seal

Guidance: level 1

:: ::

The _________ of 1977 is a United States federal law known primarily for two of its main provisions: one that addresses accounting transparency requirements under the Securities Exchange Act of 1934 and another concerning bribery of foreign officials. The Act was amended in 1988 and in 1998, and has been subject to continued congressional concerns, namely whether its enforcement discourages U.S. companies from investing abroad.

Exam Probability: **Low**

12. *Answer choices:*
(see index for correct answer)

- a. Foreign Corrupt Practices Act
- b. levels of analysis
- c. interpersonal communication
- d. open system

Guidance: level 1

:: Business ::

_________, or built-in obsolescence, in industrial design and economics is a policy of planning or designing a product with an artificially limited useful life, so that it becomes obsolete after a certain period of time. The rationale behind this strategy is to generate long-term sales volume by reducing the time between repeat purchases .

Exam Probability: **Medium**

13. *Answer choices:*
(see index for correct answer)

- a. Values scales

- b. Planned obsolescence
- c. Business partnering
- d. Equality impact assessment

Guidance: level 1

:: United States federal labor legislation ::

The _________ of 1988 is a United States federal law that generally prevents employers from using polygraph tests, either for pre-employment screening or during the course of employment, with certain exemptions.

Exam Probability: **Low**

14. *Answer choices:*
(see index for correct answer)

- a. Employee Polygraph Protection Act
- b. National Industrial Recovery Act
- c. Workforce Investment Act of 1998
- d. National Whistleblowers Center

Guidance: level 1

:: Auditing ::

_________, as defined by accounting and auditing, is a process for assuring of an organization`s objectives in operational effectiveness and efficiency, reliable financial reporting, and compliance with laws, regulations and policies. A broad concept, _________ involves everything that controls risks to an organization.

Exam Probability: **Low**

15. *Answer choices:*
(see index for correct answer)

- a. Professional Evaluation and Certification Board
- b. Internal control
- c. Certified Internal Control Auditors
- d. Technical audit

Guidance: level 1

:: False advertising law ::

The Lanham Act is the primary federal trademark statute of law in the United States. The Act prohibits a number of activities, including trademark infringement, trademark dilution, and false advertising.

Exam Probability: **Low**

16. *Answer choices:*
(see index for correct answer)

- a. Rebecca Tushnet
- b. POM Wonderful LLC v. Coca-Cola Co.

Guidance: level 1

:: Financial markets ::

The __________ is a United States federal government organization, established by Title I of the Dodd–Frank Wall Street Reform and Consumer Protection Act, which was signed into law by President Barack Obama on July 21, 2010. The Office of Financial Research is intended to provide support to the council.

Exam Probability: **High**

17. *Answer choices:*
(see index for correct answer)

- a. Consolidated Quotation System
- b. Swap spread
- c. dark pool
- d. Financial Stability Oversight Council

Guidance: level 1

:: Television terminology ::

A __________ organization , also known as a non-business entity, not-for-profit organization, or __________ institution, is dedicated to furthering a particular social cause or advocating for a shared point of view. In economic terms, it is an organization that uses its surplus of the revenues to further achieve its ultimate objective, rather than distributing its income to the organization's shareholders, leaders, or members. __________ s are tax exempt or charitable, meaning they do not pay income tax on the money that they receive for their organization. They can operate in religious, scientific, research, or educational settings.

Exam Probability: **High**

18. *Answer choices:*
(see index for correct answer)

- a. distance learning
- b. Satellite television
- c. Nonprofit
- d. multiplexing

Guidance: level 1

:: ::

A __________ is a form of business network, for example, a local organization of businesses whose goal is to further the interests of businesses. Business owners in towns and cities form these local societies to advocate on behalf of the business community. Local businesses are members, and they elect a board of directors or executive council to set policy for the chamber. The board or council then hires a President, CEO or Executive Director, plus staffing appropriate to size, to run the organization.

Exam Probability: **High**

19. *Answer choices:*
(see index for correct answer)

- a. interpersonal communication
- b. functional perspective
- c. process perspective
- d. information systems assessment

Guidance: level 1

:: Market-based policy instruments ::

Cause marketing is defined as a type of corporate social responsibility, in which a company's promotional campaign has the dual purpose of increasing profitability while bettering society.

Exam Probability: **High**

20. *Answer choices:*
(see index for correct answer)

- a. Tree credits
- b. Fiscal localism
- c. Cause-related marketing
- d. Feebate

Guidance: level 1

:: Business ethics ::

__________ is a persistent pattern of mistreatment from others in the workplace that causes either physical or emotional harm. It can include such tactics as verbal, nonverbal, psychological, physical abuse and humiliation. This type of workplace aggression is particularly difficult because, unlike the typical school bully, workplace bullies often operate within the established rules and policies of their organization and their society. In the majority of cases, bullying in the workplace is reported as having been by someone who has authority over their victim. However, bullies can also be peers, and occasionally subordinates. Research has also investigated the impact of the larger organizational context on bullying as well as the group-level processes that impact on the incidence and maintenance of bullying behaviour. Bullying can be covert or overt. It may be missed by superiors; it may be known by many throughout the organization. Negative effects are not limited to the targeted individuals, and may lead to a decline in employee morale and a change in organizational culture. It can also take place as overbearing supervision, constant criticism, and blocking promotions.

Exam Probability: **Medium**

21. *Answer choices:*
(see index for correct answer)

- a. Conscious business

- b. Workplace bullying
- c. Institute of Business Ethics
- d. Hostile work environment

Guidance: level 1

:: Ethical banking ::

A ________ or community development finance institution - abbreviated in both cases to CDFI - is a financial institution that provides credit and financial services to underserved markets and populations, primarily in the USA but also in the UK. A CDFI may be a community development bank, a community development credit union , a community development loan fund , a community development venture capital fund , a microenterprise development loan fund, or a community development corporation.

Exam Probability: **Medium**

22. *Answer choices:*

(see index for correct answer)

- a. Citizens Bank of Canada
- b. GLS Bank
- c. Reliance Bank
- d. Alfred Rexroth

Guidance: level 1

:: Social enterprise ::

Corporate social responsibility is a type of international private business self-regulation. While once it was possible to describe CSR as an internal organisational policy or a corporate ethic strategy, that time has passed as various international laws have been developed and various organisations have used their authority to push it beyond individual or even industry-wide initiatives. While it has been considered a form of corporate self-regulation for some time, over the last decade or so it has moved considerably from voluntary decisions at the level of individual organisations, to mandatory schemes at regional, national and even transnational levels.

Exam Probability: **Medium**

23. *Answer choices:*

(see index for correct answer)

- a. Social venture
- b. Corporate citizenship

Guidance: level 1

:: Statutory law ::

__________ or statute law is written law set down by a body of legislature or by a singular legislator . This is as opposed to oral or customary law; or regulatory law promulgated by the executive or common law of the judiciary. Statutes may originate with national, state legislatures or local municipalities.

Exam Probability: **High**

24. *Answer choices:*
(see index for correct answer)

- a. incorporation by reference
- b. Statutory law
- c. statute law
- d. ratification

Guidance: level 1

:: ::

In regulatory jurisdictions that provide for it , __________ is a group of laws and organizations designed to ensure the rights of consumers as well as fair trade, competition and accurate information in the marketplace. The laws are designed to prevent the businesses that engage in fraud or specified unfair practices from gaining an advantage over competitors. They may also provides additional protection for those most vulnerable in society. __________ laws are a form of government regulation that aim to protect the rights of consumers. For example, a government may require businesses to disclose detailed information about products—particularly in areas where safety or public health is an issue, such as food.

Exam Probability: **Low**

25. *Answer choices:*
(see index for correct answer)

- a. co-culture
- b. levels of analysis
- c. imperative
- d. cultural

Guidance: level 1

:: Hazard analysis ::

Broadly speaking, a _________ is the combined effort of 1. identifying and analyzing potential events that may negatively impact individuals, assets, and/or the environment ; and 2. making judgments "on the tolerability of the risk on the basis of a risk analysis" while considering influencing factors . Put in simpler terms, a _________ analyzes what can go wrong, how likely it is to happen, what the potential consequences are, and how tolerable the identified risk is. As part of this process, the resulting determination of risk may be expressed in a quantitative or qualitative fashion. The _________ is an inherent part of an overall risk management strategy, which attempts to, after a _________ , "introduce control measures to eliminate or reduce" any potential risk-related consequences.

Exam Probability: **Medium**

26. *Answer choices:*

(see index for correct answer)

- a. Risk assessment
- b. Hazard identification
- c. Hazardous Materials Identification System

Guidance: level 1

:: ::

A _________ service is an online platform which people use to build social networks or social relationship with other people who share similar personal or career interests, activities, backgrounds or real-life connections.

Exam Probability: **Medium**

27. *Answer choices:*

(see index for correct answer)

- a. functional perspective

- b. Social networking
- c. levels of analysis
- d. interpersonal communication

Guidance: level 1

:: Corporate scandals ::

The __________ was a privately held international group of financial services companies controlled by Allen Stanford, until it was seized by United States authorities in early 2009. Headquartered in the Galleria Tower II in Uptown Houston, Texas, it had 50 offices in several countries, mainly in the Americas, included the Stanford International Bank, and said it managed US$8.5 billion of assets for more than 30,000 clients in 136 countries on six continents. On February 17, 2009, U.S. Federal agents placed the company into receivership due to charges of fraud. Ten days later, the U.S. Securities and Exchange Commission amended its complaint to accuse Stanford of turning the company into a "massive Ponzi scheme".

Exam Probability: **Low**

28. *Answer choices:*

(see index for correct answer)

- a. Lynn Brewer
- b. Stanford Financial Group
- c. Peter R. Harris
- d. Lysine price-fixing conspiracy

Guidance: level 1

:: Leadership ::

__________ is leadership that is directed by respect for ethical beliefs and values and for the dignity and rights of others. It is thus related to concepts such as trust, honesty, consideration, charisma, and fairness.

Exam Probability: **High**

29. *Answer choices:*

(see index for correct answer)

- a. Moral example
- b. Evolutionary leadership theory

- c. Situational leadership theory
- d. Ethical leadership

Guidance: level 1

:: United States law ::

The ABA _________ , created by the American Bar Association , are a set of rules that prescribe baseline standards of legal ethics and professional responsibility for lawyers in the United States. They were promulgated by the ABA House of Delegates upon the recommendation of the Kutak Commission in 1983. The rules are merely recommendations, or models, and are not themselves binding. However, having a common set of Model Rules facilitates a common discourse on legal ethics, and simplifies professional responsibility training as well as the day-to-day application of such rules. As of 2015, 49 states and four territories have adopted the rules in whole or in part, of which the most recent to do so was the Commonwealth of the Northern Mariana Islands in March 2015. California is the only state that has not adopted the ABA Model Rules, while Puerto Rico is the only U.S. jurisdiction outside of confederation has not adopted them but instead has its own Código de Ética Profesional.

Exam Probability: **Medium**

30. *Answer choices:*

(see index for correct answer)

- a. Pro se
- b. Model Rules of Professional Conduct

Guidance: level 1

:: Pyramid and Ponzi schemes ::

_________ was an Italian swindler and con artist in the U.S. and Canada. His aliases include Charles Ponci, Carlo, and Charles P. Bianchi. Born and raised in Italy, he became known in the early 1920s as a swindler in North America for his money-making scheme. He promised clients a 50% profit within 45 days or 100% profit within 90 days, by buying discounted postal reply coupons in other countries and redeeming them at face value in the United States as a form of arbitrage. In reality, Ponzi was paying earlier investors using the investments of later investors. While this type of fraudulent investment scheme was not originally invented by Ponzi, it became so identified with him that it now is referred to as a "Ponzi scheme". His scheme ran for over a year before it collapsed, costing his "investors" $20 million.

Exam Probability: **Medium**

31. *Answer choices:*

(see index for correct answer)

- a. K1 fund
- b. Charles Ponzi
- c. Nevin Shapiro
- d. Donald Anthony Walker Young

Guidance: level 1

:: Business ethics ::

_________ is a type of harassment technique that relates to a sexual nature and the unwelcome or inappropriate promise of rewards in exchange for sexual favors. _________ includes a range of actions from mild transgressions to sexual abuse or assault. Harassment can occur in many different social settings such as the workplace, the home, school, churches, etc. Harassers or victims may be of any gender.

Exam Probability: **Low**

32. *Answer choices:*

(see index for correct answer)

- a. Surface Transportation Assistance Act
- b. Sexual harassment
- c. Eating your own dog food
- d. Corporate sustainable profitability

Guidance: level 1

:: ::

_________ is a bundle of characteristics, including ways of thinking, feeling, and acting, which humans are said to have naturally. The term is often regarded as capturing what it is to be human, or the essence of humanity. The term is controversial because it is disputed whether or not such an essence exists. Arguments about _________ have been a mainstay of philosophy for centuries and the concept continues to provoke lively philosophical debate. The concept also continues to play a role in science, with neuroscientists, psychologists and social scientists sometimes claiming that their results have yielded insight into _________ . _________ is traditionally contrasted with characteristics that vary among humans, such as characteristics associated with specific cultures. Debates about _________ are related to, although not the same as, debates about the comparative importance of genes and environment in development .

Exam Probability: **Medium**

33. *Answer choices:*

(see index for correct answer)

- a. interpersonal communication
- b. Sarbanes-Oxley act of 2002
- c. similarity-attraction theory
- d. cultural

Guidance: level 1

:: Real estate ::

_________ s serve several societal needs – primarily as shelter from weather, security, living space, privacy, to store belongings, and to comfortably live and work. A _________ as a shelter represents a physical division of the human habitat and the outside .

Exam Probability: **High**

34. *Answer choices:*

(see index for correct answer)

- a. Lease and release
- b. Building
- c. Monotenure

- d. Rent control in the United States

Guidance: level 1

:: Confidence tricks ::

A __________ is a business model that recruits members via a promise of payments or services for enrolling others into the scheme, rather than supplying investments or sale of products. As recruiting multiplies, recruiting becomes quickly impossible, and most members are unable to profit; as such, __________ s are unsustainable and often illegal.

Exam Probability: **Medium**

35. *Answer choices:*

(see index for correct answer)

- a. Black money scam
- b. Gem scam
- c. Great Oil Sniffer Hoax
- d. Pyramid scheme

Guidance: level 1

:: ::

A __________ is a set of rules, often written, with regards to clothing. __________ s are created out of social perceptions and norms, and vary based on purpose, circumstances and occasions. Different societies and cultures are likely to have different __________ s.

Exam Probability: **Low**

36. *Answer choices:*

(see index for correct answer)

- a. Dress code
- b. process perspective
- c. Sarbanes-Oxley act of 2002
- d. co-culture

Guidance: level 1

:: Business law ::

A _________ is an arrangement where parties, known as partners, agree to cooperate to advance their mutual interests. The partners in a _________ may be individuals, businesses, interest-based organizations, schools, governments or combinations. Organizations may partner to increase the likelihood of each achieving their mission and to amplify their reach. A _________ may result in issuing and holding equity or may be only governed by a contract.

Exam Probability: **Low**

37. *Answer choices:*
(see index for correct answer)

- a. Articles of partnership
- b. Financial Security Law of France
- c. Uniform Commercial Code
- d. Partnership

Guidance: level 1

:: Types of marketing ::

_________ is an advertisement strategy in which a company uses surprise and/or unconventional interactions in order to promote a product or service. It is a type of publicity. The term was popularized by Jay Conrad Levinson`s 1984 book _________ .

Exam Probability: **Medium**

38. *Answer choices:*
(see index for correct answer)

- a. Secret brand
- b. Customerization
- c. Project SCUM
- d. Guerrilla Marketing

Guidance: level 1

:: Product certification ::

__________ is food produced by methods that comply with the standards of organic farming. Standards vary worldwide, but organic farming features practices that cycle resources, promote ecological balance, and conserve biodiversity. Organizations regulating organic products may restrict the use of certain pesticides and fertilizers in the farming methods used to produce such products. __________ s typically are not processed using irradiation, industrial solvents, or synthetic food additives.

Exam Probability: **Medium**

39. *Answer choices:*
(see index for correct answer)

- a. SAI Global
- b. Organic food
- c. Clerk of works
- d. Organic Crop Improvement Association

Guidance: level 1

:: ::

__________ is the collection of mechanisms, processes and relations by which corporations are controlled and operated. Governance structures and principles identify the distribution of rights and responsibilities among different participants in the corporation and include the rules and procedures for making decisions in corporate affairs. __________ is necessary because of the possibility of conflicts of interests between stakeholders, primarily between shareholders and upper management or among shareholders.

Exam Probability: **Low**

40. *Answer choices:*
(see index for correct answer)

- a. information systems assessment
- b. Corporate governance
- c. co-culture
- d. hierarchical

Guidance: level 1

:: Anti-Revisionism ::

_________ , officially the German Democratic Republic , was a country that existed from 1949 to 1990, when the eastern portion of Germany was part of the Eastern Bloc during the Cold War. It described itself as a socialist "workers` and peasants` state", and the territory was administered and occupied by Soviet forces at the end of World War II — the Soviet Occupation Zone of the Potsdam Agreement, bounded on the east by the Oder–Neisse line. The Soviet zone surrounded West Berlin but did not include it; as a result, West Berlin remained outside the jurisdiction of the GDR.

Exam Probability: **Medium**

41. *Answer choices:*
(see index for correct answer)

- a. Ho Chi Minh Thought
- b. Party of Labour of Albania
- c. Anti-Revisionism
- d. East Germany

Guidance: level 1

:: Euthenics ::

_________ is an ethical framework and suggests that an entity, be it an organization or individual, has an obligation to act for the benefit of society at large. _________ is a duty every individual has to perform so as to maintain a balance between the economy and the ecosystems. A trade-off may exist between economic development, in the material sense, and the welfare of the society and environment, though this has been challenged by many reports over the past decade. _________ means sustaining the equilibrium between the two. It pertains not only to business organizations but also to everyone whose any action impacts the environment. This responsibility can be passive, by avoiding engaging in socially harmful acts, or active, by performing activities that directly advance social goals. _________ must be intergenerational since the actions of one generation have consequences on those following.

Exam Probability: **Medium**

42. *Answer choices:*
(see index for correct answer)

- a. Social responsibility
- b. Minnie Cumnock Blodgett

- c. Euthenics
- d. Family and consumer science

Guidance: level 1

:: ::

The _________ , the Calvinist work ethic or the Puritan work ethic is a work ethic concept in theology, sociology, economics and history that emphasizes that hard work, discipline and frugality are a result of a person`s subscription to the values espoused by the Protestant faith, particularly Calvinism. The phrase was initially coined in 1904–1905 by Max Weber in his book The Protestant Ethic and the Spirit of Capitalism.

Exam Probability: **Medium**

43. *Answer choices:*

(see index for correct answer)

- a. interpersonal communication
- b. functional perspective
- c. Protestant work ethic
- d. Character

Guidance: level 1

:: Competition regulators ::

The _________ is an independent agency of the United States government, established in 1914 by the _________ Act. Its principal mission is the promotion of consumer protection and the elimination and prevention of anticompetitive business practices, such as coercive monopoly. It is headquartered in the _________ Building in Washington, D.C.

Exam Probability: **Medium**

44. *Answer choices:*

(see index for correct answer)

- a. Competition Authority
- b. Superintendency of Industry and Commerce
- c. Commerce Commission
- d. Federal Trade Commission

Guidance: level 1

:: Anti-competitive behaviour ::

__________ is a secret cooperation or deceitful agreement in order to deceive others, although not necessarily illegal, as a conspiracy. A secret agreement between two or more parties to limit open competition by deceiving, misleading, or defrauding others of their legal rights, or to obtain an objective forbidden by law typically by defrauding or gaining an unfair market advantage is an example of __________ . It is an agreement among firms or individuals to divide a market, set prices, limit production or limit opportunities.It can involve "unions, wage fixing, kickbacks, or misrepresenting the independence of the relationship between the colluding parties". In legal terms, all acts effected by __________ are considered void.

Exam Probability: **Low**

45. *Answer choices:*

(see index for correct answer)

- a. Collusion
- b. Exclusive dealing
- c. Bid rigging
- d. Institute for Consumer Antitrust Studies

Guidance: level 1

:: ::

MCI, Inc. was an American telecommunication corporation, currently a subsidiary of Verizon Communications, with its main office in Ashburn, Virginia. The corporation was formed originally as a result of the merger of __________ and MCI Communications corporations, and used the name MCI __________ , succeeded by __________ , before changing its name to the present version on April 12, 2003, as part of the corporation`s ending of its bankruptcy status. The company traded on NASDAQ as WCOM and MCIP . The corporation was purchased by Verizon Communications with the deal finalizing on January 6, 2006, and is now identified as that company`s Verizon Enterprise Solutions division with the local residential divisions being integrated slowly into local Verizon subsidiaries.

Exam Probability: **Medium**

46. *Answer choices:*
(see index for correct answer)

- a. WorldCom
- b. personal values
- c. surface-level diversity
- d. deep-level diversity

Guidance: level 1

:: Auditing ::

__________ is a general term that can reflect various types of evaluations intended to identify environmental compliance and management system implementation gaps, along with related corrective actions. In this way they perform an analogous function to financial audits. There are generally two different types of __________ s: compliance audits and management systems audits. Compliance audits tend to be the primary type in the US or within US-based multinationals.

Exam Probability: **High**

47. *Answer choices:*
(see index for correct answer)

- a. Environmental audit
- b. Technical audit
- c. Audit management
- d. Management representation

Guidance: level 1

:: ::

The __________ was a severe worldwide economic depression that took place mostly during the 1930s, beginning in the United States. The timing of the __________ varied across nations; in most countries it started in 1929 and lasted until the late-1930s. It was the longest, deepest, and most widespread depression of the 20th century. In the 21st century, the __________ is commonly used as an example of how intensely the world`s economy can decline.

Exam Probability: **Low**

48. *Answer choices:*

(see index for correct answer)

- a. similarity-attraction theory
- b. Great Depression
- c. cultural
- d. surface-level diversity

Guidance: level 1

:: Private equity ::

In finance, a high-yield bond is a bond that is rated below investment grade. These bonds have a higher risk of default or other adverse credit events, but typically pay higher yields than better quality bonds in order to make them attractive to investors.

Exam Probability: **High**

49. *Answer choices:*

(see index for correct answer)

- a. Special purpose private equity fund
- b. Business Development Company
- c. Junk bond
- d. Super angel

Guidance: level 1

:: Cultural appropriation ::

__________ is a social and economic order that encourages the acquisition of goods and services in ever-increasing amounts. With the industrial revolution, but particularly in the 20th century, mass production led to an economic crisis: there was overproduction—the supply of goods would grow beyond consumer demand, and so manufacturers turned to planned obsolescence and advertising to manipulate consumer spending. In 1899, a book on _________ published by Thorstein Veblen, called The Theory of the Leisure Class, examined the widespread values and economic institutions emerging along with the widespread "leisure time" in the beginning of the 20th century. In it Veblen "views the activities and spending habits of this leisure class in terms of conspicuous and vicarious consumption and waste. Both are related to the display of status and not to functionality or usefulness."

Exam Probability: **High**

50. *Answer choices:*

(see index for correct answer)

- a. Aunt Jemima
- b. Consumerism
- c. Washington Redskins
- d. Jynx

Guidance: level 1

:: Business ethics ::

__________ is a type of international private business self-regulation. While once it was possible to describe CSR as an internal organisational policy or a corporate ethic strategy, that time has passed as various international laws have been developed and various organisations have used their authority to push it beyond individual or even industry-wide initiatives. While it has been considered a form of corporate self-regulation for some time, over the last decade or so it has moved considerably from voluntary decisions at the level of individual organisations, to mandatory schemes at regional, national and even transnational levels.

Exam Probability: **Medium**

51. *Answer choices:*

(see index for correct answer)

- a. Corporate social responsibility
- b. MBA Oath
- c. Interfaith Center on Corporate Responsibility
- d. Precarity

Guidance: level 1

:: Dutch inventions ::

The Fairtrade certification initiative was created to form a new method for economic trade. This method takes an ethical standpoint, and considers the producers first.

Exam Probability: **Low**

52. *Answer choices:*

(see index for correct answer)

- a. Dijkstra's algorithm
- b. Fairtrade

Guidance: level 1

:: Coal ::

__________ is a combustible black or brownish-black sedimentary rock, formed as rock strata called __________ seams. __________ is mostly carbon with variable amounts of other elements; chiefly hydrogen, sulfur, oxygen, and nitrogen. __________ is formed if dead plant matter decays into peat and over millions of years the heat and pressure of deep burial converts the peat into __________ . Vast deposits of __________ originates in former wetlands—called __________ forests—that covered much of the Earth`s tropical land areas during the late Carboniferous and Permian times.

Exam Probability: **High**

53. *Answer choices:*

(see index for correct answer)

- a. Carbolineum
- b. Albertite
- c. Coal
- d. Coldry Process

Guidance: level 1

:: Labour relations ::

__________ is a field of study that can have different meanings depending on the context in which it is used. In an international context, it is a subfield of labor history that studies the human relations with regard to work – in its broadest sense – and how this connects to questions of social inequality. It explicitly encompasses unregulated, historical, and non-Western forms of labor. Here, __________ define "for or with whom one works and under what rules. These rules determine the type of work, type and amount of remuneration, working hours, degrees of physical and psychological strain, as well as the degree of freedom and autonomy associated with the work."

Exam Probability: **Medium**

54. *Answer choices:*
(see index for correct answer)

- a. Union Wallonne des Entreprises
- b. Labor relations
- c. Negotiated cartelism
- d. Impasse

Guidance: level 1

:: ::

_________ , O.S.A. was a German professor of theology, composer, priest, monk, and a seminal figure in the Protestant Reformation.

Exam Probability: **High**

55. *Answer choices:*
(see index for correct answer)

- a. similarity-attraction theory
- b. Character
- c. Martin Luther
- d. open system

Guidance: level 1

:: ::

_________ was a philosopher during the Classical period in Ancient Greece, the founder of the Lyceum and the Peripatetic school of philosophy and Aristotelian tradition. Along with his teacher Plato, he is considered the "Father of Western Philosophy". His writings cover many subjects – including physics, biology, zoology, metaphysics, logic, ethics, aesthetics, poetry, theatre, music, rhetoric, psychology, linguistics, economics, politics and government. _________ provided a complex synthesis of the various philosophies existing prior to him, and it was above all from his teachings that the West inherited its intellectual lexicon, as well as problems and methods of inquiry. As a result, his philosophy has exerted a unique influence on almost every form of knowledge in the West and it continues to be a subject of contemporary philosophical discussion.

Exam Probability: **Low**

56. *Answer choices:*
(see index for correct answer)

- a. co-culture
- b. Sarbanes-Oxley act of 2002
- c. deep-level diversity
- d. process perspective

Guidance: level 1

:: ::

A _________ is a proceeding by a party or parties against another in the civil court of law.The archaic term "suit in law" is found in only a small number of laws still in effect today.The term " _________ " is used in reference to a civil action brought in a court of law in which a plaintiff, a party who claims to have incurred loss as a result of a defendant`s actions, demands a legal or equitable remedy. The defendant is required to respond to the plaintiff`s complaint. If the plaintiff is successful, judgment is in the plaintiff`s favor, and a variety of court orders may be issued to enforce a right, award damages, or impose a temporary or permanent injunction to prevent an act or compel an act. A declaratory judgment may be issued to prevent future legal disputes.

Exam Probability: **Medium**

57. *Answer choices:*
(see index for correct answer)

- a. open system
- b. deep-level diversity
- c. hierarchical perspective
- d. co-culture

Guidance: level 1

:: Fraud ::

In law, _________ is intentional deception to secure unfair or unlawful gain, or to deprive a victim of a legal right. _________ can violate civil law , a criminal law , or it may cause no loss of money, property or legal right but still be an element of another civil or criminal wrong. The purpose of _________ may be monetary gain or other benefits, for example by obtaining a passport, travel document, or driver`s license, or mortgage _________ , where the perpetrator may attempt to qualify for a mortgage by way of false statements.

Exam Probability: **Low**

58. *Answer choices:*

(see index for correct answer)

- a. Welfare queen
- b. Lip-synching in music
- c. Wine fraud
- d. Fraud

Guidance: level 1

:: Mortgage ::

In finance, _________ means making loans to people who may have difficulty maintaining the repayment schedule, sometimes reflecting setbacks, such as unemployment, divorce, medical emergencies, etc. Historically, subprime borrowers were defined as having FICO scores below 600, although "this has varied over time and circumstances."

Exam Probability: **Low**

59. *Answer choices:*

(see index for correct answer)

- a. Variable-rate mortgage
- b. Australian mortgage
- c. Subprime lending
- d. Higher lending charge

Guidance: level 1

Accounting

Accounting or accountancy is the measurement, processing, and communication of financial information about economic entities such as businesses and corporations. The modern field was established by the Italian mathematician Luca Pacioli in 1494. Accounting, which has been called the "language of business", measures the results of an organization's economic activities and conveys this information to a variety of users, including investors, creditors, management, and regulators.

:: Commerce ::

A _________ , is a document acknowledging that a person has received money or property in payment following a sale or other transfer of goods or provision of a service. All _________ s must have the date of purchase on them. If the recipient of the payment is legally required to collect sales tax or VAT from the customer, the amount would be added to the _________ and the collection would be deemed to have been on behalf of the relevant tax authority. In many countries, a retailer is required to include the sales tax or VAT in the displayed price of goods sold, from which the tax amount would be calculated at point of sale and remitted to the tax authorities in due course. Similarly, amounts may be deducted from amounts payable, as in the case of wage withholding taxes. On the other hand, tips or other gratuities given by a customer, for example in a restaurant, would not form part of the payment amount or appear on the _________ .

Exam Probability: **Low**

1. *Answer choices:*

(see index for correct answer)

- a. Bidding
- b. Export restriction
- c. Receipt

- d. Card association

Guidance: level 1

:: Financial ratios ::

In finance, the _________ , also known as the acid-test ratio is a type of liquidity ratio which measures the ability of a company to use its near cash or quick assets to extinguish or retire its current liabilities immediately. Quick assets include those current assets that presumably can be quickly converted to cash at close to their book values. It is the ratio between quickly available or liquid assets and current liabilities.

Exam Probability: **Medium**

2. *Answer choices:*

(see index for correct answer)

- a. Theoretical ex-rights price
- b. Net interest income
- c. Beta
- d. Quick ratio

Guidance: level 1

:: Accounting systems ::

In bookkeeping, a _________ statement is a process that explains the difference on a specified date between the bank balance shown in an organization`s bank statement, as supplied by the bank and the corresponding amount shown in the organization`s own accounting records.

Exam Probability: **Medium**

3. *Answer choices:*

(see index for correct answer)

- a. Standard accounting practice
- b. Invoice processing
- c. Bank reconciliation
- d. Inflation accounting

Guidance: level 1

:: ::

__________ is a means of protection from financial loss. It is a form of risk management, primarily used to hedge against the risk of a contingent or uncertain loss

Exam Probability: **Low**

4. *Answer choices:*
(see index for correct answer)

- a. corporate values
- b. information systems assessment
- c. cultural
- d. Insurance

Guidance: level 1

:: Information systems ::

__________ are formal, sociotechnical, organizational systems designed to collect, process, store, and distribute information. In a sociotechnical perspective, __________ are composed by four components: task, people, structure , and technology.

Exam Probability: **Low**

5. *Answer choices:*
(see index for correct answer)

- a. Information systems
- b. E-GMS
- c. Information engineering
- d. Semantic broker

Guidance: level 1

:: ::

_________ is the collection of mechanisms, processes and relations by which corporations are controlled and operated. Governance structures and principles identify the distribution of rights and responsibilities among different participants in the corporation and include the rules and procedures for making decisions in corporate affairs. _________ is necessary because of the possibility of conflicts of interests between stakeholders, primarily between shareholders and upper management or among shareholders.

Exam Probability: **Low**

6. *Answer choices:*

(see index for correct answer)

- a. hierarchical
- b. Corporate governance
- c. cultural
- d. corporate values

Guidance: level 1

:: Generally Accepted Accounting Principles ::

In accounting, _________ , gross margin, sales profit, or credit sales is the difference between revenue and the cost of making a product or providing a service, before deducting overheads, payroll, taxation, and interest payments. This is different from operating profit . Gross margin is the term normally used in the U.S., while _________ is the more common usage in the UK and Australia.

Exam Probability: **High**

7. *Answer choices:*

(see index for correct answer)

- a. Earnings before interest, taxes and depreciation
- b. Indian Accounting Standards
- c. Vendor-specific objective evidence
- d. Gross profit

Guidance: level 1

:: Payment systems ::

A __________ is a bond of the redeemable transaction type which is worth a certain monetary value and which may be spent only for specific reasons or on specific goods. Examples include housing, travel, and food __________ s. The term __________ is also a synonym for receipt and is often used to refer to receipts used as evidence of, for example, the declaration that a service has been performed or that an expenditure has been made. __________ is a tourist guide for using services with a guarantee of payment by the agency.

Exam Probability: **Low**

8. *Answer choices:*

(see index for correct answer)

- a. Net Element
- b. Adyen
- c. Voucher
- d. M-Pesa

Guidance: level 1

:: ::

The __________ is an American stock exchange located at 11 Wall Street, Lower Manhattan, New York City, New York. It is by far the world`s largest stock exchange by market capitalization of its listed companies at US$30.1 trillion as of February 2018. The average daily trading value was approximately US$169 billion in 2013. The NYSE trading floor is located at 11 Wall Street and is composed of 21 rooms used for the facilitation of trading. A fifth trading room, located at 30 Broad Street, was closed in February 2007. The main building and the 11 Wall Street building were designated National Historic Landmarks in 1978.

Exam Probability: **Medium**

9. *Answer choices:*

(see index for correct answer)

- a. open system
- b. empathy
- c. New York Stock Exchange
- d. surface-level diversity

Guidance: level 1

:: Basic financial concepts ::

In finance, maturity or _________ refers to the final payment date of a loan or other financial instrument, at which point the principal is due to be paid.

Exam Probability: **Medium**

10. *Answer choices:*

(see index for correct answer)

- a. Eurodollar
- b. Lodgement
- c. Tax shield
- d. Future-oriented

Guidance: level 1

:: Financial ratios ::

The _________ is a financial ratio indicating the relative proportion of shareholders` equity and debt used to finance a company`s assets. Closely related to leveraging, the ratio is also known as risk, gearing or leverage. The two components are often taken from the firm`s balance sheet or statement of financial position , but the ratio may also be calculated using market values for both, if the company`s debt and equity are publicly traded, or using a combination of book value for debt and market value for equity financially.

Exam Probability: **Medium**

11. *Answer choices:*

(see index for correct answer)

- a. Operating ratio
- b. Sustainable growth rate
- c. Debt-to-equity ratio
- d. return on invested capital

Guidance: level 1

:: ::

The __________ or just chief executive , is the most senior corporate, executive, or administrative officer in charge of managing an organization especially an independent legal entity such as a company or nonprofit institution. CEOs lead a range of organizations, including public and private corporations, non-profit organizations and even some government organizations . The CEO of a corporation or company typically reports to the board of directors and is charged with maximizing the value of the entity, which may include maximizing the share price, market share, revenues or another element. In the non-profit and government sector, CEOs typically aim at achieving outcomes related to the organization`s mission, such as reducing poverty, increasing literacy, etc.

Exam Probability: **High**

12. *Answer choices:*
(see index for correct answer)

- a. information systems assessment
- b. process perspective
- c. Chief executive officer
- d. personal values

Guidance: level 1

:: Management accounting ::

__________ is a professional certification credential in the management accounting and financial management fields. The certification signifies that the person possesses knowledge in the areas of financial planning, analysis, control, decision support, and professional ethics. The CMA is a U.S.-based, globally recognized certification offered by the Institute of Management Accountants.

Exam Probability: **High**

13. *Answer choices:*
(see index for correct answer)

- a. Certified Management Accountant
- b. Variable cost
- c. Double counting
- d. Direct material usage variance

Guidance: level 1

:: Inventory ::

Costs are associated with particular goods using one of the several formulas, including specific identification, first-in first-out , or average cost. Costs include all costs of purchase, costs of conversion and other costs that are incurred in bringing the inventories to their present location and condition. Costs of goods made by the businesses include material, labor, and allocated overhead. The costs of those goods which are not yet sold are deferred as costs of inventory until the inventory is sold or written down in value.

Exam Probability: **Low**

14. *Answer choices:*
(see index for correct answer)

- a. Reorder point
- b. Stock-taking
- c. Cost of goods sold
- d. just-in-time manufacturing

Guidance: level 1

:: Accounting ::

__________ is the recording of financial transactions, and is part of the process of accounting in business. Transactions include purchases, sales, receipts, and payments by an individual person or an organization/corporation. There are several standard methods of __________ , including the single-entry and double-entry __________ systems. While these may be viewed as "real" __________ , any process for recording financial transactions is a __________ process.

Exam Probability: **Low**

15. *Answer choices:*
(see index for correct answer)

- a. Maker-checker
- b. Efficiency-based absorption costing
- c. Pipeline planning
- d. Bookkeeping

Guidance: level 1

:: Competition (economics) ::

In taxation and accounting, _________ refers to the rules and methods for pricing transactions within and between enterprises under common ownership or control. Because of the potential for cross-border controlled transactions to distort taxable income, tax authorities in many countries can adjust intragroup transfer prices that differ from what would have been charged by unrelated enterprises dealing at arm's length . The OECD and World Bank recommend intragroup pricing rules based on the arm's-length principle, and 19 of the 20 members of the G20 have adopted similar measures through bilateral treaties and domestic legislation, regulations, or administrative practice. Countries with _________ legislation generally follow the OECD _________ Guidelines for Multinational Enterprises and Tax Administrations in most respects, although their rules can differ on some important details.

Exam Probability: **Medium**

16. *Answer choices:*

(see index for correct answer)

- a. Level playing field
- b. Blindspots analysis
- c. Economic forces
- d. Competition

Guidance: level 1

:: ::

A tax is a compulsory financial charge or some other type of levy imposed upon a taxpayer by a governmental organization in order to fund various public expenditures. A failure to pay, along with evasion of or resistance to _________ , is punishable by law. Taxes consist of direct or indirect taxes and may be paid in money or as its labour equivalent.

Exam Probability: **Medium**

17. *Answer choices:*

(see index for correct answer)

- a. deep-level diversity
- b. hierarchical perspective
- c. surface-level diversity
- d. Taxation

Guidance: level 1

:: Shareholders ::

A __________ is a payment made by a corporation to its shareholders, usually as a distribution of profits. When a corporation earns a profit or surplus, the corporation is able to re-invest the profit in the business and pay a proportion of the profit as a __________ to shareholders. Distribution to shareholders may be in cash or, if the corporation has a __________ reinvestment plan, the amount can be paid by the issue of further shares or share repurchase. When __________s are paid, shareholders typically must pay income taxes, and the corporation does not receive a corporate income tax deduction for the __________ payments.

Exam Probability: **Low**

18. *Answer choices:*

(see index for correct answer)

- a. Dividend
- b. Derivative suit
- c. Activist shareholder
- d. Proxy statement

Guidance: level 1

:: Mathematical finance ::

In economics and finance, _________ , also known as present discounted value, is the value of an expected income stream determined as of the date of valuation. The _________ is always less than or equal to the future value because money has interest-earning potential, a characteristic referred to as the time value of money, except during times of negative interest rates, when the _________ will be more than the future value. Time value can be described with the simplified phrase, "A dollar today is worth more than a dollar tomorrow". Here, `worth more` means that its value is greater. A dollar today is worth more than a dollar tomorrow because the dollar can be invested and earn a day`s worth of interest, making the total accumulate to a value more than a dollar by tomorrow. Interest can be compared to rent. Just as rent is paid to a landlord by a tenant without the ownership of the asset being transferred, interest is paid to a lender by a borrower who gains access to the money for a time before paying it back. By letting the borrower have access to the money, the lender has sacrificed the exchange value of this money, and is compensated for it in the form of interest. The initial amount of the borrowed funds is less than the total amount of money paid to the lender.

Exam Probability: **Medium**

19. *Answer choices:*

(see index for correct answer)

- a. Present value
- b. Modified Dietz method
- c. Volatility smile
- d. Frictionless market

Guidance: level 1

:: Corporations law ::

_________ , also referred to as the certificate of incorporation or the corporate charter, are a document or charter that establishes the existence of a corporation in the United States and Canada. They generally are filed with the Secretary of State or other company registrar.

Exam Probability: **Low**

20. *Answer choices:*

(see index for correct answer)

- a. Memorandum of association
- b. Drag-along right
- c. Corporate structure
- d. Benihana of Tokyo, Inc. v. Benihana, Inc.

Guidance: level 1

:: Bonds (finance) ::

A _________ is a fund established by an economic entity by setting aside revenue over a period of time to fund a future capital expense, or repayment of a long-term debt.

Exam Probability: **High**

21. *Answer choices:*

(see index for correct answer)

- a. Luxembourg Depositary Receipt
- b. Sinking fund
- c. Covered bond
- d. Exchange offer

Guidance: level 1

:: Accounting in the United States ::

The _________ is a private-sector, nonprofit corporation created by the Sarbanes–Oxley Act of 2002 to oversee the audits of public companies and other issuers in order to protect the interests of investors and further the public interest in the preparation of informative, accurate and independent audit reports. The PCAOB also oversees the audits of broker-dealers, including compliance reports filed pursuant to federal securities laws, to promote investor protection. All PCAOB rules and standards must be approved by the U.S. Securities and Exchange Commission .

Exam Probability: **High**

22. *Answer choices:*

(see index for correct answer)

- a. Association of Certified Fraud Examiners
- b. Other postemployment benefits
- c. Public Company Accounting Oversight Board
- d. Accounting Today

Guidance: level 1

:: Management accounting ::

In _________ or managerial accounting, managers use the provisions of accounting information in order to better inform themselves before they decide matters within their organizations, which aids their management and performance of control functions.

Exam Probability: **Medium**

23. *Answer choices:*

(see index for correct answer)

- a. Resource consumption accounting
- b. Management accounting
- c. Variable Costing
- d. Direct material usage variance

Guidance: level 1

:: Generally Accepted Accounting Principles ::

Expenditure is an outflow of money to another person or group to pay for an item or service, or for a category of costs. For a tenant, rent is an _________ . For students or parents, tuition is an _________ . Buying food, clothing, furniture or an automobile is often referred to as an _________ . An _________ is a cost that is "paid" or "remitted", usually in exchange for something of value. Something that seems to cost a great deal is "expensive". Something that seems to cost little is "inexpensive". " _________ s of the table" are _________ s of dining, refreshments, a feast, etc.

Exam Probability: **Low**

24. *Answer choices:*

(see index for correct answer)

- a. Expense
- b. Earnings before interest, taxes, depreciation, and amortization
- c. Pro forma
- d. Long-term liabilities

Guidance: level 1

:: Stock market ::

_________ is a form of corporate equity ownership, a type of security. The terms voting share and ordinary share are also used frequently in other parts of the world; " _________ " being primarily used in the United States. They are known as Equity shares or Ordinary shares in the UK and other Commonwealth realms. This type of share gives the stockholder the right to share in the profits of the company, and to vote on matters of corporate policy and the composition of the members of the board of directors.

Exam Probability: **Low**

25. *Answer choices:*
(see index for correct answer)

- a. Common stock
- b. Selling climax
- c. Leading stock
- d. House stock

Guidance: level 1

:: Legal terms ::

_________ is a state of prolonged public dispute or debate, usually concerning a matter of conflicting opinion or point of view. The word was coined from the Latin controversia, as a composite of controversus – "turned in an opposite direction," from contra – "against" – and vertere – to turn, or versus , hence, "to turn against."

Exam Probability: **Low**

26. *Answer choices:*
(see index for correct answer)

- a. Merger clause
- b. Misdemeanor
- c. Controversy
- d. Acceptance of responsibility

Guidance: level 1

:: Marketing ::

_________ or stock is the goods and materials that a business holds for the ultimate goal of resale .

Exam Probability: **Low**

27. *Answer choices:*

(see index for correct answer)

- a. Intent scale translation
- b. City marketing
- c. Marketing mix
- d. Lingerie party

Guidance: level 1

:: Generally Accepted Accounting Principles ::

An _________ or profit and loss account is one of the financial statements of a company and shows the company's revenues and expenses during a particular period.

Exam Probability: **Low**

28. *Answer choices:*

(see index for correct answer)

- a. Income statement
- b. Operating statement
- c. Management accounting principles
- d. Earnings before interest and taxes

Guidance: level 1

:: Expense ::

An _________ is the right to reimbursement of money spent by employees for work-related purposes. Some common _________ s are: administrative expense, amortization expense, bad debt expense, cost of goods sold, depreciation expense, freight-out, income tax expense, insurance expense, interest expense, loss on disposal of plant assets, maintenance and repairs expense, rent expense, salaries and wages expense, selling expense, supplies expense and utilities expense.

Exam Probability: **Medium**

29. *Answer choices:*

(see index for correct answer)

- a. Tax expense
- b. Corporate travel
- c. Stock option expensing
- d. Expense account

Guidance: level 1

:: Accounting in the United States ::

The _________ is the source of generally accepted accounting principles used by state and local governments in the United States. As with most of the entities involved in creating GAAP in the United States, it is a private, non-governmental organization.

Exam Probability: **High**

30. *Answer choices:*

(see index for correct answer)

- a. Legal liability of certified public accountants
- b. Governmental Accounting Standards Board
- c. Cotton Plantation Record and Account Book
- d. Accounting Principles Board

Guidance: level 1

:: ::

_________ is capital that is contributed to a corporation by investors by purchase of stock from the corporation, the primary market, not by purchase of stock in the open market from other stockholders . It includes share capital as well as additional _________ .

Exam Probability: **Medium**

31. *Answer choices:*

(see index for correct answer)

- a. open system
- b. process perspective
- c. Paid-in capital

- d. empathy

Guidance: level 1

:: Taxation and efficiency ::

_________ is the legal usage of the tax regime in a single territory to one`s own advantage to reduce the amount of tax that is payable by means that are within the law. Tax sheltering is very similar, although unlike _________ tax sheltering is not necessarily legal. Tax havens are jurisdictions which facilitate reduced taxes.

Exam Probability: **High**

32. *Answer choices:*

(see index for correct answer)

- a. Tax incentive
- b. supply-side
- c. Tax avoidance
- d. Tax advantage

Guidance: level 1

:: Management accounting ::

_________ is accounting which tracks the costs and revenues by "job" and enables standardized reporting of profitability by job. For an accounting system to support _________ , it must allow job numbers to be assigned to individual items of expenses and revenues. A job can be defined to be a specific project done for one customer, or a single unit of product manufactured, or a batch of units of the same type that are produced together.

Exam Probability: **Low**

33. *Answer choices:*

(see index for correct answer)

- a. Institute of Cost and Management Accountants of Bangladesh
- b. Contribution margin
- c. Job costing
- d. Chartered Institute of Management Accountants

Guidance: level 1

:: Hazard analysis ::

Broadly speaking, a _________ is the combined effort of 1. identifying and analyzing potential events that may negatively impact individuals, assets, and/or the environment ; and 2. making judgments "on the tolerability of the risk on the basis of a risk analysis" while considering influencing factors . Put in simpler terms, a _________ analyzes what can go wrong, how likely it is to happen, what the potential consequences are, and how tolerable the identified risk is. As part of this process, the resulting determination of risk may be expressed in a quantitative or qualitative fashion. The _________ is an inherent part of an overall risk management strategy, which attempts to, after a _________ , "introduce control measures to eliminate or reduce" any potential risk-related consequences.

Exam Probability: **Low**

34. *Answer choices:*

(see index for correct answer)

- a. Risk assessment
- b. Swiss cheese model
- c. Hazard identification
- d. Hazardous Materials Identification System

Guidance: level 1

:: Taxation ::

_________ is a type of tax law that allows a person to give assets to his or her spouse with reduced or no tax imposed upon the transfer. Some _________ laws even apply to transfers made postmortem. The right to receive property conveys ownership for tax purposes. A decree of divorce transfers the right to that property by reason of the marriage and is also a transfer within a marriage. It makes no difference whether the property itself or equivalent compensation is transferred before, or after the decree dissolves the marriage. There is no U.S. estate and gift tax on transfers of any amount between spouses, whether during their lifetime or at death. There is an important exceptions for non-citizens. The U.S. federal Estate and gift tax _________ is only available if the surviving spouse is a U.S. citizen. For a surviving spouse who is not a U.S. citizen a bequest through a Qualified Domestic Trust defers estate tax until principal is distributed by the trustee, a U.S. citizen or corporation who also withholds the estate tax. Income on principal distributed to the surviving spouse is taxed as individual income. If the surviving spouse becomes a U.S. citizen, principal remaining in a Qualifying Domestic Trust may then be distributed without further tax.

Exam Probability: **Low**

35. *Answer choices:*

(see index for correct answer)

- a. Marital deduction
- b. Suits index
- c. Hotchpot
- d. Fiscal drag

Guidance: level 1

:: Accounting in the United States ::

_________ were documents issued by the Committee on Accounting Procedure between 1938 and 1959 on various accounting problems. They were discontinued with the dissolution of the Committee in 1959 under a recommendation from the Special Committee on Research Program. In all, 17 bulletins were issued; however, the lack of binding authority over AICPA`s membership reduced the influence of, and compliance with the content of the bulletins. The _________ have all been superseded by the Accounting Standards Codification .

Exam Probability: **High**

36. *Answer choices:*
(see index for correct answer)

- a. National Association of State Boards of Accountancy
- b. Beta Alpha Psi
- c. Certified Government Financial Manager
- d. Accounting Research Bulletins

Guidance: level 1

:: Generally Accepted Accounting Principles ::

_________ s is an accounting term that refers to groups of accounts serving to express the cost of goods and service allocatable within a business or manufacturing organization. The principle behind the pool is to correlate direct and indirect costs with a specified cost driver, so to find out the total sum of expenses related to the manufacture of a product.

Exam Probability: **Medium**

37. *Answer choices:*
(see index for correct answer)

- a. Cost pool
- b. Cost principle
- c. AICPA Statements of Position
- d. Petty cash

Guidance: level 1

:: Stock market ::

A _________ , equity market or share market is the aggregation of buyers and sellers of stocks , which represent ownership claims on businesses; these may include securities listed on a public stock exchange, as well as stock that is only traded privately. Examples of the latter include shares of private companies which are sold to investors through equity crowdfunding platforms. Stock exchanges list shares of common equity as well as other security types, e.g. corporate bonds and convertible bonds.

Exam Probability: **Medium**

38. *Answer choices:*
(see index for correct answer)

- a. Prime Standard
- b. Indirect finance
- c. Matchbook FX
- d. Penny stock

Guidance: level 1

:: Accounting terminology ::

_________ is an independent, objective assurance and consulting activity designed to add value to and improve an organization's operations. It helps an organization accomplish its objectives by bringing a systematic, disciplined approach to evaluate and improve the effectiveness of risk management, control and governance processes. _________ achieves this by providing insight and recommendations based on analyses and assessments of data and business processes. With commitment to integrity and accountability, _________ provides value to governing bodies and senior management as an objective source of independent advice. Professionals called internal auditors are employed by organizations to perform the _________ activity.

Exam Probability: **High**

39. *Answer choices:*

(see index for correct answer)

- a. Internal auditing
- b. Record to report
- c. revenue recognition principle
- d. Enterprise liquidity

Guidance: level 1

:: ::

The _________ of 1934 is a law governing the secondary trading of securities in the United States of America. A landmark of wide-ranging legislation, the Act of '34 and related statutes form the basis of regulation of the financial markets and their participants in the United States. The 1934 Act also established the Securities and Exchange Commission , the agency primarily responsible for enforcement of United States federal securities law.

Exam Probability: **Medium**

40. *Answer choices:*
(see index for correct answer)

- a. corporate values
- b. open system
- c. Sarbanes-Oxley act of 2002
- d. Securities Exchange Act

Guidance: level 1

:: Generally Accepted Accounting Principles ::

_________ , also referred to as the bottom line, net income, or net earnings is a measure of the profitability of a venture after accounting for all costs and taxes. It is the actual profit, and includes the operating expenses that are excluded from gross profit.

Exam Probability: **Medium**

41. *Answer choices:*
(see index for correct answer)

- a. Goodwill
- b. Access to finance
- c. Deprival value
- d. Consolidation

Guidance: level 1

:: Finance ::

The _________ of a corporation is the accumulated net income of the corporation that is retained by the corporation at a particular point of time, such as at the end of the reporting period. At the end of that period, the net income at that point is transferred from the Profit and Loss Account to the _________ account. If the balance of the _________ account is negative it may be called accumulated losses, retained losses or accumulated deficit, or similar terminology.

Exam Probability: **High**

42. *Answer choices:*
(see index for correct answer)

- a. In-house lending

- b. Retained earnings
- c. Asset-backed commercial paper program
- d. Mohatra contract

Guidance: level 1

:: ::

A __________ is an entity that owes a debt to another entity. The entity may be an individual, a firm, a government, a company or other legal person. The counterparty is called a creditor. When the counterpart of this debt arrangement is a bank, the __________ is more often referred to as a borrower.

Exam Probability: **High**

43. *Answer choices:*

(see index for correct answer)

- a. hierarchical
- b. surface-level diversity
- c. functional perspective
- d. Debtor

Guidance: level 1

:: Generally Accepted Accounting Principles ::

The __________ principle is a cornerstone of accrual accounting together with the matching principle. They both determine the accounting period in which revenues and expenses are recognized. According to the principle, revenues are recognized when they are realized or realizable, and are earned , no matter when cash is received. In cash accounting – in contrast – revenues are recognized when cash is received no matter when goods or services are sold.

Exam Probability: **Low**

44. *Answer choices:*

(see index for correct answer)

- a. Revenue recognition
- b. Generally accepted accounting principles
- c. Long-term liabilities
- d. Profit

Guidance: level 1

:: Money ::

In economics, _________ is money in the physical form of currency, such as banknotes and coins. In bookkeeping and finance, _________ is current assets comprising currency or currency equivalents that can be accessed immediately or near-immediately . _________ is seen either as a reserve for payments, in case of a structural or incidental negative _________ flow or as a way to avoid a downturn on financial markets.

Exam Probability: **High**

45. *Answer choices:*

(see index for correct answer)

- a. Limping bimetallism
- b. Metallism
- c. Cash
- d. Leprosy colony money

Guidance: level 1

:: Tax law ::

_________ or revenue law is an area of legal study which deals with the constitutional, common-law, statutory, tax treaty, and regulatory rules that constitute the law applicable to taxation.

Exam Probability: **Low**

46. *Answer choices:*

(see index for correct answer)

- a. Tax Court of Canada
- b. Tax Law Rewrite Project
- c. Tax law
- d. De minimis fringe benefit

Guidance: level 1

:: Accounting ::

It is the period for which books are balanced and the financial statements are prepared. Generally, the _________ consists of 12 months. However the beginning of the _________ differs according to the jurisdiction. For example, one entity may follow the regular calendar year, i.e. January to December as the accounting year, while another entity may follow April to March as the _________ .

Exam Probability: **Low**

47. *Answer choices:*

(see index for correct answer)

- a. Merdiban
- b. Part exchange
- c. Accounting period
- d. amortisation

Guidance: level 1

:: Financial ratios ::

_________ is a measure of how revenue growth translates into growth in operating income. It is a measure of leverage, and of how risky, or volatile, a company`s operating income is.

Exam Probability: **High**

48. *Answer choices:*

(see index for correct answer)

- a. WHIS ratio
- b. Operating leverage
- c. Risk-adjusted return on capital
- d. Accounting rate of return

Guidance: level 1

:: Accounting ::

__________ examines how accounting is used by individuals, organizations and government as well as the consequences that these practices have. Starting from the assumption that accounting both measures and makes visible certain economic events, __________ has studied the roles of accounting in organizations and society and the consequences that these practices have for individuals, organizations, governments and capital markets. It encompasses a broad range of topics including financial __________ , management __________ , auditing research, capital market research, accountability research, social responsibility research and taxation research.

Exam Probability: **Low**

49. *Answer choices:*

(see index for correct answer)

- a. History of accounting
- b. Accounting research
- c. Clearing account
- d. Legal cashier

Guidance: level 1

:: Accounting terminology ::

__________ or capital expense is the money a company spends to buy, maintain, or improve its fixed assets, such as buildings, vehicles, equipment, or land. It is considered a __________ when the asset is newly purchased or when money is used towards extending the useful life of an existing asset, such as repairing the roof.

Exam Probability: **Low**

50. *Answer choices:*

(see index for correct answer)

- a. managerial accounting
- b. Enterprise liquidity
- c. Accounts payable
- d. Capital expenditure

Guidance: level 1

:: Banking ::

A _________ is a financial institution that accepts deposits from the public and creates credit. Lending activities can be performed either directly or indirectly through capital markets. Due to their importance in the financial stability of a country, _________ s are highly regulated in most countries. Most nations have institutionalized a system known as fractional reserve _________ ing under which _________ s hold liquid assets equal to only a portion of their current liabilities. In addition to other regulations intended to ensure liquidity, _________ s are generally subject to minimum capital requirements based on an international set of capital standards, known as the Basel Accords.

Exam Probability: **Low**

51. *Answer choices:*

(see index for correct answer)

- a. Bank
- b. Variance swap
- c. Land development bank
- d. Europeans for Financial Reform

Guidance: level 1

:: Business law ::

An _________ is a natural person, business, or corporation that provides goods or services to another entity under terms specified in a contract or within a verbal agreement. Unlike an employee, an _________ does not work regularly for an employer but works as and when required, during which time they may be subject to law of agency. _________ s are usually paid on a freelance basis. Contractors often work through a limited company or franchise, which they themselves own, or may work through an umbrella company.

Exam Probability: **Low**

52. *Answer choices:*

(see index for correct answer)

- a. Independent contractor
- b. Industrial relations
- c. Complex structured finance transactions
- d. Personal Property Security Act

Guidance: level 1

:: ::

_________ is the income that is gained by governments through taxation. Taxation is the primary source of income for a state. Revenue may be extracted from sources such as individuals, public enterprises, trade, royalties on natural resources and/or foreign aid. An inefficient collection of taxes is greater in countries characterized by poverty, a large agricultural sector and large amounts of foreign aid.

Exam Probability: **Medium**

53. *Answer choices:*

(see index for correct answer)

- a. surface-level diversity
- b. Tax revenue
- c. co-culture
- d. empathy

Guidance: level 1

:: United States federal income tax ::

Under United States tax law, the _________ is a dollar amount that non-itemizers may subtract from their income before income tax is applied. Taxpayers may choose either itemized deductions or the _________ , but usually choose whichever results in the lesser amount of tax payable. The _________ is available to US citizens and aliens who are resident for tax purposes and who are individuals, married persons, and heads of household. The _________ is based on filing status and typically increases each year. It is not available to nonresident aliens residing in the United States . Additional amounts are available for persons who are blind and/or are at least 65 years of age.

Exam Probability: **High**

54. *Answer choices:*

(see index for correct answer)

- a. Unicap
- b. Rabbi trust
- c. Standard deduction
- d. 1256 Contract

Guidance: level 1

:: Generally Accepted Accounting Principles ::

A __________ or reacquired stock is stock which is bought back by the issuing company, reducing the amount of outstanding stock on the open market .

Exam Probability: **Low**

55. *Answer choices:*

(see index for correct answer)

- a. Generally accepted accounting principles
- b. Goodwill
- c. AICPA Statements of Position
- d. Vendor-specific objective evidence

Guidance: level 1

:: Generally Accepted Accounting Principles ::

In accrual accounting, the revenue recognition principle states that expenses should be recorded during the period in which they are incurred, regardless of when the transfer of cash occurs. Conversely, cash basis accounting calls for the recognition of an expense when the cash is paid, regardless of when the expense was actually incurred.

Exam Probability: **Medium**

56. *Answer choices:*

(see index for correct answer)

- a. deferred revenue
- b. net realisable value
- c. Matching principle
- d. Income statement

Guidance: level 1

:: Asset ::

__________ s, also known as tangible assets or property, plant and equipment , is a term used in accounting for assets and property that cannot easily be converted into cash. This can be compared with current assets such as cash or bank accounts, described as liquid assets. In most cases, only tangible assets are referred to as fixed. IAS 16 defines __________ s as assets whose future economic benefit is probable to flow into the entity, whose cost can be measured reliably. __________ s belong to one of 2 types:"Freehold Assets" – assets which are purchased with legal right of ownership and used,and "Leasehold Assets" – assets used by owner without legal right for a particular period of time.

Exam Probability: **High**

57. *Answer choices:*

(see index for correct answer)

- a. Fixed asset
- b. Asset

Guidance: level 1

:: E-commerce ::

A __________ is a plastic payment card that can be used instead of cash when making purchases. It is similar to a credit card, but unlike a credit card, the money is immediately transferred directly from the cardholder`s bank account when performing a transaction.

Exam Probability: **Low**

58. *Answer choices:*

(see index for correct answer)

- a. Center for the Connected Consumer
- b. Debit card
- c. Hukkster
- d. Computer security

Guidance: level 1

:: Expense ::

An __________ , operating expenditure, operational expense, operational expenditure or opex is an ongoing cost for running a product, business, or system. Its counterpart, a capital expenditure , is the cost of developing or providing non-consumable parts for the product or system. For example, the purchase of a photocopier involves capex, and the annual paper, toner, power and maintenance costs represents opex. For larger systems like businesses, opex may also include the cost of workers and facility expenses such as rent and utilities.

Exam Probability: **High**

59. *Answer choices:*

(see index for correct answer)

- a. Momentem
- b. Business overhead expense disability insurance
- c. Interest expense
- d. Tax expense

Guidance: level 1

INDEX: Correct Answers

Foundations of Business

1. b: Market segmentation

2. a: Property

3. d: Debt

4. : Purchasing

5. d: Duty

6. d: E-commerce

7. b: ITeM

8. a: Target market

9. b: Globalization

10. a: Free trade

11. : Empowerment

12. b: Budget

13. b: Project management

14. d: Analysis

15. c: Benchmarking

16. d: Quality control

17. c: ASEAN

18. a: Risk management

19. a: Six Sigma

20. a: Price

21. b: Present value

22. c: Stock

23. : INDEX

24. : Industry

25. b: Loan

26. c: Gross domestic product

27. c: Commerce

28. b: Franchising

29. : Size

30. : Quality management

31. b: Interest rate

32. b: Authority

33. b: Competitor

34. a: Security

35. : Revenue

36. : Incentive

37. c: Payment

38. b: Stock exchange

39. d: Career

40. : Audience

41. b: Limited liability

42. a: Mission statement

43. c: Life

44. b: Bankruptcy

45. d: Evaluation

46. a: Common stock

47. c: Solution

48. b: Bribery

49. c: Initiative

50. : Import

51. b: Competitive advantage

52. : Patent

53. : Credit

54. d: Scheduling

55. b: Marketing strategy

56. : Law

57. c: Description

58. d: Technology

59. a: Outsourcing

Management

1. b: Gantt chart

2. b: Autonomy

3. b: Board of directors

4. a: Organizational commitment

5. d: Management by objectives

6. : Market share

7. d: Interdependence

8. d: Bureaucracy

9. : Entrepreneurship

10. : Cost leadership

11. b: Leadership style

12. : Supply chain management

13. : Performance

14. c: Supply chain

15. c: Checklist

16. a: Project manager

17. a: Political risk

18. c: Emotional intelligence

19. c: Profit sharing

20. a: World Trade Organization

21. a: Review

22. : Utility

23. d: Interaction

24. : Accounting

25. b: Ratio

26. a: Leadership development

27. : Wage

28. d: Senior management

29. b: Certification

30. a: European Union

31. : Integrity

32. a: Inventory

33. a: Organizational culture

34. b: Facilitator

35. : Statistic

36. d: Tariff

37. c: Creativity

38. b: Property

39. c: Job enlargement

40. d: Project

41. c: Partnership

42. a: Strategy

43. a: Firm

44. c: Goal

45. c: Halo effect

46. b: Choice

47. : Scientific management

48. c: Trade

49. : Assembly line

50. c: Corporate governance

51. : Control chart

52. d: Time management

53. c: Decision tree

54. b: Quality control

55. b: Pension

56. a: Problem solving

57. a: Situational leadership

58. a: Operations management

59. c: Absenteeism

Business law

1. b: Aid

2. a: Procedural law

3. : Supreme Court

4. d: Contract Clause

5. d: Offeror

6. : Product liability

7. c: Federal Trade Commission

8. b: Good faith

9. b: Trade

10. b: Mediation

11. d: Implied authority

12. d: Economic Espionage Act

13. a: Precedent

14. d: Service mark

15. c: Wire fraud

16. : Affidavit

17. d: Warehouse receipt

18. c: Cyberspace

19. a: Parol evidence

20. d: Criminal law

21. d: Merger

22. d: Industry

23. : Perfect tender

24. b: Subsidiary

25. : Implied warranty

26. b: Judicial review

27. : Guarantee

28. b: Presentment

29. : Resource

30. c: Categorical imperative

31. a: World Trade Organization

32. a: Assignee

33. c: Computer fraud

34. d: Accord and satisfaction

35. a: Criminal procedure

36. a: Commerce

37. a: Subrogation

38. : Foreign Corrupt Practices Act

39. : Real property

40. d: Writ

41. c: Apparent authority

42. c: Garnishment

43. c: Relevant market

44. c: Shareholder

45. b: Employment discrimination

46. d: Security

47. : Duty of care

48. b: Sexual harassment

49. d: Secured transaction

50. c: Standing

51. b: Mens rea

52. a: Intellectual property

53. c: Presumption

54. c: Warehouse

55. c: Property

56. d: Federal Arbitration Act

57. d: Utilitarianism

58. a: Negotiation

59. c: Purchasing

Finance

1. c: Bank

2. b: Financial crisis

3. c: Residual value

4. d: Income tax

5. c: Board of directors

6. d: Debt

7. b: Coupon

8. b: Quick ratio

9. b: Bad debt

10. d: Retained earnings

11. b: Financial Accounting Standards Board

12. b: Double taxation

13. a: Source document

14. c: Accounting

15. c: Net asset

16. d: Annual report

17. a: Finance

18. : Stock split

19. : Property

20. : Rate of return

21. a: Corporate governance

22. b: Break-even

23. : Public company

24. c: Liquidity

25. a: Indirect costs

26. b: Stock

27. : Earnings per share

28. a: Conservatism

29. a: Current asset

30. a: Generally accepted accounting principles

31. a: Opportunity cost

32. : Face

33. d: Compound interest

34. b: Pricing

35. : Patent

36. b: Accrued liabilities

37. a: Enron

38. c: Need

39. a: Intangible asset

40. d: Time value of money

41. d: Strategy

42. a: Bank account

43. d: Interest expense

44. d: Annuity

45. a: Normal balance

46. b: Schedule

47. c: Hedge fund

48. : Loan

49. d: Accrued interest

50. : Capital budgeting

51. : Limited liability

52. a: Debit card

53. d: Compounding

54. c: Market price

55. a: Creditor

56. c: Monetary policy

57. b: Internal Revenue Service

58. a: Partnership

59. a: Buyer

Human resource management

1. : Six Sigma

2. : Bottom line

3. a: Expatriate

4. a: Bargaining unit

5. a: Parental leave

6. b: Best practice

7. c: Job rotation

8. a: Flexible spending account

9. d: Reasonable person

10. d: Pension

11. b: Congress

12. a: Progressive discipline

13. c: Workforce planning

14. c: Undue hardship

15. b: Authoritarianism

16. : Employee assistance program

17. a: Wage

18. d: Trade union

19. : Occupational Safety and Health Act

20. b: Employee engagement

21. : Employee retention

22. c: Hostile work environment

23. : Xerox Corporation

24. : National Institute for Occupational Safety and Health

25. : Recruitment

26. c: Open shop

27. b: Flextime

28. : Wage curve

29. a: Job satisfaction

30. : Case interview

31. d: Selection ratio

32. : Performance measurement

33. : Faragher v. City of Boca Raton

34. d: Overtime

35. d: Discipline

36. b: Outplacement

37. b: Affirmative action

38. b: Job security

39. b: Impression management

40. b: International Brotherhood of Teamsters

41. c: Virtual team

42. c: Training and development

43. a: Global workforce

44. a: Cost

45. c: Phantom stock

46. d: Test validity

47. : Eustress

48. a: Worker Adjustment and Retraining Notification Act

49. : Schedule

50. : Labor force

51. c: Performance appraisal

52. : Sick leave

53. c: Knowledge worker

54. b: Health Reimbursement Account

55. : Physician

56. b: Aptitude

57. : Perception

58. : Ownership

59. : Material safety data sheet

Information systems

1. c: Data cleansing

2. : Verisign

3. a: Benchmarking

4. b: Magnetic tape

5. a: Computer fraud

6. b: Total cost

7. a: Information technology

8. d: Digital rights management

9. : QR code

10. a: M-Pesa

11. d: Avatar

12. c: Diagram

13. : E-commerce

14. d: Network management

15. d: Social network

16. : Web page

17. d: Transport Layer Security

18. c: World Wide Web

19. a: Fault tolerance

20. b: Enterprise resource planning

21. d: Galileo

22. d: Gmail

23. d: Data element

24. d: Carnivore

25. b: Innovation

26. c: Second Life

27. b: Information systems

28. d: Supply chain management

29. b: Blogger

30. d: Sustainable

31. c: Collision

32. : Packet switching

33. d: Decision support system

34. c: Property

35. c: Availability

36. a: Interactivity

37. d: Star

38. a: Service level agreement

39. d: Information management

40. d: Google Calendar

41. : Structured query language

42. a: Artificial intelligence

43. : Zynga

44. a: Wiki

45. a: Competitive advantage

46. d: Data field

47. : Freemium

48. b: Threat

49. d: Radio-frequency identification

50. d: Data integrity

51. a: Service-oriented architecture

52. d: Total cost of ownership

53. d: Smart card

54. a: Interview

55. : Bit rate

56. b: COBIT

57. b: Authentication protocol

58. : Search engine

59. c: Click-through

Marketing

1. b: Hearing

2. c: Database marketing

3. : Customer retention

4. : Sherman Antitrust Act

5. b: Firm

6. c: Brand awareness

7. b: Federal Trade Commission

8. d: Need

9. : Credit

10. : Strategic alliance

11. d: Information technology

12. d: Publicity

13. a: New product development

14. a: Outsourcing

15. c: Resource

16. b: Marketing communications

17. : Customer experience

18. a: Personnel

19. b: Trademark

20. : Total cost

21. : Logo

22. d: Code

23. b: Product development

24. d: Vendor

25. c: Wall Street Journal

26. : Cooperative

27. a: Sales management

28. c: Derived demand

29. d: Merchandising

30. d: Market segments

31. : Respondent

32. d: Revenue

33. c: Mission statement

34. : Supermarket

35. d: Brand management

36. : Demand

37. a: Advertising

38. c: Viral marketing

39. : Target audience

40. c: Partnership

41. a: Authority

42. c: Market research

43. : Primary data

44. d: Cost

45. d: Presentation

46. d: Trade association

47. b: Goal

48. d: Dimension

49. : Integrated marketing

50. c: Empowerment

51. a: Inventory

52. d: Product placement

53. b: Green marketing

54. a: Strategic planning

55. c: Target market

56. : Household

57. : North American Free Trade Agreement

58. : Services marketing

59. d: Customer value

Manufacturing

1. c: Quality by Design

2. c: Extended enterprise

3. d: Turbine

4. b: Tool

5. : Supply chain network

6. b: Sony

7. b: Six Sigma

8. : Kaizen

9. d: PDCA

10. : Reorder point

11. : Process engineering

12. a: Quality management

13. d: Electronic data interchange

14. c: Quality costs

15. b: Synergy

16. b: Authority

17. d: Catalyst

18. d: Distillation

19. d: American Society for Quality

20. : Reverse auction

21. : Root cause

22. b: Thomas Register

23. : Consensus

24. : Customer

25. c: E-commerce

26. c: DMAIC

27. b: New product development

28. d: Reboiler

29. : Chemical reaction

30. : Furnace

31. : Lean manufacturing

32. b: Sunk costs

33. : Consortium

34. b: Asset

35. b: Expediting

36. a: Goal

37. c: Stakeholder management

38. b: Steel

39. : Joint Commission

40. c: Process capital

41. : Certification

42. c: Aggregate planning

43. b: Vendor

44. : Capacity planning

45. b: Total cost of ownership

46. d: Property

47. c: Project team

48. : Check sheet

49. a: Service quality

50. : Accreditation

51. b: Economic order quantity

52. : Design of experiments

53. d: Vendor relationship management

54. d: Materials management

55. d: Indirect costs

56. : Histogram

57. d: Performance

58. c: Minitab

59. c: Concurrent engineering

Commerce

1. c: Outsourcing

2. b: Trade

3. c: Tourism

4. c: Initiative

5. d: Minimum wage

6. a: Compromise

7. d: Supervisor

8. b: Inflation

9. c: Quality management

10. c: Jury

11. b: Board of directors

12. c: Subsidy

13. b: Authority

14. : Entrepreneur

15. : Forward auction

16. c: Federal government

17. a: Lycos

18. b: Antitrust

19. a: Information technology

20. b: Strategic alliance

21. a: Mining

22. a: Electronic data interchange

23. b: Credit

24. : Fixed cost

25. a: Deregulation

26. d: Invoice

27. : Short run

28. c: Goal

29. d: Automation

30. c: Enabling

31. a: Hospitality

32. d: Vickrey auction

33. d: Sexual harassment

34. : Performance

35. d: Collaborative filtering

36. d: Webvan

37. b: Subsidiary

38. b: Monopoly

39. : Economies of scale

40. b: Overhead cost

41. b: Charter

42. d: Firm

43. a: Case study

44. : Loyalty

45. : Leadership

46. c: Land

47. c: Labor union

48. : Reverse auction

49. d: Cost structure

50. d: Inventory

51. b: Project

52. c: Automated Clearing House

53. d: English auction

54. d: Pizza Hut

55. b: Payment card

56. c: Shopping cart

57. a: Welfare

58. a: Publicity

59. b: Advertisement

Business ethics

1. b: Perception

2. a: Arthur Andersen

3. b: Sullivan principles

4. a: Empowerment

5. c: Exxon Valdez

6. a: Undue hardship

7. a: Principal Financial

8. c: Vigilance committee

9. b: Insider trading

10. c: Cultural relativism

11. a: Corporate structure

12. a: Foreign Corrupt Practices Act

13. b: Planned obsolescence

14. a: Employee Polygraph Protection Act

15. b: Internal control

16. c: Lanham Act

17. d: Financial Stability Oversight Council

18. c: Nonprofit

19. : Chamber of Commerce

20. c: Cause-related marketing

21. b: Workplace bullying

22. : Community development financial institution

23. b: Corporate citizenship

24. b: Statutory law

25. : Consumer Protection

26. a: Risk assessment

27. b: Social networking

28. b: Stanford Financial Group

29. d: Ethical leadership

30. b: Model Rules of Professional Conduct

31. b: Charles Ponzi

32. b: Sexual harassment

33. : Human nature

34. b: Building

35. d: Pyramid scheme

36. a: Dress code

37. d: Partnership

38. d: Guerrilla Marketing

39. b: Organic food

40. b: Corporate governance

41. d: East Germany

42. a: Social responsibility

43. c: Protestant work ethic

44. d: Federal Trade Commission

45. a: Collusion

46. a: WorldCom

47. a: Environmental audit

48. b: Great Depression

49. c: Junk bond

50. b: Consumerism

51. a: Corporate social responsibility

52. c: Fair Trade Certified

53. c: Coal

54. b: Labor relations

55. c: Martin Luther

56. : Aristotle

57. : Lawsuit

58. d: Fraud

59. c: Subprime lending

Accounting

1. c: Receipt

2. d: Quick ratio

3. c: Bank reconciliation

4. d: Insurance

5. a: Information systems

6. b: Corporate governance

7. d: Gross profit

8. c: Voucher

9. c: New York Stock Exchange

10. : Maturity date

11. c: Debt-to-equity ratio

12. c: Chief executive officer

13. a: Certified Management Accountant

14. c: Cost of goods sold

15. d: Bookkeeping

16. : Transfer pricing

17. d: Taxation

18. a: Dividend

19. a: Present value

20. : Articles of incorporation

21. b: Sinking fund

22. c: Public Company Accounting Oversight Board

23. b: Management accounting

24. a: Expense

25. a: Common stock

26. c: Controversy

27. : Inventory

28. a: Income statement

29. d: Expense account

30. b: Governmental Accounting Standards Board

31. c: Paid-in capital

32. c: Tax avoidance

33. c: Job costing

34. a: Risk assessment

35. a: Marital deduction

36. d: Accounting Research Bulletins

37. a: Cost pool

38. : Stock Market

39. a: Internal auditing

40. d: Securities Exchange Act

41. : Net profit

42. b: Retained earnings

43. d: Debtor

44. a: Revenue recognition

45. c: Cash

46. c: Tax law

47. c: Accounting period

48. b: Operating leverage

49. b: Accounting research

50. d: Capital expenditure

51. a: Bank

52. a: Independent contractor

53. b: Tax revenue

54. c: Standard deduction

55. : Treasury stock

56. c: Matching principle

57. a: Fixed asset

58. b: Debit card

59. : Operating expense

CPSIA information can be obtained
at www.ICGtesting.com
Printed in the USA
LVHW051624301019
635718LV00005B/732/P

CW01652689

allez-y!

Bienvenue!

Julia Batters • Anneli McLachlan

HEINEMANN EDUCATIONAL

1 On se présente

In this unit you will learn how to:

- introduce yourself to visitors
- introduce others to visitors

1 Qui est-ce?

écoutez! Write down 1–8. Find out who is who. Listen to the tape. Now add the right letter.

Guest List

a Kamal Ramdani
b Paul Thibault
c Sadia Baida
d Marc Ledieu
e Raymond Pouget
f Anne Valette
g Julie Coussin
h Sylvie Aubert

2 Je m'appelle ...

parlez! What would you say? Pretend you are these people. Introduce yourself.

a Prince Charles

b Lenny Henry

c Whitney Houston

d Cleopatra

e Madonna

f Gary Lineker

3 Ma famille

écoutez! Write down 1–6. Who is being introduced? Listen to the tape. Now add the right letter.

- a mother
- b sister
- c brother
- d father
- e friend
- f colleague

4 Je vous présente ...

parlez! Practise introducing someone. What would you say for each bubble in activity 3? Make sure you know how to ask someone how they are.

5 Allez-y!

parlez! Work in groups of three. Act out this conversation.

A: Greet the visitor and introduce yourself.
B: Say you're very well.
A: Introduce your colleague.
C: Say hello.
B: Say hello.

Now try and act out the scene with your books closed.

Changez de rôle!

Now fill in your progress sheet ✓

mots clés

A

Bonjour. Bonsoir.	Je me présente: je m'appelle . . .
Comment ça va?	
Je vous présente	mon/ma collègue, . . . mon ami(e), . . . ma mère. mon père. ma soeur, . . . mon frère, . . .

B

Très bien merci.
Bonjour. Bonsoir.

2 *Tu es comment?*

In this unit you will learn how to:

- ask people what they look like
- understand people saying what they look like
- say what you look like

1 C'est qui?

écoutez! Write down 1–6.
You are meeting some French visitors at the station.
You have been given these descriptions over the phone.
Which description fits which person?
Add the right letter.

a b c d e f

2 Je suis ...

écoutez! Write down 1–8.
Listen to the tape.
Who is speaking? Add the right letter.

		height and build		hair colour and type	eye colour
a	Nathalie	tall	slim	red, long, straight	green
b	André	small	slim	brown, long	blue
c	Mathieu	tall	quite fat	black, straight	grey
d	Carole	medium	fat	red, curly, long	blue
e	Younes	small	slim	black, short	brown
f	Mireille	medium	quite fat	blonde, straight	brown
g	Sylvie	tall	slim	grey, short	blue
h	Luc	small	quite slim	black, long	green

3 A vous!

parlez! Can you remember how to ask someone what they look like?

4 Rappel!

parlez! Work with a partner.
Pretend to be one of the people in activity 2.
Say what you look like.
Can your partner guess who you are?

If you need help, listen again to the tape for activities 1 and 2 and look at the mots-clés on page 7.

5 Allez-y!

parlez! Work with a partner.

One of you chooses to be one of the people below.
Your partner asks you what you look like.
Say what you look like.
Your partner points to the right picture to show that he or she has understood.

Changez de rôle!

6 J'ai ...

lisez!

1 J'ai les cheveux noirs.

2 J'ai les yeux verts.

3 J'ai les cheveux frisés et les yeux bleus.

4 J'ai les cheveux raides.

5 J'ai les cheveux longs et blonds.

6 Je suis assez grand, j'ai les yeux bleus et j'ai les cheveux gris.

7 Je suis petit et j'ai les cheveux noirs et frisés

Copy out a chart like this one. Fill in the details from the letters above.

	Height	Build	Hair	Eyes
1	–	–	black	–

7 Je suis assez grand

écrivez! How would the people on page 6 fill in this form? The first one has been done for you.

	Taille	Yeux	Cheveux
a	grand	bleus	blonds, courts

Now fill in your progress sheet

Fini déjà? Tournez à la page 22.

mots clés

A

Tu es Vous êtes	comment?

Tu or vous?

Use *tu* for friends of your own age.

Use *vous* for people older than you and people you don't know.

B

Je suis	assez	grand(e). petit(e).	gros(se). mince.
	de taille moyenne.		
J'ai	les yeux	marron. noirs. gris.	bleus. verts. noisette.
	les cheveux	noirs. châtain. blonds. roux. gris.	longs. courts. raides. frisés.

3 *Ma ville*

In this unit you will learn how to:

- describe your town or area
- understand people talking about where they live

1 C'est quelle ville?

écoutez! Write down 1–6.
You will hear six places being talked about.
Listen to the tape and add the right letter.

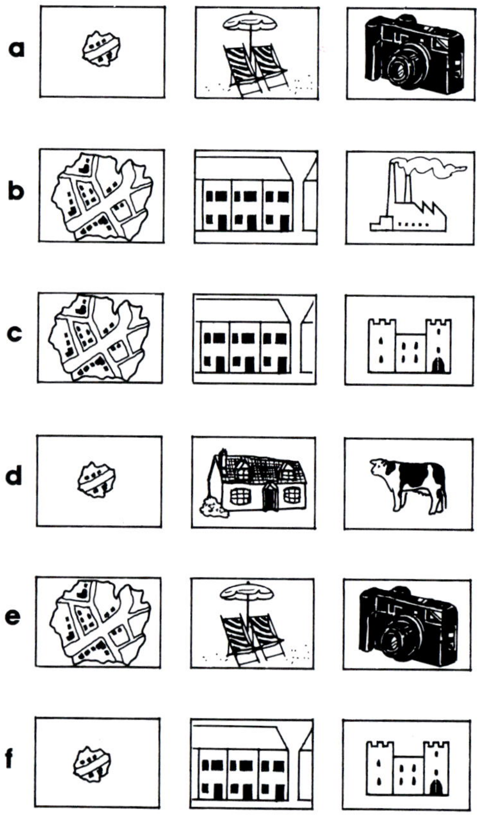

2 C'est où?

écoutez! Write down 1–6.
You will hear six more places being talked about. Make a note of the right country and the right direction for each place.

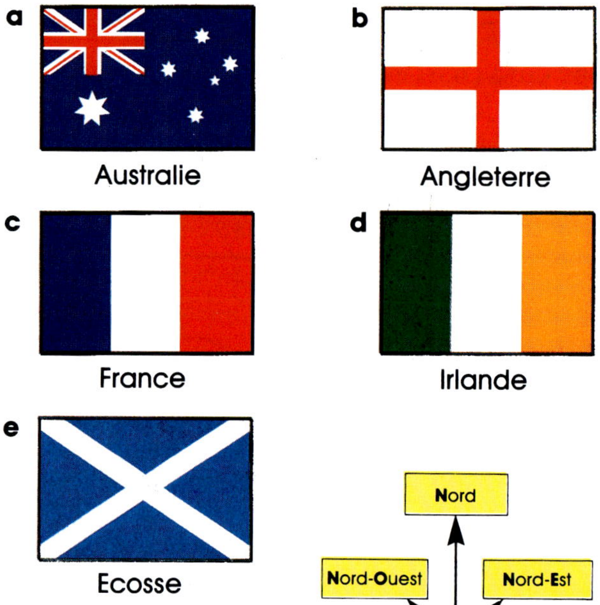

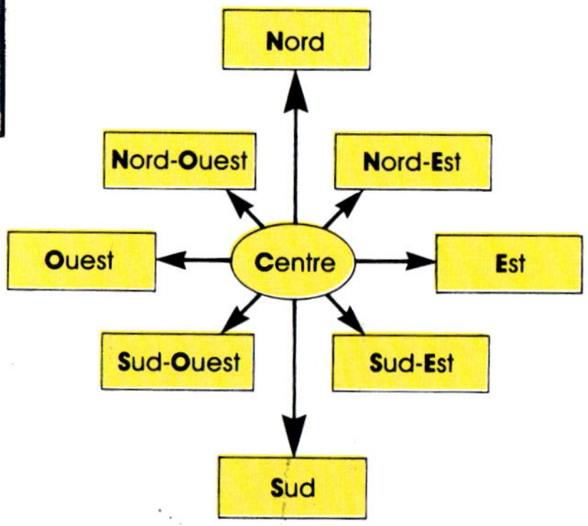

3 A vous!

parlez!

- Practise saying what places are like using the symbols in activity 1.
- Practise saying where places are using the words in activity 2.

4 Rappel!

parlez! Check that you can ask someone what a place is like.

5 Allez-y!

parlez! Work with a partner.
One of you asks about a town and the other describes it.
Changez de rôle!

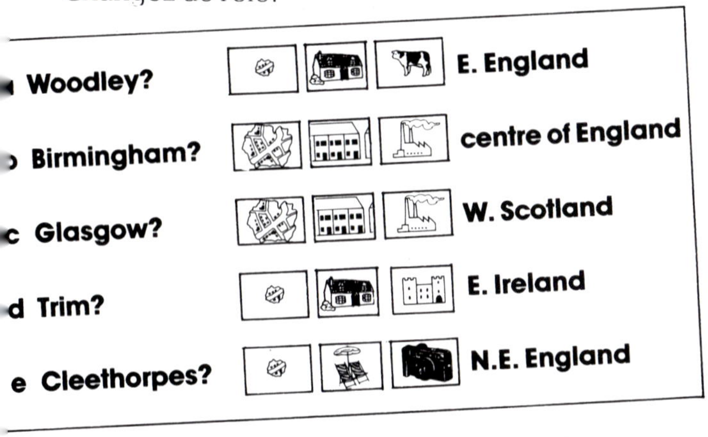

6 Une ville française

lisez! Which description goes with which place?

1 C'est une grande ville touristique.
2 C'est un petit village rural.
3 C'est une grande station balnéaire.
4 C'est une grande ville industrielle.
5 C'est une grande ville historique.

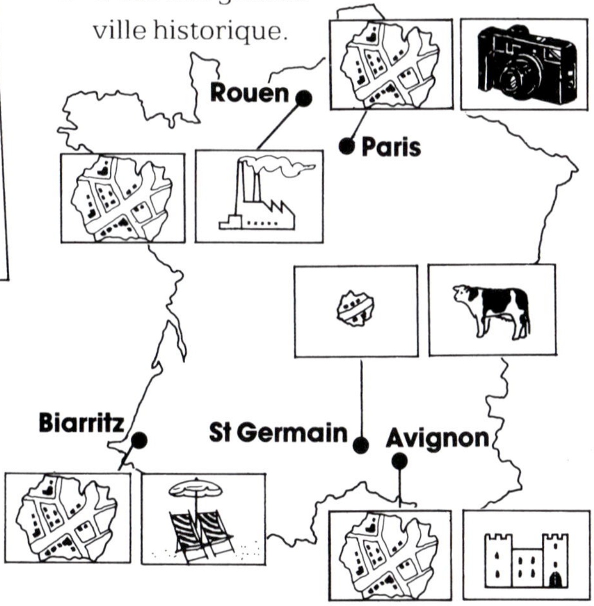

7 Une description

écrivez! Write up the descriptions of the towns in activity 5 for French-speaking visitors to your local tourist office.

mots clés

A

Sheffield, Melbourne, Fort William,	c'est comment?

B

C'est	une grande petite	ville station balnéaire	touristique, historique, industriel(le), rural(e),
	un petit	village	
situé(e)	dans le nord le sud l'ouest l'est	le nord-ouest le nord-est le sud-ouest le sud-est	de l'Angleterre. de l'Ecosse. de l'Irlande. du pays de Galles. de l'Australie. de la France.
	au centre		

Now fill in your progress sheet ✓

Fini déjà? Tournez à la page 23.

4 *A la maison*

In this unit you will learn how to:

- talk about the rooms in a house or flat
- understand people when they talk about their house or flat

1 Il y a ...

écoutez! Write down 1–9.
Some French visitors are describing their home. In what order are the rooms mentioned?
Listen to the tape. Now add the right letter.

a

b

c

d

e

f

g

h

i

2 A vous!

parlez! Can you remember what the rooms are called?
Practise saying what the rooms in the photos are.

3 C'est quelle maison?

écoutez! Write down 1–5.
Which house or flat is being described?
Listen to the tape.
Now add the right letter.

a kitch, liv. room, din. room, garden, bathroom, 3 beds.
b kitch, liv. room, bathroom, 2 beds.
c kitch, liv. room, din. room, shower, bathroom, 4 beds, garden, garage.
d kitch, liv. room, shower, 1 bed.
e kitch, liv. room, din. room, bathroom, 3 beds, garage.

4 Rappel!

parlez! Can you remember how to ask what rooms there are?
Check that you can ask if there is a garden.

5 Allez-y!

parlez!

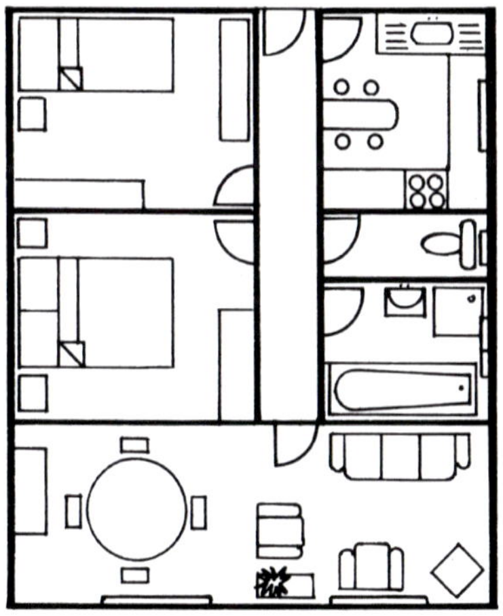

a

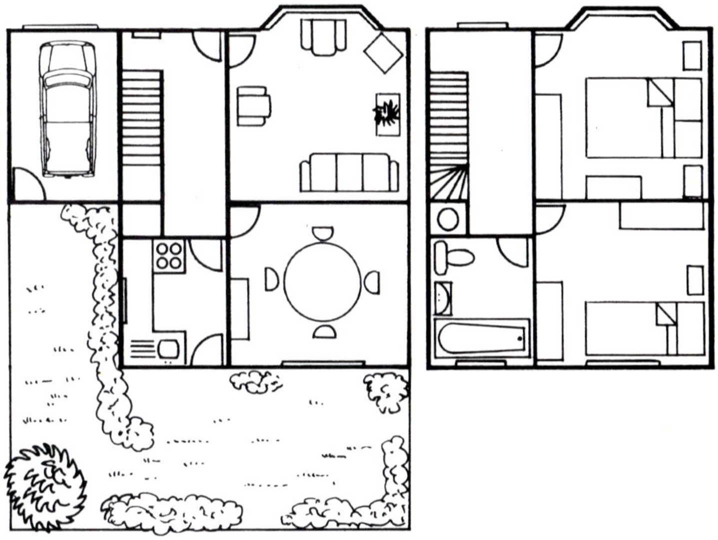

b

Look at the plans above with your partner.
Act out this conversation.

For example:

A: Ask what rooms there are.
B: List some of the rooms.
A: Ask if there is a garden.
B: Say if there is a garden.

Changez de rôle!

mots clés

A

Il y a combien de pièces?

B

Il y a . . .

A

Il y a . . . ?

B

Oui, il y a . . .

un	jardin(?) salon(?) garage(?) wc(?)
une	salle à manger(?) salle de bains(?) cuisine(?) douche(?)
une deux trois quatre	chambre(s) (?)

Now fill in your progress sheet

Fini déjà? Tournez à la page 24.

5 Chez nous

In this unit you will learn how to:

- say what different houses and flats are like
- understand people saying what their homes are like

a

b

c

d

e

f

1 C'est comment?

écoutez! Write down 1–6. Which house or flat is being described? Listen to the tape. Add the right letter.

2 A vous!

parlez! Make sure that you can ask people if they live in a house or flat. Can you remember how to ask what the house or flat is like?

	grand	petit	moderne	vieux	calme	confortable
	✓	–	✓	–	✓	✓
	–	✓	✓	–	✗	✓
	✓	–	–	✓	✓	✗
	–	✓	–	✓	✗	✓

3 Rappel!

parlez! Use the grid on the left to practise describing houses and flats.

4 Allez-y!

parlez! Make up conversations with a partner. Tell your partner about your home and find out about your partner's home. You can invent the details.

Par exemple:

A:  ?

B: 

A: C'est comment?

B: pet. ✓ mod. ✓ calme ✗

Bonus! Can you describe your own home to a French-speaking visitor?

Changez de rôle!

5 C'est grand

lisez! Match the right text to the right house or flat.

a 

b 

c 

d 

e 

1 C'est grand
2 C'est moderne
3 C'est petit
4 C'est calme
5 C'est vieux

Now fill in your progress sheet ✓

Fini déjà? Tournez à la page 25 et 26.

mots clés

A

Vous habitez Tu habites	une maison? un appartement?
C'est comment?	

B

J'habite	une maison. un appartement.	
C'est	assez très	grand petit moderne. vieux. calme. confortable. agréable.
Ce n'est pas	très	

6 *Qu'est-ce que tu aimes faire?*

In this unit you will learn how to:

- ask your visitors what they like doing and what they would like to do
- tell someone what you like doing

1 Et toi?

écoutez! Write down 1–11. What do these people like doing? Listen to the tape. Now add the right letter.

a

b

c

d

e

f

g

h

i

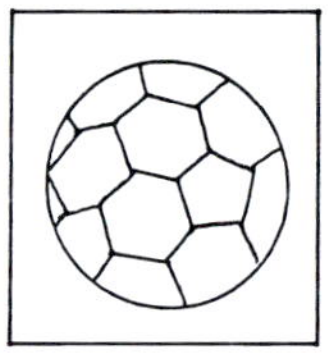
j

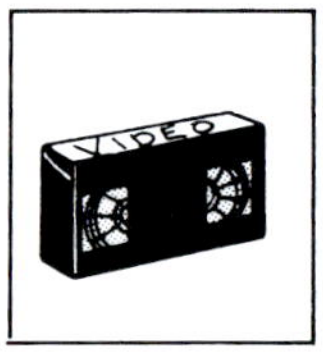
k

2 J'adore ...

écoutez! Write down 1–8. Do these people like doing these things or not? Listen to the tape. Now add the right letter. You will have to use some more than once. Jot down the activities as well if you like.

a 

b 

c 

d 

3 A vous!

parlez! Look back at activity 1. Ask your visitors if they like to do the things shown in the pictures.

4 Rappel!

parlez! Look at the pictures below. Practise saying whether you like the things shown or not.

If you like, look back at the pictures in activity 1 and give your own answers.

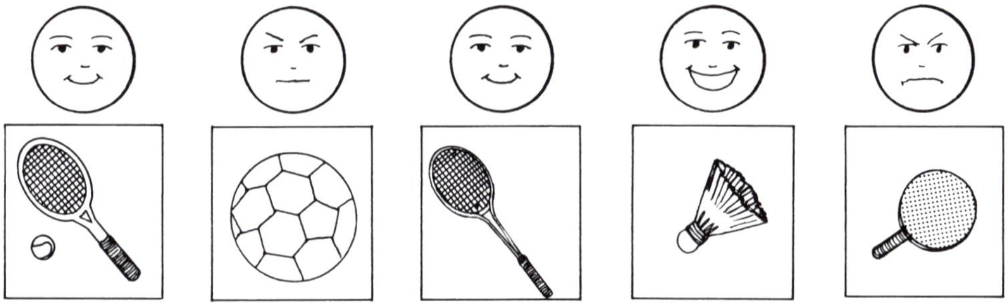

5 Allez-y!

parlez! Find out what people in your group like and don't like. Draw up a grid like the one on the right and note down the answers you are given.

Activities				
squash	II	III	~~IIII~~	IIII
tennis	IIII	II	III	I

Now fill in your progress sheet

Fini déjà? Tournez à la page 27.

mots clés

A

Qu'est-ce que tu aimes faire?

Tu veux . . . ?
Tu aimes . . . ?

jouer au

squash (?)
badminton (?)
ping-pong (?)
tennis (?)
football (?)
scrabble (?)

B

J'aime . . .
Je n'aime pas . . .
Je déteste . . .
J'adore . . .

regarder la télé (?)
regarder les vidéos(?)
écouter la radio (?)
aller au cinéma (?)
danser (?)

7 *Au cinéma*

In this unit you will learn how to:

- say what films are on at the cinema
- agree which film to go and see
- understand what films are on at a cinema and say what you prefer

1 Qu'est-ce qu'on joue?

a	Bambi
b	Presumed Innocent
c	Indiana Jones
d	The Return of the Thing
e	The Good, the Bad and the Ugly
f	Dad's Army
g	Platoon
h	Dracula
i	Star Wars
j	Eternal Love

écoutez! Write down 1–5.

a Which two films are showing in each case?
Listen to the tape and make a note of the two films.

b What sort of films are they?
Listen to the tape again.
Now choose the right letter for each film.

a

b

c

d

e

f

g

h

i

c Finally, which film do they decide to go and see in each case?

2 C'est un film de ...

parlez! Test your partner.
Point to one of the pictures and ask:
Qu'est-ce que c'est comme film?

Your partner answers:
C'est un film . . .

3 A vous!

parlez! Make sure that you can

- ask someone if they want to go to the cinema
- say what is on
- ask what the person prefers

4 Rappel!

parlez! Make sure that you can

- accept an invitation to the cinema
- ask what is on
- say what you prefer

5 Allez-y!

parlez! Work with a partner.

These are the films that are showing.

A: Ask your partner if he or she wants to go to the cinema.
B: Say yes. Ask what is on.
A: Say what films are on.
B: Ask what sort of film each one is.
A: Reply and ask your partner what he or she prefers.
B: Say what you want to see.

Changez de rôle!

mots clés

A

Tu veux aller au cinéma?

Star Trek 2.
Love Story.

C'est	un film	de science-fiction. de guerre. d'horreur. d'amour. d'aventure. comique.
	un policier. un dessin animé. un western.	

Qu'est-ce que tu préfères?

D'accord.

B

Oui, je veux bien. Qu'est-ce qu'on joue?

Star Trek 2, qu'est-ce que c'est comme film?

Je préfère . . .

Now fill in your progress sheet

Fini déjà? Tournez à la page 28.

8 La télévision

In this unit you will learn how to:

- ask your visitors what kind of TV programmes they like
- tell someone what kind of TV programmes you like

1 Tu veux regarder la télé?

écoutez! Write down 1–10.

a What sort of programmes are suggested?
Listen to the tape.
Now add the right letter.

a

b

c

d

e

f

g

h

i

j

b What do they think of the programmes suggested?
Listen to the tape again.
Write down the correct letter.

2 A vous!

parlez! Ask if someone wants to watch these programmes.
Say what sort of programme each one is.

Newsnight

Tom and Jerry

The Bill

3 Rappel!

parlez! Can you remember how to ask what sort of programme something is and say what you think of it?

Look back at activity 1 and say what you think of each type of programme shown.

4 Allez-y!

parlez! Work with a partner.
Act out these conversations.

A: Ask a guest if he or she wants to watch..

B: Ask what kind of programme it is.

A: Answer.

B: Say whether you want to watch the programme.

Now fill in your progress sheet

Fini déjà? Tournez à la page 29 et 30.

mots clés

A

Tu veux regarder	Panorama? A Question of Sport?	
C'est	un programme	de sport. pour enfants.
	un jeu. un policier. un documentaire. un dessin animé. un film. un feuilleton. la météo	
Ce sont	les informations	

B

Qu'est-ce que c'est comme programme?		
Oh oui,	j'adore j'aime	les programmes de sport. les programmes pour enfants. les jeux. les policiers. les documentaires. les dessins animés. les films. les feuilletons. les informations. la météo.
Oh non,	je n'aime pas je déteste	

Bande dessinée Les vidéos.

Quelle histoire!

Activités

1 Copy the grid below and complete it in English.

	Carole	David
Likes		
Dislikes		

2 Unjumble these words from the story

a EDETSET
b OOLSUTIN
c ERIOPLIC
d REEDGRAR
e SEDNIS MAINE

3 Write a different story by changing any details you like.

Tu es comment?

1 Les descriptions

écrivez! These are three faxes from business partners whom you must meet at the station.
Make notes in English to make sure you will recognise them.
Now write a similar message to send to them so that they will recognise you.

Chère Susie,

J'espère que vous allez bien. J'attends le voyage d'affaires en Grande Bretagne avec impatience. Je vais me décrire pour que vous puissiez me reconnaître à mon arrivée.

Je suis de taille moyenne. J'ai les cheveux longs, frisés et noirs. J'ai les yeux bleus et je suis assez mince.

J'espère que nous nous retrouverons facilement.

Sentiments distingués,

Laure Richard

Chère Susie,

Veuillez trouver ci-joint ma description: je suis grand, j'ai les cheveux blonds et raides et les yeux marron. Je porterai une rose jaune!

Sentiments distingués,

Alain Duminier

Chère Susie,

La date de notre rendez-vous approche. Je crois que ma description pourrait vous être utile.

Je suis de taille moyenne, j'ai les cheveux courts et noirs, j'ai les yeux verts. Je suis assez mince.

En attendant votre réponse,

Sentiments distingués,

Leila Chaba.

Ma ville

1 C'est une petite ville ...

écrivez! Use the word blocks below to write a description of each of the places below.

a

c

d

f

g

	située dans le sud-ouest	
C'est une petite station balnéaire	située dans le nord-ouest	
C'est une petite ville historique	située dans le nord-est	de l'Angleterre
C'est une grande ville historique	situé(e) dans le sud	de l'Australie
C'est un petit village	situé(e) dans l'est	de l'Ecosse
C'est une grande ville touristique	situé dans l'ouest	du pays de Galles

A la maison

1 C'est quelle pièce?

lisez! You have found a flat for a French friend. This is a plan of the flat. Can you label it?

1 salle à manger
2 salle de bains
3 cuisine
4 chambre
5 WC
6 salon

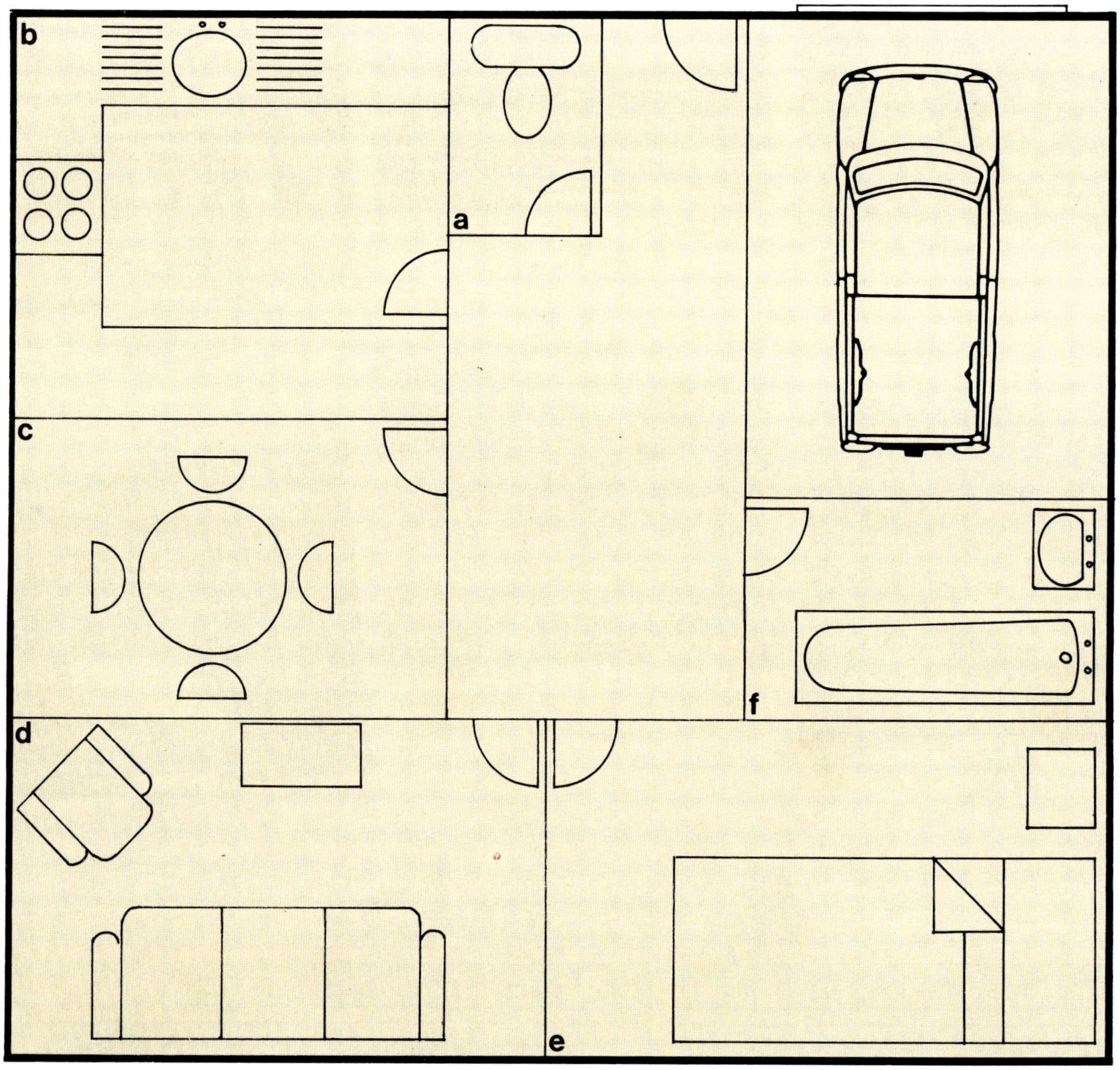

2 Mon appartement idéal

écrivez! Design a flat of your own. Draw a plan and label it.

Chez nous

1 Où habitent-ils?

lisez! Match the descriptions to the pictures.

1

Oui, j'habite Lille, j'habite une maison, c'est une grande maison moderne, tres confortable. Il y a beaucoup de distractions tout près.

2

C'est un très grand appartement de luxe, tout confort. Je vous conseille de le considérer.

3

A Longwy, il s'agit d'un appartement qui est assez petit, mais très bien aménagé. Il est assez vieux.

4

Pour ma part, j'habite un appartement. C'est un petit appartement mais j'ai quand même un jardin, ce qui est très pratique.

5

Il vous faut une description de la propriété. C'est une petite maison très calme au bord du lac.

2 C'est comment?

écrivez! Write one or two sentences about each house or flat.

Use this grid to help you.

C'est	assez très	grand(e) petit(e) moderne vieux calme confortable agréable
Ce n'est pas	très	

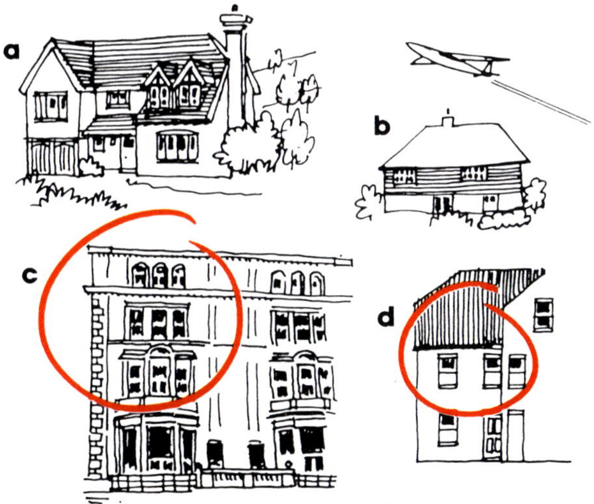

3 A vendre!

écrivez! Write a letter like this one describing a house that you want to sell to a French customer.
The house you are suggesting has a kitchen, three bedrooms, a bathroom, a dining room, a living room and a garage. It's large and is in a quiet position.

Oxford le 6 août

Monsieur,

Voici la maison que je vous propose. Il y a deux chambres, un salon, une cuisine, une salle de bains et une salle à manger. Il y a aussi un garage et un jardin.

C'est petit et agréable.

Sentiments distingués,

James Prior.

4 Quel appartement?

lisez! Which of these estate agent's descriptions go with each floor plan? Use the key to help you.

a 1 ch. sal. cuis. s. de b.
b 2ch. cuis./s. à m. gar. s.de b.
c 4ch. sal. s.à m. cuis. s. de b. gar.

1

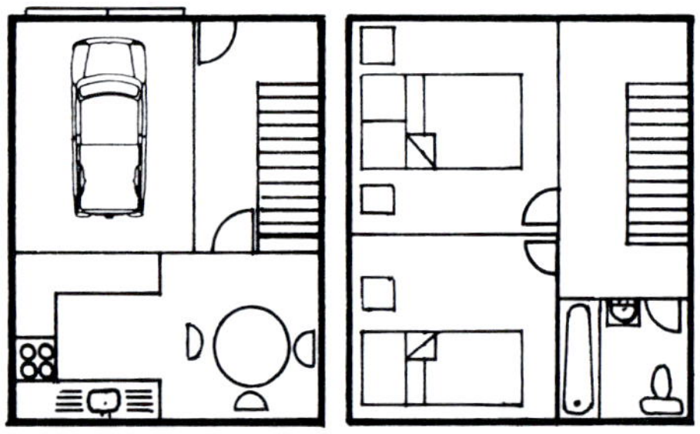

3

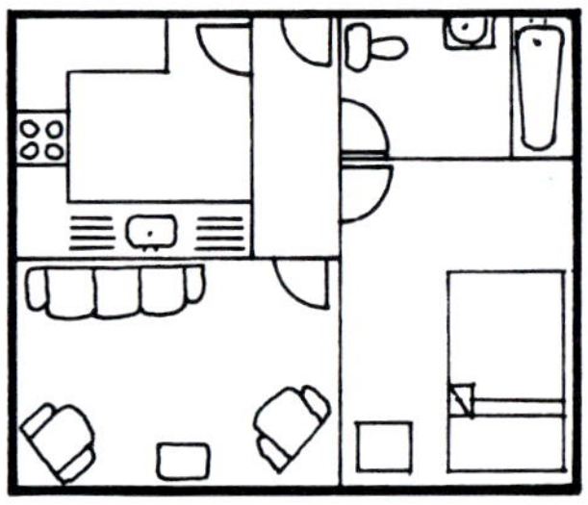

2

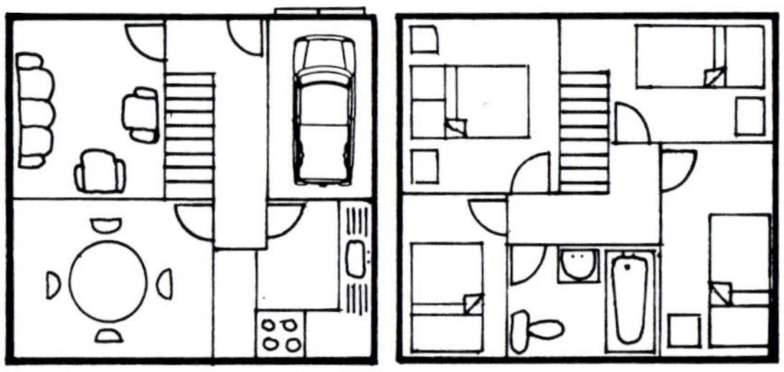

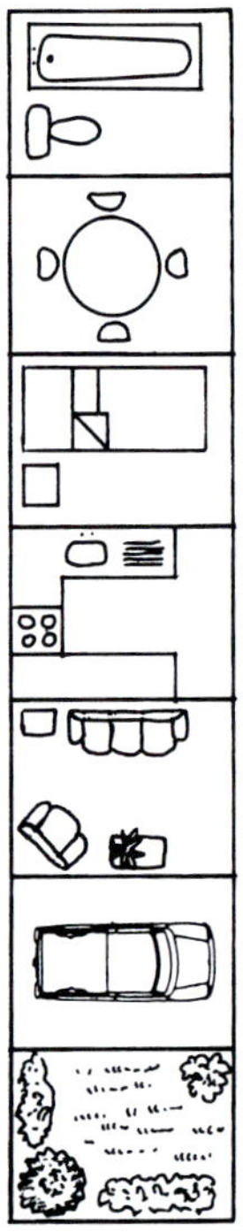

a s. de b.
b s. à m.
c ch.
d cuis.
e sal.
f gar.
g jar.

5 Une petite annonce

écrivez! Now write your own advertisements!

Qu'est-ce que tu aimes faire?

1 Le week-end

écrivez! Put the French version of this weekend programme in order.

dimanche après-midi
restaurant
dimanche matin
scrabble
télé
ping pong
disco
ou squash
samedi après-midi
tennis
cinéma
samedi soir
dimanche soir
samedi matin
vendredi soir
le week-end

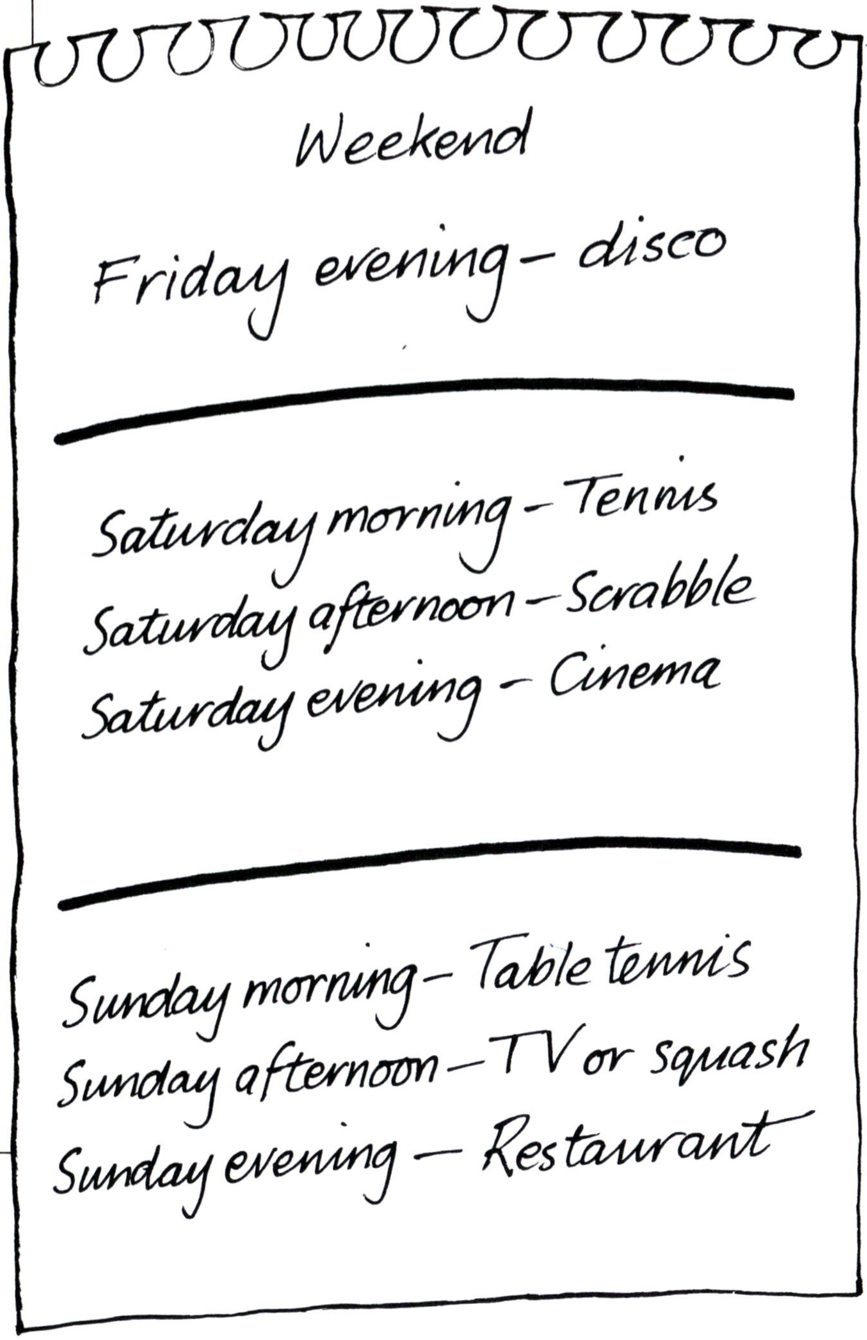

Au cinéma

1 Qu'est-ce qu'on joue?

lisez! You are helping out a group of British people in France.
Tell them what is on at the cinema. Say what kind of film each one is.
Remember, v.o. means 'version originale', so it will be in English.

CROCODILE DUNDEE. 1985. 1h35. Film d'aventures australien en couleurs de Peter Faiman avec Paul Hogan, Linda Kozlowski, John Meillon, David Gulpilil, Mark Blum, Michael Lombard.
♦**Pathé Francais 92** v.f.

LE DECLIN DE L'EMPIRE AMERICAIN. The decline of the american empire. 1986. 1h35. Comédie canadienne en couleurs de Denys Arcand avec Dominique Michel, Dorothée Berryman, Louise Portal, Geneviève Rioux, Pierre Curzi.
♦**Cinoche 45**

LE DERNIER EMPEREUR. The last emperor. 1987. 2h45. Film à grand spectacle américain en couleurs de Bernardo Bertolucci avec John Lone, Joan Chen, Peter O'Toole, Ying Ruocheng, Victor Wong.
♦**Les Forums Cinémas Arc-en-Ciel 2** v.o. ♦**Pathé Marignan Concorde 70** v.o. ♦**Kinopanorama 140** v.o. ♦**Pathé Francais 92** v.f. ♦**Le Galaxie 118** v.f. ♦**Pathé Montparnasse 129** v.f.

DIRTY DANCING. 1987. 1h40. Comédie musicale américaine en couleurs d'Emile Ardolino avec Patrick Swayze, Jennifer Grey, Jerry Orbach, Cynthia Rhodes, Jane Brucker.
L'été 1963, dans un village de vacances. Une jeune fille découvre la liberté à travers la danse et l'amour. Une chronique sociale sur un rythme endiablé. Un grand succès au box-office américain. ♦**George V 69** v.o.

DOWN BY LAW. 1985. 1h45. Comédie américaine en noir et blanc de Jim Jarmusch avec Tom Waits, John Lurie, Roberto Benigni, Nicoletta Braschi, Ellen Barkin.
♦**Cinoche 45** v.o.

ENGRENAGES. House of games. 1987. 1h50. Film policier américain en couleurs de David Mamet avec Lindsay Crouse, Joe Mantegna, Mike Nussbaum, Lilia Skala, J.-T. Walsh. ♦**Ciné Beaubourg Les Halles 19** v.o. ♦**UGC Danton 58** v.o. ♦**UGC Rotonde Montparnasse 61** v.o. ♦**UGC Champs-Elysées 78** v.o. ♦**Les 14 Juillet Bastille 109** v.o. ♦**14 Juillet Beaugrenelle 142** v.o. ♦**UGC Montparnasse 59** v.f. ♦**UGC Opera 95** v.f. ♦**UGC Gobelins 119** v.f.

La télévision

1 Tu veux regarder ... ?

lisez! You are doing a survey for a British magazine.
Look at this TV section from a French newspaper.
Make a list of all the different types of programmes you recognise.

AGENDA

TÉLÉVISION

TF 1

14.25 Série : Julien Fontanes magistrat.
16.05 Série : Tribunal.
16.35 Club Dorothée.
17.35 Série : Starsky et Hutch.
18.25 Jeu : Une famille en or.
18.55 Feuilleton : Santa-Barbara.
19.25 Jeu : La roue de la fortune.
19.50 Divertissement : Pas folles, les bêtes !
20.00 Journal, Météo et Tapis vert.
20.35 Variétés : Tous à la Une.
Avec Michel Boujenah, Francis Cabrel, Eddy Mitchell, Maurane, Zouk Machine...
22.40 Magazine : Et si on se disait tout ?
23.40 Journal, Météo et Bourse.
0.05 Concert : The Wall.

CANAL PLUS

15.30 Magazine : Rapido (rediff.).
16.00 Cinéma : Suivez cet avion. □
Film français de Patrice Ambard (1989).
17.25 Documentaire : Les allumés...
Le géant de Tignes.
18.00 Cabou cadin.

En clair jusqu'à 20.30

18.30 Dessins animés : Ça cartoon.
18.50 Top albums.
19.20 Magazine : Nulle part ailleurs.
20.05 Sport : Football. Championnat de France. Caen-Auxerre, en direct.
22.40 Flash d'informations.
22.45 Magazine : Exploits.
Présenté par Marc Toesca.
23.00 Cinéma : Le maître de guerre. ■
Film américain de Clint Eastwood (1986).

A 2

14.35 Série : Les enquêtes du commissaire Maigret.
Le témoignage d'un enfant de chœur.
16.05 Feuilleton : Un seul être vous manque
(2ᵉ épisode).
17.00 Magazine : Giga.
17.35 Jeu : Des chiffres et des lettres.
18.00 Magazine : Eve raconte.
Gabrielle Chanel (dernière partie).
18.15 Série : Quoi de neuf, docteur ?
18.51 Divertissement : Drôles de têtes.
19.00 Série : Mac Gyver.
19.59 Journal et Météo.
20.40 Variétés : Avant que le ciel ne nous tombe sur la tête.
Avec Alain Souchon, Eddy Mitchell, Jean-Marie Bigard, Liane Foly, Bruno Masure...
21.55 Caractères.
Magazine littéraire de Bernard Rapp. L'amour. Invités : Boris Cyrulnik *(Sous le signe du lien)*, Marc Lambron *(La nuit des masques)*, Jean-Didier Wolfromm *(La leçon inaugurale)*, Marie Nimier *(Anatomie d'un chœur)*.
23.15 24 heures sur l'A 2.
23.30 Journal et Météo.
23.35 Cinéma : Géant. ■■
Film américain de George Stevens (1955). Avec Elizabeth Taylor, Rock Hudson, James Dean (v.o.).

1 Une visite d'échange

lisez! You are helping to match up people for an exchange visit with a French twin town.

Will you match Karim with Jack, Sally or Ian?

Montpellier le 4 mai

Salut !

Je me présente, je m'appelle Karim. J'ai seize ans. Je suis assez grand. J'ai les cheveux courts et frisés. J'ai les yeux marron.

J'habite Montpellier. C'est une grande ville assez historique, située dans le sud-est de la France. J'habite un appartement moderne. Il y a trois chambres, une salle de bains, une cuisine et un salon.

J'aime jouer au ping-pong et regarder la télé. J'aime les dessins animés. Je vais souvent au cinéma. J'aime les films comiques.

J'espère que tu voudras bien être mon partenaire,

Amitiés

Karim

a Name: Jack
Age: 14
Interests: tennis, computers, cartoon books, war films.

b Name: Sally
Age: 15
Interests: table tennis, reading, watching TV, favourite programmes - soaps and cartoons, likes comedy.

c Name: Ian
Age: 16
Interests: squash, badminton, watching TV, going to the cinema, horror films.

2 Une lettre

écrivez! Now write a letter like Karim's to find a partner for yourself.

Vocabulaire

Unit 1

bonjour hello
bonsoir good evening
je me présente let me introduce myself
je m'appelle my name is
comment ça va? how are you?
très bien, merci very well, thank you
je vous présente ... let me introduce ...

mon/ma collègue my colleague
mon ami(e) my friend
ma mère my mother
mon père my father
ma soeur my sister
mon frère my brother

Unit 2

je suis I am
je suis assez ... I am quite ...

grand(e) tall
petit(e) small
gros(se) fat
mince thin
de taille moyenne medium height

j'ai ... I have ...
les yeux eyes
marron brown
noirs black
gris grey
bleus blue
verts green
noisette hazel

les cheveux hair
noirs black
châtain brown
blonds fair
roux red
gris grey
longs long
courts short
raides straight
frisés curly

Unit 3

c'est comment? what is it like?
c'est une grande ville it's a large town
petit(e) small
un petit village a small village
une station balnéaire a coastal resort
touristique tourist
historique historic
industriel(le) industrial
rural(e) rural

situé(e) dans le nord situated in the north
le sud south
l'ouest west
l'est east
le nord-ouest northwest
le nord-est northeast
le sud-ouest southwest
sud-est southeast
au centre de in the middle of

l'Angleterre England
l'Ecosse Scotland
l'Irlande Ireland
pays de Galles Wales
l'Australie Australia
la France France

Unit 4

il y a combien de pièces? how many rooms are there?
il y a ... there is/there are ...
il y a ... ? is there ... ?

un jardin a garden
un salon a sitting room
un garage a garage
un WC a toilet
une salle à manger a dining room
une salle de bains a bathroom
une cuisine a kitchen
une douche a shower
une chambre a bedroom
deux two
trois three
quatre four

Unit 5

vous habitez une maison? do you live in a house?
vous habitez un appartement? do you live in a flat?
j'habite I live
c'est comment? what's it like?

c'est assez grand it's quite big
c'est très petit it's very small
moderne modern
vieux old
calme quiet
confortable comfortable
agréable pleasant

Unit 6

qu'est-ce que tu aimes faire? what do you like doing?
tu veux ... ? do you want ... ?
tu aimes ... ? do you like ... ?

jouer au squash playing squash
badminton badminton
ping-pong table tennis
tennis tennis
football football
scrabble scrabble
regarder la télé watching TV
regarder les vidéos watching videos
écouter la radio listening to the radio
aller au cinéma going to the cinema
danser dancing

j'aime I like
je n'aime pas I don't like
je déteste I hate
j'adore I love

Unit 7

tu veux aller au cinéma? do you want to go to the cinema?
qu'est-ce qu'on joue? what's on?
qu'est-ce que c'est comme film? what kind of film is it?
c'est un film de science fiction it's a science fiction film
de guerre war
d'horreur horror
d'amour love
d'aventure adventure
comique comedy
un policier a police story
un film comique a comedy
un dessin animé a cartoon
un western a western

qu'est-ce que tu préfères? what do you prefer?
je préfère ... I prefer ...
d'accord I agree

Unit 8

tu veux regarder ... ? do you want to watch ... ?
qu'est-ce que c'est comme programme? what kind of programme is it?
c'est un programme de sport it's a sports programme

pour enfants for children
un jeu a quiz
un policier a police thriller
un documentaire a documentary
un dessin animé a cartoon
un film a film
un feuilleton a serial
la météo the weather
les informations the news

j'adore I love
j'aime I like
je n'aime pas I don't like
je déteste I hate

Grip Op Koolhydraten

'Koolhydraten lijken hot en happening. Ze vliegen om je oren in de winkels, leefstijladviezen en damesbladen. We weten de laatste jaren ineens dat ze "niet zo goed zijn". Yvonne Lemmers wist al heel veel jaren eerder dat het niet zo goed is om er veel van te eten. Je kunt er zwaar en ziek van worden op de lange termijn. Ze heeft als diëtist goed ingezien dat de ene koolhydraat de andere niet is, dat koolhydraatarm (low carb) verstandig klinkt, maar hóe arm/low dan? En geen koolhydraten eten? Is dat dan goed? Op die vragen geeft Yvonne met haar GOK-principe een antwoord. Het antwoord is namelijk: je moet ze niet te veel eten, je moet ze ook niet weglaten... Je moet er GRIP op krijgen. Voor nu en voor altijd. Dus je leert ermee te dealen. En dat is heerlijk. Als gezondheidsprofessional zie ik juist deze GOK-methode voor onze patiënten goed werken. En als "stevige dame" weet ik dat het voor mij ook al zes jaar werkt.

In de spreekkamer leg ik het vaak zo uit: bij koolhydraten en andere voedingstoffen heb je the good, the bad and the ugly... Je zou kunnen zeggen dat Yvonne dat mooi voor je in groen, oranje en rood heeft verdeeld. Dat is een fijne leidraad voor je leven.

En ja, af en toe mag het even bad!
Heerlijk toch?

En het fijne van GOK is dat je het helemaal zelf kunt inrichten. Dat doe ik graag. Lekker puur en eenvoudig eten waar ik op dat moment zin in heb. Maar als je dat lastiger vindt, zijn er veel eenvoudige recepten en zelfs complete weekmenu's. Dat is heerlijk om ongestoord af te vallen. Dan kun je ondertussen gewoon lekker door met je leven. De fitheid komt vanzelf.

- Martje

Grip Op Koolhydraten

SNELLE EN MAKKELIJKE WEEKMENU'S

Yvonne Lemmers

KOSMOS

Kosmos Uitgevers, Utrecht/Antwerpen

KOSMOS

www.kosmosuitgevers.nl

kosmos.uitgevers

kosmosuitgevers

Eerste druk, november 2018
Tweede druk, maart 2019
Derde druk, april 2019
Vierde druk, juli 2019

Auteur: Yvonne Lemmers
Receptuur en bereiding: Thea Bremer
Foodstyling: Goran Todorovic
Fotografie: Joshua Rood
Omslagontwerp en lay-out binnenwerk: Sven van Pel

ISBN 978 90 215 7060 0
NUR 443

Reeds verschenen:

9789090243481 Grip op Koolhydraten - Opgewicht

9789081556316 Grip op Koolhydraten - Kookboek 1

9789081556309 Grip op Koolhydraten - Kookboek 2

9789021564555 Grip op Koolhydraten dagmenu's, richtlijnen en recepten

9789021567860 Grip op Koolhydraten Voedingsplanner

9789081556323 Grip op Koolhydraten Productenwijzer

9789021572895 Slank en energiek met Grip Op Koolhydraten

INHOUD

SNELLE EN MAKKELIJKE WEEKMENU'S

Steeds meer mensen ontdekken het gemak, het genot en de lichamelijke en geestelijke voordelen van de koolhydraatbeperkte eetmethode van *Grip op Koolhydraten* (= GOK) met het zo gewaardeerde koolhydratenuur.
Om tegemoet te komen aan de vraag naar nóg meer makkelijke en snelle recepten en vooral ook weekmenu's hebben we dit boek *Grip op Koolhydraten – Weekmenu's* samengesteld. Om GOK nóg makkelijker en toepasbaarder te maken voor iedereen. Dus ook voor kinderen, ouderen, maar ook voor mensen die een maagverkleining hebben. Met die groepen hebben we dan ook rekening gehouden en daarvoor hebben we aparte weekmenu's samengesteld. Dit boek bevat meer dan 120 mooie nieuwe verrassende koolhydraatarme (GOK-groene) en koolhydraatbeperkte (GOK-oranje) recepten. De recepten zijn vrijwel allemaal met weinig ingrediënten samengesteld én snel te maken. Snelle en makkelijke recepten dus. Bijvoorbeeld van koolhydraatarme vezelcrackers, broden, soepen, tussendoortjes, poké bowls, kip-, kalkoen-, eier- en groentegerechten. In de 12 makkelijke en snelle weekmenu's zijn veel van deze nieuwe recepten verwerkt.

Er zijn 10 fase 1-weekmenu's – voor elk wat wils – om op gewicht te komen en 2 fase 2-weekmenu's om op gewicht te blijven.
De fase 1-weekmenu's zijn ingedeeld in categorieën. Drie gewone weekmenu's, een weekmenu met dagelijkse broodmaaltijden, een weekmenu zonder vlees, een weekmenu zonder vlees en vis, twee weekmenu's met tussendoortjes, geschikt voor kleine eters, zoals mensen met een maagverkleining, kinderen en ouderen, maar ook voor mensen die net starten met GOK.

De kracht van Grip op Koolhydraten is dat er zoveel ruimte is voor eigen keuze van je eetschema. Iedereen eet immers op zijn eigen manier en heeft zijn eigen specifieke voorkeuren en dingen die je niet wilt eten, zoals kaas of vlees. Daarom staat in de weekmenu's bijvoorbeeld: 'koolhydratenuur naar keuze', 'vezelcracker met beleg naar keuze', 'GOK-groene maaltijd naar keuze', met daarbij ideeën uit dit boek.
Je kunt dus naar hartenlust variëren in de weekmenu's, dagdelen wisselen of je favoriete recepten uit de voorgaande GOK-boeken in je eigen weekmenu's gebruiken.
Blijf wel altijd rekening houden met de richtlijnen van Grip op Koolhydraten fase 1 of 2 (zie voor de volledige richtlijnen van fase 1 en meer uitleg over het koolhydratenuur het basisboek *Opgewicht* (ISBN 978 90 902 4348 1) en *Grip op Koolhydraten – dagmenu's, richtlijnen en recepten* (ISBN 978 90 215 6455 5).

Eigen keuze staat voorop, dus mixen en matchen maar!
'Wissel af en varieer' is en blijft een van de richtlijnen van GOK!
Hou vast aan Grip op koolhydraten en hou vol!

Succes gewenst met Grip op Koolhydraten en geniet van de lichamelijke én geestelijke voordelen.
Veel kook- en bakplezier en eet smakelijk.
Tot slot mijn speciale dank aan hobbykok Thea Bremer die net als in de Grip op Koolhydraten Kookboeken 1 en 2 weer mooie smaakvolle en makkelijke recepten samengesteld heeft.

Yvonne Lemmers diëtist
Beneden-Leeuwen

RECEPTEN VOOR 2 PERSONEN / PORTIES

Alle recepten zijn voor 2 personen/porties tenzij anders vermeld.
1 eetlepel is altijd een afgestreken eetlepel.

Een maaltijd of tussendoortje mag niet uit alleen groenten bestaan. Eet groenten altijd in combinatie met eiwitrijke producten

HOUD REKENING MET...

De hoeveelheden die aangegeven zijn in de recepten en bij de menu's passen bij een gemiddeld persoon in fase 1 (op gewicht komen) met een gemiddelde activiteit. Houd daarom rekening met je eigen lengte, dagelijkse beweging en gewicht. Pas de hoeveelheden naar behoefte aan. Bijvoorbeeld: een grote man met veel lichamelijke arbeid mag meer eten dan de aangegeven hoeveelheden en een kleine vrouw zal wat minder moeten eten om op gewicht te komen.

KOOLHYDRATEN IN KOOLHYDRATENUUR

De voorbeelden van koolhydratenuren zijn zo samengesteld dat ze allemaal ongeveer dezelfde hoeveelheid koolhydraten bevatten. Daarom is er in het ene dagmenu wel ruimte voor een toetje, en in een ander dagmenu niet. Alleen in de balansmenu's wordt hiervan afgeweken De koolhydratenuren kunnen naar wens aangepast worden met een ander recept of producten met dezelfde GOK-kleur (zie de verkorte richtlijnen van GOK-fase 1 op blz. 10 van dit boek).

UITLEG KLEURCODE RECEPTEN:

Groen: Een recept is groen als alle producten GOK-groen zijn, dat wil zeggen van de groene lijst van GOK afkomstig zijn. Dit zijn voornamelijk koolhydraatarme voedingsmiddelen zonder kunstmatige zoetstoffen.
Oranje: Een recept is oranje bij minimaal 1 GOK-oranje product (van de oranje lijst van GOK) en geen product van de rode lijst (zoals kunstmatige zoetstoffen, transvetzuren en glucose-fructosestroop). Dit zijn de koolhydraatbeperkte of koolhydraatrijke voedingsmiddelen die alleen in het koolhydratenuur gebruikt mogen worden.
GOK-rood = vermijden. Vanzelfsprekend bevatten de recepten en de weekmenu's in dit boek géén producten van de rode lijst.

RICHTLIJNEN FASE 1: OP GEWICHT KOMEN

- Iedere dag een koolhydratenuur
- Zorg voor balans in het koolhydratenuur, zodat het (op het oog) ongeveer evenveel is:
  - ¼ eiwitten /vetten (groene lijst)
  - ¼ zetmeelvrije groenten en vezels (groene lijst)
  - ¼ fruit (oranje lijst)
  - ¼ alle overige koolhydraatrijke producten (oranje lijst)
- Beperk je in het koolhydratenuur tot één doorlopende maaltijd zonder lange pauzes. Duur van de maaltijd: maximaal 60 minuten, korter mag ook en is nog beter.

Voor de overige maaltijden/tussendoortjes geldt:
- Kies alleen producten van de groene lijst
- Combinatie: groenten en eiwitten/vetten. Een maaltijd of tussendoortje mag niet uit alleen groenten bestaan. Eet groenten altijd in combinatie met eiwitrijke producten zoals kaas, vlees, kip, ei of vis.
- Solo: eiwitten/vetten. Kaas, vlees, kip, ei, vis, noten mogen wel zonder groenten gegeten worden.
- Tussendoortjes afbouwen tot zo min mogelijk.
- Alleen dranken van de groene lijst. Drink géén kunstmatig gezoete dranken.
- Zit minder en beweeg dagelijks. Dat is goed voor lichaam én geest.
- Veel Omega 3 (vette vis) en omega 9 (olijfolie) en weinig omega 6 (linolzuur).
- Wees niet bang voor vet.
- Neem dagelijks voedingssupplementen om de eventuele tekorten aan vitamines en mineralen in je voeding op te lossen. Voedingssupplementen zijn geen medicijnen! Je hebt alle vitamines en mineralen nodig voor een goede stofwisseling en een optimaal afvalvermogen.
- Wissel af en varieer: Wissel af in hoeveelheid eten en varieer in je voeding. Je lichaam mag niet lui worden en zich erop instellen dat het die dag weer hetzelfde te verwerken heeft als de vorige dag. Blijf daarom je lichaam verrassen, dan werkt het kunstje met Grip op Koolhydraten iedere keer weer.

Zie voor meer tekst en uitleg, de uitgebreide richtlijnen van fase 1 en de groene, oranje en rode lijsten, het basisboek *Opgewicht* (ISBN 978 90 902 43481) en *Grip op Koolhydraten – dagmenu's, richtlijnen en recepten* (ISBN 978 90 215 6455 5).

RICHTLIJNEN VOOR HET SAMENSTELLEN VAN JE MAALTIJDEN

Maak de porties zo groot dat je met een verzadigd gevoel van tafel gaat. (Natuurlijk niet overdrijven qua hoeveelheden.) Je moet uitgaan van ongeveer 100 gram vlees, vis, kaas, eieren (1 ei is 50 gram) per maaltijd. In het koolhydratenuur mag de portie eventueel wat groter zijn. Per persoon verschilt het natuurlijk. Bijvoorbeeld: een man van 120 kilo mag meer hebben dan een vrouw van 80 kilo. Naarmate je minder gaat wegen, kunnen de porties kleiner worden. Je lijf geeft het vanzelf aan. Je zult dus voor jezelf de juiste portiegrootte moeten zien te vinden, met inachtneming van de richtlijn 4 x ¼ in het koolhydratenuur. En let wel, vol = vol.

MAAK HET VOOR JEZELF SNEL EN MAKKELIJK!

Ga goed voorbereid aan de slag!
Maak een plan de campagne en houd je daaraan!

BRODEN EN CRACKERS:

Het is lekker, snel én makkelijk om koolhydraatarm brood of vezelcrackers als ontbijt of lunch te kiezen. In de weekmenu's zie je die dan ook vaak staan.
Omdat het vrijwel ondoenlijk is om voor al die eetmomenten verse crackers en broden te bakken is het aan te raden om grotere hoeveelheden tegelijk te bakken. Neem hier wekelijks even de tijd voor. Zo heb je genoeg op voorraad. De broden en crackers zijn allemaal lang houdbaar.
De brood- en crackerrecepten zijn bovendien allemaal snel en makkelijk te maken. Het is een kwestie van afwegen, mengen en dan uitsmeren op een bakplaat (voor crackers) of in een bakvorm gieten (broden). De oven/magnetron doet de rest. Leer wel je oven kennen. De baktijden die aangegeven zijn, kunnen afwijkend zijn voor jouw apparatuur. Schrijf daarom gerust in je boek als er aanpassingen nodig zijn qua temperatuur of baktijden. Een kookboek is ervoor om eigen aantekeningen in te maken.

- Bak crackers goed droog en bewaar ze luchtdicht afgesloten, dan zijn ze dagen / weken lekker. Mochten ze wat minder knapperig geworden zijn, dan zijn ze in enkele minuten op te piepen in de broodrooster, magnetron of oven tot ze weer droog en knapperig zijn.
- De broden – die meestal eieren bevatten en daarom bederfelijk zijn – moeten koel bewaard worden. In de koelkast zijn ze ten minste 3 dagen houdbaar. In de diepvries enkele maanden.
  Snel en makkelijk: invriezen per portie.

QUICHES, SALADES EN POKÉ BOWLS

- Quiches, salades en poké bowls zijn ook van tevoren klaar te maken.
  Koel bewaard zijn deze gerechten drie dagen houdbaar. Prima mee te nemen in bijvoorbeeld een lunchbox met aparte vakjes.
- Quiches kun je ook in vriezen. Snel en makkelijk: invriezen per portie. Handig om mee te nemen in een lunchbox. Koud opeten of even opwarmen in de magnetron.

SOEPEN

- Ook soepen kun je van tevoren klaarmaken en makkelijk opwarmen.
  Lekker voor een snelle warme lunch of desgewenst als opkikkertje tussendoor.
- In een thermosfles met brede hals zijn soepen makkelijk mee te nemen naar kantoor of school voor een snelle warme lunch.

NOODVOORRADEN

- Maak noodvoorraden aan van GOK-groene gerechten zodat je altijd de goede keuze kunt maken. Zorg dus voor koolhydraatarme broden en quiches in de diepvries en vezelcrackers in een afgesloten doosje.
- En zorg dat je altijd een zakje gemengde noten of eigengemaakte gekruide nootjes (recept op blz. 106) op voorraad hebt (en meeneemt in je tas).
- Weet dat je altijd de mogelijkheid hebt om maximaal 50 gram noten te eten als GOK-groene maaltijd. Dat is snel en makkelijk als je eens een keer geen tijd of mogelijkheid hebt voor een andere GOK-groene maaltijd.

TOELICHTING BIJ DE MENU'S

In de weekmenu's zie je vaak een * staan achter een menukeuze of gerecht. Hieronder staat de toelichting van deze sterretjes. Lees deze informatie regelmatig goed door, zodat je de richtlijnen van GOK door en door leert kennen en in de praktijk weet toe te passen.

*) KH-UUR (KOOLHYDRATEN-UUR) NAAR KEUZE

Maak een keuze uit producten van de groene en oranje lijst. Houd wel rekening met de 4 x ¼ indeling om het koolhydratenuur in balans te houden. Want als je te veel koolhydraten in het uur neemt, dan is de kans groot dat je snel weer honger krijgt en wat aankomt.

4 X ¼ INDELING:
Op het oog:

- ¼ eiwitten /vetten (groene lijst)
- ¼ zetmeelvrije groenten en vezels (groene lijst)
- ¼ fruit (oranje lijst)
- ¼ alle overige koolhydraatrijke producten (oranje lijst)

Zie voor de volledige richtlijnen van fase 1 en meer uitleg over het koolhydratenuur het basisboek *Opgewicht* (ISBN 978 90 902 43481) en *Grip op Koolhydraten – dagmenu's, richtlijnen en recepten* (ISBN 978 90 215 64555)

*) BELEG NAAR KEUZE

Maak een keuze uit beleg van de groene lijst. Kies uit vlees(waren), vis, kaas of notenpasta, ei of eiersalade.. Maak ook gerust combinaties van eiwitrijk belegsoorten zoals wat plakjes ei op vleeswaren. Dit maakt het lekker smeuïg en voedzamer. Met naar wens nog wat groente (rauwkost, gekookte groenten, kiemgroenten) erbij of erop. Left-overs (restjes) van de warme maaltijd zijn makkelijk om te gebruiken als beleg op een (eigengemaakte) sneetje koolhydraatarm brood of cracker.

*) BROODMAALTIJD NAAR KEUZE (KH-UUR) = GOK-ORANJE

In het koolhydratenuur kan naar wens ook gewoon (= koolhydraatrijk) brood gegeten worden.
In fase 2 (zie weekmenu's 11 en 12) zijn buiten het koolhydratenuur om ook broodmaaltijden mogelijk.
Om de hoeveelheid koolhydraten beperkt te houden zijn dit de richtlijnen voor de GOK-oranje broodmaaltijden:

- Neem nooit dubbele boterhammen, behalve bij tosti's
- Snijd broodjes in twee helften.
- Iedere snee brood of helft van het broodje besmeer je ruim met roomboter.
- Daarna dik beleggen met je favoriete beleg naar keuze (zie de toelichting 'Beleg naar keuze' op blz. 13). Op deze manier hoef je geen 4 sneden (of misschien zelfs meer) te eten maar heb je genoeg aan 1 of 2 sneden. Dat scheelt je heel wat koolhydraten (1 snee gewoon brood bevat ca. 15 g koolhydraten). Maak dus van elke snee brood 'een feestje', flink belegd en versierd met rauwkost. Paar schijfjes paprika op wat vleeswaren of kaas, heerlijk. Neem een voorbeeld aan goed-gezond-belegde broodjes in restaurants. Daar krijg je ook meer beleg dan brood, en zo hoort het ook.
- Om het koolhydratenuur compleet te maken neem er dan wat groenten (bijv. in de vorm van rauwkost) en 1 portie fruit bij. Zie de voorbeelden in weekmenu 4.
- In fase 2 hoeft je er geen fruit bij te doen, als je in het koolhydratenuur al een portie fruit eet.

Naar keuze kun je natuurlijk altijd je eigengebakken koolhydraatarme brood eten. Dat scheelt in koolhydraten. Als je gevoelig bent voor gluten is het zeker aan te raden.
Let wel, kant en klaar gekocht koolhydraatarm brood bevat meestal wél gluten en meestal ook soja. Dat is dan weer wat minder goed voor je lijf.

*) KOOLHYDRAATARM BROOD NAAR KEUZE

Neem als koolhydraatarm brood het liefst een eigengebakken voedzaam vezelrijk brood met noten(meel), zemelen, zaden en pitten. Kies bijvoorbeeld uit een naanbroodje, platbrood, champignon-spekbrood of een MIM. Of kies een van de GOK-groene broodrecepten in de eerder verschenen GOK-boeken, zoals voedzaam vezelbrood, Noors platbrood. Erg lekker allemaal!

Koolhydraatarm brood met sojameel, tarwe-eiwit (= gluten) en tarwemeel is niet geschikt om dagelijks te eten.

*) VEZELCRACKERS NAAR KEUZE

Kies, net als bij het koolhydraatarme brood, ook bij crackers voor (eigengemaakte) vezelrijke crackers met als hoofdingrediënten zemelen, noten(meel), zaden en pitten. Als bij de eerste drie ingrediënten van kant-en-klare crackers zowel sojameel, tarwe-eiwit (= gluten) en tarwemeel staat, dan zijn deze niet geschikt om dagelijks te eten. Ze kunnen dan wel koolhydraatarm zijn, maar ze geven niet echt eetrust en ook je darmen geven ze geen rust. De kans is groot dat je er nog steeds een opgeblazen gevoel van krijgt. Kies daarom voor eigengebakken vezelcrackers met de recepten uit dit boek en de andere GOK-boeken, zoals lijnzaadcrackers, zaden-pittencrackers en Yvonne's favorites. Er zijn ook koolhydraatarme vezelcrackers (met als eerste ingrediënt zemelen) te koop die heel lang goed blijven. Neem daar gerust een voorraadje van in huis voor een snelle en makkelijke GOK-groene koolhydraatarme maaltijd.

*) PSYLLIUMVEZELS

Op diverse dagen in de weekmenu's staat bijvoorbeeld vermeld: 'Goed om er nog wat psylliumvezels bij te nemen.' Daarmee wordt bedoeld de oplosbare psylliumvezels, en ook de combinatie psylliumvezels/inuline.
Begin met 1 theelepel psylliumvezels opgelost in een glas water, goed roeren, direct opdrinken (anders wordt het te dik) en dan nog een glas water extra drinken. De vezels trekken veel vocht aan en als je er te weinig bij drinkt kan dat weer een ongemakkelijk gevoel geven.
Valt het goed dan kun je de volgende keer 2 of 3 theelepels (of 1 afgestreken eetlepel) psylliumvezels nemen in een groot glas water.
Het geeft een lekker vol gevoel en de vezels zijn goed voor je darmen. En doordat de oplosbare vezels vetten en gifstoffen binden is het extra aan te bevelen, vooral als je veel overgewicht hebt.
Je kunt ook op tijdstippen waarop je eigenlijk trek zou hebben in een tussendoortje (bijv. om 16.00 uur of 21.00 uur) een glas opgeloste psylliumvezels nemen. Maag vol, trek weg ;-)
Ook als er geen psylliumvezels bij de menu's vermeld staat, mogen ze altijd dagelijks 1 – 3 keer ingenomen worden. Psylliumvezels en inuline zijn pre- en probiotica en dragen bij tot een soepele ontlasting en zijn goed voor je afvalvermogen.
Echt een aanrader en een van de troeven van het GOK-programma. Lees in het basisboek *Opgewicht* meer over het belang van psylliumvezels.

De koolhydraten in de psylliumvezels zijn niet opneembaar en hebben daarom geen invloed op de bloedsuiker en er hoeft geen insuline aangemaakt te worden. De vezels zijn voedsel voor de darmbacteriën. Ze functioneren er erg goed op en je krijgt er een aangename soepele ontlasting van. De darmen worden er niet lui van en je kunt ze dus gerust een hele tijd gebruiken. Zorg wel dat je er voldoende bij drinkt.

*) CHOCOLADE

Hoe puurder, des te meer cacao en des te minder suiker er in zit.
Kies daarom voor chocolade met minimaal 72% cacao en eet maximaal 20 gram chocolade als afsluiter van je koolhydratenuur. Eet langzaam en geniet van elk stukje.

GEBRUIK ZOUT MET JODIUM!

In veel recepten staat zout vermeld. Zout is een natuurlijke smaakmaker.
Belangrijk!
Met zout wordt '(keuken)zout met jodium' bedoeld.
Gebruik gejodeerd zout (zout met jodium) in je maaltijden. Op die manier krijg je meer jodium binnen dan met gewoon zout of zeezout (= zonder jodium).
Zout met jodium is te koop in de supermarkt onder de naam JOZO (JOdium ZOut) in de rode verpakking en groene verpakking, dus niet de blauwe verpakking , want daar zit geen jodium in. Ook steeds meer huismerken verkopen zout met jodium. Gebruiken dus!

UITLEG
Bakkers zijn verplicht om brood te bakken met gejodeerd bakkerszout om tekorten aan jodium in voeding te voorkomen. Omdat bij Grip op Koolhydraten veelal weinig door bakkers-gebakken-brood gegeten wordt, moet je - voor behoud van een goede schildklierfunctie - zout met jodium gebruiken om aan de benodigde hoeveelheid jodium te komen.
Zeezout, Keltisch zout en Himalaya zout bevatten vrijwel geen jodium. En de zo geprezen mineralen die in deze zouten zitten, blijken minimale hoeveelheden te zijn. Bij inname van een dagelijkse multivitamine krijg je ook al de nodige mineralen extra binnen.
Kies daarom voor keukenzout met jodium, omdat het mineraal jodium van essentieel belang is voor onder andere een goede schildklierwerking. In een normale multivitamine zit veelal niet genoeg jodium om aan de dagelijkse behoefte te voldoen.

EIEREN: EEN EI HOORT ERBIJ

Neem gerust iedere dag één, twee of zelfs meer eieren.
Ze bevatten de goede eiwitten, vetten, veel vitamines en mineralen. Ze bevatten geen koolhydraten. Eieren zijn enorm voedzaam en verzadigend. Én goedkoop en volop verkrijgbaar.
In de weekmenu's vind je dan ook veel eetmomenten met eieren.
Houd je niet van gekookte eieren, verwerk eieren dan in een omelet, muffin (MIM), quiche of bak ze gewoon lekker met wat spek eronder. En wil je iedere dag twee eieren met spek, doe dat dan gewoon. Lekker met een augurkje erbij. Zo makkelijk kan GOK zijn.

HELP, IK VAL NIET GENOEG AF?

Het streven is om in fase 1 gemiddeld 0,5 tot 1 kg per week – al schommelend - af te vallen.

VAL JE MINDER AF?
- Maak dan de portie koolhydraten in het koolhydratenuur eens een paar dagen kleiner en zie wat er gebeurt. In de balansmenu's vind je voorbeelden van dagen met minder koolhydraten.
- Als de maaltijd (in je koolhydratenuur) niet als verzadigend gevoeld wordt, maak dan vooral de niet-koolhydraten-porties (van de groene lijst) groter.
- Maak eens een tijdje de porties van de niet-koolhydratenmaaltijden (= GOK-groene maaltijden) kleiner en zie wat er gebeurt. Waarschijnlijk zul je - ondanks de misschien voor jouw doen kleine porties - geen honger hebben. Neem bijvoorbeeld geen twee maar één cracker of sneetje koolhydraatarm vezelbrood. Dat scheelt niet alleen de cracker of het brood maar vooral de hoeveelheid beleg. En je zult merken dat je toch verzadigd blijft. Voor je eigen gemoedsrust geef je jezelf de ruimte om een gekookt ei als eventueel tussendoortje bij de hand te hebben.
  Met een glas water met psylliumvezels erbij zul je zeker

lange tijd een vol gevoel hebben.
- Let op de tussendoortjes. Liefst zo min mogelijk tussendoortjes. Vooral te veel noten en kaas tussendoor kunnen saboteurs zijn van je eigen afvalproject. Lees op blz. 16 meer uitleg hierover.
- Pas je dagelijkse beweging aan. Want door extra bewegen verbruik je je voorraadje glycogeen (=reservesuiker in de spieren) en ben je weer sneller je eigen lichaamsvetten aan het verbranden.
- Neem eens een ander merk multivitaminen. Wellicht kom je toch nog een vitamine- of mineraal tekort, door een slechtere opname van vooral de mineralen, waardoor de stofwisseling niet optimaal werkt.

Als je op bovenstaande punten let, val je wellicht wel weer af.

LET OP:
- Bij mensen die bij de aanvang van het GOK-programma slecht enkele kilo's overgewicht hebben, kan het zelfs zijn dat ze qua gewicht weinig merken, maar dat ze wel één of twee kledingmaten minder krijgen naarmate ze langer bezig zijn met GOK fase 1. Dat komt omdat je met GOK koolhydraatbeperkt én eiwitrijk eet en daardoor meer spieren aanmaakt en vetten afvalt. En aangezien spieren meer wegen dan vet, merk je dan vrijwel niets op de weegschaal. Dus laat je niet van de wijs brengen door de weegschaal. De weegschaal zegt immers niet alles. Je broekriem des te meer!

STREEFGEWICHT IN ZICHT?

Naarmate je meer afvalt en dus minder gewicht hebt zul je merken dat je met dezelfde portiegrootte, waar je ettelijke kilo's mee afgevallen bent, nu niet meer zo snel afvalt. Je lijf heeft immers minder energie nodig omdat het eenvoudigweg minder hóeft te onderhouden, de basale stofwisseling is lager geworden. Vooral als je al veel bent afgevallen en nu steeds dichter bij je gewenste kledingmaat bent zul je nog even nauwlettend de richtlijnen van fase 1 GOK moeten volgen. Het is aan te raden om vooral variatie in je voeding en leefstijl te blijven brengen om je lichaam alert te houden.

Aanraders
1. Maak de portiegrootte kleiner. Vooral in het koolhydratenuur zou je kunnen minderen, met name de GOK-oranje producten.
2. Afwisselend wat meer en wat minder koolhydraten.
3. Geef het afvallen een nieuwe impuls door eens een keer een maaltijd uit te stellen of over te slaan.
4. Minder zitten en wat extra bewegen (vooral via interval training HIIT).
5. Doorbreek je eetpatroon: verwissel eens een tijdje het koolhydratenuur. Bijvoorbeeld van de avond naar de middag of naar de ochtend. Dit kan net weer even het zetje geven om af te gaan vallen.

Voor de punten 2 en 3 kun je de balansmenu's 9 en 10 als voorbeeld nemen.

RICHTLIJN HOEVEELHEDEN VAN DE KOOLHYDRAATRIJKE PRODUCTEN IN HET KOOLHYDRATENUUR

VOOR EEN GEMIDDELDE ETER

Brood	60 gram (2 sneetjes)
Aardappelen	100 gram (2 kleine aardappelen)
Pasta	150 gram gaar (3 opscheplepels) / 50 gram rauw
Rijst	75 - 100 gram gaar (2 opscheplepels) / 40 gram rauw
Peulvruchten	150 gram gaar (2 opscheplepels)
Quinoa	50 gram rauw
Puree (voor stamppot)	150 gram gaar (2 opscheplepels)
Vleesvervanger	150 gram
Friet	75 gram (bereid)
Toetje	150 gram
Fruit	Gemiddelde portie bijv. • 1 appel, sinaasappel, peer, citrusfruit, kleine banaan etc. • 100 - 150 gram roodfruit (o.a. aardbeien, bosbessen, bramen, kersen, blauwe bessen) Een portie roodfruit bevat de minste koolhydraten. Kies hier vaak voor. • 100 gram druiven (15 – 20 grote druiven) • 150 gram meloen (1/8 kleine meloen) • 15-20 druiven • 4 – 5 pruimen • 2 kiwi's

LAAT DE TUSSENDOORTJES GEEN SABOTEUR WORDEN VAN JE EIGEN GEWICHTS-PROJECT!

In de menu's met tussendoortjes (weekmenu 7 en 8) is het zaak om de portiegrootte van de hoofdmaaltijden klein te houden. Want als je én drie grote maaltijden eet en nog eens drie tussendoortjes eet, dan is de kans klein dat je afvalt. De weekmenu's 7 en 8 zijn vooral bedoeld voor mensen die geen grote porties per maaltijd (kunnen) eten. Zoals mensen met een maagverkleining, kinderen en (verzwakte) oude mensen. Juist als er weinig gegeten kan worden, is het zo fijn om jezelf in de drie hoofdmaaltijden goed te voeden met eiwitrijke niet-vetarme voeding. Dat voedt en verzadigt. En om aan voldoende calorieën te komen zijn er tussendoortjes nodig, omdat eenvoudigweg in drie kleine maaltijden vaak niet eens aan de 1000 kcal gekomen kan worden.

NOTEN TUSSENDOOR: PAS OP!

Val je niet af en neem je dagelijks meer dan een handje noten tussendoor? Eet dan eens een paar weken geen noten als tussendoortje en zie wat het met je gewicht doet.

UITLEG

Noten zijn vetrijk en daardoor energierijk. Én noten hebben een hoge dooreet-factor. Je eet er snel te veel van. Met als gevolg dat je ongemerkt te veel calorieën binnen krijgt. We tellen bij GOK dan wel geen calorieën maar het zal voor iedereen begrijpelijk zijn dat je ook te veel GOK-groen kunt eten en dat je daardoor niet afvalt. Vooral mensen die niet veel (extra) bewegen zullen toch enigszins spaarzaam moeten eten. Het fijne van GOK is dat je geen honger hebt en dus niet hoeft te vervallen in veel en vaak eten en snaaien. Eetrust dus. Het streven is om maximaal 3 voedzame maaltijden te eten en zo min mogelijk tussendoortjes waardoor je tussen de 1200 en 1500-1700 kcal binnenkrijgt. Maak daar gebruik van en blijf de tussendoortjes beperken. Dat kan immers het verschil maken in wel of niet afvallen.

KAAS TUSSENDOOR: PAS OP!
Alles wat op de vorige bladzijde over noten gezegd is, geldt ook voor kaas. Vooral mensen die tussendoor van de kaas blíjven eten – met het idee: het is GOK-groen, dus het mag – zullen waarschijnlijk verschil gaan merken op de weegschaal of aan de broekriem, als ze eens een tijdje géén kaas tussendoor eten.

ALGEMENE VOEDINGSTIPS

Let hierop:

- Goed kauwen. Zodat de voedingsstoffen zo goed mogelijk opgenomen kunnen worden. Voorvertering begint al in de mond. In het mondslijmvlies zitten enzymen die zetmeel afbreken.
- Liefst geen grote hoeveelheden water drinken tijdens de maaltijd. Laat je speeksel zijn werk doen. Dat komt de spijsvertering ten goede.
- Voeg vet (roomboter of olijfolie) toe aan de maaltijd. Vetten zijn van belang voor de opname van in vetoplosbare vitamines en vetten zijn voedzaam. Ook je darmen gaan goed op wat meer vet in de maaltijden. Vezels, vocht en vetten zijn een goede combinatie.
- Eieren zijn voedzaam en zitten bomvol nutriënten. Iedere dag twee eieren mag gerust. Gekookte eitjes zo los uit de hand zijn makkelijke tussendoortjes. Kook dus altijd wat eitjes van tevoren.
- Fruit hoeft niet in het koolhydratenuur als het niet past of als je al 'vol' zit. Dit is vooral van belang bij mensen met een maagverkleining. Bij een sleeve kan vaak wel fruit in het koolhydratenuur.
- Sla dus gerust een dag het fruit over. Zorg die dag dan wel voor voldoende vezels in groenten. Extra groenten kun je toevoegen in een tussendoortje in combinatie met wat vlees, vis of kaas. Of voeg wat oplosbare vezels, zoals psylliumvezels, toe aan je dagmenu. Deze oplosbare vezels kun je los van een maaltijd innemen of in plaats van een tussendoortje.
- Kies vaker voor rood klein fruit, zoals aardbeien, frambozen, bramen, bosbessen. Rood fruit zit vol met goede stoffen en heeft een kleiner volume én het bevat minder koolhydraten dan de grote vruchten die vooral vol met vocht en fruitsuikers zitten.
- Rood fruit is ook als diepvriesfruit te koop en zeer geschikt en snel en makkelijk in een toetje te verwerken in het koolhydratenuur. Het hele jaar door verkrijgbaar voor een schappelijke prijs.
- Zorg voor GOK-groene hapjes in de koelkast. Zodat je altijd voor de eventuele trek tussendoor iets GOK-proofs hebt liggen. Dit maakt een goede GOK-keuze makkelijker. Maar houd de tussendoortjes beperkt. Hoe minder hoe beter.

VASTEN / INTERMITTENT FASTING

Als je goed in de vetverbranding zit, is het makkelijk om een tijdje niets te eten. Je bloedsuikers worden door je lichaam in stand gehouden. Probeer de eerste maaltijd zo lang mogelijk uit te stellen zodat je een periode van minimaal 15 uur niets eet. Dit geeft het afvallen vaak een boost.
Neem naar wens een glas psylliumvezels.
Drink veel vocht in de vorm van (heet) water, thee, koffie.
Laat je lekker afleiden door bezigheden, dus ga gewoon aan de slag, lichamelijk of geestelijk. Voor je er erg in hebt is de ochtend voorbij. En zul je gemerkt hebben dat je eigenlijk geen honger gehad hebt, geen dipjes en een helder hoofd :-)

SEIZOENSFRUIT IN OVERVLOED EN ZO'N TREK ERIN! WAT NU?

Vooral in de zomermaanden is er vers fruit in overvloed. Als je zin hebt in behoorlijk wat fruit, plan dat dan in het koolhydratenuur in. Je eet dan een dubbele portie fruit en geen overige koolhydraten. Dus als je veel fruit eet in je koolhydratenuur, neem dan geen aardappels, rijst, pasta of andere zetmeelbronnen en suikers.
Een koolhydratenuur kan er dan als volgt uit zien:

- portie vlees of vis
- portie groente of een lekkere gemengde sla
- dubbele portie fruit.

Zo houd je de balans in het koolhydratenuur.
De helft GOK-groen en de helft GOK-oranje.
En houd je aan de richtlijn om alleen in het koolhydratenuur fruit te eten! Veel en vaak fruit eten en afvallen gaat helaas niet samen. Dan saboteer je je eigen afvalproces. Dat zou jammer zijn.

WANNEER SUPPLEMENTEN INNEMEN?

- Een multivitamine en vitamine D moeten altijd in combinatie met een vet-bevattende maaltijd ingenomen worden. Anders worden de in-vet-oplosbare vitamines A, D, E en K niet goed opgenomen.
- In water oplosbare vitamines en mineralen zoals vitamine C en magnesium kunnen wel los van een maaltijd ingenomen worden.
- Psylliumvezels kunnen ook los van een maaltijd ingenomen worden. Prima om dit voor het ontbijt in te nemen, of bijvoorbeeld rond 16.00 of 21.00 uur. Op tijdstippen waarop je anders geneigd zou zijn om een tussendoortje te nemen. Buik gevuld en verlost van 'trek'.

GASTRIC BYPASS (GBP = MAAGVERKLEINING) (WEEKMENU'S 7 EN 8)

GOK en GBP gaan goed samen

UITLEG

Met een maagverkleining is het van groot belang dat wat je eet, je lichaam 'voedt' en niet alleen maar 'vult'. Dat je voldoende eiwitten en goede vetten binnen krijgt. En dat je ook strikt de voorgeschreven supplementen in blijft nemen. Nutriëntentekorten (een tekort aan vitamines, mineralen en sporenelementen) liggen op de loer. En als je op celniveau tekorten hebt, dan gaat het lichaam 'schreeuwen' om voeding in de vorm van honger!
Omdat door de kleine maaginhoud in het koolhydratenuur veelal niet voldoende gegeten kan worden, zijn er meerdere kleine tussendoortjes van de GOK-groene lijst toegestaan. Laat je inspireren door de vele voorbeelden in de weekmenu's 7 en 8.
Het koolhydratenuur blijft hetzelfde als voor mensen zonder maagverkleining, maar de kwarten op het bord zijn wat kleiner. Van alles wat minder dus! Maar nog steeds de balans van 4 x ¼.

GOK-STARTERS (WEEKMENU'S 7 EN 8)

Vrijwel iedereen die begint met Grip op Koolhydraten, kan zich niet voorstellen dat 3 hoofdmaaltijden voldoende kunnen zijn. In de meeste koolhydraatrijke 'normale' eetpatronen worden immers naast de 3 hoofdmaaltijden meerdere tussendoortjes gegeten.
Om de overgang naar een GOK-eetpatroon met zo min mogelijk tussendoortjes makkelijk te maken, kan het handig zijn om de weekmenu's 7 en 8 te gebruiken.
Als je trek hebt, neem dan een GOK-groen tussendoortje, maar zorg wel dat de porties in de hoofdmaaltijden niet al te groot zijn. Anders val je nog niet af. Het blijft immers zaak om minder calorieën tot je te nemen dan dat je verbruikt. Gaandeweg de dagen/weken zul je merken dat je steeds minder behoefte aan tussendoortjes hebt. Stap dan over op een van de andere weekmenu's.

IN OVERLEG MET JE HUISARTS

Ga je beginnen met Grip op koolhydraten, dan raad ik je aan om dit in overleg met je huisarts te doen. Het is je eigen verantwoordelijkheid om met dit programma te beginnen. Gebruik je medicatie (voor schildklier of diabetes), dan kan het zijn dat de medicatie gaandeweg het programma aangepast dient te worden. Doe dit nooit op eigen houtje, maar altijd in overleg met je huisarts/specialist. Vooropgesteld dat Grip op koolhydraten voor de meeste mensen zeker een verbetering van de gezondheid teweeg zal brengen, zullen er altijd mensen zijn die, vooral de eerste dagen, wat klachten krijgen. Geef het de tijd en de klachten zullen verdwijnen. Houden de klachten aan, dan is het prettig dat je huisarts al op de hoogte is van je goede voornemen om definitief iets aan je gewicht te doen. Je kunt dan in overleg met de huisarts iets aan de klachten doen.

OUDEREN EN KLEINE PORTIES (WEEKMENU'S 7 EN 8)

Ook ouderen (60, 70+ers) kunnen vaak maar kleine porties eten. Vooral als je ouder wordt is het van belang om voldoende eiwitrijke voeding te eten voor behoud van je spieren. Want naarmate je ouder wordt, gaat je lichaam meer spieren afbreken. Dit heet *sarcopenie*. Het wordt gekenmerkt door een aan leeftijd gerelateerde afname van spiermassa en spierkracht. Niet alleen veroudering, maar ook (in)activiteit, ziekte en voeding hebben invloed op het ontstaan van sarcopenie. Daarnaast is het van belang dat de vitamine- en mineralenstatus goed is. Aanvullende voedingssupplementen, zoals een goed opneembare multivitamine - speciaal voor ouderen - en extra vit D zijn ten zeerste aan te bevelen. Ook dagelijkse beweging en wat krachttraining zijn nodig voor je conditie en spierbehoud.
Qua voeding is het belangrijk om in iedere maaltijd eiwitrijke voeding met goede vetten te gebruiken. Hierdoor vertraag je de spierafbraak en blijf je langer fit en energiek. De weekmenu's 7 en 8 kunnen gebruikt worden voor ouderen. En laat je vooral ook inspireren door voorbeelden in de andere dagmenu's.
Voor gewichtsbehoud is GOK-fase 2 aan te raden. Want voeding beperkt aan koolhydraten, met behoorlijk wat eiwitten en goede vetten, blijft de basis voor een energiek fit lijf en een heldere geest.

- 20-25 gram noten (als tussendoortje en in de yoghurt)

- 50 gram noten (als GOK-groene maaltijd, eventueel met nog wat rauwkost of een gekookt eitje)

KINDEREN (WEEKMENU'S 7, 8, 11 EN 12)

Bij Grip op Koolhydraten adviseren we voor opgroeiende kinderen die te zwaar zijn, om twee weken de richtlijnen van GOK-fase 1 te volgen. De honger neemt dan snel af en het kind komt in de vetverbranding. Hierdoor krijgt het als vanzelf weer meer energie en meer zin om te bewegen. De eerste kilo's zijn er dan af. Omdat kinderen – sociaal gezien – veelal meerdere tussendoortjes willen eten, is het mogelijk om in fase 1 bijvoorbeeld de weekmenu's 7 en 8 te volgen. Dat zijn voorbeeldmenu's met in het koolhydratenuur geen al te grote maaltijden en maximaal drie GOK-groene tussendoortjes.

Na twee weken GOK-fase 1 gevolgd te hebben, kan overgestapt worden op fase 2. Weekmenu 11 (fase 2) met dagelijks twee koolhydraatrijke maaltijden is geschikt voor kinderen. Hiermee kan het gewicht gehandhaafd blijven of langzaam nog wat afnemen. Meestal groeien kinderen dan vanzelf in hun gewicht. Van belang blijft om kinderen van het graaien en snaaien van koolhydraatrijke tussendoortjes en dranken af te houden. Blijf vooral ook de rode-lijstproducten vermijden zoals kunstmatige zoetstoffen en glucose-fructosestroop.

Als de porties van de drie hoofdmaaltijden wat klein gehouden worden, dan zijn er desgewenst nog wat GOK-groene tussendoortjes mogelijk. Zie daarvoor de voorbeelden van tussendoortjes in de weekmenu's 7 en 8.

Grip op koolhydraten heeft mijn leven veranderd. Was ik jaren gewend om magere producten te eten om af te vallen. De laatste jaren lukte dat niet meer. Geen gram viel ik af. Een gewichtsconsulent had al eens aangegeven dat ik een goede kandidaat zou zijn voor koolhydraatarm. Tien maanden geleden ging de knop om en begon ik met GOK. Ik ben nu 10 kilo kwijt. Ik eet lekker en ben weer lekker aan het bakken. De recepten zijn gemakkelijk te maken. Voor iedereen een aanrader, die niet wil snaaien maar lekker en gezond wil eten.

- Sietske

WEEKMENU 1

WEEKMENU'S 1 T/M 3

DIT ZIJN FASE 1 'GEWONE' WEEKMENU'S.

Met in het koolhydratenuur de warme maaltijd. Naar wens kan de middag- en avondmaaltijd gewisseld worden, net zoals het uitkomt. Wisselen met dagen uit andere weekmenu's is altijd mogelijk. Kijk bijvoorbeeld voor een dagje 'geen vlees en vis' bij weekmenu 6 of voor een dagje 'pas op de plaats' bij de balansweekmenu's 9 en 10.

MAANDAG

O 1-2 gekookte eieren. Goed om ook nog een glas water met psylliumvezels erbij te nemen.
* Makkelijk, snel en voedzaam. Hier kun je uren op werken zonder honger.

M koolhydraatarme salade bijv.
bloemkoolsalade – blz. 88
Handig om mee te nemen. Deze salade kan een dag van tevoren gemaakt worden en is een paar dagen houdbaar. Dus maak ook alvast voor de volgende dag een portie. Wel koel bewaren.

A KH-uur naar keuze * bijv.
easy chicken – blz. 111
met 1-2 aardappelen, yoghurt met fruit

DINSDAG

O MIM met beleg bijv.
MIM met zongedroogde tomaat en olijven - blz. 74
met ham

M koolhydraatarme salade bijv.
bloemkoolsalade – blz. 88
of een omeletwrap met roomkaas, plakjes ham of kipfilet of zalm, sla en lente-ui
zie recept **omelettaart** – blz. 84

A KH-uur naar keuze * bijv.
zalmmoot, sperziebonen, aardappelen, appel, stukje pure chocolade

WOENSDAG

O 1-2 vezelcrackers met beleg naar keuze* bijv.
bijv. **zonnige cracker** – blz. 60
met notenpasta of eiersalade

M tapas hapjes (worst, kaas, vis, olijven, noten en rauwkost naar keuze) bijv.
kipkluifjes – blz. 100
met rauwkost bijv. plakjes komkommer, stukje paprika, augurk, asperges uit potje
ook makkelijk om mee te nemen in de lunchbox

A KH-uur naar keuze * bijv.
tartaartje, witlof met ham en kaas, druiven en chocolade
Druiven bevatten vrij veel kh, dus als je daar behoorlijk van 'snoept' dan liever geen andere kh-bron bij.

O = ochtend **M** =middag **A** =avond

DONDERDAG

O 1-2 vezelcrackers met beleg naar keuze* bijv.
hennepcracker – blz. 60
met kaas en plakjes komkommer

M **komkommerquiche uit de koekenpan**
– blz. 78
dit kan van tevoren klaargemaakt worden en per portie ingevroren

A KH-uur naar keuze * bijv.
asperge-zalmsalade – blz. 88
wat krielaardappeltjes
fruit en stukje pure chocolade

VRIJDAG

O 100 gram Griekse yoghurt met 20 gram KH-arme notenmuesli of lijnzaad en walnoten. Stevia naar smaak.

M lunch(box) met 1 gekookt ei in 4 parten omwikkeld met rookvlees, paar blokjes kaas, stukje komkommer, ca. 5 olijven, paar snacktomaatjes en 4 halve walnoten.

A vis-maaltijd (KH-uur) bijv.
kiwi, lekkerbekje, frietjes, gemengde sla,
glaasje wijn

ZATERDAG

O 1-2 gebakken eieren met spek (of kaas) en augurk

M Gemengde salade of poké bowl naar keuze bijv.
poké bowl met beefreepjes – blz. 99

A KH-uur naar keuze * bijv.
shoarmavlees met pitabroodje, saus
tomatensalade – blz. 147
glaasje wijn

ZONDAG

O 1-2 vezelcrackers met beleg naar keuze* bijv.
1 Parmezaanse cracker – blz. 61
met paprikapesto – blz. 65
of **eiersalade** – blz. 68

M gemengde salade met ei, vis of vlees of bijv.
gerookte kip met gamba's – blz. 101
of **Spaanse kip** – blz. 113

A KH-uur naar keuze * bijv. uit-eten maaltijd
carpaccio, zalm met groenten, aardappels of pasta,
ijs met vruchten

WEEKMENU 2

MAANDAG

O 1-2 gebakken eieren met spek (of kaas) en augurk of 1-2 gekookte eieren met een beetje zout en/of mayonaise
* goed om ook nog een glas water met psyllium erbij te nemen.

M **champignon-spekbrood** – blz. 72
met roomboter en salami

A KH-uur naar keuze * bijv.
gevulde kipfilet – blz. 111
met bloemkool, 2 kleine aardappels, kiwi, stukje pure chocolade

DINSDAG

O 1-2 vezelcrackers of snee koolhydraatarm brood met beleg* naar keuze bijv.
amandelcrackers – blz. 61
kaas of notenpasta

M **gekruide noten ca. 50 gram** – blz. 106
1 gekookt ei in vieren omwikkeld met plakjes rookvlees

A KH-uur naar keuze * bijv.
boerenkoolstamppot of andijviestamppot, karbonade, spek en worst, piccalilly, 2 mandarijntjes

WOENSDAG

O 100 g Griekse yoghurt met 20 gram KH-arme notenmuesli* of lijnzaad en walnoten. Stevia naar smaak

M **omeletwrap-spinazie met roomkaas, zalm**
zie **omelettaart** – blz. 84 (derde omelet met spinazie)

A KH-uur naar keuze * bijv.
kalkoenschnitzel – blz. 115
of
zalmpakketje – blz. 137
spinazie, penne en Parmezaanse kaas. Sinaasappel.

DONDERDAG

O 1-2 vezelcrackers met beleg naar keuze* bijv.
amandelcrackers – blz. 61
met kipfilet en kiemgroenten

M **quiche salami/brie** - blz. 78
of
3 à 4 rolletjes ham met asperges met een gekookt eitje

A KH-uur naar keuze* bijv. peulvruchtenmaaltijd
chili con carne, roomyoghurt met appel

VRIJDAG

O 1-2 gebakken eieren met spek (of kaas) en augurk of 1-2 gekookte eieren met een beetje zout en/of mayonaise
* goed om ook nog een glas water met psyllium erbij te nemen.

M gemengde sla met vis, vlees of ei bijv.
krulsla met kip en mozzarella – blz. 93

A KH-uur naar keuze* bijv.
gehaktbal, worteltjes en doperwten
fruit, klein toetje en stukje pure chocolade
Houd rekening met de 4 x 1/4 indeling. worteltjes en doperwten zijn GOK-oranje, daarom beter geen of slechts 1 klein aardappeltje erbij.

O = ochtend M =middag A =avond

ZATERDAG

O 1-2 gebakken eieren met spek (of kaas) en augurk of 1-2 gekookte eieren met een beetje zout en/of mayonaise
* goed om ook nog een glas water met psyllium erbij te nemen.

M **poké bowl met garnaaltjes (**GOK-oranje) – blz. 99
of
1-2 snee koolhydraatarm brood met beleg naar keuze* bijv.
half **naanbroodje** – blz. 72
met makreel of shoarma

A KH-uur naar keuze * bijv. maaltijdsoep met brood
* dubbele portie maken. Snel en makkelijk voor morgen.
bijv. gegrilde rode uiensoep (GOK-oranje) – blz. 161
of **bataat/peersoep (GOK-oranje)** – blz. 161
half **naanbroodje** – blz. 72
met (kruiden)boter of olijfolie
fruit en een stukje pure chocolade

ZONDAG

O 1-2 vezelcrackers met beleg naar keuze* bijv.
1 **Parmezaanse cracker** – blz. 61
met gerookte zalm
of
avocadocrème – blz. 64

M **kalkoenroerbak** – blz. 115
met fijngesneden ijsbergsla

A KH-uur naar keuze * bijv. soep met salade en tapas
soep van de vorige dag
fruitige kipsalade – blz. 181
tapas hapjes (worst, kaas, vis, olijven, noten en rauwkost naar keuze)

* Voor recepten KH-arme notenmuesli zie *Grip op koolhydraten - Dagmenu's, richtlijnen en recepten*, blz. 83.

WEEKMENU 3

MAANDAG

O 1 - 2 gekookte eieren of gebakken eieren (met spek). Goed om ook nog wat psylliumvezels erbij te nemen.

M 1 - 2 vezelcrackers of snee koolhydraatarm brood met beleg naar keuze* bijv.
cracker met serranoham - blz. 62
* maak een dubbele portie. Snel en makkelijk voor overmorgen

A KH-uur naar keuze * bijv.
komkommer-bleekselderij salade - blz. 93
met **gemarineerde gamba's** - blz. 139
of zalmmoot
toetje naar keuze en stukje chocolade

DINSDAG

O rolletjes vleeswaren met augurk en/of blokjes kaas met komkommer. Eventueel nog een eitje erbij

M koolhydraatarm vezelbrood met beleg naar keuze* bijv.
platbrood met tonijn - blz. 72
paprikapesto - blz. 65

A KH-uur naar keuze * bijv.
kippendijen met sesamolie - blz. 170
zoete chilisaus - blz. 149
kleine portie rijst
Wil je het beperkt houden qua koolhydraten eet er dan bloemkoolrijst of broccolirijst bij in plaats van gewone rijst.
komkommersalade - blz. 94
* Maak een dubbele portie. Snel en makkelijk voor morgen
yoghurt met stukjes appel, lijnzaad, walnoten, kaneel en stevia naar smaak.

WOENSDAG

O 100 gram Griekse yoghurt met 20 gram KH-arme notenmuesli of lijnzaad en walnoten. Stevia naar smaak

M 1- 2 vezelcrackers of snee koolhydraatarm brood met beleg naar keuze* bijv.
cracker met serranoham - blz. 62

A KH-uur naar keuze * bijv.
steak met worcestersaus - blz. 131
komkommersalade - blz. 94
gebakken aardappeltjes
fruit en een stukje pure chocolade

DONDERDAG

O 100 gram Griekse yoghurt met 20 gram KH-arme notenmuesli of lijnzaad en walnoten. Stevia naar smaak
* eventueel nog een eitje of wat kaas erbij.

M **quiche salami/brie** - blz. 78
* een quiche is koud en warm lekker en makkelijk mee te nemen. Per portie invriezen.

A KH-uur naar keuze * bijv.
Indische gehaktballen - blz. 123
zoete chilisaus - blz. 149
kleine portie rijst
* Wil je het beperkt houden qua koolhydraten eet er dan bloemkoolrijst of broccolirijst bij in plaats van gewone rijst
haricots verts of sperzieboontjes
Kook wat meer boontjes voor de haricots-vertssalade voor morgen. Wil je de salade morgen meenemen in je lunchbox bereid hem dan alvast in de loop van de avond.
Griekse yoghurt met stukjes appel, kaneel, lepel gebroken lijnzaad en all bran flakes
latte macchiatto en stukje chocolade

O = ochtend **M** =middag **A** =avond

VRIJDAG

O roerei met zalm of 1-2 gebakken eieren met spek of kaas

M **haricots-vertssalade** - blz. 91
* eventueel nog een eitje of wat kaas erbij.
* handig om mee te nemen. Kan een dag van te voren gemaakt worden.

A KH-uur naar keuze * bijv.
chili con carne, gemengde sla met dressing
romig warm fruit - blz. 185

ZATERDAG

O koolhydraatarm vezelbrood met beleg naar keuze* bijv.
champignon-spekbrood - blz. 72
*Dit brood kun je van tevoren al maken. Makkelijk en snel om per portie in te vriezen.
met roomboter en salami

M koolhydraatarm vezelbrood met beleg naar keuze* bijv.
champignon-spekbrood - blz. 72
met roomboter en kaas

A KH-uur naar keuze * bijv.
shoarmavlees met pitabroodje, saus
tomatensalade - blz. 147
fruit

ZONDAG

O 1- 2 vezelcrackers of snee koolhydraatarm brood met beleg naar keuze* bijv.
cracker met serranoham - blz. 62

M tapas hapjes (worst, kaas, vis, olijven, noten en rauwkost naar keuze)
of bijv. **chorizochips, brie met truffelsalami, kipkluifjes, gevulde komkommer** - blz. 100-107
of
poké bowl met zalm - blz. 99

A KH-uur naar keuze* Houd wel rekening met de 4 x ¼ indeling bijv.
olijfjes, gerookte zalm, biefstuk met groenten, paar frietjes, ananas met slagroom
* uit-eten maaltijd. Olijfjes en gerookte zalm als voorgerecht

WEEKMENU 4 BROODMAALTIJDEN ALS KH-UUR

Dit is een weekmenu met in het koolhydratenuur een broodmaaltijd. Vooral voor mensen die buitenshuis werken kan het makkelijk zijn om de keuze te maken om als lunch een broodmaaltijd te plannen en dan thuis bij de warme maaltijd geen koolhydraten te eten.
In het weekend staan hier twee voorbeelden van broodmaaltijden in de ochtend. Dat kan ook weleens lekker zijn.
Naar wens kun je switchen met een andere dag uit een van de andere weekmenu's .
Eigen keuze blijft immers. De weekmenu's zijn als leidraad te gebruiken.

MAANDAG

O 1 - 2 gebakken eieren met spek en augurk of 2 gekookte eieren

M broodmaaltijd naar keuze (KH-uur) * bijv.
2 snee brood, ruim besmeerd met roomboter, ruim belegd met kaas, vis, vlees en/of ei
wat rauwkost en een stukje fruit, bijv. een kiwi

A GOK-groene maaltijd naar keuze bijv.
koolhydraatarme salade met ei, kaas, vlees en/of vis
of
poké bowl met beefreepjes – blz. 99

DINSDAG

O 1 - 2 vezelcrackers met beleg naar keuze* bijv.
krokante cracker - blz. 60
eiersalade - blz. 68

M broodmaaltijd naar keuze (KH-uur) * bijv.
tosti met ham en kaas en ananas
als groente kun je bijv. kiezen voor wat rauwkost of glas tomatensap of kop groentesoep of
komkommercocktail (oranje) - blz. 50

A GOK-groene maaltijd naar keuze bijv.
omeletwrap-tomaat met mayonaise, tonijn en rucola
*zie recept 1ste omelet van de **omelettaart** - blz. 84
of
vitello tonnato - blz. 125

WOENSDAG

O rosbiefrolletjes (rosbief met partjes gekookt ei, wat kiemgroenten en peper en zout)

M broodmaaltijd naar keuze (KH-uur) * bijv.
2 geroosterde sneetjes brood met
filet americain met makreel - blz. 65
wat rauwkost bijv. worteltjes en paprika of
tomatensalade - blz. 147
als je nog zin hebt: yoghurt met roodfruit

A GOK-groene maaltijd naar keuze bijv.
roerei met zalm - blz. 83
of
kabeljauw in kruidenolie - blz. 139
In de loop van de avond een glas water met psylliumvezels. Dat vult het aantal vezels van deze dag aan

O = ochtend **M** =middag **A** =avond

DONDERDAG

O rosbiefrolletjes (rosbief met partjes gekookt ei, wat kiemgroenten en peper en zout)
of 100 g Griekse yoghurt met walnoten, lijnzaad en kaneel. Stevia naar smaak
* eventueel nog een eitje of wat kaas erbij.

M broodmaaltijd naar keuze (KH-uur) * bijv.
1 - 2 sneetjes brood met roomboter en oude kaas
wat rauwkost zoals worteltjes, paprika en komkommer
2 mandarijntjes

A GOK-groene maaltijd naar keuze bijv.
varkenshaas met maanzaadkorst - blz. 129
broccoli
of
poké bowl met tonijn - blz. 96

VRIJDAG

O plakjes ham met augurk, gekookt eitje

M broodmaaltijd naar keuze (KH-uur) * bijv.
broodje haring met een zure bom, 2 mandarijntjes

A GOK-groene maaltijd naar keuze bijv.
lasagne - blz. 126
of
steak met worcestersaus - blz. 130
en gemengde salade

ZATERDAG

O broodmaaltijd naar keuze (KH-uur) * bijv.
1 kiwi vooraf of een klein glaasje (vers geperst) sinaasappelsap
1- 2 geroosterde sneetjes brood met
beleg naar keuze* bijv.
roomboter, ham en kaas. Met wat rauwkost of kiemgroenten erop of ernaast
Misschien heb je aan 1 of 1,5 sneetje brood al genoeg. Des te beter. Kies altijd voor hartig beleg anders wordt de portie koolhydraten te groot en krijg je snel weer honger en wordt de verleiding groter.

M makreelsalade met sperzieboontjes
of
koolsalade - blz. 94
aangevuld met wat noten of blokjes kaas

A GOK-groene maaltijd naar keuze bijv.
tapashapjes (worst, kaas, vis, olijven, noten en rauwkost naar keuze)
of bijv. **caprese balletjes, pittige notenmix, beef jerky, snackgroenten** en/of **gerookte kip met gamba's** - blz. 101-107

ZONDAG

O broodmaaltijd naar keuze (KH-uur) * bijv.
1 kiwi vooraf
1 - 2 broodjes
met beleg naar keuze* bijv.
filet americain of rosbief met wat plakjes ei, komkommer en snoeptomaatje
Misschien heb je aan 1 of 1,5 broodje al genoeg. Des te beter. Houd de rest van de dag GOK-groen!

M **tuinkerssoep** (GOK-groen) - blz. 153
met stukjes gerookte zalm

A GOK-groene maaltijd naar keuze bijv.
tartaartje met serranoham - blz. 121
gegrilde paksoi - blz. 143

WEEKMENU 5
GEEN VLEES

Een weekmenu zonder vlees.
Wel met de dierlijke eiwitbronnen: vis, eieren, melkproducten.

MAANDAG

O 1 - 2 gekookte eieren met een beetje zout en/of mayonaise
of 1 - 2 gebakken eieren met een plakje kaas erop .
* goed om ook nog een glas water met psyllium-vezels erbij te nemen

M **gekruide noten max. 50 gram** - blz. 106
wat rauwkost en kaas erbij

A KH-uur naar keuze* bijv.
zalmpakketje - blz. 136
quinoa
fruit en een stukje pure chocolade of
romig warm fruit - blz. 185

DINSDAG

O **skyr met avocado** - blz. 56
eventueel nog een eitje, wat kaas of noten ernaast

M **gekruide noten** max. 50 gram - blz. 106
wat rauwkost en kaas erbij

A KH-uur naar keuze* bijv.
tuinkerssoep (GOK-groen) - blz. 153
stokbrood met
avocadocrème - blz. 64
fruit en een stukje pure chocolade

WOENSDAG

O **MIM met Parmezaanse kaas** – blz. 74
met **bruschetta** – blz. 64 of gewoon met wat roomboter

M 1 - 2 vezelcrackers met beleg naar keuze* bijv.
hennepcracker - blz. 60
met
frisse komkommersalade - blz. 64

A KH-uur naar keuze* bijv.
smoothie (GOK-oranje) 1 persoon - blz. 179
tomaat met ei (GOK-oranje) - blz. 173
stukje chocola

O = ochtend **M** =middag **A** =avond

DONDERDAG

O 1 - 2 vezelcrackers met beleg naar keuze* bijv.
hennepcracker - blz. 60
met **eiersalade** – blz. 68 of
avocadocrème - blz. 64

M 1 - 2 vezelcrackers met beleg naar keuze* bijv.
hennepcracker - blz. 60
met
frisse komkommersalade - blz. 64

A KH-uur naar keuze* bijv.
gele paprikasoep (GOK-oranje) - blz. 162
frittata - blz. 81
* vegetarische variant
fruit en een stukje pure chocolade

VRIJDAG

O 1 - 2 vezelcrackers met beleg naar keuze* bijv.
zonnige cracker - blz. 60
met roomboter, oude kaas en kiemgroenten en plakje tomaat

M **gemarineerde kaasblokjes** - blz. 104
met wat rauwkost (komkommer, stukje paprika, snoeptomaatje)

A KH-uur naar keuze* bijv.
kabeljauw in kruidenolie - blz. 139
spruitjes
romig warm fruit - blz. 185
koekje bij de koffie

ZATERDAG

O 1 - 2 vezelcrackers met beleg naar keuze* bijv.
zonnige cracker - blz. 60
met roomboter, oude kaas en kiemgroenten en plakje tomaat

M **omelet met asperges** - blz. 81

A KH-uur naar keuze* bijv.
pompoen/currysoep (variant met cashewnoten) (GOK-oranje) - blz. 160
paar plakjes stokbrood of toast met roomboter met gerookte zalm of forelfilet of
zalmtartaartje - blz. 140
brie met druiven (GOK-oranje) - blz. 185
of
kersensalade - blz. 183

ZONDAG

O 100 gram Griekse yoghurt met 20 gram KH-arme notenmuesli of lijnzaad en walnoten. Stevia naar smaak.

M eventueel nog een eitje of wat kaas erbij
koolhydraatarm brood met beleg naar keuze* bijv.
broccoli-broodjes - blz. 69
tonijnsalade - blz. 140

A KH-uur naar keuze* bijv.
asperge-zalmsalade - blz. 88
gebakken aardappeltjes
kiwi

WEEKMENU 6
GEEN VLEES EN GEEN VIS

Dit weekmenu is zonder vlees én zonder vis.
Wel met de dierlijke eiwitbronnen: eieren en melkproducten.
Kijk ook eens bij de andere weekmenu's. In diverse dagdelen staan mooie menusuggesties zonder vlees en vis.

MAANDAG

O 1 - 2 vezelcrackers met beleg naar keuze* bijv.
hennepcracker - blz. 60
met notenpasta, komkommersalade of eiersalade

M **choco MIM** - blz. 77
met wat slagroom (met stevia gezoet) of wat roomboter

A KH-uur naar keuze* bijv.
frittata (vegetarische variant) - blz. 81
quinoa
gemengde salade naar keuze
yoghurt met stukjes appel, wat noten en kaneel

DINSDAG

O 100 g Griekse yoghurt met KH-arme notenmuesli of wat gemengde noten met kaneel. Stevia naar smaak. Eventueel aanvullen met een gekookt eitje of wat blokjes kaas

M 1 - 2 vezelcrackers met beleg naar keuze* bijv.
krokante cracker - blz. 61
courgettetapenade - blz. 64

A KH-uur naar keuze* bijv. de voedzame combinatie van eieren en spinazie:
gevulde eieren uit de oven - blz. 83
spinazie met kipfilet en een Limburgs kaasje - blz. 116
met aardappelen
fruit naar keuze en een stukje chocolade

WOENSDAG

O 100 g Griekse yoghurt met KH-arme notenmuesli of wat gemengde noten met kaneel. Stevia naar smaak. Eventueel aanvullen met een gekookt eitje.

M gemengde salade of poké bowl naar keuze bijv:
poké bowl kaas - blz. 96

A KH-uur naar keuze* bijv.
mosterd/preisoep (GOK-groen) - blz. 156
tomaat met ei (GOK-oranje) - blz. 173
pasta of groentepasta
fruit en een stukje pure chocolade

O = ochtend **M** =middag **A** =avond

DONDERDAG

O 1 - 2 crackers of snee koolhydraatarm brood met beleg naar keuze* bijv.
rookkaascracker* met gekookt eitje

M **koolsalade** - blz. 94
*dubbele portie maken – ook voor zaterdag
aangevuld met wat noten of blokjes kaas

A KH-uur naar keuze* bijv.
1 kiwi vooraf
vleesvervanger naar keuze met groenten bijv.
komkommer-bleekselderij salade - blz. 93
of
gegrilde paksoi - blz. 143
met wat aardappelen of quinoa óf
toetje naar keuze
stukje chocolade

VRIJDAG

O 100 g Griekse yoghurt met 20 gram KH-arme notenmuesli. Eventueel aanvullen met een gekookt eitje of glas water met psylliumvezels.

M **gemarineerde kaasblokjes** - blz. 104
met rauwkost bijv. plakjes komkommer, stukje paprika, augurk, asperges uit potje

A KH-uur naar keuze* bijv.
zoete aardappel röstirondjes - blz. 172
fruitsalade bijv.
kersensalade - blz. 183
stukje chocolade

ZATERDAG

O 1 - 2 vezelcrackers met beleg naar keuze* bijv.
1 **Parmezaanse cracker** - blz. 61
met gekookt ei, kiemgroente en plakje tomaat

M koolhydraatarm brood met beleg naar keuze* bijv.
broccoli-broodjes - blz. 69
met oude kaas

A KH-uur naar keuze* bijv.
koolsalade - blz. 94
*overgehouden van donderdag
bataat/peersoep (GOK-oranje) - blz. 161
of peulvruchtenmaaltijd met quinoa
fruit en een stukje chocolade

ZONDAG

O 1 - 2 vezelcrackers met beleg naar keuze* bijv.
hennepcracker - blz. 60
met notenpasta, komkommersalade of eiersalade
kaneelkoffie - blz. 53
*lekkere verwenkoffie op de zondagochtend

M **rucolasoep** (GOK-groen) - blz. 153
half **naanbroodje** - blz. 72

A KH-uur naar keuze* bijv.
poké bowl kaas - blz. 96
met sushirijst erbij
yoghurt met stukjes appel, wat noten en kaneel

* Voor het recept van rookkaascrackers zie blz. 90 van *Grip op koolhydraten - Dagmenu's, richtlijnen en recepten.*

WEEKMENU 7 MET TUSSENDOORTJES

WEEKMENU'S 7 EN 8

DIT ZIJN WEEKMENU'S MET KLEINERE PORTIEGROOTTE IN HET KOOLHYDRATENUUR EN MAXIMAAL 3 TUSSENDOORTJES.

Geschikt voor
- mensen met een maagverkleining (Gastric Bypass = GBP)
- kinderen
- ouderen met weinig eetlust
- mensen die beginnen met GOK (die nog gewend zijn aan dagelijkse tussendoortjes.) Als startweken.

Lees vooral de Algemene voedingstips op blz. 17 goed door.

MAANDAG

O 1 vezelcracker met beleg naar keuze* bijv.
1 **amandelcracker** - blz. 61
met roomboter, plakje kipfilet en kiemgroenten of plakjes komkommer
* het recept van amandelcrackers is goed voor 4 eetmomenten

T **gekruide noten** – max. 20 gram - blz. 106
maak meerdere porties zodat je een voorraadje hebt om als gepland tussendoortje te nemen.

M 1 vezelcracker met beleg naar keuze* bijv.
1 **amandelcracker** - blz. 61
met roomboter plakje kipfilet en kiemgroenten of plakjes komkommer

T 1 gekookt ei (met mayonaise)

A KH-uur naar keuze* - kleine porties - bijv.
gehaktbal
frisse fruitsalade met ham - blz. 183

T **brie met truffelsalami** - blz. 107 (halve portie)
of paar stukjes kaas

O = ochtend **M** =middag **A** =avond **T** =tussendoor

DINSDAG

O 1 vezelcracker met beleg naar keuze* bijv.
1 **amandelcracker** - blz. 61
met brie en kiemgroenten

T wat kaas, worst of plakjes vleeswaren met wat rauwkost of als je zin hebt in zoet:
stracciatellaverwennerij – halve portie
- blz. 109

M 1 vezelcracker met beleg naar keuze* bijv.
1 **amandelcracker** - blz. 61
met brie en kiemgroenten

T **chorizochips** - blz. 105
* maak meerdere porties zodat je een voorraadje hebt om als gepland tussendoortje te nemen.

A KH-uur naar keuze* - kleine porties - bijv.
kipfilet, groenten, toetje naar keuze, roodfruit

T **gekruide noten** – max. 20 gram - blz. 106
of een rolletje rauwe ham met roomkaas, rucola en pijnboompitjes

WOENSDAG

O 1 vezelcracker met beleg naar keuze* bijv.
zonnige cracker - blz. 60
met **frisse komkommersalade** - blz. 64

T 1 gekookt ei (met mayonaise)

M 1 vezelcracker met beleg naar keuze* bijv.
zonnige cracker - blz. 60
met **frisse komkommersalade** - blz. 64

T stukjes kaas of droge worst met olijfjes of komkommer of bijv.
chorizochips - blz. 105

A KH-uur naar keuze* - kleine porties - bijv.
vis, groente, aardappeltje, bramen en stukje chocolade

T **gekruide noten** – max. 20 gram - blz. 106
of bijv.
brie met truffelsalami - blz. 107
(halve portie)

DONDERDAG

O 100 gram skyr of Griekse yoghurt met 20 gram KH-arme notenmuesli of bijv.
skyr met avocado - blz. 56

T handje noten max. 20 gram of
pittige notenmix max. 20 gram- blz. 107
of een rolletje rauwe ham met roomkaas, rucola en pijnboompitjes

M wat kaas, worst of plakjes vleeswaren met wat rauwkost of bijv.
gerookte kip met gamba's - blz. 101
(halve portie)

T olijven of wat blokjes kaas

A KH-uur naar keuze* - kleine porties - bijv.
tartaartje met serranoham - blz. 121
spruitjes, 1 kleine aardappel, bramen en een stukje chocolade

T handje noten max. 20 gram of
pittige notenmix max. 20 gram - blz. 107
of rest van
gerookte kip met gamba's - blz. 101

VRIJDAG

O 100 gram skyr of Griekse yoghurt met 20 gram KH-arme notenmuesli of bijv.
of bijv. **skyr met avocado** - blz. 56

T 1 gekookt ei (met mayonaise)

M 1 cracker met beleg naar keuze* bijv.
1 rookkaascracker met tonijnsalade

T **kipkluifjes** - blz. 100
of
caprese balletjes - blz. 104

A KH-uur naar keuze* - kleine porties - bijv.
kipfilet of **kipkluifjes** - blz. 100
of
caprese balletjes - blz. 104
spinazie, penne en Parmezaanse kaas. Mandarijn toe

T plakjes komkommer met tonijnsalade of ossenworst

ZATERDAG

O MIM naar keuze en in 6 plakjes snijden bijv.
MIM met zongedroogde tomaat en olijven - blz. 74
3 plakjes MIM met beleg naar keuze* bijv. ossenworst

T rolletjes runderrookvlees met roomkaas of eiersalade

M **MIM met zongedroogde tomaat en olijven** - blz. 74
3 plakjes MIM met beleg naar keuze* bijv. smeerkaas

T **zalmtartaartje** - halve portie - blz. 140

A KH-uur naar keuze* - kleine porties - bijv.
kipfilet, spruitjes, toetje, 1 kiwi

T **zalmtartaartje** - halve portie - blz. 140

ZONDAG

O 1 vezelcracker met beleg naar keuze* bijv.
zonnige cracker - blz. 60
met notenpasta

T wat kaas, worst of plakjes vleeswaren met wat rauwkost of bijv.
chorizochips - blz. 105

M 2 rolletjes ham met asperges
of 2 rolletjes boterhamworst met augurk

T **gevulde komkommer!** - blz. 106
gemengde noten max 20 gram of
pittige notenmix max. 20 gram - blz. 107

A KH-uur naar keuze* - kleine porties - bijv.
fruitige kipsalade - blz. 181
* dit is een lekkere voedzame en frisse salade

T wat kaas, worst of plakjes vleeswaren met wat rauwkost of bijv.
chorizochips – blz. 105

WEEKMENU 8 MET TUSSENDOORTJES

MAANDAG

O MIM naar keuze en in 6 plakjes snijden bijv.
MIM met Parmezaanse kaas – blz. 74
3 plakjes MIM met roomboter en kipfilet of parmaham

T 1 gekookt ei (met mayonaise)

M MIM naar keuze bijv.
MIM met Parmezaanse kaas – blz. 74
3 plakjes met
bruschetta – blz. 64

T max. 20 gram gemengde noten of
pittige notenmix max. 20 gram - blz. 107

A KH-uur naar keuze* – kleine porties - bijv.
Duits biefstukje, broccoli of bloemkool, wat frietjes, mandarijntje

T plakjes komkommer met ossenworst of bruschetta

DINSDAG

O 100 g Griekse yoghurt of roomkwark met lijnzaad en 20 gram walnoten

T stukje droge worst met olijfjes of komkommer

M **frittata** – kleine portie – blz. 81

T rookkaascracker

A KH-uur naar keuze* - kleine porties - bijv.
asperges (vers of uit een potje) met plak gekookte ham, gekookte ei, botersausje, aardappeltje, fruit

T plakjes komkommer met zalm of roomkaas

WOENSDAG

O 1 gekookt ei (met mayonaise)

T **choco-MIM** – blz. 77
* MIM in 6 plakjes snijden
3 plakjes MIM met wat slagroom (met stevia gezoet) of wat roomboter

M 1 cracker of koolhydraatarm brood met beleg naar keuze* bijv.
rookkaascracker met roomboter en plakje kipfilet

T **choco-MIM** – blz. 77
3 plakjes MIM met wat slagroom (met stevia gezoet) of wat roomboter

A KH-uur naar keuze* - kleine porties - bijv.
tartaartje met serranoham - blz. 121
bietjes (mag ook uit een pot), fruit

T max. 20 gram gemengde noten of
gekruide noten – max. 20 gram - blz. 106

DONDERDAG

O 1 snee koolhydraatarm brood met beleg naar keuze*
bijv. **champignon-spekbrood** - blz. 72
Dit brood kun je van tevoren al maken. Makkelijk en snel om per portie in te vriezen.
met roomboter en salami

T **Indische gehaktballen** - blz. 123

M 1 snee koolhydraatarm brood met beleg naar keuze*
bijv. **champignon-spekbrood** - blz. 72
met roomboter en kaas en kiemgroenten

T **Indische gehaktballen** - blz. 123

A KH-uur naar keuze* - kleine porties - bijv.
kipkluifjes - blz. 100
met bloemkoolnasi, satésaus, kroepoek, fruit, stukje chocolade

T stukje worst of kaas of olijfjes

O = ochtend M =middag A =avond T =tussendoor

VRIJDAG

O 100 g Griekse yoghurt met KH-arme notenmuesli of 20 g walnoten en een lepel lijnzaad. Stevia naar smaak

T **gekruide noten – max. 20 gram** - blz. 106

M omeletwrap ham of kipfilet, blaadjes sla, roomkaas en lente-ui
Ook makkelijk om mee te nemen in de lunchbox

T **gekruide noten – max. 20 gram** – blz. 106

A KH-uur naar keuze* - kleine porties - bijv. maaltijdsoep bijv.
tom kha kai - blz. 157
Maak een extra portie voor de lunch van morgen of in de wintermaanden erwtensoep
rood fruit en een stukje pure chocolade

T plakjes komkommer met roomkaas

ZATERDAG

O 1 gekookt ei (met mayonaise)

T 2 rolletjes ham met asperges
of 2 rolletjes rauwe ham met roomkaas, rucola en pijnboompitjes
* maak een dubbele portie voor de middag

M GOK-groene maaltijd naar keuze bijv.
tom kha kai - blz. 157
of **kipburger** - blz. 113
* maak wat extra's om morgen als middag-tussendoortje te nemen

T 2 rolletjes ham met asperges
of 2 rolletjes rauwe ham met roomkaas, rucola en pijnboompitjes

A KH-uur naar keuze* - kleine porties - bijv.
gegrilde paksoi - blz. 143
brie met druiven (GOK-oranje) - blz. 185

T max. 20 gram gemengde noten of
gekruide noten – max. 20 gram - blz. 106

ZONDAG

O 1 gekookt ei in vieren omwikkeld met plakjes rookvlees

T rookkaascracker

M **roerei met zalm** – kleine portie – blz. 83

T **tom kha kai** – blz. 157
of **kipburger** - blz. 113
* over van gisteren

A KH-uur naar keuze* - kleine porties - bijv.
Indische gehaktballen - blz. 123
of stukje zalm
roerbakgroenten met wat nasi
fruit en een stukje pure chocolade

T plakjes komkommer met roomkaas

WEEKMENU 9 BALANSMENU

WEEKMENU 9 EN 10

Balansmenu's met GOK-groene dagen of dagen met maximaal twee maaltijden.
Naar wens volg je deze balansmenu's enkele dagen of enkele weken. Ga daarna weer over op een van de 'normale' weekmenu's met dagelijks een koolhydratenuur.
Geschikt voor:

- Als je even een boost nodig hebt. Om van een 'plateau' af te komen. Dat wil zeggen als je al een tijdje stilstaat qua gewicht en centimeters. Dan is het goed om even een tijdje anders te eten. Dan dwing je je lichaam tot actie. Kans is groot dat je weer af gaat vallen.
- Als je een of meerdere dagen te veel koolhydraten gegeten hebt. Via deze balansmenu's ben je weer snel van de honger af. Je reservesuikers raken snel op en de vetverbranding kan dan weer beginnen.

MAANDAG

O Vasten / Intermittent Fasting: Als je goed in de vetverbranding zit, is het makkelijk om een tijdje niets te eten en dus je ontbijt uit te stellen. Lees verder de aanwijzingen op blz. 17.
Neem naar wens een glas psylliumvezels.

M 1 - 2 vezelcrackers met beleg naar keuze* bijv.
hennepcracker - blz. 60
met eiersalade of kaas of
filet americain met makreel - blz. 65

A KH-uur naar keuze* bijv.
kalkoenschnitzel - blz. 115
gegrilde paksoi - blz. 143
yoghurt met fruit, lijnzaad, walnoten, kaneel en stevia naar smaak
stukje pure chocolade

DINSDAG

O glas water met 1 eetlepel psylliumvezels en gekookt eitje of blokjes kaas of worst of bijv.

M ca. 50 g gemengde noten of macadamia's of
gekruide noten max. 50 g - blz. 106
of rolletjes rauwe ham met roomkaas, rucola en pijnboompitjes

A KH-uur met beperkt koolhydraten naar keuze bijv:
auberginelasagne - blz. 174
en **komkommersalade** - blz. 94
stukje chocolade

WOENSDAG

O glas water met 1 eetlepel psylliumvezels en gekookt eitje of blokjes kaas of worst of bijv.
gemarineerde kaasblokjes - blz. 104

M salade met vis bijv.
haricots-vertssalade - blz. 91

A **spinazie met kipfilet en een Limburgs kaasje** - blz. 116
* of dit recept zonder kaas en met een gekookte ei er doorheen gemengd.
met kipfilet of stukje zalm

O = ochtend M =middag A =avond T =tussendoor

DONDERDAG

O Vasten / Intermittent Fasting* Als je goed in de vetverbranding zit, is het makkelijk om een tijdje niets te eten en dus je ontbijt uit te stellen. Lees verder de aanwijzingen op blz. 17.
Neem naar wens een glas psylliumvezels.

M MIM of vezelcrackers met beleg naar keuze* bijv.
2 **hennepcrackers** - blz. 60
Met kaas, ham, ei en wat rauwkost of kiemgroenten

A KH-uur naar keuze * bijv.
sudderlappen of pulled pork met gestoofde prei, appel, stukje pure chocolade

VRIJDAG

O bulletproof koffie
of **kaneelkoffie met slagroom** gezoet met stevia – blz. 53

M **quiche salami/brie** - blz. 78

A taughetti bolognese
chia yoghurt met 20 gram gehakte noten of
stracciatellaverwennerij - blz. 109

T In de loop van de avond een glas water met psylliumvezels.

ZATERDAG

O 1 gekookt ei (met mayonaise)
2 à 3 rolletjes achterham met asperges

M koolhydraatarm brood met beleg naar keuze* bijv.
broccoli-broodjes - blz. 69
met eiersalade of kaas

A GOK-groene maaltijd naar keuze bijv.
poké bowl met beefreepjes – blz. 99
100 g Griekse yoghurt met KH-arme notenmuesli of 20 g gehakte noten met kaneel, stevia naar smaak
of **stracciatellaverwennerij** – blz. 109

T In de loop van de avond een glas water met psylliumvezels.

ZONDAG

O 1 gekookt ei (met mayonaise)
2 à 3 rolletjes achterham met asperges
Lekker en makkelijk een kopie van de vorige ochtend. Andere helft van het potje asperges en van de achterham opmaken.

M **choco-MIM** - blz. 77
met wat slagroom (met stevia gezoet) of wat roomboter
of **krulsla met kip en mozzarella** - blz. 93

A GOK-groene maaltijd naar keuze bijv.
vissoep (GOK-groen) - blz. 152
en
easy chicken - blz. 111

WEEKMENU 10 BALANSMENU

MAANDAG

O glas water met 1 eetlepel psylliumvezels
gekookt eitje of paar blokjes kaas of worst

M Koolhydraatarm brood met beleg naar keuze* bijv.
broccoli-broodjes - blz. 69
met eiersalade of kaas

A GOK-groene maaltijd naar keuze bijv.
zalm met
gegrilde paksoi - blz. 143
stracciatellaverwennerij - blz. 109

DINSDAG

O 100 gram Griekse yoghurt met KH-arme noten-muesli of 20 gram gehakte noten met kaneel, stevia naar smaak
1 gekookt ei (met mayonaise)

M gemengde salade met vis of bijv.
tonijnsalade - blz. 140

A GOK-groene maaltijd naar keuze bijv.
mosterd/preisoep (GOK-groen) - blz. 156
tartaartje met broccoli

WOENSDAG

O 2 gebakken eieren met spek of kaas

M 1 - 2 vezelcrackers met beleg naar keuze* bijv.
amandelcrackers - blz. 61
filet americain met makreel - blz. 65

A GOK-groene maaltijd naar keuze bijv.
lof/kaassoep (GOK-groen) - blz. 157
kippendijen met sesamolie - blz. 170
veldsla-salade - blz. 91

DONDERDAG

O MIM of 1-2 crackers naar keuze bijv.
MIM met Parmezaanse kaas - blz. 74
met achterham of eiersalade

M 1 - 2 vezelcrackers met beleg naar keuze* bijv.
amandelcrackers - blz. 61
met notenpasta

A GOK-groene maaltijd naar keuze bijv.
steak met worcestersaus - blz. 130
broccoli
stracciatellaverwennerij - blz. 109

O = ochtend M =middag A =avond

VRIJDAG

O Vasten / Intermittent Fasting: Als je goed in de vetverbranding zit, is het makkelijk om een tijdje niets te eten en dus je ontbijt uit te stellen. Lees verder de aanwijzingen op blz. 17.
Neem naar wens een glas psylliumvezels.

M omeletrol van 2 eieren met kip en komkommer – zie **omelettaart** - blz. 84

A KH-uur met beperkt koolhydraten naar keuze bijv:
snoepsoep (GOK-oranje) - blz. 166
varkenshaas met maanzaadkorst - blz. 129
Griekse yoghurt met roodfruit, kaneel, paar walnoten en stevia naar smaak
roodfruit bevat de minste koolhydraten qua fruit

ZATERDAG

O Nog een ochtend vasten en - als je niet hoeft te werken - lekker uitslapen. Neem vervolgens de tijd voor een heerlijke brunch/lunch.
of neem 1 gekookt eitje. Dat voedt goed en heeft geen hoge dooreetfactor.

M **zalmcarpaccio** - blz. 133

A GOK-groene maaltijd naar keuze bijv.
cannelloni - blz. 119
yoghurt met wat walnoten, lijnzaad, kaneel en stevia naar smaak
Als je nog zin hebt een lekkere kop **kaneelkoffie met slagroom** gezoet met stevia - blz. 53
In de loop van de avond een glas water met psylliumvezels. Dat vult het aantal vezels van deze dag aan.

ZONDAG

O 100 gram Griekse yoghurt met KH-arme notenmuesli of 20 gram walnoten en een lepel lijnzaad.
stevia naar smaak
of
skyr met avocado - blz. 56

M **komkommerquiche uit de koekenpan** - blz. 78

A GOK-groene maaltijd naar keuze bijv.
lasagne - blz. 126
of **Spaanse kip** – blz. 113
met gemengde sla
kaneelkoffie toe

WEEKMENU 11
FASE 2 - STRATEGIE 2

PER DAG 2 KH-MOMENTEN

TOELICHTING FASE 2 - WEEKMENU'S 11 EN 12
Deze menu's zijn geschikt voor:

- Als je je streefgewicht behaald hebt en via fase 2 op gewicht wilt blijven.
- Als je je streefgewicht nog niet behaald hebt, maar even rustig aan wilt doen. Van belang is dat je niet helemaal afzwakt naar een eetpatroon met nog veel meer koolhydraatrijke eetmomenten, want dan keert de honger snel weer terug en begint het graaien en snaaien weer en gaat je lichaam weer vetten opslaan.
- Kinderen als ze na 2 weken fase 1 over kunnen gaan op een eetpatroon met wat meer koolhydraten. Belangrijk bij kinderen is dat het hongergevoel in toom gehouden wordt. Zodat ze niet te veel gaan eten en te veel aankomen. Zodra een kind weer meer honger gaat krijgen, kun je het weer een of twee weken fase 1 (weekmenu 7 en 8) laten volgen.. Kinderen die nog in de groei zijn, kunnen zo groeien in hun gewicht. 1 centimeter groei staat gelijk met 1 kilo gewicht.

In het basisboek *Opgewicht* staan (vanaf blz. 141) 5 strategieën vermeld voor fase 2, om op gewicht te blijven. Want dat is toch ons aller streven, om op gewicht te komen, maar vooral om daarna makkelijk op gewicht te kunnen blijven. Grip op je eigen gewicht met Grip op Koolhydraten. Met deze makkelijke en snelle weekmenu's als leidraad moet dat gaan lukken. En weet, dat je altijd weer even terug kunt gaan naar fase 1. Geen gejojo, maar al schommelend (1- 1,5 kg verschil) op gewicht blijven.

Weten is nog geen doen.
Daarom, pak jezelf aan en ga het gewoon DOEN!
Je lichaam en geest zullen je dankbaar zijn.
Laat koolhydraatbeperkte voeding je - preventieve - medicijn zijn.
Echt je kunt het!
Yes you can!

MAANDAG

O 1 - 2 gekookte eieren of gebakken eieren (met spek). Goed om ook nog wat psylliumvezels erbij te nemen.

M 2 sneetjes brood met beleg naar keuze* en wat rauwkost
bijv. 2 sneetjes volkorenbrood met roomboter, plak ham, plak kaas, blaadjes sla, tomaat

A KH-uur naar keuze * bijv.
zalmpakketje - blz. 137
worteltjes, aardappelen, fruit, stukje chocolade

DINSDAG

O Griekse yoghurt met appel, kaneel en 20 gram noten (of KH-arme notenmuesli)
of 2 gebakken eieren met spek en
smoothie (GOK-oranje) 1 persoon - blz. 179

M 1 - 2 sneeën koolhydraatarm brood met beleg naar keuze* en wat rauwkost
of
koolhydraatarme salade bijv.
haricots-vertssalade - blz. 91

A KH-uur naar keuze * bijv.
tomatensoep, speltbroodje met kaas en sla, fruit en stukje pure chocolade

Als je in fase 2 nog blijft afvallen, terwijl dat niet je bedoeling meer is, maak dan de porties in de maaltijden wat groter of neem dagelijks wat extra's als tussendoortje. Neem dan wel zo veel mogelijk GOK-groene tussendoortjes.

O = ochtend **M** =middag **A** =avond **T** =tussendoor

WOENSDAG

O 1 - 2 vezelcrackers met beleg naar keuze* bijv.
zonnige cracker - blz. 60
notenpasta met kiemgroenten

M 2 sneetjes brood met beleg naar keuze* en fruit
bijv. 2 sneetjes volkorenbrood met roomboter, plak ham, plak kaas, blaadjes sla, tomaat.
1 appel

A KH-uur naar keuze * bijv.
kalkoenroerbak - blz. 115
ijsbergsla, rijst
limoenyoghurt met munt (GOK-oranje) - blz. 179

DONDERDAG

O 1- 2 vezelcrackers met beleg naar keuze* bijv.
1 **Parmezaanse cracker** – blz. 61
bijv. plak fricandeau met kiemgroenten

M 2 sneetjes brood met beleg naar keuze* bijv.
volkorenbrood met gerookte zalm, avocado en kiemgroenten

A KH-uur naar keuze * bijv.
kippendijen met zwarte rijst – blz. 171
sinaasappel en een stukje chocolade

VRIJDAG

O MIM met beleg naar keuze* bijv.
MIM met Parmezaanse kaas - blz. 74

M 2 sneetjes brood met beleg naar keuze* en wat rauwkost bijv.
volkorenbrood met pindakaas en komkommer
of
fruitige kipsalade – blz. 181

A KH-uur naar keuze * bijv.
lasagne van aardappel – blz. 175
broccoli of spruitjes
yoghurttoetje en een stukje fruit

ZATERDAG

O 1- 2 vezelcrackers met beleg naar keuze* bijv.
zonnige cracker - blz. 60
beleg naar keuze* bijv. Zeeuws spek met mosterd

M **poké bowl met garnaaltjes** (GOK-oranje)
- blz. 99

A KH-uur naar keuze * bijv.
bataat/peersoep (GOK-oranje) - blz. 161
stukjes stokbrood met
paprikapesto – blz. 65
gevulde kalkoenfilet – blz. 115
stukje chocolade

ZONDAG

O **smoothie** (GOK-oranje) 1 persoon – blz. 179
roerei met zalm - blz. 83

M tapashapjes (worst, kaas, vis, olijven, noten en rauwkost naar keuze)
of bijv. **chorizochips, brie met truffelsalami, kipkluifjes, gevulde komkommer, stukjes paprika**
– blz. 100-107

A KH-uur naar keuze * bijv.
snoepsoep (GOK-oranje) – blz. 166
spareribs, paar frietjes en gemengde sla

T **choco-MIM** - blz. 77
met wat slagroom (met stevia gezoet) of wat roomboter

A GOK-groene maaltijd naar keuze bijv.
vissoep (GOK-groen) - blz. 152
en
easy chicken - blz. 111

WEEKMENU 12
FASE 2 - STRATEGIE 5

HET VIER-DRIESTRAMIEN

MAANDAG

O 1 - 2 gekookte eieren of gebakken eieren met spek. Goed om ook nog wat psylliumvezels erbij te nemen. Je bent zo urenlang verzadigd en zonder honger.
Als je fase 2 strategie 5 al wat langer volgt, dan weeg je op de maandagochtend waarschijnlijk 1 à 1,5 kilo meer dan op de vrijdagochtend. Daarom nu weer strikt 4 dagen fase 1. Een 'saai' ontbijt met eieren is een goede hongerstiller.

M een voedzame salade bijv.
witlofsalade met zalm, gekookt ei en stukjes walnoten of
haricots-vertssalade – blz. 91

A KH-uur naar keuze * bijv.
kabeljauw in kruidenolie - blz. 139
worteltjes met peultjes, fruit, stukje chocolade
* worteltjes en peultjes zijn GOK-oranje, daarom liever geen aardappels of toetje erbij

DINSDAG

O 1 - 2 vezelcrackers met beleg naar keuze* bijv.
zonnige cracker - blz. 60
met notenpasta, serranoham of eiersalade

M **omelet met asperges** - blz. 81
of omeletrol met tonijn, mayonaise en sla – zie bij
omelettaart - blz. 84

A KH-uur naar keuze * bijv.
zoete aardappel röstirondjes - blz. 172
met sperziebonen en spekjes
fruit en een stukje pure chocolade

WOENSDAG

O MIM naar keuze en in 6 plakjes snijden
bijv.
MIM met Parmezaanse kaas - blz. 74
3 plakjes MIM met roomboter en kipfilet, parmaham of kaas

M MIM naar keuze bijv.
MIM met Parmezaanse kaas - blz. 74
3 plakjes MIM met roomboter en kipfilet, parmaham of kaas

A KH-uur naar keuze * bijv.
gegrilde paksoi - blz. 143
met zalm, 1-2 kleine aardappelen, fruit, stukje chocolade

DONDERDAG

O 100 g Griekse yoghurt met lijnzaad, 20 gram walnoten, kaneel en stevia naar smaak
glas psylliumvezels en/of gekookt eitje

M 2 rookkaascrackers met tonijnsalade, eiersalade of kaas (voor het recept rookkaascrackers zie: *Grip op koolhydraten, Dagmenu's, richtlijnen en recepten,* blz. 90)
of **krulsla met kip en mozzarella** - blz. 93

A KH-uur naar keuze * bijv.
meloen met ham
groentewrap - blz. 119
beetje rijst of aardappeltjes
stukje chocolade

O = ochtend **M** =middag **A** =avond

VRIJDAG

O 1- 2 vezelcrackers met beleg naar keuze* bijv.
zonnige cracker - blz. 60
met notenpasta

M **frittata** – blz. 81
of boerenomelet

A KH-uur naar keuze * bijv.
curry met banaan – blz. 181
toetje naar keuze en stukje chocolade

T lekker chill-avondje, bijv.
paar stukjes stokbrood of toastjes met kaas, vlees of vis
of met **filet americain met makreel** – blz. 65
of kies een van de recepten bij Tussendoortjes en hapjes
als je zin hebt een glaasje wijn

ZATERDAG

O **smoothie** (GOK-oranje) 1 persoon - blz. 179
met een gekookt eitje erbij of een koolhydraatarme cracker met beleg
Heb je 's avonds een feestje of uitgaansavond met koolhydraten, kies dan in de ochtend of middag voor GOK-groen. Dan heb je wat ruimte voor wat extra koolhydraten in de avond.

M salade met fruit erdoor
of **poké bowl garnaaltjes (oranje)** blz. 99
of **kersensalade** - blz. 183

A KH-uur naar keuze* bijv.
nasimaaltijd
of kippendijen met zwarte rijst - blz. 171
toetje naar keuze en stukje chocolade

ZONDAG

O 1 broodje of 2 sneetjes 'normaal' brood met ruim beleg naar keuze*, glaasje verse jus d'orange of bijv. latte macchiatto. Heb je nog trek, neem dan een vezelrijke cracker of knäckebröt erbij. Of wat yoghurt met fruit.

M Lunch naar keuze. Als je weer kiest voor koolhydraatrijke voedingsmiddelen van de oranje lijst, combineer dit dan met GOK-groene producten. Of ga voor bijv.
gevulde peer - blz. 186
of **brie met druiven** - blz. 185

A KH-uur naar keuze * bijv.
gegrilde rode uiensoep (GOK-oranje) - blz. 161
toast met roomboter
fruit en een stukje pure chocolade

Als je in fase 2 nog blijft afvallen, terwijl dat niet je bedoeling meer is, maak dan de porties in de maaltijden wat groter of neem dagelijks wat extra's als tussendoortje. Neem dan wel zo veel mogelijk GOK-groene tussendoortjes.

8 mooie kruidenmixen om zelf samen te stellen.
Zodat je weet wat erin zit en ook weet wat er níet in zit.
Dus vrij van smaakversterkers en andere toevoegingen.
Werk netjes en met schone spullen.
Meng de kruiden en bewaar de kruidenmixen in mooie potjes of blikjes op een droge en donkere plaats. Met natuurlijk de naam op een mooi etiket.
Ook leuk om cadeau te geven.

Aardappelkruiden
Za'atar
Seroendeng
Cajunkruiden

RODE CURRYKRUIDEN

Zeker het niezen waard!
Deze mix kun je in verschillende recepten gebruiken.

- 35 g paprikapoeder
- 10 g gemalen anijszaad
- 10 g cayennepeper
- 8 g anijszaadjes
- 8 g gemalen komijnzaad
- 5 g knoflookpoeder
- 4 g gedroogde tijm
- 3 g zwarte peper
- 2 g gemberpoeder
- 2 g gemalen citroengras
- 2 g gemalen kardemom
- 2 g basilicum
- 1 g gemalen koriander
- 1 g gemalen kruidnagel

Voeg alle kruiden samen en meng ze goed.

SEROENDENG

Deze kruidenmix wordt gebruikt in de Indische gehaktballetjes op blz. 123

- 30 ml olijfolie
- 15 g komijnpoeder
- 15 g korianderpoeder
- 1 serehstengel
- 50 g gemalen kokos
- 50 g grofgehakte amandelen

Verhit de olijfolie in een koekenpan.
Strooi het komijnpoeder en het korianderpoeder in de pan.
Kneus de serehstengel en leg die ook in de pan, draai het vuur op middelmatig.
Voeg de gemalen kokos toe en blijf omscheppen tot het licht verkleurd is.
Voeg grofgehakte amandelen toe, warm deze nog even mee, maar let op dat de kokos niet verbrandt.
Laat het geheel afkoelen.

Lekker bij verschillende oosterse gerechten.

CAJUNKRUIDEN

Kant-en-klare cajunkruiden zitten meestal boordevol zout. Het is beter om zelf een samenstelling te maken, zoals hieronder.

- 30 g paprikapoeder
- 15 g uienpoeder
- 15 g knoflookpoeder
- 12 g cayennepeper
- 8 g zwarte peper
- 8 g oregano
- 8 g gedroogde tijm
- 4 g zout

Voeg alle kruiden samen en meng ze goed.

SHICHIMI TOGARASHI

(Japanse 7 kruidenmix)

Deze kruidenmix wordt gebruikt in het recept 'kippendijen met zwarte rijst' op blz. 171

- 30 g sichuanpeper
- 25 g chillipepervlokken
- 20 g sinaasappelschil poeder
- 20 g sesamzaadjes (wit en/of zwart)
- 15 g hennepzaadjes
- 8 g gemberpoeder
- ½ blad nori, fijngemalen

Voeg alle kruiden samen en meng ze goed.

LASAGNEKRUIDENMIX

Deze kruidenmix wordt gebruikt in het recept 'lasagne' op blz. 126

- 1 el gedroogde basilicum
- 1 tl gedroogde oregano
- 1 tl gedroogde peterselie
- 1 tl gedroogde tijm
- 1 tl paprikapoeder
- ½ tl chilipoeder
- mespunt zout

Voeg alle kruiden samen en meng ze goed.

ZA'ATAR

Deze kruidenmix wordt gebruikt in het recept 'tomaat met ei' op blz. 173
Een heerlijk kruidenmengsel uit het Midden-Oosten.

- 2 el sumak (Turkse winkel)
- 1 el sesamzaad, geroosterd
- 1 el komijnzaad, geroosterd
- 1 el gedroogde tijm
- 1 el gedroogde marjolein

Voeg alle kruiden samen en meng ze goed.

ITALIAANSE KRUIDENMIX

Deze kruidenmix wordt gebruikt in de recepten 'Parmezaanse cracker', 'caprese balletjes', 'groentewrap' en 'tonijnsalade'.

- 2 el gedroogde basilicum
- 2 el gedroogde peterselie
- 1 el gedroogde oregano
- 1 el gedroogde uiensnippers
- ½ el gedroogde salie
- ½ el gedroogde tijm
- ½ el knoflookpoeder
- ½ tl zwarte peper
- mespunt zout

Voeg alle kruiden samen en meng ze goed.

AARDAPPELKRUIDEN

- 1 el knoflookpoeder
- 1 el paprikapoeder
- 1 el uienpoeder
- ½ el gedroogde bieslook
- ½ el cayennepeper
- ½ el knoflookpoeder
- ½ el zwarte peper
- 1 tl zout

Voeg alle kruiden samen en meng ze goed.

Lekker om aardappelgerechten van extra smaak te voorzien

KOKOSLIMO

Voor 1 glas

Een lekker fris kokosdrankje.

- 1 glas water
- scheutje kokosmelk
- citroensap (vers of uit een druppelflesje)
- stevia naar smaak (ca. 2 - 5 druppels)

Voeg naar smaak een scheutje kokosmelk, het citroensap en de stevia aan het water toe.
Vind je het te waterig voeg dan iets kokosmelk toe.
Pas de smaak naar behoefte aan.
Extra lekker met wat ijsklontjes.

KOMKOMMERCOCKTAIL

Voor 2 glazen

- 100 g komkommer, geschild
- 100 g watermeloen, zonder pitten
- 200 ml bruiswater (sodawater / spa rood)
- stevia naar smaak

Mix de ingrediënten in een blender.
Je kunt eventueel stevia naar smaak toevoegen.

Bruiswater / sodawater is gewoon kraanwater dat met koolzuurgas onder druk is ingespoten. Ook voor thuisgebruik zijn er handige apparaten om zelf bruiswater te maken. Geen gesleep meer met flessen bruisend mineraalwater.

GRAPEFRUIT SPRITZEL

Voor meerdere glazen

- 1 deel grapefruitsap
- 7 delen (bruisend) mineraalwater
- stevia naar smaak (een goed uitgangspunt is ca. 5 druppels per glas)

Giet het grapefruitsap in een glas of karaf en doe er 7 keer zoveel mineraalwater bij. Voeg eventueel wat stevia toe.
Roer alles even door en geniet van dit enigszins bittere drankje. Een prima alternatief voor een glas wijn of als aperatiefje.
Maak gerust wat meer en bewaar het in een afgesloten karaf of fles in de koelkast.
Geschikt voor fase 2 en in het koolhydratenuur.

Vervang grapefruitsap voor sinaasappelsap en je hebt koolhydraatarme sinas!

Let op: Als de naam van het recept in het oranje is (zoals komkommercocktail), dan is het GOK-oranje. In fase 1 dan alleen gebruiken in het koolhydratenuur.

Icetea
Kokoslimo
Komkommercocktail
Grapefruit spritzel

ICETEA

Recept van Cira, Femke, Karlijn en Jet
Voor 1 liter

- 1 liter water
- 4 g thee (liefst losse thee)
- 1 el citroensap of limoensap (vers of uit een flesje)
- stevia naar smaak (10 à 25 druppels)

Schenk 750 ml koud water in een grote kan.
Voeg 250 ml kokend water toe en zet hier thee van.
Laat de thee gerust een tijdje trekken, bijvoorbeeld 1 uur.
Doordat de temperatuur laag is, kan de thee niet bitter worden.
Voeg het citroen- of limoensap toe. Vers sap is het lekkerst, maar voor het gemak voldoet sap uit een flesje ook.
Voeg naar smaak stevia toe.
Zet de kan minstens een paar uur in de koelkast.
Drink de thee ijs- en ijskoud. Nog lekkerder met een ijsklontje erin.

Je kunt diverse theesoorten gebruiken.
Zo krijg je telkens een ander smaakje icetea en verveelt het nooit.

Gebruik je muntblaadjes in de thee, spoel de takjes munt dan eerst even af.
Zwarte, groene of rooibosthee - zowel theezakjes als losse thee - kun je ook rustig even onder de koude kraan afspoelen. Best een fris idee ;-)

'Gok is geen kwestie van volhouden, maar van doorgaan. Bewuster stilstaan bij wat je écht lekker vindt en hier volop van kunnen genieten!'

- Marlieke

KANEELKOFFIE

Voor 1 kopje

- 1 tl kaneel
- 1 kop koffie
- flinke toef opgeklopte slagroom (eventueel naar smaak met stevia gezoet)
- stevia naar smaak

Doe wat kaneel in een koffiemok, schenk de koffie (met eventueel wat stevia) erbij en roer even goed door. Schep de slagroom er bovenop en strooi hier nog een beetje kaneel over.

GEMBERTHEE

Voor 1 glas

- 1 glas water
- schijfje gember
- ½ in de lengte gesneden serehstengel
- 3 à 4 takjes munt
- stevia naar smaak

Kook water en doe dat in een glas. Voeg de gember, sereh en munt toe.
Voeg eventueel stevia naar smaak toe.
Laat de thee een paar minuten trekken.

Hoe fijner je de gember snijdt, hoe intenser de smaak wordt.

Deze thee bevat geen cafeïne en kan dus gerust in de avond gedronken worden. Lekker en gezond!

Tomatensap
Limoenade
Gemberthee
Kaneelkoffie

TOMATENSAP

Voor 1 glas

- 2 flinke el tomatenpuree
- 250 ml water
- 1 el verse peterselie, fijngehakt
- peper en zout naar smaak

Kook het water.
Schep de tomatenpuree in een groot theeglas en schenk er het kokende water op. Voeg de peterselie en eventueel peper en zout toe.
Laat het tomatensap afkoelen in de koelkast.

LIMOENADE

Voor 1 glas
Lekker als je zin hebt om wat anders te drinken dan water, thee of koffie.
Kinderen vinden dit ook erg lekker.

- 1 glas (bruisend) mineraalwater (250 ml)
- 1 el limoensap (vers of uit een flesje)
- stevia naar smaak

Voeg limoensap en stevia toe aan het mineraalwater.

Makkelijk en snel:
Maak gelijk 1,5 liter limoenade en zet die in de koelkast. Dan heb je altijd GOK-groene frisdrank op voorraad.

VIRGIN COLADA

Voor 1 glas
- 100 g verse ananas, in stukjes gesneden of 100 ml ananassap
- 50 ml kokosmelk
- 5 à 6 ijsblokjes
- 1 schijfje ananas ter versiering

Mix de ingrediënten in de blender tot het ijs is gecrushed en de melk en de sap schuimt.
Schenk de drank in een
mooi glas en versier het glas met het schijfje ananas.

Variant: schenk er een scheutje rum bij

SKYR MET AVOCADO

Voor 1 portie

- 100 g skyr
- 50 g avocadocrème (zie recept blz. 64)
- citroensap, naar smaak (vers of uit een flesje)
- stevia, naar smaak

Meng de avocadocrème door de skyr en breng het op smaak met citroensap en stevia.

Skyr is een eiwitrijke magere yoghurt/kwark variant. Om het nog voedzamer te maken is avocadocrème een heel gezonde en lekkere toevoeging.

'One year from now you'll wish you started today.

Deze quote helpt me om door te gaan. omdat ik weet dat over een jaar mijn lichaam gezonder en slanker zal zijn als ik me aan de GOK-leefstijl houd.'

- Babette

KH-ARME CRACKERS

AANWIJZINGEN EN BAKINSTRUCTIES MAGNETRON EN OVEN

Koolhydraatarme vezel/noten/pittencrackers zijn gemakkelijk klaar te maken. Eenvoudigweg de ingrediënten goed mengen en uitsmeren op bakpapier of een siliconenbakmat. En dan bakken in een magnetron of in de oven. Voor het lekkerste resultaat wel goed droogbakken, maar niet laten verbranden. Blijf aan het einde van de baktijd bij de oven/magnetron in de buurt en controleer regelmatig het resultaat. Ovenkijken dus.

MAGNETRON:
Bakken in de magnetron doe je op de hoogste stand (bijv.900 watt). De baktijd is afhankelijk van de hoeveelheid. Variërend van ca. 9 minuten tot ca. 30 minuten.

OVEN:
In de oven is de baktijd ca. 30-40 minuten.
Baktemperatuur 150 of 160 °C. Niet hoger! Zet daarna de oven uit en laat de crackers nadrogen in de oven om ze droog en krokant te krijgen voor de beste bite!

Het aantal bakminuten varieert door de hoeveelheid toegevoegd water, de dikte van de cracker, het wateropnemend vermogen van de ingrediënten en het vermogen van de magnetron/oven. Ook als je nog bakplaten of roosters in de magnetron/oven hebt staan, kan dit invloed hebben op de baktijd. Bij gebruik van een 100% siliconen bakmat is de baktijd ca. 10% korter. Experimenteer daar even mee. Al doende leer je je magnetron en oven kennen en weet je hoeveel minuten nodig zijn voor je baksels. Handig om de baktijden in dit boek bij het betreffende recept te noteren.
Bij een kleine hoeveelheid is de magnetron makkelijk en snel. Bij grotere hoeveelheden heeft de oven de voorkeur. Heb je geen oven en wil je bijvoorbeeld 16 crackers bakken, bak dan liever 4 x 4 crackers. Dat werkt beter.

Bedenk dat iedere magnetron en oven anders werkt, dus blijf er de eerste keer bij. Als de crackers te bruin worden kun je ze de volgende keer ietsjes korter bakken.
Zijn de crackers in het midden nog iets te zacht doordat er nog vocht in zit, dan mogen ze wat langer in de magnetron/ oven totdat ze droog en knapperig zijn.
Bewaar de crackers luchtdicht. Zo blijven ze zeker enkele dagen lekker krokant.
Zijn de crackers niet meer helemaal krokant, piep ze dan in enkele minuten even op in de magnetron, oven of broodrooster tot ze weer droog en knapperig zijn.

Parmezaanse cracker
Amandelcracker
Zonnige cracker

Hennepcracker
Krokante cracker

HENNEPCRACKER

Voor 4 crackers

- 100 g gepeld hennepzaad
- 7 g kokosmeel
- 5 g psylliumvezels
- mespunt zout
- 75 ml water

Rooster het hennepzaad lichtjes in een droge koekepan op een lage stand.
Bekleed een bakplaat met bakpapier. Voeg alle ingrediënten bij elkaar en roer dit goed door.
Maak hier vier hoopjes van op het bakpapier en smeer dit met de bolle kant van een lepel uit tot er een platte vorm ontstaat van circa 3 mm dik.
Bak 5 minuten in de magnetron (900 watt), draai de crackers voorzichtig om en bak ze nog eens 5 minuten.

Hennepzaad is behoorlijk eiwitrijk en bevat omega 3-vetzuren. Gezond zaad dus, vooral ook voor vegetariërs en mensen die slechts kleine porties kunnen eten, zoals bijvoorbeeld mensen met een maagverkleining. Hennepzaad heeft een nootachtige smaak en bevat geen THC, dus stoned worden van deze cracker gaat niet lukken ;-)

Liever bakken in de oven? Zie de bakinstructies op blz. 57

ZONNIGE CRACKER

Voor 4 crackers (max. 2 per maaltijd)

- 100 g zonnebloempitten, geroosterd
- 15 g haverzemelen
- 7 g kokosmeel
- 5 g psylliumvezels
- mespunt zout
- 100 ml water

Met deze cracker halen we het zonnetje in huis.
Hak de zonnebloempitten fijn.
Bekleed een bakplaat met bakpapier. Voeg alle ingrediënten bij elkaar en roer dit goed door.
Maak hier vier hoopjes van op het bakpapier en smeer dit met de bolle kant van een lepel uit tot er een platte vorm ontstaat van ± 3 mm dik.
Bak 7 - 10 minuten in de magnetron (900 watt), draai de crackers voorzichtig om en bak ze nog eens 2 - 5 minuten.
Bedenk dat iedere magnetron anders werkt, dus blijf er de eerste keer bij.
Als de crackers te bruin worden kun je ze de volgende keer ietsjes korter bakken.

Verslavend lekker!!

Liever bakken in de oven? Zie de bakinstructies op blz. 57

AMANDELCRACKERS

4 crackers (max. 2 per maaltijd)

- 15 g sesamzaad
- 25 g gebroken lijnzaad
- 30 g pittenmix (pompoenpitten, pijnboompitten, zonnebloempitten)
- 30 g amandelmeel
- 10 g psylliumvezels
- mespunt zout
- 100 ml water

Voeg alle ingrediënten samen en meng dit goed. Verdeel in 4 hoopjes en strijk deze uit over een vel bakpapier of bakmat. Ongeveer 3 à 4 millimeter dikte.
Bak dit 11 à 12 minuten in de magnetron.

Liever bakken in de oven? Zie de bakinstructies op blz. 57

PARMEZAANSE CRACKER

Voor 2 crackers (max. 1 per maaltijd)

- 40 g Parmezaanse kaas, geraspt
- 60 g amandelmeel
- 5 g psylliumvezels
- 2 tl Italiaanse kruidenmix (zie recept blz. 49)
- 75 ml water

Bekleed een bakplaat met bakpapier. Voeg alle ingrediënten bij elkaar en roer dit goed door.
Maak hier twee hoopjes van op het bakpapier en smeer dit met de bolle kant van een lepel uit tot er een platte vorm ontstaat van 3 mm dik.
Bak 5 minuten op de hoogste stand in de magnetron, draai de crackers voorzichtig om en bak ze nog ca. 5 minuten tot ze droog en knapperig zijn.

Laat ze afkoelen.

Lekker met bijvoorbeeld (paprika)pesto en avocado.

Liever bakken in de oven? Zie de bakinstructies op blz. 57

KROKANTE CRACKERS

Voor 4 crackers (max. 2 per maaltijd)

- 20 g haverzemelen
- 10 g sesamzaad
- 10 g lijnzaad, gebroken of gemalen
- 10 g pompoenpitten
- 5 g psylliumvezels
- mespunt zout
- 75 ml water

Meng alle ingrediënten goed door. Gebruik kokend water, dit werkt het snelst doordat de vezels sneller opzwellen. Zorg dat het een deeg soepel wordt want dat is makkelijk uit te smeren is op een bakplaat. Verdun het eventueel nog met een beetje water.
Bekleed een bakplaat met bakpapier.
Smeer het mengsel goed uit op de bakplaat. Verdeel met een mes in vieren.

Bak de crackers 7 - 10 minuten in de magnetron op de hoogste stand. Draai ze om en bak nog 2 à 5 minuten tot ze droog en krokant zijn.

Liever bakken in de oven? Zie de bakinstructies op blz. 57

CRACKER MET SERRANOHAM

- 60 g serranoham, in stukjes
- 2 zelfgemaakte crackers (zie recept op blz. 60 e.v.)
- 4 plakken kaas naar keuze
- ½ avocado, in plakjes
- 2 macadamianoten, geraspt
- knoflookpoeder en/of peper naar smaak

Bak in een koekenpan de stukjes serranoham totdat deze krokant zijn. Beleg de zelfgemaakte crackers met kaas. Leg hier de plakjes avocado op en voeg de serranoham toe. Bestrooi met de geraspte macadamianoten en breng het op smaak met knoflookpoeder en/of peper.

Een mix van knoflookpoeder en peper is kant en klaar te koop in de supermarkt onder dan naam 'knoflookpeper'.

Cracker met serranoham
Bruschetta

AVOCADOCRÈME

- 1 rijpe avocado
- 5 druppels citroensap (vers of uit een flesje)
- 50 g slagroom, geklopt
- peper en zout naar smaak

Snijd de avocado in de lengte doormidden en haal de pit eruit. Lepel het zachte vruchtvlees eruit en prak dit fijn. Meng het citroensap en de slagroom erdoor.
Breng op smaak met peper en zout.

COURGETTETAPENADE

- ½ courgette, in blokjes gesneden
- klontje roomboter
- 4 el feta uit een potje
- handvol verse muntblaadjes
- 30 g pijnboompitten, geroosterd
- peper en zout naar smaak

Bak de courgette in wat roomboter zacht en laat afkoelen. Snijd feta uit een potje (eventueel met olijven) in kleine stukjes en hak de muntblaadjes fijn.
Voeg dit samen met de pijnboompitten bij de courgette en breng op smaak met peper en zout.
Heerlijk voor op brood of een toastje!

BRUSCHETTA

- 20 snoeptomaatjes (max. 200 gram in totaal)
- 1 sjalotje, fijngesneden
- 1 knoflookteen, geperst
- 30 g Parmezaanse kaas, geraspt
- handvol basilicumblaadjes, gesneden
- peper en zout naar smaak

Ontdoe de snoeptomaatjes van de zaadjes en snijd ze klein. Voeg hier de overige ingrediënten aan toe en breng op smaak met peper en zout.

Dit is zo lekker op koolhydraatarm brood.
Vooral als het brood nog even met een beetje (knoflook) olijfolie onder de grill of even in de koekenpan gebakken is.

Hier kan toch geen uit potjes of bakjes, kant en klare smurrie tegenop?
Zeg nou zelf!

FRISSE KOMKOMMERSALADE

- 150 g komkommer
- 2 eetlepels slasaus (zie recept blz. 148)
- 1 el Griekse yoghurt

Snijd de komkommer in flinterdunne plakjes en meng goed met de slasaus en yoghurt.
Eventueel op smaak brengen met peper en zout.
Heerlijk fris op een cracker of als bijgerecht.

PAPRIKAPESTO

- 2 stuks rode paprika (max. 100 gram in totaal)
- 1 knoflookteentje, geperst
- 30 g pijnboompitten, geroosterd
- 60 g Parmezaanse kaas, geraspt
- ± 50 ml extra vierge olijfolie
- zout en peper naar smaak

Snijd de paprika's door de helft en verwijder de zaadlijsten. Leg de paprika's onder de grill met de buitenkant naar boven. Grill de paprika's tot ze donker tot zwart geblakerd zijn. Haal ze uit de oven en dek ongeveer 5 minuten af met aluminiumfolie.
Hierna kun je het vel gemakkelijk verwijderen.
Pureer de paprika en voeg de andere ingrediënten toe. Blijf pureren en giet de olie er beetje bij beetje bij.
Hoeveel olijfolie erbij moet, hangt af van de grote van de paprika's.

De pesto is lang houdbaar als je deze in een potje/bakje doet, dit gladstrijkt en er een laagje olijfolie op schenkt. Voor gebruik giet je de overtollige olijfolie af, restjes doorroeren en vervolgens weer met een nieuw laagje olijfolie terugzetten in de koelkast.
Lekker op koolhydraatarm brood of cracker of door de (groente)pasta.

FILET AMERICAIN MET MAKREEL

- 100 g filet americain
- 80 g gerookte makreel, flakes
- 30 g kappertjes, fijngesneden
- peper en zout naar smaak
- 1 zachtgekookt ei, in stukjes
- 1 el bieslook, fijngeknipt
- alfalfa, naar smaak

Meng de filet americain met de makreel en kappertjes en breng het op smaak met peper en zout.
Verdeel over 2 crackers. Verdeel ook het ei erover en bestrooi met wat bieslook en alfalfa.
Ook lekker met plakjes gerookte kip als tussendoortje of feestelijk hapje.

Variant: ben je geen makreelliefhebber? Zonder vis is dit ook een heerlijke combinatie.

Frisse komkommersalade
Eiersalade
Zalmrillette

Courgettetapenade
Paprikapesto
Filet americain
met makreel

EIERSALADE

- 4 eieren, gekookt
- 2 à 3 el mayonaise
- uienpoeder, kurkuma en currykruiden (zie recept blz. 48) naar smaak
- peper en zout naar smaak
- vloeibare room (slagroom onbereid of koffieroom)
- 1 el bieslook, fijngeknipt ter garnering

Scheid het eigeel van het eiwit.
Meng het eigeel met de mayonaise, het uienpoeder, kurkuma, de currykruiden en peper en zout.
Maak hier een romig smeersel van door naar smaak vloeibare room toe te voegen.
Snijd het eiwit in grove stukken en meng dit door het eigeelmengsel.
Serveer met bieslook.

ZALMRILLETTE

Voor 4 porties

- 300 ml groentebouillon
- 120 g zalmfilet
- 100 g gerookte zalm, zeer fijngesneden
- ½ avocado, fijngeprakt
- 1 flinke el kappertjes
- zwarte peper naar smaak

Pocheer de zalmfilet in de bouillon in 5 à 6 minuten gaar.
Haal de zalmfilet eruit en laat het afkoelen.
Meng alle ingrediënten en zet dit minimaal een half uur in de koelkast.

Deze zalmrilette smaakt lekker op crackers of schijfjes komkommer.
De overgebleven bouillon kan voor de vissoep gebruikt worden.
Een rillette is een smeuïge pastei. Het is afgeleid van het Franse woord rille dat varkensvlees betekent. Tegenwoordig worden er ook rillettes gemaakt van vis, eend en wild.

BROCCOLI-BROODJES

- 150 g broccoli, fijngemalen
- 1 groot ei
- 1 el room/water
- 40 g amandelmeel
- 1 el psylliumvezels
- ½ tl baking soda
- 2 el slakruiden
- 50 g mozzarella/pizzakaas, geraspt
- snufje zout

Snijd de broccoli in stukjes, spoel goed af en maal of hak de broccoli zeer fijn. Klop het ei los met 1 lepel room of water. Meng alle ingrediënten door elkaar en maak er 4 hoopjes van op een bakplaat. Bak de broodjes 40 minuten in een op 160 °C voorverwarmde oven.
Strooi er eventueel in de laatste 5 minuten nog wat kaas over.

Lekker met tonijnsalade.

Broccolibroodjes
Champignon-spekbrood

Platbrood met tonijn

Naanbroodje

NAANBROODJE

1 naanbroodje voor 2 porties

- 2 eieren
- 60 g mascarpone
- 2 el amandelmeel
- 4 el psylliumvezels
- 1 tl baking soda
- zout, naar smaak
- ½ knoflookteen, geperst
- korianderblad (gedroogd), naar smaak

Roer de eieren met de mascarpone en voeg er amandelmeel, psylliumvezels, baking soda, zout en knoflook aan toe. Roer tot het iets begint in te dikken. Schep het mengsel op een vel bakpapier en smeer het uit tot ongeveer 1 centimeter dik.
Strooi er koriander over en zet het 2 minuten in de magnetron.

Lekker met verschillende soorten beleg of gevuld met warm vlees of vis.

Liever in de oven?
Bak het naanbroodje in ca. 30-40 minuten goudbruin in een op 150 – 160 °C voorverwarmde oven.

½ naanbroodje per eetmoment.

Mascarpone over?
Maak er dan het heerlijke choco-MIM of stracciatellatoetje van.
In plaats van mascarpone kan Griekse yoghurt gebruikt worden. Voeg dan 1 eetlepel kokosolie toe.

CHAMPIGNON-SPEKBROOD

Voor 8 porties

- 4 grote eieren
- 200 g pecannoten, zeer fijn gemalen
- 20 g kokosmeel
- 2 el psylliumvezels
- 1 tl baking soda
- blaadjes van 2 takjes verse tijm
- 100 g champignons, in plakjes gesneden
- 100 g kalkoen spekreepjes, uitgebakken
- peper en zout, naar smaak

Mix de eieren 5 minuten en schep er een voor een de overige ingrediënten luchtig doorheen.
Schenk het mengsel in een taartvorm en bak het 40 à 45 minuten in een op 160 °C voorverwarmde oven.

Lekker met een beetje roomboter, kaas, salami, kruidenboter enzovoort.

PLATBROOD MET TONIJN

Voor 4 porties

- 75 g tonijn uit blik
- 3 eieren
- 50 g crème fraîche
- 50 g kaas, geraspt
- 50 g courgette, geraspt
- 5 g psylliumvezels
- ½ tl baking soda
- peper en zout naar smaak

Prak de tonijn door de rauwe eieren en voeg de overige ingrediënten toe.
Schep het mengsel op een vel bakpapier en smeer dit uit tot het ongeveer een halve centimeter dik is.
Zet het circa 8 minuten in de magnetron op de hoogste stand tot al het vocht gestold is en het platbrood goudbruin van kleur is.

Liever in de oven?
Bak het platbrood in ca. 30-40 minuten goudbruin in een op 150 – 160 °C voorverwarmde oven.

Kaas: Kies de kaas die jij het lekkerst vindt. Jong, belegen of oud. Het smaakt allemaal. Heerlijk met gezouten roomboter of paprikapesto.

MIM = MUFFIN IN EEN MOK

AANWIJZINGEN EN BAKINSTRUCTIES MAGNETRON EN OVEN

Het leuke van een muffin in een mok is dat hij zo lekker snel bereid kan worden in de magnetron. Binnen een paar minuutjes heb je een heerlijk luchtig 'broodje'.

MAGNETRON:
Bak ca. 1,5 à 2,5 minuten op het hoogste vermogen tot een structuur die lijkt op cake. Is de muffin nog wat te vochtig, bak dan nog een extra half minuutje.

OVEN:
Wil je liever in een gewone oven? Dat gaat ook prima, maar duurt iets langer. Neem dan wel een ovenbestendige mok of schaaltje. Bak de muffin 12 tot 15 minuten in een op 175 °C voorverwarmde oven.

'GOK is een levenswijze die mij lichter heeft gemaakt in gewicht en in afbouw medicatie hoge bloeddruk. Letterlijk en figuurlijk is de lichtheid van mijn bestaan terug.'

- Hannah

MIM MET ZONGEDROOGDE TOMAAT EN OLIJVEN

Afhankelijk van of je een grote of kleine eter bent en ook afhankelijk van wat je er op of er bij eet, is dit recept voor 1 of 2 porties.

- 1 ei
- 2 el haverzemelen
- 1 el psylliumvezels
- ½ tl baking soda
- 3 olijven, in plakjes gesneden
- 1 zongedroogde tomaat, in stukjes gesneden
- peper en zout, naar smaak

Roer de ingrediënten door elkaar en schep ze in een mok.
Zet ± 2 minuten in de magnetron.
Laat afkoelen.
Heerlijk met roomboter of dippen in olijfolie.

Liever bakken in de oven? Zie de bakinstructies op blz. 73

MIM MET KNOFLOOK EN PARMEZAANSE KAAS

Afhankelijk van of je een grote of kleine eter bent en ook afhankelijk van wat je er op of er bij eet, is dit recept voor 1 of 2 porties.

- 1 ei
- 1 knoflookteen, geperst
- 30 g Parmezaanse kaas, geraspt
- 2 el tarwezemelen
- 1 el psylliumvezels
- ½ tl baking soda
- peper en zout, naar smaak

Roer de ingrediënten door elkaar en schep ze in een mok.
Zet ± 2 minuten in de magnetron op de hoogste stand.
Laat afkoelen.
Dit broodje is uitermate geschikt om even in plakjes te snijden, te roosteren en te gebruiken als toast.
Lekker met bruschetta.

Zonder knoflook kan natuurlijk ook.

Liever bakken in de oven? Zie de bakinstructies op blz. 73

CHOCO-MIM

Voor 1 portie

Als tussendoortje voor 2 porties
Voor als je eens zin hebt in zoet én in chocolade.

- 1 ei
- 20 g boter (op kamertemperatuur)
- 20 g mascarpone
- stevia, naar smaak
- 4 druppels vanille extract
- 5 el amandelmeel
- 1 el cacao
- ½ tl baking soda

Roer de ingrediënten door elkaar en schep ze in een mok. Zet ongeveer 2 à 2,5 minuten in de magnetron op de hoogste stand tot het een structuur is die lijkt op een cake. Is de muffin nog wat vochtig, bak dan nog een halve minuut. Laat afkoelen.
Heerlijk met een toef slagroom (met stevia gezoet)!
Ook lekker als je de choco-MIM in plakjes snijdt en dan met roomboter besmeert.

Liever bakken in de oven? Zie de bakinstructies op blz. 73

'Ik ben een verwoed verzamelaar van GOK-recepten. Ik heb er inmiddels zoveel dat ik wel honderd mag worden (ben een zeventiger) voor ik ze allemaal uitgeprobeerd en gegeten zou hebben. Mijn man moet altijd lachen omdat ik per dag wel 3 x zeg: we eten dit en iedere keer verandert dat weer, want dan zie ik weer een recept dat ik misschien nog lekkerder vind.
GOK is en blijft voor ons een levenswijze en geen dieet.'

- Coby

QUICHE SALAMI/BRIE

- 3 eieren
- halve ui, gesneden
- knoflook, geperst
- 2 el mascarpone
- 75 g salami, in blokjes
- 75 g brie, in plakjes

Klop de eieren luchtig.
Fruit de ui en de knoflook glazig. Schep dit door de eieren samen met de mascarpone, de salami en ± de helft van de brie. Schep dit in een quichevorm van 15 cm doorsnede en leg er de laatste plakjes brie op en bak de quiche 40 minuten in een op 180 °C voorverwarmde oven.

KOMKOMMERQUICHE UIT DE KOEKENPAN

Voor 6 porties

- 500 g gehakt
- 1 prei, in ringen gesneden
- 1 komkommer, in blokjes gesneden
- 2 knoflooktenen, geperst
- peper en zout naar smaak
- piripiri naar smaak
- 5 eieren
- 3 el room (slagroom onbereid of crème fraiche)
- 100 g geraspte kaas naar keuze

Bak het gehakt rul in een grote koekenpan en voeg vervolgens de prei, komkommer en knoflook toe. Bak mee totdat het vocht verdwenen is. Breng op smaak met peper, zout en piripiri. Maak een vel bakpapier nat onder de kraan en knijp dit uit. Leg het bakpapier op de bodem van een kleine koekenpan. Schep het gehakt-komkommermengsel hier bovenop.
Kluts de eieren met de room los en giet dit over het gehakt-komkommermengsel. Druk het geheel een beetje aan met een spatel. Verdeel de geraspte kaas erover.
Leg een deksel op de pan en bak de quiche op laag vuur circa 30 - 40 minuten totdat al het ei gestold is.
Giet het overtollig vet dat vrijgekomen is af en keer de quiche ondersteboven op een bord.

Deze quiche is zowel warm als koud lekker.
Ook goed in te vriezen; vries per portie in.
Makkelijk en snel mee te nemen in de lunchbox.

Quiche salami/brie
Komkommerquiche
uit de pan

'Ik ben zo iemand die al z'n hele leven (vanaf m'n jeugd) aan het 'lijnen' was. Je kent het wel, magere vleeswaren en halvarine op brood, mager vlees bij de aardappels, magere vla na, koffie met zoetjes, light frisdranken enz. enz. Ik viel soms een korte tijd enorm af, maar nooit was het vol te houden. Ik voelde me slap, lusteloos en zonder energie. Als ik dan stopte, werd ik zwaarder dan ik voor die tijd was, zo enorm frustrerend!
Omdat "normaal diëten" niet lukte, ben ik ook shakes en andere rotzooi gaan proberen, maar steeds met hetzelfde slechte resultaat.
Omdat verandering van eten nooit werkte ben ik zo'n 25 jaar geleden begonnen met sporten. M'n lichaam veranderde, maar afvallen lukte nog steeds niet. Zelfs niet toen ik in 2004 spinning instructeur werd. Ik gaf vijf lessen per week en viel uiteindelijk niets af.
Ik was zo enorm gefrustreerd dat ik maar besloot om het los te laten en ik werd zwaarder en zwaarder.
Na een heftige mountainbike crash, waardoor ik door m'n verwondingen zes weken niet meer kon sporten en m'n gewicht opliep tot 106 kg was voor mijn vrouw de maat vol. Ze maakte zich al jaren ernstig zorgen, omdat ik ieder jaar wel een kilootje zwaarder werd.
Ze is gaan zoeken op internet en kwam terecht bij "koolhydraatbeperking" en jouw boeken. Ze heeft ze besteld en vanaf het moment dat ik ze binnenkreeg, is mijn leven veranderd. Dat klinkt dramatisch, maar het is echt zo. Ik heb als een klein kind zitten janken bij het lezen van het basisboek, het was mijn verhaal, mijn frustratie's die jij beschreef, zo herkenbaar!
Mijn vrouw deed de boodschappen en ik maakte zo goed en zo kwaad als het ging jouw recepten uit de beide kookboeken. Al in die eerste week verloor ik zo'n vier kilo, ondanks dat ik niet kon sporten, ik kon het bijna niet geloven! De weegschaal werd m'n vriend en uiteindelijk ben ik 22 kilo afgevallen en ik ben die kilo's nog steeds kwijt!
Wat me het meest opvalt, is de "eetrust", ik denk bijna nooit meer aan eten, m'n lichaam geeft het zelf wel aan als ik honger heb.
Maar ook de energie die ik nu voel, zeker in vergelijking met leeftijdgenoten die KHrijk eten is enorm! Ik ben nu 58 jaar en fulltime buschauffeur, geef nog steeds 2 à 3 spinninglessen per week, treedt regelmatig op als zanger/entertainer en heb dan ook nog genoeg energie over voor m'n vrouw, 4 kinderen en 5 kleinkinderen.
Mijn vrouw en ik zijn echte levensgenieters, houden van uit eten gaan, een wijntje in een bar, vakantie enz. Maar nooit hoef ik me meer zorgen te maken over m'n gewicht, want grip op koolhydraten werkt iedere keer weer...'

- Erik

OMELET MET ASPERGES

- 150 g groene aspergetips, in stukjes gesneden
- 2 slalotjes, gesnipperd
- 4 eieren
- 2 el room (slagroom onbereid of crème fraiche)
- 50 g Parmezaanse kaas, geraspt
- handvol verse muntblaadjes, fijngesneden
- peper en zout naar smaak
- 1 tl paprikapoeder

Fruit de sjalotjes en bak de asperges 4 minuten mee. Klop intussen de eieren samen met de room, kaas, munt, peper en zout.
Schenk dit over de asperges en zet het vuur op de laagste stand en bak de omelet met de deksel op de pan.
Strooi het paprikapoeder erover zodra het ei is gestold. De omelet is klaar!

FRITTATA

- 150 g courgette, geraspt
- 40 g mozzarella, geraspt
- 20 g Parmezaanse kaas, geraspt
- 50 g salami, in kleine blokjes gesneden
- 2 grote eieren, geklutst
- gerookt paprikapoeder
- peper en zout naar smaak

Knijp het vocht uit de courgetterasp. Meng alle ingrediënten en schenk dit in een koekenpan. Gaar de frittata op matig vuur met de deksel op de pan. Draai om zodra de bovenkant is gestold en bak de frittata nog 2 minuten.

Voor een vegetarische variant: vervang de salami door 50 – 100 gram gekookte champignons.

Gevulde eieren uit de oven

Roerei met zalm

ROEREI MET ZALM

- 4 eieren
- 40 g roomboter, in blokjes
- 1 flinke el crème fraîche
- peper en zout naar smaak
- 200 g gerookte zalm

Breek de eieren en giet in een steelpan met dikke bodem. Voeg de blokjes roomboter erbij.
Zet de pan op het vuur en roer tot het geheel iets romig wordt.
Haal de pan van het vuur en blijf 1 minuut roeren. Plaats de pan weer op het vuur.
Verwarm het mengsel al roerend totdat het begint te stollen.
Haal de pan weer van het vuur af.
Het eimengsel zal door de warmte van de pan doorgaan met stollen.
Schep de crème fraîche erbij en blijf roeren tot het een smeuïge massa is geworden.
Breng op smaak met peper en zout.
Beleg de bordjes met de gerookte zalm. Verdeel het roerei over de zalm.

GEVULDE EIEREN UIT DE OVEN

- 1 sjalotje, gesnipperd
- 1 el olijfolie
- 2 eieren, hardgekookt
- 1 el crème fraîche
- 1 tl mosterd
- 20 g geraspte kaas naar keuze
- twee takjes bieslook, fijngeknipt
- 1 el blaadjes peterselie, fijngesneden
- peper en zout naar smaak
- kerriepoeder naar smaak
- mespunt paprikapoeder

Verwarm de olijfolie in een koekenpan en fruit het sjalotje hierin. Snijd de eieren doormidden, haal het eigeel eruit en houd de eiwithelften apart. Prak het eigeel fijn en voeg de crème fraîche, mosterd en kaas hieraan toe. Breng op smaak met de bieslook, peterselie en eventueel wat zout, peper en kerriepoeder. Vul de eiwithelften met het eigeelmengsel. Bestrooi met het paprikapoeder en bak de eieren 15 minuten in een op 190 °C voorverwarmde oven.

OMELETTAART

Voor 4 porties

1ste omelet
- 2 eieren, geklutst
- 10 g tomatenpuree
- 1 tomaat, kleingesneden
- paprikapoeder naar smaak
- peper en zout naar smaak

2de omelet
- 2 eieren, geklutst
- 50 g geraspte kaas naar keuze
- kurkuma of kerrie naar smaak
- peper en zout naar smaak

3de omelet
- 2 eieren, geklutst
- flinke handvol verse spinazie
- 30 g kruidenkaas
- peper en zout naar smaak

Meng de ingrediënten per omelet.
Voor de derde omelet is dit het makkelijkste om met een blender te doen.
Bak de omeletten een voor een in een kleine koekenpan, niet te snel en met een deksel op de pan.
De bovenkant moet gestold zijn voorat je de omlet kunt omdraaien.
Na omdraaien de omelet nog 1 minuutje bakken en dan op elkaar op een bord leggen.
Hoe kleiner de pan, hoe dikker de omelet, hoe hoger de taart.
En nóg 3 lagen erop is natuurlijk ook leuk.

Nog lekkerder: besmeer de tussenlagen met wat roomkaas en beleg met vleeswaren of wat rauwkost naar wens.

Omeletwrap: De omeletten kunnen afzonderlijk ook gebruikt worden om een omeletwrap van te maken. Bak de omeletten dan lekker dun. Besmeren met wat roomkaas, beleggen met ham, kipfilet of zalm en wat slablaadjes. Oprollen en in handzame stukken snijden. Warm en koud lekker én makkelijk mee te nemen.

Frittata
Omelettaart

LASAGNEBLADEN/ TAGLIATELLE VAN BLOEMKOOLRIJST

Voor 4 porties

Wat een vondst!
Koolhydraatarme groentepasta.
En best snel en makkelijk te maken.

- 125 g bloemkoolrijst
- 4 eieren
- 6 el psylliumvezels
- zout, naar smaak
- 40 g Parmezaanse kaas, geraspt

Verwarm de bloemkoolrijst 2 à 3 minuten in de magnetron totdat deze zacht is.
Meng alle ingrediënten tot een gladde massa.
Schep de helft hiervan op een vel bakpapier, leg hier een ander vel bakpapier bovenop en rol dit uit totdat het deeg van bloemkoolrijst een dikte van ongeveer 2 à 3 millimeter heeft.
Bak dit 2 à 3 minuten op de hoogste stand in de magnetron totdat het bovenste vel bakpapier zonder moeite loslaat als je het verwijdert.
Snijd het deeg in de gewenste maat voor lasagnebladen of in smalle repen voor tagliatelle.

Let op: bak op de hoogste stand van je magnetron. Iedere magnetron is anders, dus controleer regelmatig - zeker bij de eerste bereiding van een nieuw recept - hoe het bakproces verloopt.

Is het deeg te stevig om goed uit te rollen? Roer hier dan 1 à 2 eetlepels Griekse yoghurt doorheen.
Geen magnetron? In de oven is dit ook te bakken, maar dat duurt beduidend langer.

Verwarm de bloemkoolrijst dan een paar minuten in een koekenpan. En bak het uitgerolde mengsel op circa 175°C in ongeveer 30 minuten tot het mooi vast qua structuur is en loskomt van het bakpapier.

Bloemkoolrijst is kant-en-klaar te koop op de groenteafdeling van de supermarkt. Of eenvoudig zelf te maken door bloemkoolroosjes fijn te hakken tot de grootte van rijstkorrels. Gebruik ook gerust de stelen van de bloemkool.

Geen kaasliefhebber? Zonder kaas lukt het ook. Is het beslag dan te stevig om goed uit te rollen, meng er dan nog een extra ei doorheen.

ASPERGE-ZALMSALADE

- ca. 50 ml sojasaus
- paar druppels citroensap (vers of uit een flesje)
- 2 zalmfilets
- 150 g groene aspergetips, gehalveerd
- 1 el olijfolie
- 100 g komkommer
- blaadjes romeinse sla of ijsbergsla
- ½ rode ui, gesneden
- zout en peper naar smaak
- flinke el truffelmayonaise

Meng de sojasaus, het citroensap en wat peper en laat de zalm hierin een half uurtje marineren.
Bak de aspergetips ongeveer 3 minuten in de olijfolie.
Schep de asperges uit de pan en bak de zalm in de overgebleven olijfolie gaar.
Snijd komkommer eerst in plakken en daarna in vier partjes.
Leg de slabladeren in diepe borden, schep hier de asperges, de ui en komkommer op.
Leg de zalm hier bovenop met erop een flinke lepel truffelmayonaise.

Aspergetips zijn jonge asperges met een fijnere smaak dan volgroeide asperge.
Ze zijn kruidiger en sterker van smaak dan witte asperges.
Deze asperges worden boven de grond geteeld en zijn vrijwel het gehele jaar door te koop.

BLOEMKOOLSALADE

- 100 g bloemkool, in stukjes gesneden
- 60 g kalkoen spekreepjes, uitgebakken
- 60 g gerookte kip, in blokjes gesneden
- 60 g snoeppaprika's, in stukjes gesneden
- 6 snoeptomaatjes, in vieren gesneden
- 2 augurken, in blokjes gesneden
- 2 flinke el slasaus met kruiden (zie recept blz. 148)
- peper en zout naar smaak

Meng alle ingrediënten en voeg hier naar smaak peper en zout toe.

Deze bloemkoolsalade is makkelijk en handig als meeneemlunch.
Verdeel de ingrediënten van de sla dan in 2 bakjes.
De eerste 4 ingrediënten in het ene, de laatste 4 ingrediënten in het andere bakje.
En mengen ter plaatse. Eet ze!
Voedzaam, fris en lekker!
Makkelijk en snel: maak meerdere porties tegelijk.
De salade is een dag van tevoren al klaar te maken en enkele dagen houdbaar in de koelkast.

Asperge zalmsalade

Bloemkoolsalade

Haricots-vertssalade
Veldsla salade

VELDSLA-SALADE

- zakje gemengde veldsla
- 1 sjalot, fijngesneden
- 1 bakje Boursin knoflook & fijne kruiden mini's
- ½ puntpaprika, in stukjes gesneden
- 40 g pijnboompitjes, geroosterd
- 10 snoeptomaatjes, in vieren gesneden
- 1 el olijfolie
- peper en zout naar smaak

Meng alle ingrediënten en breng op smaak met peper en zout.

HARICOTS-VERTSSALADE

- 100 g haricots verts, gekookt
- 4 snoeppaprika's, klein gesneden
- 2 gekookte eieren, in vieren gesneden
- 100 g tonijn op water (blikje), afgegoten
- 3 el zelfgemaakte slasaus (zie recept blz. 148)
- peper en zout naar smaak

Meng alles en breng op smaak met peper en zout.

Variatie:
Gebruik sperzieboontjes in plaats van haricots verts.

Snoeppaprika's?
Net als snoeptomaatjes zijn er nu ook snoeppaprika's en snoepkomkommers. Een kleurrijk setje snackgroenten.

Komkommer-bleekselderij salade

Krulsla met kip
en mozzarella

KOMKOMMER-BLEEKSELDERIJ SALADE

- 150 g komkommer
- 100 g bleekselderij
- 100 g extra belegen kaas
- handvol verse muntblaadjes, fijngesneden
- 2 el slasaus met kruiden (zie recept blz. 148)

Snijd de komkommer, de bleekselderij en de kaas in gelijke kleine blokjes.
Meng de munt en de slasaus er doorheen.

Dit is de enige manier om bleekselderij lekker te vinden als je er niet van houdt.
Deze salade is overal lekker bij.

En heerlijk te combineren met de gemarineerde gamba's op blz. 139
Een mooi lunchgerecht of onderdeel van een koolhydraten-uur!

KRULSLA MET KIP EN MOZZARELLA

- 1 zak gemengde krulsla (100-150 g)
- 1 gerookte kipfilet, in stukjes gesneden
- 10 snoeptomaatjes, in vieren gesneden
- 1 rode puntpaprika, in ringen gesneden
- 1 buffelmozzarella, in stukjes
- 50 g uitgebakken spekjes
- 40 ml olijfolie
- 15 ml balsamico
- peper en zout naar smaak

Meng alle ingrediënten en breng op smaak met peper en zout.
De rode puntpaprika is ook te vervangen voor een oranje of lichtgroene.

Genieten met de hoofdletter G!

KOOLSALADE

- 150 g witte kool, in reepjes gesneden
- 100 g venkel, in reepjes gesneden
- 50 g rode kool, in reepjes gesneden
- 4 (snoep)paprika's, in reepjes gesneden
- 2 sjalotjes, fijngesneden
- 30 g kappertjes
- 50 g Kernhem kaas, in blokjes gesneden
- 30 g pijnboompitjes, geroosterd
- oma lemmers dressing, naar smaak
- peper en zout naar smaak

Meng alle ingrediënten, schenk de dressing erover en breng op smaak met peper en zout.

Complexiteit ontstaat, eenvoud moet je creëren.

Wikiweetje: Kernhem is een Nederlandse gewassen korstkaas. De kaas blijft van binnen enigszins zacht en heeft een milde smaak. De kaas wordt gemaakt in diverse kaasfabrieken in Nederland.

De kaas is ontwikkeld door het Nederlands Instituut voor Zuivelonderzoek, het NIZO (nu NIZO Food Research) in Ede. Vele kazen worden genoemd naar de plaats waarin de kaas traditioneel werd gemaakt, zoals Goudse kaas en Leidse kaas. Voor Kernhem ligt dat anders; het is, net als bijvoorbeeld Leerdammer, een moderne kaas zonder historische traditie. De kaas 'Ede' of Edese kaas te noemen klonk niet erg aantrekkelijk. Daarom is de kaas genoemd naar het voormalige landgoed Kernhem, waarin het NIZO ligt.
(bron: Wikipedia)

Het recept van de Oma Lemmers dressing (een vinaigrette) staat in *Grip op Koolhydraten, dagmenu's richtlijnen en recepten en in Grip op Koolhydraten kookboek 2.*

KOMKOMMERSALADE

- 300 g komkommer, in staafjes gesneden (julienne)
- 1 rode paprika, in blokjes gesneden
- (of als je het liever pittiger wilt: 1 rode peper)
- 1 lente-ui, in ringetjes gesneden
- 1 handvol muntblaadjes, fijngesneden
- 2 el olijfolie
- paar druppels citroensap naar smaak (vers of uit een flesje)
- 2 el maanzaad
- peper en zout naar smaak

Meng alle ingrediënten en breng op smaak met peper en zout.
Het is zo lekker snel klaar.

De komkommer in staafjes gesneden staat leuk, maar je kunt de komkommer natuurlijk ook gewoon blokjes of schijfjes snijden.

Komkommersalade
Koolsalade

POKÉ BOWLS

De nieuwe sushi!
Poké staat voor 'in blokjes gesneden'.
En bowls zijn de kommetjes waaruit gegeten wordt. Er zijn tegenwoordig enorm mooie bowls te koop. Leuk voor op je verlanglijstje. Tip!

Poké bowl is een typisch traditioneel gerecht uit Hawaï. Meestal met verse rauwe vis en groenten in blokjes gesneden met (sushi)rijst of glasnoedels als basis. Je kunt er ook een vlees- of vegetarisch gerecht van maken. En natuurlijk laten we de rijst buiten het koolhydratenuur weg of vervangen dit voor bloemkoolrijst.
Wat zo fijn is aan een poké bowl is dat je hierin de restjes uit je koelkast kunt verwerken. Daarom staan er geen hoeveelheden bij de ingrediënten.
Gebruik je rijst erbij, roer dan wat rijstazijn door de rijst. Rijstazijn is een Japanse azijn met een milde, lichtzoete smaak. Het versterkt de smaken in Aziatische gerechten.

Zo maak je een poké bowl:
Combineer je favoriete producten tot een smaakvol gerecht.
Snijd alle ingrediënten in mooie blokjes van ongeveer 1 centimeter of dunne schijfjes.
Doe alles in een mooie kom en maak er een kleurrijke combinatie van.
Strooi hier nog wat pitjes of zaden overheen.

Meng de ingrediënten voor de dressing.
Verhouding: sojasaus 3 delen, rijstazijn 2 delen.
Dus bijvoorbeeld 3 eetlepels sojasaus en 2 eetlepels rijstazijn.
Sprenkel de dressing als laatste eroverheen.

Een feestje in je kom :-)
Makkelijk en snel: Maak een grotere hoeveelheid dressing voor meerdere keren en bewaar dit in de koelkast.

Een aantal heerlijke combinaties:
Variatie: Bij al deze poké bowls kun je naar wens nog bloemkoolrijst, broccolirijst (GOK-groen) of sushirijst (GOK-oranje) toevoegen.

POKÉ BOWL KAAS

- kaas naar keuze
- ei
- augurk
- rettich
- komkommer
- ui
- rode peper
- sesamzaadjes, geroosterd

Dressing naar smaak;
- sojasaus
- rijstazijn
- verse gember, geraspt
- balsamico
- zwarte peper

POKÉ BOWL MET TONIJN

- tonijn
- taugé
- rode puntpaprika
- ei, gekookt
- komkommer
- sesamzaadjes, geroosterd

Dressing naar smaak;
- sojasaus
- rijstazijn
- zwarte peper
- knoflook, geperst

Poké bowl
met tonijn
Poké bowl kaas

Poké bowl met beefreepjes
Poké bowl met zalm
Poké bowl met garnaaltjes

POKÉ BOWL MET BEEFREEPJES

- biefstuk, gebakken en in reepjes gesneden
- champignons, gebakken
- broccoli, gekookt
- rucola
- radijs
- rode peper, ter garnering
- sesamzaadjes, geroosterd

Dressing;
- sojasaus
- rijstazijn
- donkere sesamolie, enkele druppels
- knoflook
- gember
- zwarte peper

POKÉ BOWL MET ZALM

- zalm
- alfalfa
- wakame
- oranje paprika
- rode paprika
- avocado
- sesamzaadjes wit of zwart, geroosterd

Dressing naar smaak;
- sojasaus
- rijstazijn
- donkere sesamolie, enkele druppels
- verse gember, geraspt
- zwarte peper

Laat de blokjes zalm eerst even een half uurtje in de dressing marineren.
Schenk de overgebleven dressing over de gevulde bowl.

POKÉ BOWL MET GARNAALTJES

- noordzeegarnalen
- mango
- wakame
- wortel
- paprika
- sesamzaadjes, geroosterd

Dressing naar smaak;
- sojasaus
- rijstazijn
- knoflook, geperst
- verse gember, geraspt
- zwarte peper

PORTIEGROOTTE TUSSENDOORTJES

Bij de tussendoortjes is het aantal porties niet goed aan te geven.
De ene persoon heeft als tussendoortje een iets grotere behoefte dan een ander. En als onderdeel van een tapasmaaltijd zijn de hoeveelheden ook anders dan wanneer het tussendoortje solo gegeten wordt.
En sommige tussendoortjes zijn ook lekker bij de hoofdmaaltijd en dan gebruik je een grotere hoeveelheid.

KIPKLUIFJES

- ca. 500 gram kipkluifjes
- 50 ml olijfolie
- 10 druppels citroensap (vers of uit een flesje)
- 8 g gerookt paprikapoeder
- 15 ml sojasaus
- 1 knoflookteen, geperst
- sambal en zout naar smaak
- peterselie of koriander als garnering

Maak een marinade van de olijfolie, het citroensap, gerookt paprikapoeder, de sojasaus, knoflook,
sambal en zout.
Marineer de kipkluifjes hierin minimaal een uur.
Bak de kluifjes ca. 30 minuten in de oven of airfryer tot ze gaar en mooi van kleur zijn.
Bestrooi met wat peterselie of koriander.

Smullen maar!!!

BEEF JERKY

Voor meerdere porties

Dit heerlijke beef jerky (gedroogd vlees) recept is lekker als tussendoortje of gewoon bij de borrel als je visite hebt. En omdat het niet gekoeld hoeft te worden is het lekker makkelijk om mee te nemen als je op stap gaat. Beef jerky blijft maandenlang goed, zonder dat het gekoeld hoeft te worden.
Het ziet er misschien uit als een hondensnack maar geloof me, het smaakt echt heerlijk.

- 3 bavette steaks
- 1 flinke teen knoflook, geperst
- 50 ml sojasaus
- peper en zout naar smaak

Maak een marinade van de sojasaus, de knoflook en peper en zout. Snijd de bavette in repen van ongeveer een halve centimeter dik. Hussel door de marinade en laat dit een half uurtje intrekken.
Verdeel de repen op een ovenrek. Bij een kleine oven kan dit boven elkaar.
Droog de bavette in circa 1 uur en 45 minuten in een op 100 °C voorverwarmde oven.
Om het nog een beetje mooi op de foto te krijgen heb ik het op een kampvuur bereid.
Serveer met 3 kleuren rauwe paprika.
Smaakt er nog lekker bij ook.

Bavette is vlees van de flank van het rund. In plaats van bavette kun je ook entrecote gebruiken.

GEROOKTE KIP MET GAMBA'S

- kruidenboter kruiden
- kruidenboterkruiden
- peper en zout
- 1 knoflookteen, geperst
- 1 el olijfolie
- 6 gamba's
- 6 toefjes avocadocrème (zie recept blz. 64)
- 6 plakjes gerookte kipfilet

Maak een marinade van de kruiden, peper en zout, knoflook en de olie. Meng dit met de gamba's en laat het een half uurtje marineren. Bak de gamba's op hoog vuur gaar.
Schep een toefje avocadocrème op een plakje kip en leg daar een gamba op.
Herhaal dit nog 5 keer.

Ook leuk op een verjaardag of feestje. Kruidenboterkruiden zijn kant en klaar te koop in de supermarkt in het kruidenvak.

Brie met truffelsalami
Gekruide noten
Gemarineerde kaasblokjes
Chorizochips
Kipkluifjes
Chorizo met coquilles
Beef jerky

Gevulde komkommer!
Stracciatella
verwennerij
Pittige notenmix
Caprese balletjes
Gerookte kip
met gamba's

GEMARINEERDE KAASBLOKJES

- stuk extra belegen kaas
- flinke scheut oude balsamico *
- chillipeper en zout naar smaak

Snijd de extra belegen kaas in blokjes en giet hier een flinke scheut (oude) balsamico overheen.
Voeg chilipeper en zout naar smaak toe.
Bewaar dit in een afgesloten bakje in de koelkast en schud dit af en toe even om.
Laat de kaas een nachtje in de koelkast staan.
Lekker makkelijk om van te tevoren klaar te maken als je visite krijg of om mee te nemen naar het werk.
Extra lekker met Maldon zeezoutvlokken.

*) oude balsamico is stroperig en blijft beter aan de kaas 'hangen'. Op het etiket staat vaak vermeld 'oude balsamico' en kan wel meer dan 10 - 100 jaar oud zijn. Een goede 'tradizionale' balsamico heeft als eerste ingrediënt 'most'. Bij industriële balsamico's staat druivenazijn als eerste = hoofdingrediënt vermeld en wordt met 'caramel' donker gekleurd wordt. Scan dus even het etiket om de juiste balsamico te kiezen.

CAPRESE BALLETJES

Voor meerdere porties

- 4 gedroogde tomaten, fijngesneden
- handvol verse basilicumblaadjes, fijngesneden
- Italiaanse kruidenmix (zie recept blz. 49)
- peper en zout, naar smaak
- 400 g rundergehakt
- 1 pot mini buffelmozzarella

Meng de gedroogde tomaat, verse basilicum, Italiaanse kruiden en peper en zout met het rundergehakt.
Bekleed de mini buffelmozzarella met het gehakt en bak de gehaktballetjes in een koekenpan gaar.
Heerlijk voor bij de borrel, door tomatensaus en pasta, etc.

Capisce?

CHORIZO MET COQUILLES

- 1 el roomboter
- 4 verse salieblaadjes
- 4 coquilles
- 6 cm chorizoworst, in vier plakken gesneden
- peper en zout naar smaak

Verhit de boter op hoog vuur.
Zodra de boter gaat schuimen, de salie en coquilles toevoegen.
Haal de salieblaadjes uit de pan zodra ze bruin worden.
Laat de coquilles 1 à 2 minuten stil liggen en keer ze dan pas om.
Bak ze aan beide kanten bruin, maar wel zodat het midden nog doorzichtig is.
Leg de coquilles op een bord rusten.
Bak de chorizo anderhalve minuut aan beide kanten.
Leg de chorizo op een bord, leg daarop de coquilles en de salie, en strooi her een beetje peper en zout over.

Coquilles worden ook sint-jakobsschelpen genoemd.
In plaats van coquilles kun je ook 'mantelschelpen' gebruiken.

CHORIZOCHIPS

Voor meerdere porties

- 1 chorizoworstje
- olie om in te bakken (olijfolie, kokosolie of arachideolie)

Snijd de chorizo in zo dun mogelijke plakjes en bak ze in een laagje olie 2 à 3 minuten tot ze knapperig zijn.
De tijd hangt af van hoe dun het gesneden is.

Makkelijk en snel: koop kant-en-klaar gesneden chorizo plakjes en bak die lekker knapperig.
Gooi na het bakken de olie niet weg, maar bewaar deze in een afgesloten bakje en laat het afkoelen. Gebruik de olie bij de volgende bakbeurt van vlees, vis of eieren. Door het uitgebakken vet van de chorizo zit hier extra smaak aan..
Het gestolde vet is ook te gebruiken als smeersel op een stukje (koolhydraatarm) brood of cracker.

GEVULDE KOMKOMMER!

Voor meerdere porties

Deze gevulde komkommer is in verschillende varianten te maken en doet het erg leuk op een verjaardag.
Het is maar net wat je lekker vindt. Groenten, fruit, kruiden, vlees, vis of kaas.
Alles kan. Maar let wel op de kleurcombinatie, die deze schijfjes zo mooi maakt.

Maak met een appelboor een gat in een stuk komkommer. Snijd al vulling naar keuze groenten, fruit etc. julienne. Rol de vulling stevig op in een blad rode kool.
Schuif deze rol in het gat van de komkommer en snijd hier mooie plakjes van!!

Rode kool over? Maak er dan een lekkere rode koolsalade van of een klassiek rode koolrecept met appel voor in je koolhydratenuur. Lekker, voedzaam en gezond!
Kijk in een basiskookboek of zoek op internet naar een makkelijk recept met rode kool. En ja, je kunt rode kool ook lekker op smaak brengen met 1 of 2 druppeltjes stevia.

GEKRUIDE NOTEN

Voor meerdere porties

- 100 g gemengde noten, ongebrand
- 1 flinke el kruidenboterkruiden
- ½ el roomboter, olijfolie of kokosolie

Bak de noten met de kruiden in de boter of olie 8 à 10 minuten op matig vuur. Schep een aantal keer even om. De noten mogen wel een beetje verkleuren maar pas op dat ze niet verbranden.
Zodra ze mooi van kleur zijn, dan snel uit de pan!

In fase 1: maximaal 25 gram als tussendoortje. Als GOK-groene maaltijd 50 gram.
Zie blz. 16 'Noten tussendoor'.
Kruidenboterkruiden zijn te koop in de supermarkt.

PITTIGE NOTENMIX

Voor meerdere porties

- 200 g gemengde noten
- 1 el olijfolie
- 50 g kalkoen spekreepjes
- 1 ui, gesnipperd
- 1 knoflookteen, geperst
- chilipeper en zout naar smaak

Bak de noten in een olijfolie in de koekenpan.
Bak de spekreepjes, ui en knoflook kort mee.
Schep de chilipeper en zout erdoor en verspreid de notenmix op een bakplaat.
Bak de mix circa 15 minuten droog in een op 160 °C voorverwarmde oven.

Let op dat er geen cashewnoten en pinda's in de notenmix zitten om de notenmix GOK-groen te houden.

In fase 1: maximaal 25 gram als tussendoortje. Als GOK-groene maaltijd 50 gram.
Zie blz. 16 'Noten tussendoor'.

BRIE MET TRUFFELSALAMI

Voor meerdere porties

- stuk roombrie
- 1 ons truffelsalami

Wikkel een plakje truffelsalami om een plakje brie.
Een overheerlijk tussendoortje!!!

Vijf jaar geleden ben ik begonnen op advies van een vriendin met Grip op Koolhydraten, omdat ik al mijn hele leven last had van prikkelbaar darm syndroom.
Ik stond er wat sceptisch tegenover, aangezien meer vetten eten zo tegen mijn gevoel in was, omdat ik ook bezig was met afvallen en juist alleen maar mager en light at.
Maar omdat ik het resultaat bij mijn vriendin zag, ben ik er toch aan begonnen, gelijk het eerste basisboek gekocht en na het lezen van dit boek erg enthousiast geworden.
Ik ben geen kokkin, maar de weekmenu's gaven mij vooral heel veel eetrust en omdat in de boeken ook veel en makkelijke recepten staan was het gemakkelijk vol te houden.
Inmiddels zijn we vijf jaar verder, mijn klachten van mijn prikkelbare darm zijn echt helemaal verdwenen, iets waar ik zo blij mee ben, omdat ik jarenlang ziekenhuis in en uit ben gegaan zonder dat de artsen mij konden helpen.
Afvallen is daarbij een mooie bijkomstigheid, ook al ben ik af en toe afgedwaald naar een andere methode. Toch ben ik altijd weer bij Grip op Koolhydraten teruggekomen, omdat dit gewoon het beste werkte voor mij.
Inmiddels is ook mijn behandelend arts in het ziekenhuis voor mijn buik- en darmproblemen helemaal om en beveelt deze methode bij zijn patiënten met dezelfde klachten aan en mét resultaat.
Kortom, ik ben blij dat ik dit concept of eigenlijk deze levenswijze destijds ben tegengekomen.

Een lieve groet van Heidi

STRACCIATELLA VERWENNERIJ

Voor 4 porties

- 100 g mascarpone
- 100 g slagroom zonder suiker, opgeklopt
- 15 g chocolade puur, fijngeraspt
- stevia naar smaak

Roer de slagroom en de geraspte chocolade door de mascarpone en breng op smaak met stevia.
Chocolade raspen gaat makkelijk als je de chocoladereep (uit de koelkast) op zijn kant houdt en dan langs een omgekeerde kaasschaaf schaaft.

Extra lekker met wat geschaafde amandelen erover.
Let op: Deze lekkernij is een calorierijk 'vetbommetje'. Houd de porties klein, neem kleine hapjes, eet langzaam en geniet van iedere hap.
Chocolade puur staat wel op de oranje lijst van GOK. Maar aangezien in dit gerecht weinig chocolade gebruikt wordt en het gecombineerd wordt met vetrijke producten, hebben die paar gram koolhydraten weinig invloed op je bloedsuiker. Hoe puurder de chocolade des te minder suiker. Er is zelfs pure chocolade 99%.

Easy chicken
Gevulde kipfilets

GEVULDE KIPFILETS

- 2 kipfilets
- 80 g kruidenkaas
- 2 takjes verse peterselie, fijngesneden
- 50 g serranoham, in stukjes gesneden en krokant gebakken
- sambal naar smaak
- peper en zout naar smaak
- paprikapoeder naar smaak

Meng de kruidenkaas met verse peterselie, serranoham en sambal.
Snijd de kipfilets aan de zijkant in en vul ze met het kaasmengsel. Vouw de kipfilets dicht en zet dit vast met cocktailprikkers of een stukje keukentouw.
Kruid de kipfilets met peper, zout en paprikapoeder.
Bak de kipfilets in een koekenpan in circa 10 minuten rondom gaar.

EASY CHICKEN

Zo makkelijk en zo snel!

- 2 kippendijfilets, in blokjes gesneden
- peper, zout en paprikapoeder naar smaak
- 200 g groene asperges, in stukjes van 1 à 2 cm gesneden
- 6 zongedroogde tomaten op oliebasis, fijngesneden
- 2 el olie uit het potje van de zongedroogde tomaten

Kruid de kipblokjes met de peper, het zout en paprikapoeder.
Verhit de olie uit het potje van de tomaten en bak de kip hierin gaar.
Voeg de asperges en de zongedroogde tomaten toe en bak nog 2 à 3 minuten mee.

Spaanse kip
Kipburger

SPAANSE KIP

- 2 kipfilets, met vel
- 1 el olijfolie
- 1 ui, gesnipperd
- 2 knoflooktenen, geperst
- 75 g chorizo, in blokjes gesneden
- 10 snoeptomaatjes, gehalveerd
- 10 pikante olijven, gehalveerd
- zout en tijm naar smaak
- 200 g courgette, in blokjes gesneden
- paar takjes verse peterselie, fijngesneden

Bak de kipfilets in een koekenpan in de olijfolie, 3 minuten aan iedere kant.
Neem de kipfilets uit de pan en verhit de grill.
Fruit de ui in de achtergebleven olie.
Voeg de knoflook en de chorizo toe en bak circa 5 minuutjes.
Voeg de snoeptomaatjes en de pikante olijven toe.
Breng op smaak met zout en tijm.
Leg een deksel op de pan en laat het 10 minuten op matig vuur pruttelen.
Roer af en toe om.
Voeg de courgette toe en bak hem nog 10 minuten mee.
Leg de kipfilets met het vel naar boven nog circa 10 minuten onder de hete grill.
Strooi er voor het opdienen nog wat verse peterselie over.

KIPBURGER

- 2 sjalotjes, gesnipperd
- 1 el olijfolie
- kruidenboterkruiden naar smaak
- peper en zout naar smaak
- 2 eieren, geklutst
- 25 g haverzemelen
- 2 kipfilets à 125 gram per stuk, zeer fijngesneden

Fruit de sjalotjes in wat olijfolie en meng dit met lekker veel kruidenboterkruiden, peper en zout, de geklutste eieren en de haverzemelen. Voeg dit bij de fijngesneden kipfilets en maak hier burgers van.
Bak de kipfiletburgers om en om in circa 10 minuten in een koekenpan bruin en gaar.

Kruidenboterkruiden zijn kant en klaar te koop in de supermarkt.
Ook lekker: in reepjes snijden en koud eten als tussendoortje of bij een tapasmaaltijd.

Kalkoenschnitzel
Gevulde kalkoenfilet
Kalkoen roerbak

KALKOENSCHNITZEL

Een koolhydraatarme gepaneerde kalkoenschnitzel! In dit recept gebruiken we fijngemalen knabbelspek en Parmezaanse kaas voor een knapperig hartige korst. Knabbelspek is makkelijk fijn te malen in een hakmolen.

- 40 g knabbelspek, fijngemalen
- 20 g Parmezaanse kaas, geraspt
- 2 kalkoenfilets à la minute
- 2 eieren, geklutst
- peper en zout naar smaak

Meng de knabbelspek met de Parmezaanse kaas.
Haal de kalkoenfilets door het ei en en vervolgens door het knabbelspek-kaasmengsel.
Bestooi met peper naar smaak en eventueel – spaarzaam – wat zout.
Denk er aan dat knabbelspek en kaas ook al zout zijn.
Bak de kalkoenfilets in 10 minuten in een koekenpan om en om gaar.

KALKOENROERBAK

- 1 rode ui, gesnipperd
- 1 kalkoenfilet, in blokjes gesneden
- peper en zout naar smaak
- paprikapoeder naar smaak
- 15 pikante olijven, in plakjes gesneden
- rode puntpaprika, gesneden
- 1 knoflookteen, geperst
- 50 g crème fraîche
- mosterd naar smaak
- ijsbergsla, optioneel

Fruit de rode ui. Voeg de kalkoen, de kruiden, olijven, paprika en knoflook toe. Roerbak tot de kalkoen gaar is.
Maak een sausje door de crème fraîche te verwarmen en hier naar smaak mosterd aan toe te voegen.
Eventueel zout en peper toevoegen.
Lekker met wat dun gesneden ijsbergsla.

GEVULDE KALKOENFILET

- 1 kalkoenfilet
- takje verse oregano
- takje verse tijm
- 40 g gorgonzola
- ½ el olijfolie
- peper en zout naar smaak

Snijd de kalkoenfilet aan de zijkant in.
Ris de blaadjes van de takjes kruiden, roer ze met een vork door de gorgonzola en vul de kalkoenfilet met dit mengsel.
Bind keukentouw eromheen en smeer de kalkoenfilet in met olijfolie.
Bestrooi met peper en zout en gaar circa 9 à 10 minuten in de contactgrill.
That's it.

En zo blijven we genieten!

SPINAZIE MET KIPFILET EN EEN LIMBURGS KAASJE

Simpele gerechten kunnen toch zo lekker zijn hè . Dat is dit recept zeker.

- 1 el olijfolie
- 2 kipfilets
- 1 rode ui, gesnipperd
- 2 knoflooktenen, geperst
- 600 g verse spinazie
- 2 'de echte Limburger' kaasjes
- peper en zout, naar smaak

Verwarm de olijfolie in een koekenpan en bak de kipfilet in 10 minuten rondom gaar.
Fruit de ui kort mee.
Voeg de knoflook toe en beetje bij beetje de spinazie.
Roerbak dit tot het grootste gedeelte van het vocht dat uit de spinazie komt, is verdampt.
Voeg de kaasjes toe en laat deze al roerend smelten.
Breng op smaak met peper en zout.

Een Limburgs kaasje is befaamd om de sterke geur en de plakkerige korst. Onder de korst zit een smaakvol, romig kaasje met een licht kruidige smaak. De korst is eetbaar. Naar wens kun je de korst ook wegsnijden. Ieder zijn smaak.

CANNELLONI

Voor 4 porties

- 2 komkommers
- 500 g rundergehakt
- 1 grote ui, gesnipperd
- 100 g olijven, in plakjes gesneden
- 2 knoflooktenen, geperst
- 20 snoeptomaatjes, in vieren gesneden
- 400 g gezeefde tomaat
- 1 el sambal brandal
- zout naar smaak
- 100 g gorgonzola
- 100 g kaas

Was de komkommers en snijd ze in stukken (2 - 4 centimeter). Hol de stukken komkommer uit tot er rondom 0,5 centimeter dikte overblijft.
Zet de komkommer rechtop in een ovenschaal.
Rul het gehakt en bak de ui, de olijven, de knoflook en de tomaatjes mee.
Schenk er de gezeefde tomaat bij en breng op smaak met sambal brandal en zout.
Vul de komkommer met het gehaktmengsel, leg er een paar stukjes gorgonzola op en rasp de kaas erover.
Bak de komkommers in 45 minuten gaar in een op 180 °C voorverwarmde oven.

Het vruchtvlees van de komkommer kun je gebruiken voor een frisse komkommersalade.

Variatie: je kunt de komkommer natuurlijk ook vullen met je eigen favoriete pastasaus.

GROENTEWRAP

- 250 g rundergehakt of kippengehakt
- 1 ui, gesnipperd
- 1 paprika, in stukjes gesneden
- ½ courgette, in blokjes gesneden
- ½ blik gezeefde tomaten
- Italiaanse kruidenmix (zie recept blz. 49)
- peper en zout naar smaak
- 4 grote bladeren ijsbergsla
- 100 g kaas, geraspt
- 50 g Parmezaanse kaas (of gorgonzola of pecorino)

Rul het gehakt en bak de ui, de paprika en de courgette mee. Schenk de gezeefde tomaten erbij en breng op smaak met de Italiaanse kruiden, peper en zout.
Dompel de bladeren kort in kokend heet water, net zolang totdat je ziet dat ze ietsjes slap worden. Leg ze op een bord.
Verdeel de saus over de bladeren, rol de bladeren op en leg ze in een ovenschaal.
Strooi de kaas erover en zet de schaal even onder de grill, net zolang totdat de kaas gesmolten is.
Super lekker.

Variant: je kunt dit recept ook maken met een blad van witte kool, rode kool, spitskool, Chinese kool, boerenkool of paksoi.

TARTAARTJE MET SERRANOHAM

Op deze manier wil je wel iedere dag een tartaartje.

- 1 rode ui, gesneden
- 50 g serranoham, in stukjes gesneden
- klontje roomboter
- 2 tartaartjes
- kruidenboterkruiden
- peper en zout naar smaak
- takje peterselie, fijngesneden

Doe wat roomboter in een koekenpan en bak hierin de rode ui en de serranoham.
Kruid de tartaar met de kruidenboterkruiden, zout en peper.
Als de ui glazig is en de ham zacht en gaar wordt, schep je ze een beetje opzij en bak je daarnaast de tartaar tot de gewenste gaarheid.
Serveer de tartaar met een beetje verse peterselie.

INDISCHE GEHAKTBALLEN

Meerdere porties

Ook lekker voor bij de borrel of als tussendoortje.

- 500 g rundergehakt
- 4 flinke el seroendeng (zie recept blz. 48)
- sambal brandal naar smaak
- zout naar smaak
- 1 tl komijnpoeder
- 1 tl koriander
- 1 ei, losgeklopt
- zoete chilisaus (zie recept blz. 149)

Meng het gehakt met de seroendeng, kruiden en het ei.
Rol er ballen van 3 à 4 centimeter doorsnede van.
Braad de gehaktballen in een koekenpan in 15 minuten gaar.
Serveer de gehaktballen met de zoete chilisaus.

Snel en makkelijk:
Maak een ruime hoeveelheid gehaktballen en vries deze portiegewijs in.
De gehaktballen zijn ook makkelijk mee te nemen in de lunchbox.

VITELLO TONNATO

- 2 kalfslendes van ca. 100 g
- peper en zout naar smaak
- blikje tonijn op basis van olijfolie (200 g)
- 2 flinke el mayonaise
- 20 g kappertjes plus een beetje voor de garnering
- 1 ansjovisfilet

Bestrooi de kalfslendes met wat peper en zout en bak aan iedere kant in ongeveer 4 minuutjes.
Haal de kalfslendes uit de pan, wikkel ze in folie en laat afkoelen.
Giet de olijfolie uit het blikje tonijn grotendeels af.
Mix in een blender de tonijn, de mayonaise, de kappertjes en de ansjovisfilet tot een gladde massa.
Snijd de afgekoelde kalfslende in dunne plakken en leg de plakken op een bord.
Schep het tonijnmengsel erop en maak het af met wat kappertjes en peper en zout naar smaak.

Snelle en makkelijke Vitello tonato: plakjes kalfsfricandeau met tonijnsaus

LASAGNE

Voor 4 porties

- 500 g rundergehakt
- 2 (rode) uien, gesnipperd
- 1 groene paprika, in blokjes gesneden
- 1 (gele) courgette, in blokjes gesneden
- 400 g tomatenblokjes (uit blik)
- 1 x lasagnekruidenmix (zie recept blz. 49)
- 1 el olijfolie
- lasagnebladen (zie recept blz. 87)
- 200 g kaas naar keuze, in plakken of geraspt

Rul het gehakt in wat olie en bak de uien, de paprika en de courgette mee.
Voeg als de groenten gaar zijn de tomatenblokjes en de lasagnekruiden erbij.
Laat het geheel 4 minuutjes zachtjes pruttelen.
Vet ondertussen een ovenschaal met olijfolie in.
Schep er 1/3 van het gehaktmengsel in en bedek dit met lasagnebladen.
Herhaal dit nog 2 keer en leg hier als laatste de kaas op.
Bak de lasagneschotel 15 minuten op 190 °C in de voorverwarmde oven.

VARKENSHAAS MET MAANZAADKORST

- 250 g varkenshaas
- 3 el maanzaad
- 2 tl mosterd
- 1 el citroensap (vers of uit een flesje)
- 1 knoflookteen, geperst
- 1 el olijfolie
- peper en zout naar smaak

Verdeel de varkenshaas in twee gelijke stukken. Meng de ingrediënten, behalve het vlees. Bestrijk dit mengsel over de twee stukken varkenshaas. Leg de varkenshaas in een ingevette ovenschaal en bak het vlees 25 minuten in een op 220 °C voorverwarmde oven gaar.

Lekker bij allerlei soorten groenten en pasta, rijst of aardappelen.

STEAK MET WORCESTERSAUS

Kost voor Kerels
Nou ik maak mezelf er ook blij mee hoor.

- 1 groente- of rundvleesbouillonblokje à 10 g
- 1 el olijfolie
- 2 biefstukken
- 50 g roomboter
- 50 ml worcestersaus
- 90 ml slagroom (onbereid)
- 1 el whisky

Verkruimel het bouillonblokje en meng dit met de olijfolie totdat je een soort pasta hebt. Smeer de biefstukken met de pasta in.
Verhit een flinke klont roomboter in een koekenpan en bak hierin je biefstuk tot de gewenste gaarheid.
Haal de biefstukken uit de pan, laat ze op een bord rusten, afgedekt met aluminiumfolie.
Schenk de wocesteraus bij de overgebleven boter en voeg de slagroom en whisky toe. Blijf roeren totdat de saus warm en iets ingedikt is.
Breng de saus op smaak met peper en serveer dit bij de biefstuk.

Heerlijk met gegrilde paprika.

ZALMCARPACCIO

- 200 g gerookte zalm, in plakken
- 100 g feta
- 2 lente-ui, gesneden
- 1 flinke el kappertjes
- 60 g Parmezaanse kaas, grof geraspt
- 3 el pijnboompitten, geroosterd
- peper naar smaak
- scheutje olijfolie
- citroensap naar smaak (vers of uit een flesje)

Verdeel de plakken gerookte zalm op een bord.
Hak de feta fijn en schep hem over de zalm.
Bestrooi met de lente-ui, de kappertjes, de Parmezaanse kaas, de pijnboompitten en peper.
Sprenkel er wat olijfolie en citroensap over.

GARNALENCOCKTAIL

- 1 el whiskycocktailsaus (zie recept blz. 148)
- 100 g Noordzeegarnalen
- 1 lente-ui, fijngesneden
- ¼ paprika, rood of groen, in kleine blokjes gesneden
- 4 snoeptomaatjes, in blokjes gesneden
- peper en zout naar smaak
- 4 witlofblaadjes

Meng de whiskycocktailsaus met de garnaaltjes en voeg hier de lente-ui, de paprika en de tomaatjes aan toe. Breng op smaak met wat peper en zout. Serveer de garnalencocktail in een blaadje witlof.

'Gok heeft gewoon invloed op zoveel dingen qua gezondheid maar ook geestelijk en ook echt voor mensen met emotionele problemen die in eetbuien vastzitten.'

- Jessica

ZALMPAKKETJE

- 300 g groene aspergetips
- 2 zalmfilets
- 2 flinke el verse pesto groen
- 2 romatomaten, in plakken gesneden
- 2 el olijfolie
- peper en zout naar smaak

Verdeel de groene aspergetips over twee vellen bakpapier of aluminiumfolie.
Leg hier een zalmfilet bovenop en smeer dit in met een lepel pesto.
Garneer met plakken romatomaat, besprenkel met wat olijfolie en bestrooi met peper en zout naar smaak.
Vouw de aluminiumfolie/het bakpapier dicht en bak de zalm 20 minuten in een op 200 °C voorverwarmde oven.
Bak een bevroren zalmfilet ca. 5 minuten langer.
De zalm mag van binnen nog rosé zijn.

Errugggg lekkerrr!

Romatomaten laten minder vocht los dan de meeste andere tomaten.
Gebruik je bakpapier, maak er dan eerst even een prop van, maak die nat met water, knijp er het vocht uit en strijk het papier weer uit. Zo is bakpapier makkelijker hanteerbaar.

Kabeljauw in kruidenolie

KABELJAUW IN KRUIDENOLIE

- 15 g verse platte peterselie
- 15 g verse bieslook
- 15 g verse tuinkers
- peper en zout naar smaak
- 50 ml olijfolie
- 250 g kabeljauw
- 40 g Parmezaanse kaas, grof geraspt

Doe de kruiden samen met de olijfolie in een hakmolen en maal alles fijn totdat er een gladde massa ontstaat.
Breng op smaak met peper en zout. Leg de kabeljauw in een ovenschaal en schenk de kruidenolie eroverheen.
Bak de kabeljauw circa 12 minuten in een op 200 °C voorverwarmde oven.
Rasp bij opdienen nog wat Parmezaanse kaas over de kabeljauw.
Heerlijk om in de overgebleven olie koolhydraatarm brood te dopen.

GEMARINEERDE GAMBA'S

- 40 ml (oude) balsamico
- 1 knoflookteen, geperst
- peper en zout naar smaak
- 8 gamba's

Maak een marinade van de balsamico, de knoflook en peper en zout en laat de gamba's op zijn minst een uur marineren.
Bak de gamba's in de koekenpan of tussen de contactgrill gaar.
Lekker met de komkommer-bleekselderij-salade op blz. 93.

Kijk voor meer uitleg over oude balsamico bij het recept 'Gemarineerde kaasblokjes' op blz. 104

ZALMTARTAARTJE

Ohhhhhwwww, dit is zooooooo lekker (en gezond)!!!!

- 200 g gerookte zalm, fijngesneden
- 2 sjalotjes, gesnipperd
- 4 el kappertjes, fijngesneden
- 4 el pijnboompitten, geroosterd
- 1 el mayonaise
- peper, zout en dille naar smaak
- citroensap (optioneel) (vers of uit een flesje)

Meng alle ingrediënten.
Plaats een kookring op ieder bord en schep hier de helft van het zalmmengsel in.
Druk het geheel een beetje aan en haal de kookring weg.

Sprenkel eventueel een paar druppels citroen over het zalmtartaartje.

TONIJNSALADE

- 4 eieren, hardgekookt
- 1 blikje tonijn à 200 g
- 2 zongedroogde tomaatjes, fijngesneden
- 1 sjalotje, fijngesneden
- 20 taggiasche olijfjes, fijngesneden
- 30 g kappertjes, fijngesneden
- mayonaise, tot gewenste smeuïgheid
- Italiaanse kruidenmix naar smaak, zie recept blz. 49
- knoflookpoeder en peper, naar smaak
- zout naar smaak

Prak de eieren door de tonijn en voeg de overige ingrediënten toe.
Breng het geheel op smaak met de Italiaanse kruiden, de knoflookpoeder, peper en zout.

Heerlijk op een cracker of als bijgerecht.

Taggiasche olijven zijn kleine, donker paarsige, ontpitte olijven van topkwaliteit uit de Italiaanse streek Taggia.
Een mix van knoflookpoeder en peper is kant en klaar te koop in de supermarkt onder dan naam 'knoflookpeper'.

Tonijnsalade
Zalmtartaartje

Gegrilde paksoi
Sperziebonensalade met knoflook

GEGRILDE PAKSOI

- 2 mini-paksoi
- olijfolie
- peper en zout naar smaak
- kruidenboterkruiden naar smaak
- geroosterde sesamzaadjes naar smaak
- 2 zachtgekookte eieren, in plakjes

Snijd het uiterste kontje van de paksoi weg. Verwijder eventuele losse bladeren. Snijd dan de mini- paksoi doormidden. Besprenkel de binnenkanten van de paksoi met olijfolie en strooi hier de kruiden overheen.
Leg de helften ongeveer 10 tot 15 minuten tussen de contactgrill, naargelang de warmte stand van de grill.
Leg de helften op een bord, strooi er wat sesamzaadjes over en leg de plakjes ei erop.

Ook lekker: nog een paar druppels zwarte sesamolie erover.

Kruidenboterkruiden zijn te koop in de supermarkt.

SPERZIEBONENSALADE MET KNOFLOOK

1-2 porties, bijgerecht

Als je snel van je visite af wilt moet je dit eten voor ze komen.... Knoflookkegel!

- 200 g sperziebonen
- ½ bol knoflook, geperst
- sap van 1 citroen
- 30 ml olijfolie
- flinke handvol muntblaadjes, fijngesneden
- peper en zout naar smaak

Kook de sperziebonen in circa 8 - 10 minuten beetgaar en laat ze afkoelen.
Meng dit vervolgens met de overige ingrediënten en breng op smaak met peper en zout.

Groen tuinhek
Komkommer met ui

KOMKOMMER MET UI

Bijgerecht, 1 à 2 porties

- 200 g komkommer, in dunne schijfjes gesneden
- 1 rode ui, dun gesneden
- verse koriander naar smaak
- scheutje olijfolie
- paar druppels limoensap naar smaak
- peper en zout naar smaak

Meng alle ingrediënten en breng het op smaak met peper en zout.
Vervang de koriander ook eens door verse peterselie, salie, of munt.

GROEN TUINHEK

1 à 2 porties, bijgerecht

Heerlijk voor op de bbq!!!

- 200 g groene aspergetips
- olijfolie om in te smeren
- zout en peper naar smaak
- knoflook naar smaak, uitgepers

Rijg de aspergetips aan de onderkant en aan de bovenkant naast elkaar op 2 sateprikkers, smeer in met olijfolie en bestrooi met zout en peper en eventueel wat knoflook.
Even 1 à 2 minuten aan weerskanten bakken op de bbq en dan intens genieten.
Om je vingers bij af te likken

Kan ook onder de grill worden bereid.
Aspergetips zijn jonge asperges met een fijnere smaak dan een volgroeide asperge.
Ze zijn kruidiger en sterker van smaak dan witte asperges.
Deze asperges worden boven de grond geteeld en zijn vrijwel het gehele jaar door te koop.

Tomatensalade
Gestoofde komkommer

TOMATENSALADE

Bijgerecht

- 40 g verse pesto groen
- 200 g snoeptomaatjes, in vieren gesneden
- handvol basilicum- of muntblaadjes, gesneden
- peper en zout naar smaak

Schep de pesto door de tomaatjes en breng op smaak met de verse kruiden, peper en zout.

Ook lekker op een cracker.

Variant: Rucola heeft ook een peperachtige smaak en is een goede vervanger van basilicum in deze tomatensalade.

Basilicum heeft een vrij sterke overheersende peperachtige smaak.
Begin met een beetje toe te voegen en proef even. Zo nodig nog wat erbij doen.
Basilicum en tomaat is een lekkere combinatie die in de Italiaanse keuken veel gebruikt wordt. Ook veel pesto's bevatten basilicum.

GESTOOFDE KOMKOMMER

1 à 2 porties, bijgerecht

- 1 grote ui, gesnipperd
- 1 el olijfolie
- 250 g komkommer, in grove blokjes gesneden
- 100 ml water
- bouillonblokje (5 gr)
- 12 knoflookolijven, in 4 delen gesneden

Fruit de ui in een scheut olijfolie.
Voeg de komkommer en het bouillonblokje toe en bak dit omscheppend 2 minuten mee.
Voeg het water toe en laat dit met de deksel op de pan 6 minuten stoven.
Schep de olijven erdoor en laat het vocht verdampen.

SLASAUS MET KRUIDEN

Meerdere porties

- 1 pot Zaanse mayonaise
- 15 ml citroensap (vers of uit een flesje)
- 15 g mosterd
- 10 druppels worcestersaus
- 8 druppels stevia
- saladekruiden naar smaak
- knoflook naar smaak, geperst
- peper en zout naar smaak

Meng alles door elkaar en verdun het met wat water tot het de gewenste dikte van een slasaus heeft.
Heerlijk als je deze saus standaard in je koelkast hebt staan. Je kunt de saus ook als basis gebruiken en bijvoorbeeld andere kruiden en/of drank toevoegen.

Deze slasaus wordt gebruikt in de volgende recepten: frisse komkommersalade, bloemkoolsalade, haricots verts salade, komkommer-bleekselderij salade, fruitige kipsalade

WHISKYCOCKTAILSAUS

Meerdere porties

- 4 flinke el mayonaise
- 2 el whisky
- 1 tl tomatenpuree
- ½ tl cayennepeper
- 2 druppels stevia
- zout naar smaak

Meng de mayonaise met de whisky, de tomatenpuree, de cayennepeper en stevia.
Breng op smaak met een beetje zout.

TRUFFELMAYONAISE

Meerdere porties

- ½ pot Zaanse mayonaise
- 3 tl truffelpasta of truffeltapenade
- zout naar smaak

Mayonaise en truffelpasta of truffeltapenade mengen en op smaak brengen met een mespunt zout.
Een kind kan de was doen!!

ZOETE CHILISAUS

Meerdere porties

- 4 rode pepers
- 1 tl zout
- 1 knoflookteen, geperst
- 1 el olijfolie
- 100 ml rijstazijn
- 120 ml water
- 50 g honing
- 5 druppels stevia
- 4 g (1 zakje) agar agar

Snijd of hak de pepers (zonder zaadjes) heel fijn.
Meng hier 7 gram zout door en zet het even weg.
Smoor de knoflook kort in een beetje olijfolie.
Voeg dit bij de pepers zodra het is afgekoeld.
Breng de rijstazijn, het water, de honing, de stevia en het zakje agar agar aan de kook.
Kook op matig vuur het geheel tot ongeveer de helft in.
Neem de pan van het vuur en roer de pepers erdoor.
Laat afkoelen in de koelkast.

Truffelmayonaise
Whiskycocktailsaus

Slasaus met kruiden
Zoete chilisaus

MAAK EENS EEN SOEPJE!

Als je gewend bent dat soep maken erg lang duurt, wees gerust, deze soepen zijn allemaal snel te maken. Als basis kun je een eigengemaakte bouillon gebruiken, maar om het snel en makkelijk te maken zijn bouillonblokjes (liefst zonder smaakversterkers E621) prima te gebruiken.
Ga er eens mee aan de slag.
Soepen kunnen ook heel makkelijk in een thermosfles met brede hals mee naar het werk of school. Een lekkere warme opkikker. En nog voedzaam ook, deze soepjes.

VISSOEP

- 1 sjalot, gesnipperd
- klontje roomboter
- 50 g kreeftenpasta
- 1 el tomatenpuree
- 300 à 400 ml water
- 50 g groene of rode paprika, in blokjes
- 100 g kabeljauwfilet, in stukjes
- 100 g zalmfilet, in stukjes
- 8 grote garnalen (voorgekookt en gepeld)
- 2 el crème fraîche
- peper en zout naar smaak

Fruit een sjalot in een beetje roomboter.
Voeg de kreeftenpasta en de tomatenpuree toe.
Roer goed door en voeg beetje voor beetje het water toe. Kies zelf de gewenste dikte van de soep door meer of minder water toe te voegen.
Breng het geheel zachtjes aan de kook en voeg vervolgens de paprika, de kabeljauw, de zalmfilet en de grote garnalen toe. Roer als de vis na 5 à 10 minuten gaar is, de crème fraîche erdoor en breng de soep op smaak met peper en zout.

Snel, lekker en voedzaam met een MIM erbij. (zie recept op blz. 74)

Kreeftenpasta is een delicatesse en is te koop in een viswinkel. Heb je kreeftenpasta over? Smeer het dan op een (geroosterd) sneetje koolhydraatarm brood of cracker, lekker!

Let op: Omdat garnalen gevoelig zijn voor besmetting van bacteriën is het advies om voorgekookte garnalen goed af te spoelen en nogmaals te verhitten. Daarom laat ik ze even meekoken in deze vissoep.
Ook als je garnalen in een salade gaat verwerken, is het aan te raden om ze nogmaals goed door te koken en goed uit te laten lekken. Of even afdrogen met keukenpapier.
Je kunt het verschil in (voor)gekookte en rauwe garnalen snel zien aan de kleur. Gekookte garnalen zijn roze, rauwe garnalen zijn grijs.

RUCOLASOEP

Voor 1 portie

- scheutje olijfolie
- 1 sjalotje, gesnipperd
- 1 knoflookteen, geperst
- 250 ml groente- of rundvleesbouillon
- 40 g rucola
- 30 ml slagroom onbereid
- peper en zout naar smaak
- 40 g gerookte zalm
- 40 g gerookte forel

Fruit het sjalotje en bak de knoflook heel kort mee. Blus af met de bouillon.
Voeg de rucola toe en laat 4 minuutjes koken.
Pureer de soep met een (staaf)mixer en voeg de slagroom toe.
Verwarm nog even zonder te koken.
Breng de soep op smaak met peper en zout

Verdeel de zalm en forel in stukjes in een soepkom.
Schenk er de warme soep overheen en genieten maar.
Yammmm …..

TUINKERSSOEP

- 2 sjalotjes, gesneden
- 1 el olijfolie
- 1 knoflookteen, geperst
- 1 groente- of rundvleesbouillonblokje à 10 g
- 500 ml water
- 2 bakjes tuinkers
- 100 g crème fraîche
- peper en zout naar smaak
- 150 g gerookte zalmsnippers

Fruit de sjalotjes in een scheutje olijfolie.
Voeg de knoflook en het bouillonblokje toe en roer tot blokje is gesmolten.
Voeg het water toe en laat 5 minuutjes koken.
Roer de tuinkers erdoor, maar bewaar een beetje voor de garnering.
Voeg ook de crème fraîche toe en pureer de soep met een staafmixer.
Verwarm nog even goed door, breng op smaak met peper en zout en verdeel de soep over 2 kommen.
Serveer met de zalm en de overige tuinkers.

Rucolasoep
Vissoep

Tuinkerssoep

TOMATENCRÈMESOEP

Voor 4 porties

- 400 g gezeefde tomaten
- 100 ml water
- handvol verse basilicumblaadjes, fijngesneden
- groente- of rundvleesbouillonblokje à 10 g
- 100 ml slagroom (onbereid)
- 2 eierdooiers, geklutst
- peper naar smaak
- eventueel een toef geklopte slagroom

Verwarm de gezeefde tomaat met het water en voeg de basilicum en het bouillonblokje toe.
Als de soep warm is, 100 ml slagroom erbij schenken en verwarmen, maar niet meer koken.
Voeg vervolgens heel langzaam en al roerend de eierdooiers door de soep tot deze weer warm en lobbig is.
Breng op smaak met peper en serveer eventueel met een toef geklopte slagroom.

MOSTERD/PREISOEP

Voor 4 porties

- 1 grote prei, gesneden
- 1 courgette, in blokjes gesneden
- 1 el olijfolie
- 1 liter groente- of rundvleesbouillon
- 5 el mosterd (of naar smaak)
- 2 el crème fraîche
- peper naar smaak

Fruit de prei en de courgette in een scheutje olie. Voeg de bouillon toe als de groenten zacht zijn en breng de soep aan de kook. Voeg de mosterd en de crème fraîche toe en verwarm dit al roerend.
Breng de soep op smaak met peper.
Variant: maak de soep eiwitrijker met wat omeletreepjes, stukjes ham, kipfilet of uitgebakken spekjes. Een gekookt ei in vieren gesneden staat ook leuk en maakt de soep extra voedzaam.

LOF/KAASSOEP

- 3 dikke stronken witlof
- scheutje olijfolie
- 500 ml groente- of rundvleesbouillon
- 50 g geraspte kaas naar keuze
- 50 g Parmezaanse kaas
- peper en zout naar smaak
- takje verse peterselie, fijngesneden

Haal de buitenste bladen van de witlof en snijd de bittere kern eruit. Snijd de witlof in repen en roerbak circa 2 minuten in de olie. Schenk de bouillon erbij.
Kook de witlof gaar en pureer met een staafmixer.
Voeg de kaas toe en breng op smaak met peper en zout.
Strooi bij het opdienen nog lekker wat Parmezaanse en peterselie erover.

TOM KHA KAI

- 400 ml kippenbouillon
- 150 ml kokosmelk
- 2 stengels sereh, doormidden gesneden
- 3 schijfjes verse gemberwortel
- ½ rode paprika, klein gesneden
- 1 gerookte kipfilet, in reepjes gesneden
- 2 bosuitjes, gesnipperd

Schenk de bouillon en de kokosmelk in een soeppan en breng aan de kook.
Voeg de sereh en de gember toe en laat dit 10 minuutjes zachtjes meekoken.
Als je de smaak van de sereh en gember goed proeft, kun je de stengel en wortel verwijderen.
Voeg de paprika, de kipfilet en bosui toe en warm de soep nog 5 minuten door!

Als je een iets pittigere variant wilt, kun je de paprika vervangen door rode pepers.

Tomatencrèmesoep
Lof/kaassoep

Mosterd preisoep
Tom kha kai

POMPOEN/CURRYSOEP

Voor 4 porties

- 1 Hokkaido pompoen
- 1 rode ui, grof gesneden
- 1 zoete aardappel, geschild en in stukken gesneden
- 2 knoflooktenen
- 40 ml olijfolie
- 200 ml kokosmelk
- 2 groente- of runderbouillonblokjes à 10 g
- ca. 300 à 500 ml water
- 2 el currykruiden (zie blz. 48)
- peper en zout naar smaak
- 1 kipfilet
- peper, zout en paprikapoeder naar smaak
- takje peterselie, fijngesneden

Verwijder de pitten en draden van een Hokkaido pompoen* en snijd de pompoen in stukken.
Fruit de rode ui, de pompoen, de aardappel en de knoflooktenen in de olijfolie. Schep regelmatig om.
Voeg, zodra de groenten iets zacht worden, de kokosmelk en de bouillonblokjes toe. Voeg water toe tot de groenten onder water staan.
Voeg de currykruiden toe en breng het aan de kook.
Pureer de soep zodra de groenten helemaal zacht zijn.
Het wordt een dikke brij en je kunt hem steeds verdunnen met water tot je de gewenste dikte hebt.
Breng hem verder op smaak door extra curry, zout en peper.

Wrijf een kipfilet (of meer) in met zout, peper en paprikapoeder en bak hem in een koekenpan gaar en bruin.
Snijd de kip in stukjes, serveer op een bord en schenk de soep er bij.
Een beetje peterselie maakt het af.

Omdat de grootte van de gebruikte groenten (pompoen en zoete aardappel) enorm kan verschillen, is het moeilijk om de hoeveelheid water in dit recept aan te geven. Bepaal dus zelf hoeveel water je toevoegt en maak de soep zo dik of dun als je zelf wilt. Wel goed proeven en goed op smaak brengen met de kruiden en het zout.

Vegetarische variant: voeg in plaats van kipfilet 50 gram grof gehakte cashewnoten aan dit recept toe.

* Hokkaido pompoen (= Japanse pompoen) is een kleine brede ronde pompoen die met schil en al gegeten kan worden. Was de pompoen zorgvuldig. Snijd de vrucht verticaal doormidden, verwijder de draden en pitjes en snijd de pompoen in blokjes.

BATAAT/PEERSOEP

- 1 flinke ui, gesneden
- 1 el olijfolie
- 1 zoete aardappel, geschild
- 1 peer, geschild
- 500 ml groente- of rundvleesbouillon
- 125 ml crème fraîche
- cayennepeper en zout naar smaak

Fruit de ui in een scheutje olijfolie.
Snijd de zoete aardappel en een peer in stukken en bak even kort mee met de ui.
Voeg vervolgens de bouillon toe en kook gedurende circa 20 minuten tot de aardappel zacht is.
Roer de crème fraîche erdoor en pureer het geheel met de staafmixer.
Breng op smaak met de cayennepeper en eventueel nog wat zout.

Wist je dat bataat een andere naam is voor zoete aardappel?

GEGRILDE RODE UIENSOEP

4 porties

- 2 rode paprika's
- 2 knoflooktenen
- 5 rode uien, in vieren gesneden
- 1 el olijfolie
- 200 g rundergehakt
- paprikapoeder naar smaak
- peper en zout naar smaak
- ca. 1 liter groente- of rundvleesbouillon

Leg de paprika's, de knoflooktenen met schil en de rode uien (ontdaan van buitenste schil) in een ovenschaal en besprenkel ze met olie. Plaats de ovenschaal in de oven op grillstand en grill de groenten tot de paprika's aan beide kanten hier en daar zwart geblakerd zijn.
Draai in de tussentijd soepballetjes van het rundergehakt met het paprikapoeder, peper en zout. Bak de balletjes in een koekenpan gaar.
Laat de soepballetjes uitlekken op keukenpapier.
Bedek de groenten met aluminiumfolie.
Verwijder na circa 10 minuten het velletje en zaadjes van de paprika.
Probeer zoveel mogelijk van de vrij gekomen smaakvolle sappen te bewaren om die aan de soep toe te voegen.
Snijd de paprika in stukjes, knijp de knoflooktenen uit hun schil en voeg ze samen met de uien in een soeppannetje.
Schenk de bouillon erbij tot de groenten net onder staan.
Voeg daarna de gehaktballetjes toe en verwarm het geheel nog even door.

GELE PAPRIKASOEP

Met dit receptje heb je het zonnetje in huis gehaald!!!

- 2 sjalotjes, gesnipperd
- 1 knoflookteen, geperst
- 2 gele paprika's, in blokjes
- ½ tl kurkuma
- 1 tl kerriepoeder
- scheutje olijfolie
- 500 ml groente- of rundvleesbouillon
- 1 zalmfilet (zonder huid), in plakjes gesneden
- 2 el crème fraîche
- zwarte peper en zout naar smaak
- 1 el verse peterselie, fijngesneden

Fruit de sjalotjes, de knoflook, de paprika's, kurkuma en kerriepoeder zo'n 5 minuten in de olijfolie.
Schenk de bouillon erbij en laat de soep 15 minuten zachtjes koken.
Pureer de soep met een staafmixer en zeef hem, zodat alle velletjes van de paprika eruit zijn.
Voeg de zalm toe en laat hem 2 minuten garen.
Roer dan de crème fraîche erdoor, verwarm nog even, breng op smaak met zwarte peper en zout en dien op met de peterselie.

Zo simpel kan lekker zijn.

De combinatie kurkuma en zwarte peper is heilzaam. Altijd tegelijk met wat vetten eten, zodat de kruiden goed in het lichaam opgenomen kunnen worden.
Kurkuma is het hoofdbestanddeel van kerrie en geeft kerrie zijn zonnige gele kleur.

GEROOSTERDE PAPRIKASOEP

Misschien iets meer werk, maar dan heb je ook wat hoor.

- 3 rode paprika's
- 3 hele knoflooktenen
- 200 g rundergehakt
- 2 el satékruiden (of paprikapoeder, peper en zout)
- 1 rode ui, gesneden
- scheut olijfolie
- 1 groente- of rundvleesbouillonblokje à 10 g
- 400 ml water
- peper en zout naar smaak

Optioneel:
50 ml slagroom (eventueel wat gezoet met stevia) of geraspte kaas voor garnering

Leg de paprika's en knoflooktenen in zijn geheel in een ovenschaal, schenk hier olijfolie overheen en grill in de oven op de grillstand totdat ze zwart beginnen te worden. Draai de groenten om en grill ook de andere kant.
Dek ze daarna af met aluminiumfolie.
Na afkoelen, de velletjes en pitjes verwijderen.
Haal de knoflook uit de schil.
Bewaar het bakvocht.

Meng het gehakt met de satékruiden en breng op smaak met zout.
Draai er balletjes van en bak ze circa 10 minuten in een koekenpan.
Laat ze uitlekken op keukenpapier.

Fruit de ui in olijfolie op hoog vuur.
Blijf omscheppen.
Voeg bouillonblokjes en 200 ml water toe.
Blijf roeren tot het een beetje lobbig lijkt te worden, voeg daarna overig water toe.
Draai dan het gas iets lager en kook de ui gaar.
Voeg de paprika, knoflook en het overgebleven bakvocht toe en pureer de soep met een staafmixer.
Breng op smaak met peper en zout en verwarm goed door.
Voeg room en gehaktballetjes toe en verwarm nogmaals zonder te koken.
Dien de soep op met geraspte kaas of een toef slagroom.

(Gebruik liever geen geroosterde paprika uit pot.
Die zijn door de azijn te zuur. Dan krijgt de soep echt een andere smaak.)

Bataat/peersoep
Pompoen/currysoep
Gegrilde rode uiensoep

Gele paprikasoep
Snoepsoep
Geroosterde paprikasoep

SNOEPSOEP

Voor 4 porties

Deze soep is zo lekker en zo simpel te maken.

- 750 g snoeppaprika's, grof gesneden
- ½ rode peper, grof gesneden
- 1 grote ui, grof gesneden
- 3 knoflooktenen, in 4 stukken
- 250 g snoeptomaatjes
- ca. 50 ml olijfolie
- groente- of rundvleesbouillon
- crème fraîche naar smaak (optioneel)

Was de groenten.
Snijd van de snoeppaprika's en een halve rode peper alleen het groen weg en voeg de grof gesneden stukken samen in een soeppan.
Voeg de ui en de knoflooktenen toe aan de soeppan.
Voeg de snoeptomaatjes erbij en giet de olijfolie erover.
Bak dit al omscheppend, ongeveer 10 minuten.
Schenk er zoveel bouillon bij tot de groenten bijna onder staan.
Laat het geheel zachtjes koken tot je met een botte lepel een stuk paprika zonder kracht kunt halveren.
Pureer de soep met een staafmixer en roer deze door een zeef.
Soms is de soep al zoet van zichzelf en heerlijk, maar soms is crème fraîche erdoor ook errruggg lekker.

Snoeppaprika's?
Net als snoeptomaatjes zijn er nu ook snoeppaprika's en snoepkomkommers.
Een kleurrijk setje snackgroenten.

'Ik GOK eigenlijk niet omdat ik af wil vallen, hoewel er best een paar kilootjes af mogen, maar omdat ik me fitter voel. Ik heb meer energie, eet veel gevarieerder, kan toch met de pot mee-eten en heb bijna geen bloedsuikerschommelingen meer. En ik raak heel langzaam kilo's kwijt, waardoor ik me nog fitter voel. Win-win situatie!'

- Bianca

'Weet je wat voor mij het fijnste is aan de GOK-methode, die ik sinds dit jaar toepas? Antwoord: "Het dagmenu, met een koolhydratenuur erin!" Het is heerlijk praktisch voor jezelf en je huisgenoten. Daarbij verrukkelijke recepten, die echt nooit saai zijn! Wat wil je nog meer, en zei ik al gezond en easy?'

- Henny

'Gok is geen dieet, maar een andere manier van eten. Je moet je dat wel even eigen maken door je er even in te verdiepen, maar het is niet ingewikkeld. In de boeken krijg je de heerlijkste recepten en kant en klare weekmenu's aangereikt. Eenmaal onderweg val je af en verandert je figuur prettig doordat je buik verdwijnt. Ik lijn niet, ik Gok.'

- Anne Marie

'Sinds 2009 ben ik een GOK-ster. Het is een leefwijze geworden. Ik voel mij fitter en energieker. Als ik wel eens "zondig" voel ik dat wel in mijn lijf. Maar na bijvorrbeeld een feestje, pak ik de GOK-draad weer op en voel mij snel weer beter. Met alle boeken van GOK in mijn bezit, heb ik voldoende inspiratie om lekker te eten. GOK is mijn beste vriendin!!!!!'

- Yvonne

'Eetrust is lekker koolhydraatbeperkt eten, eetrust is niet meer snaaien, eetrust is je goed voelen, eetrust is Grip op Koolhydraten. Grip op Koolhydraten is mijn leven.'

- Lisenka

KIPPENDIJEN MET SESAMOLIE

- 2 kippendijen, zonder bot
- peper, zout en paprikapoeder naar smaak
- sojasaus
- zoete chilisaus (zie recept op blz. 149)
- donkere sesamolie

Kruid de kippendijen met peper, zout en paprikapoeder.
Bak de kippendijen in de koekenpan gaar, en schenk er tijdens het bakken een scheutje sojasaus en eigengemaakte chilisaus bij .
Leg de kip op een bord en druppel hier een beetje donkere sesamolie overheen.
Niet te veel, anders overheerst de smaak van de sesamolie te veel.

KIPPENDIJEN MET ZWARTE RIJST

- 150 g zwarte rijst
- 2 kippendijen, in stukjes gesneden
- 1 el olijfolie
- Shichimi togarashi kruidenmix naar smaak
- ½ rode puntpaprika, in blokjes
- ½ krop paksoi, klein gesneden
- 40 ml Shao Xing (of sherry)
- 1 bosui, fijngesneden
- zout naar smaak
- donkere sesamolie naar smaak

Daar zijn die lekkere malse kippendijtjes weer.

Kook de zwarte rijst volgens de verpakking gaar.
Bak de kippendijtjes in een scheutje olie en voeg de Shichimi togarashi kruiden naar smaak toe.
Als de kip bijna gaar is, even kort de rode paprika en gesneden paksoi meebakken.
Zorg dat ze lekker knapperig blijven.
Blus het af met een scheutje Shao Xing.
Laat de alcohol verdampen en zet dan het vuur uit.
Voeg de rijst toe en een fijngesneden bosuitje.
Breng op smaak met zout en een paar druppels donkere sesamolie.

(Donkere sesamolie kan erg overheersen dus niet te veel.)

Let op: 75 gram rijst per portie is een behoorlijke hoeveelheid koolhydraten. Kleine eters max. 50 gram rijst. Zonder rijst is dit recept GOK-groen.

ZOETE AARDAPPEL RÖSTIRONDJES

- 2 zoete aardappelen, geschild
- 1 grote ui, geschild
- 75 g kaas naar keuze
- 3 grote eieren
- peper en zout naar smaak

Rasp de zoete aardappel in een keukenmachine.
Rasp daarna ook meteen de ui en de kaas mee.
Kluts de eieren en voeg ze samen met peper en zout, toe aan de rasp.
Spatel dit door elkaar.
Schep met een eetlepel hoopjes in een koekenpan en druk ze plat.
Bak de rösti aan beide kanten bruin.

Variatie: Je kunt ook stukjes spek of chorizo etc. toevoegen.

BIETENSALADE

Heerlijke bietensalade of gewoon op zijn Rotterdams: krotensalade

- 2 gekookte rode bieten, in blokjes gesneden
- 200 g komkommer, in blokjes gesneden
- 2 bosuitjes, fijngesneden
- 50 g pijnboompitjes, geroosterd
- paar takjes peterselie, fijngesneden

Dressing:
- 50 ml olijfolie
- paar druppels citroensap (vers of uit een flesje)
- peper en zout naar smaak

Schep de ingrediënten door elkaar en schenk de dressing erover.

TOMAAT MET EI

- 1 ui, gesnipperd
- 1 rode paprika, in blokjes gesneden
- 2 tenen knoflook, geperst
- scheutje olijfolie
- 400 g gepelde tomaten, in blokjes
- 1 flinke el tomatenpuree
- ½ tl komijnzaadpoeder
- ½ tl paprikapoeder
- ¼ tl chilipeper
- 3 eieren
- za'atarkruiden naar smaak

Fruit de ui, de paprika en de knoflook in olijfolie in een koekenpan. Schenk als de groenten zacht zijn de tomaten en tomatenpuree erbij. Breng op smaak met het komijnzaadpoeder, paprikapoeder en de chilipeper. Laat 2 minuten zachtjes pruttelen.
Maak 3 kuiltjes in de pan en breek daar de eieren in. Zet het vuur op de laagste stand, plaats een deksel op de pan en laat de eieren stollen.
Bestrooi voor het opdienen met nog wat za'atarkruiden naar smaak.

Heerlijk als ontbijt of lunch!

AUBERGINELASAGNE

Voor 4 porties

- 3 aubergines, in plakken gesneden
- 1 el olijfolie
- peper en zout naar smaak
- 500 g rundergehakt
- 1 ui, gesneden
- ½ courgette, in blokjes gesneden
- 400 g tomatensaus
- 100 g Parmezaanse kaas, geraspt
- 200 g extra belegen kaas, geraspt

Smeer de aubergines in met de olijfolie en bestrooi met wat peper en zout.
Grill de plakken mooi bruin in de oven op de grillstand.
Bak in een koekenpan het gehakt rul.
Bak de ui en de courgette mee.
Voeg de tomatensaus toe en breng het geheel op smaak met peper en zout.
Laat even inkoken tot een dik mengsel.
Vet een ovenschaaltje in en schep hier 1/3 gehaktmengsel in.
Bedek met 1/3 gegrilde aubergine en bestrooi met 1/3 Parmezaanse en extra belegen kaas.
Herhaal dit nog 2 keer.
Bak de schotel een kwartiertje op 190 °C in een voorverwarmde oven.

Vegetarische variant: maak deze lasagne met vegetarisch gehakt.

LASAGNE VAN AARDAPPEL EN HAM

- 2 grote aardappelen, ongekookt
- scheutje olijfolie
- 8 plakken raclette kaas
- 2 el whisky
- 4 el mayonaise
- sambal brandal naar smaak
- zout naar smaak
- 8 plakken rauwe ham
- bosje bieslook, fijngesneden

Snijd de aardappels in de lengte in plakken van ongeveer 1 centimeter totdat je in totaal 8 plakken hebt.
Smeer de plakken in met een beetje olijfolie en gaar ze in de oven onder de grill.
Leg er in de laatste 1 à 2 minuten een plakje raclette kaas op en laat dit smelten.
Maak intussen een saus met de whisky, mayonaise, sambal brandal en zout.
Nu gaan we stapelen, te beginnen met een plak aardappel, een plak rauwe ham, saus en bieslook tot alle plakken aardappel zijn gebruikt.
En dan genieten.

Kies voor een vrij vastkokende aardappelsoort, bijvoorbeeld Bildstar. Naar wens schil je de aardappels wel of juist niet. Als je ze niet schilt, was de aardappels dan goed en snijd de slechte stukjes er uit.

GROENTECHIPS

Voor meerdere porties

Bak zelf je eigen groentechips. Lekker en gezond. Geschikte groenten om chips van te maken zijn zoete aardappel, wortels, gekookte bieten, courgette, pastinaak. Voornamelijk koolhydraatrijkere groenten, daarom alleen eten in het koolhydratenuur. In fase 2 kan het als tussendoortje gegeten worden.
Lekkere kruiden zijn: zout, peper, koek- en speculaaskruiden, oregano, aardappelkruiden, ras el hanout.
Snijd de gewassen (en geschilde) groente in hele dunne plakjes, dit gaat het makkelijkst met een (kaas)schaaf. Sprenkel er wat olijfolie over en doe de groenten in een plastic zak.
Hussel goed zodat de olie over alle plakjes verdeeld wordt. Leg de groenteplakjes los van elkaar op een bakblik bekleed met bakpapier. Strooi de kruiden over de groenten.

Oven:
Warm de oven voor op 180 °C.
Bak 10 tot 15 minuten op 180 °C. Houd wel in de gaten dat de chips niet verbranden. Laat ze daarna nog 30 tot 60 minuten op een hele lage stand (70 °C) in de oven. De chips zijn klaar als ze knapperig zijn.
In een heteluchtoven kun je meerdere lagen tegelijk bakken.

Magnetron:
Bak circa 10 minuten op 600 watt.
Let op: in de magnetron gaat het om hoeveelheid. Dus hoe minder chips hoe korter op 600 watt. Laat de chips vervolgens op 60 tot 180 watt in de magnetron tot ze knapperig zijn. Controleer regelmatig of lekker krokant zijn.
Als je de chips makkelijk doormidden kunt breken dan zijn ze goed gebakken.
Laat ze nog even afkoelen, en eten maar!!!!

Met dank aan Cira, Karlijn, Jet en Femke van basisschool de Leeuwenkuil in Beneden-Leeuwen voor het uittesten van de chips en de verrassende kruidensmaakjes.

'Mijn man heeft 25 jaar gesmeekt of ik eens wat variatie in de keuken kon brengen en hij kan nu zijn geluk niet op met jouw lekkere recepten, mijn toenemende plezier bij het bereiden en waar wij ook nog eens allebei van afvallen.'

- Thea

Zoete chilisaus
(zie recept blz. 149)
Smoothie
Limoenyoghurt
met munt

SMOOTHIE

Voor 1 portie

- 100 ml kokosmelk
- 60 g verse spinazie
- 50 g avocado
- 50 g banaan
- 50 g bosvruchten
- eventueel water om te verdunnen

Mix alles in een blender tot een gladde smoothie.

LIMOENYOGHURT MET MUNT

- 2½ blaadjes gelatine
- 1 limoen
- 250 g Griekse yoghurt
- 8 druppels stevia, of naar smaak
- 5 blaadjes munt, fijngesneden
- 75 ml water

Week in een kommetje 1½ blaadje gelatine en in een ander kommetje 1 blaadje in water. Was de limoen met heet water en rasp een beetje van de schil af. Houd de rasp apart en pers de limoen uit. Haal de inmiddels zacht geworden gelatine uit het water en knijp er zoveel mogelijk vocht uit. Verwarm de gelatine in een steelpannetje tot hij opgelost is en roer er 2 eetlepels yoghurt door. Roer dit samen met 5 druppels stevia en 1 eetlepel limoensap door de yoghurt. Schep het in mooie glaasjes en zet het 1 uur in de koelkast om op te stijven.
Verwarm het water met 1 eetlepel limoensap en los hier het overige blaadje gelatine in op. Voeg de munt, de limoenrasp en de stevia toe en laat het 1 minuut koken. Laat het even afkoelen zonder op te stijven. Verdeel dit over de yoghurt en zet deze terug in de koelkast totdat het stijf is geworden.

Curry met banaan
Fruitige
kipsalade

CURRY MET BANAAN

(bijgerecht)

- 2 uien, gesneden
- currykruiden (zie blz. 48) naar smaak
- 1 courgette, in blokjes gesneden
- 100 ml kokosmelk
- 1 banaan
- handvol cashewnoten
- peper en zout naar smaak

Fruit de uien met de currykruiden en voeg er de courgette aan toe.
Schenk de kokosmelk erbij op het moment dat de courgette zacht begint te worden. Laat het zachtjes pruttelen tot het begint in te dikken.
Snijd in de tussentijd de banaan in plakjes en rooster de cashewnoten.
Verwarm de banaan nog heel even mee en serveer met de cashewnoten.

FRUITIGE KIPSALADE

- ½ gerookte kipfilet, in blokjes
- 15 druiven gehalveerd
- handvol gedroogde cranberry's
- ½ appel, in blokjes (golden delicious)
- ¼ rode ui, gesnipperd
- 1 el slasaus met kruiden (zie recept blz. 148)
- peper en zout naar smaak

Meng alles en smullen maar!
Heerlijk zomers bij de bbq.

Kersensalade

Frisse fruitsalade met ham

KERSENSALADE

Voor 1 à 2 porties

- 100 g kersen
- 50 g Boursin mini's
- 50 g pecannoten, gehakt
- handvol muntblaadjes, gesneden
- scheutje walnotenolie naar smaak
- peper en zout naar smaak

Ontpit de kersen en snijd ze doormidden.
Meng alle ingrediënten en breng op smaak met peper en zout.
Het ziet er ook zo mooi uit op een bord, bijna te mooi om op te eten.
Bijna...

Snel en makkelijk trucje om kersen te ontpitten:
Nodig:
- Flesje met een opening die kleiner is dan de kersen.
- Een eetstokje of een rietje

Leg een kers op de opening van de fles.
Prik de kers door met het stokje of het rietje.
De pit valt in het flesje.
Een kersenontpitter is dus niet nodig. Scheelt je weer wat ruimte in de keukenkast.

Geen verse kersen te koop? Gebruik dan kersen uit de diepvries. Deze zijn ook al ontpit. Lekker makkelijk en smaakt ook prima

FRISSE FRUITSALADE MET HAM

Voor 1 à 2 porties

- 50 g blauwe bessen
- ½ appel, in schijfjes gesneden
- 40 g pijnboompitten, geroosterd
- 50 g serranoham, in stukjes krokant gebakken

Dressing:
- 2 el mayonaise
- verse bieslook naar smaak
- citroensap naar smaak (vers of uit een flesje)
- peper en zout naar smaak

Schep de ingrediënten door elkaar en verdeel de dressing erover.
Makkelijk en snel én erg lekker.

Brie met druiven
Romig
warm fruit
Gevulde peer

BRIE MET DRUIVEN

Voor 1 à 2 porties

- 100 g roombrie, in plakjes
- 15 druiven, gehalveerd
- 15 g pijnboompitten, geroosterd
- scheutje honing
- peper en zout naar smaak

Leg een paar plakjes brie op een bord.
Verdeel de druiven en pijnboompitjes erover.
Schenk hier een beetje honing overheen.
Bestrooi naar smaak met peper en zout en zet het geheel even in een hete oven of onder de grill.
Let er op dat het niet TE bruin wordt.

Lekker als nagerecht in je koolhydratenuur.
Het is behoorlijk voedzaam, dus eet als hoofdmaaltijd een lekkere salade of poké bowl.

ROMIG WARM FRUIT

Voor 1 portie

- 100 g gemengd fruit, in stukjes gesneden
- merg van 1 vanillestokje
- 4 el kokosmelk

Maak een stuk bakpapier goed nat (in een prop) en knijp het uit.
Leg het natte bakpapier in een kommetje.
Schep hier het fruit in. Meng het vanillemerg met de kokosmelk, giet dit over het fruit en vouw het bakpapier dicht.
Verwarm dit in 20 minuten in een op 200 °C voorverwarmde oven.

GEVULDE PEER

Voor 1 à 2 porties

- water
- scheutje citroensap (vers of uit een flesje)
- 1 zoete peer
- 2 el crème fraîche
- 2 el Zaanse mayonaise
- 1 el kappertjes, fijngesneden
- 1 el zilveruitjes, fijngesneden
- 1 el augurk, fijngesneden
- 1 tl verse dille
- 1 takje verse peterselie, fijngesneden
- peper en zout naar smaak
- 4 plakken fricandeau

Schenk in een bakje met water wat citroensap.
Schil de peer, snijd deze door de helft en schep het klokhuis eruit.
Leg de peer in het citroenwater om verkleuren tegen te gaan.
Meng de overige ingrediënten (behalve de fricandeau en verse kruiden) en breng op smaak met de dille, peterselie en peper en zout.
Dep de peer droog met keukenpapier, leg de 2 helften op een bord.
Verdeel de fricandeau erover, maak een kuiltje en schep in het kuiltje het crème fraîche mengsel.

MIJN WOORD VAN DANK

Zo'n mooi boek met én veel informatie, én veel nieuwe recepten én de mooiste foto's, dat maak je niet zomaar en al helemaal niet in je eentje. Daar zit een heel team achter. Graag wil ik dan ook een aantal mensen bedanken voor de samenwerking aan dit boek.

Allereerst hobbykok Thea Bremer die weer met smaak voor mooie en makkelijke GOK-proof-recepten gezorgd heeft. Ook voor de fotoshoot heeft Thea zorggedragen voor de bereiding van de gerechten. Ze heeft echt keihard gewerkt. Thea vormde als koksmaatje een goed koppel met ervaren foodstylist Goran Todorovic. Met zijn professionele oog voor kleur en detail maakte Goran van zelfs een eenvoudig uitziend gerecht telkens weer een feestelijk en aanlokkelijk geheel. Zijn composities werden met uiterste zorg belicht en in beeld gebracht door topfotograaf Joshua Rood. 'De gerechten moeten er vooral lekker en smakelijk uitzien. Zodat je zin krijgt om het te gaan maken. En het juiste licht doet zoveel!' En dat is gelukt! Met uiterste precisie speelde Joshua met lichtvangers, schermen, statieven en trapjes. En door zijn uitmuntende fotobewerking heeft hij de foto's nóg mooier en aantrekkelijker gemaakt.

Vier dagen fotoshoot in mijn eigen keuken was telkens een ware happening. Ik vormde de vliegende keep, verzorgde hand- en spandiensten en zocht regelmatig met Goran mooie combinaties van ondergrond en serviesgoed uit. De interactie tussen ons vieren ging uitstekend.
Tussendoor en in de lunchpauze werd er natuurlijk heerlijk gesmuld van alle lekkere en voedzame gerechten.
Hulde dus aan het topteam Thea Bremer, Goran Todorovic en Joshua Rood!

Verder dank aan Kosmos Uitgevers, met name vormgever Sven van Pel en coördinator en eindredactrice Yolande Michon. Dagen- en avondenlang is door Yolande, Sven en mij gewerkt om het boek op tijd bij de drukker te krijgen.
Dank ook aan Marieke Soons, Marit Hester en Ingrid Hamers van Kosmos uitgevers voor het meedenken en de PR.

Ook dank aan de GOK-kers die met hun eigen ervaringsverhaal of quote in dit boek staan. Na een oproep in de Grip op Koolhydraten facebookgroep en op het forum kregen we vele mooie reacties binnen. Een selectie hieruit hebben we geplaatst in dit boek ter inspiratie, maar vooral voor ieders motivatie. Op de website www.gripopkoolhydraten.nl zijn nog meer ervaringsverhalen te lezen.

Als laatste mijn dank aan mijn lieve, zorgzame, meewerkende man en maatje Hans, die mij weer heel wat dagen en avonden als een zombie met de teksten en weekmenu's bezig gezien heeft en die mij, al vele jaren, altijd in mijn waarde laat en alles op mijn eigen wijze laat doen en bij lief en leed mijn rots in de branding is.

Ik wens iedereen heel veel lees- en kookplezier met dit boek.
Succes gewenst met Grip op Koolhydraten.
Geniet van alle lichamelijke en geestelijke voordelen en eet smakelijk!

Lieve groet,
Yvonne Lemmers

REGISTER